In The Name of Allah

In The Name of Allah

A History of Clarence 13X (Allah)
And The Five Percenters.

By Wakeel Allah

A TEAM PUBLISHING
ATLANTA

IN THE NAME OF ALLAH

Second Printing: Second Edition

March 2007

COPYRIGHT © 2007

By

A-TEAM PUBLISHING

Published by

A-TEAM PUBLISHING
A division of
A-TEAM PRODUCTIONS
P.O. Box 551036
Atlanta, GA 30355

To order additional copies or to reach Wakeel Allah for speaking engagements, please contact the Publisher.
WakeelAllah@allahteam.org

ISBN 978-1-59916-200-3

To the fallen soldiers Lord Rajuahn Allah, Rahman Allah, Divine Power Allah , First Born Prince Allah, Siheem Allah, Brother Jackie Muhammad and Dr. Khallid Abdul Muhammad (RIP).
To all the Five Percenters throughout the world who remain committed, dedicated and steadfast in the divine culture of Islam.

CONTENTS

Acknowledgements

I would like to thank everyone who participated in some shape form or fashion in the completion of this project. Long is the list as many contributed in their own way and in their own good time.

First and foremost, thanks and praises to Allah Who Came In The Person of Master Fard Muhammad to Whom Praises are Forever Due, The Most Honorable Elijah Muhammad who is The Exalted Christ, The Father Allah (Clarence 13X Smith) who taught and showed us the Babies Are The Greatest and the Honorable Minister Louis Farrakhan the Divine Reminder in our midst who has done an outstanding job reaching the masses of our people. I could never ever repay each of you for what you all have done for me. Much respect and praises due to Allah for each of those mighty strong Black Men.

Thank you to my immediate family (Old Dad Hugo, Old Earth Susie, Brother Edward and Sister Joann) for being very supportive when I accepted Islam as a youth. Thanks to Vanessa B. for always being down.

I would like to thank and say peace to all of the Gods and Earths the world over for keeping Allah's teachings (the lessons) at the forefront and on the minds of the youth. Extended thanks to the some of the great institutions we have produced: The Allah School In Mecca, The Allah School In Medina, The Allah Youth Center, The Allah Team (All in All and A Team Productions), The Sun of Man Publications, The Word Newspaper, The Five Percenter Newspaper, Allah's Universal Development Inc., The Black Family Newsletter, The Universal Truth, Thy Kingdom Come Productions, The National Statement, The Great Enlightener, NGE Power Paper, Black 7 On-line magazine and last but not least the numerous Earth Committees that support the cause.

Homage and respect to the original Elders of the Five Percent Nation: Father Allah, Old Man Justice, Abu Shahid, Hebekha, Rajab and numerous others. The First Nine Born of The Five Percent Nation: Black Messiah, Uhuru, Al-Salaam, 1st Born Prince Allah, Al-Jamel, Bismillah, ABG#7, Akbar and Kihiem. The First Born of Medina: Universal Shaamguadd, Gykee Mathematics, Hasheem, Byheem, Uhuso Lakee, Sha Sha, Gamal,

Waleak, Ahmad, Raleak, Akim, Bali, Ali and Siheem. To all of the brave Five Percenters that accepted the teachings under Allah when he was here in the physical, much respect due for your perseverance and courage.

Thanks to the great Gods of ALLAH TEAM and friends: True Islam, Komdallah, Understanding, Born Righteous, U-God Myking, Rakil, Born Talib, Je'ri Understanding, Self Justice, Sayyed Munajj, Wadud Bishme, Izlaam, Omar Muhammad, Ashahed Muhammad and Barnar Cushmeer.

Thanks to the members of the Nation of Islam under the guidance of The Honorable Minister Louis Farrakhan. Thanks to Mosque Maryam (Chicago), Mosque #7 (Harlem, NY), Mosque #80 (Plainfield, NJ) and Mosque #15 (Atlanta, GA). Thanks to Minister Khallid Abdul Muhammad (Former National Spokesman), Minister Abdul Akbar Muhammad (International Representative), Minister Tony Muhammad (Western Regional Minister), Minister Karriem Muhammad (Former Eastern Regional Minister), Minister Keith Muhammad (Former Plainfield Minister), Minister James 7X (Mosque #7-A in 60's) Brother Ramza Mahmud, Minister Jabril Muhammad and the entire Cushmeer family.

Thanks to some of the Gods from Power Force, New Jerusalem (Plainfield, NJ): B.I.D.S.A.C. 7 360, Righteous So Natural, Dr. KAOS Born, Bilal Allah, Dr. Divine, True Understanding, Master Right Guidance 360, Righteous O'Real, Talee Supreme, Kindu, Al-Qwawee, Lord Rajauhn "Flip", Sincere, Divine Star, God Cipher Divine, True Born Understanding, Black Man and Jamil Ali-Quan.

Thanks to the Gods of Allah's Garden (Atlanta, GA) hey days: Pure Mathematics, Born Powerful Islam, Rommel Original Wise Man, True Islam, Ullah Biene'me, Jusmine, Everlasting Wise Malik, Born Universal Truth, Dominant, Hajj, Rasheed, Lord Magnetic, Allah Christ, Aklam, Talib Shabazz, Shahid, Justice, Jus Wise, G Supreme, Lord Savior, Tajir Asiatic, Bashir, Mumeet, Born, Rashon, Hyrek, Supreme, Knowledge, Understanding and countless others. Including all the Gods at Morehouse College in the early 90's who are too numerous to name here but you all know who you are.

Special thanks to all the Gods who wrote much of the history throughout the years and whose writings provided a lot of material for the book: Abu Shahid, Universal Shaamguadd, Gykee Mathematics, Allah B., Born Allah, Beloved Allah, Allah's Born God (ABG#7), Al-Jamel, Shahid M. Allah, Prince A. Cuba, Um Allah, Dawud Understanding Supreme, G. Kalim, Lord Jamel, U-Allah, Almighty Dawud, Shabazz Adew, Dumar Wa'de, Infinite Al'jaa'maar and Eye God.

Thanks to the Gods and Muslims in the Hip Hop community: The World Famous Supreme Team, Rakim Allah, Poor Righteous Teachers, Brand Nubians, Wu-Tang Clan, Public Enemy, Ice Cube, Black Moon, NAS & AZ, Paris, King Sun, Mc Ren, Kam, Fugees, Just-Ice, Lakim Shabazz, Digable Planets and Big Daddy Kane.

Thanks to Benjamin Karim, Barry Gottehrer, C. Eric Lincoln, Alex Haley, Les Matthews and Yusuf Nuruddin for writing on the subject matter and other related topics.

A special thanks to everyone who made this book possible, for all of those not mentioned, please accept my apologies. Charge it to my mind and not to my heart.

Peace,

Wakeel Allah

Preface

The first time I ever recall hearing of the Five Percenters was in 1981 when I was about 12 year's old while living in Plainfield, New Jersey. While still in middle school, my best friend Felix and I were at these two brothers Kerry and Yogi's house listening to music and talking about some of the local street organizations. The brothers had originally grown up in the Bronx and they began to talk about the youth organizations that were prevalent in their old neighborhood. They mentioned a few groups that caught my attention such as "The Zulu Nation" but one youth organization they spoke about in particular really did pique my interest. They name of the group was called "The Five Percenters." I thought to myself that this was a real odd name for a crew and apparently the name was just the beginning of the uniqueness of this group that separated it from so many others. The brothers explained the group's custom of asking each of its members a question about "mathematics." They went on to say that when asked the question of one another, if the members didn't give the correct response they were subject to be reprimanded. This could take the form of a verbal chastisement or even a physical punishment. I remember that last statement leaving me puzzled more than impressed. My reaction was like "what?" I couldn't comprehend why would a crew care about mathematics which to me was only a subject studied in school -- not in the streets. Besides that math was my hardest and least favorite subject in school. Even with that I found it interesting that this group had a challenge to determine who really was down with the organization. It appeared to me to be some kind of fraternal custom that again was a strange characteristic for some brothers on the street. The two explained how Five Percenters spoke real fast and sounded real smart but contrary to the smart kid stereotype, they had a real tough reputation in the streets and it was known not to mess with them. The brothers revealed The Five Percenters startling claim that eac⌐ member viewed themselves as "Gods." Initially I had mista¹ this to mean they referred to themselves as "Guards" bodyguards or something like that. I recall thinking theᵛ have adopted that name instead of a math term sincᵉ appeared to sound more militant. When I asked fᵣ man told me "No, they refer to themselves as 'Gods' as in G-O-D." This compounded the confusion of my first impression of The Five Percenters. I had to think about them naming themselves after a percentage, priding its members of knowing the subject math and then referring to themselves as deities. Although calling themselves God didn't offend me, because at this point in my life I really didn't believe any kind of God based on what I seen in America and the Black Man's condition. Ironically it would be the G.OD.s I would eventually thank for giving me the clear understanding on "who and what God is." But before knowing that I found the Gods interesting enough but I dismissed it in my mind as being a strange group of cats not knowing the major impact it would have on my life.

The City of Plainfield appeared to have a demographic specifically built for a doctrine such as The Five Percenters or The Nation of Islam. The city represented every aspect of Black life that included talent, intelligentsia, education, religion, the underworld, athletics, organization, lower and middle class, Black Pride, Black Power and Black Nationalism. I was born and raised in the city of about 50,000 people located about 20 miles outside of New York City. The city's population was predominately African-American earning it the coveted label as a "chocolate city" meaning it was a majority Black city complete with a Black mayor, a Black administration and a Black populace. Plainfield's artistic claim to fame was that it was the birthplace of the music genre known as "P-Funk" and home to legendary funk band "Parliament" aka "Funkadelic" earning the town the nickname of "P-Funk City".

In the late 1960's, Plainfield played an important role in the "Black Power" movement. The city earned a tough reputation when it served as one of the precursors for the nationwide '68 riots by having one of its own in 1967. The events began as local Plainfield residents attacked and murdered a white police officer that depending on whom you believe was either attempting crowd control or harassing Black patrons in the middle of a protest in the center of the "The Projects." Just prior to what escalated into a riot, a band of local Black militants heisted an enormous supply of weapons from a local gun armory in the neighboring town of Somerset. This heist helped the city serve s an underground gun running center for Black militant cells throughout the East Coast. This was evident in the Plainfield riots as some militants and disenchanted Blacks in the city took on the National Guard in a battle that lasted a couple of days. As in a martial law like approach, the entire city was shut down and surrounded by tanks and The National Guard. From what the elders say, you could hear gunshots night and day, as the city became a war zone prepared for a race riot. The stark situation terrified any white people left in the city and spawned what demographers refer as "white flight" which meant the remaining white residents eventually moved out of the city sooner than later. As a result, Blacks had successfully seized political and residential control over the city.

The Black Power movement in the area continued to be a force throughout the 1970's via established movements such as The Black Panthers, Nation of Islam, Black Liberation Army and other local youth organizations aka social clubs. Growing up as a kid in the 70's, social clubs or what some would eventually refer to as gangs had a strong presence. Each neighborhood or block seemed to have its own organization. Many of the organizations exemplified the Black machismo captured in the "Blaxploitation" movies of that era. Movies such as "The Black Six", "Shaft", "Superfly", "The Mack", "Three The Hard Way", "Black Caesar" and "The Spook Who Sat By The Door" appeared to give you a glimpse of the energy of young Black America in that day. It was like every young brother's fantasy to have a crew that knew karate or boxing, was sophisticated in weaponry, had the coolest nicknames, wore the best threads, donned the cultural hairstyles (afro, waves, braids or corn rows), listened to the best music, ate the best soul food, had the prettiest girls and the best transportation even if it was a ten-speed bicycle. Given all the aspirations young people had, I think the most desired attribute in the community at the time was a person's reputation. It was about being BLACK in your expression of life.

Young people in an attempt to capture and preserve this lifestyle began to form entities that captured and preserved these expressions. Another important reason was the necessity for young Blacks to protect themselves against hostile whites. In Plainfield, it wasn't unlikely for clubs to band together when it was time to fight the whites of neighboring towns. These were still earlier times, fresh off the heels of Martin Luther King's assassination and it seemed like it was always rumors of riots still lurking out there.

In my city each social club had a senior crew and a junior crew. Usually a "senior" crew consisted of high school age teens and "junior" crews represented the elementary and middle school age kids. In many cases, instead of taking on the name senior or junior, other crews opted to refer to each part by the numbers 1 & 2 respectively. Some clubs had culturally significant names such as a social club named "Shabazz" (Shabazz "1" was the senior crew and Shabazz "2" was the junior crew). I vividly remember while in elementary school, when I was in the 2nd or 3rd grade during recess we noticed that the words Shabazz 1 & 2 were spray painted on the backboards of the basketball court. I think that this was my first introduction to that name. I remember thinking that it was a cool name but I wasn't familiar with its origins but I could still tell it was a Black name of cultural significance. To this day I don't know if that club took its name from The Honorable Elijah Muhammad's teachings that all Black People in North America was from "The Tribe of Shabazz" or whether Malcolm X taking Shabazz as a surname inspired them. Another popular group was called "The Black Dragons". In other cases, all groups didn't have historically significant names. Some of the rival crews to the former were named "Country Club", "Hulk 1 & 2", and "Mad Dog 20/ 20". The latter taking its name from a popular brand name of alcoholic drinks in the Black community of that day.

For me, the thought of being part of a street organization was appealing but at the time I was too young to think about realistically joining any kind of social club. Beside that I was just like any other kid who was interested in sport and play. I was a major football, basketball and baseball fan. Like any other kid I had a strong interest in toys too. I was looking to score or steal water guns, action figures, matchbox cars, electric football, popular board games and the newly introduced electronic games, etc. Many kids were big on art too as in the likes of graffiti or cartoon caricatures seen on Parliament/ Funkadelic album covers such as "Sir Nose D Void of Funk", "Starchild," and "Dr. Funkenstein."

I can remember these pastimes as I began to enter into my rites of passage during my formative years. When I was in my 4th or 5th grade years, many more crews were formed and it seemed everyone had to choose what group to be down with. Among the top crews listed respectively by their senior and junior counterparts were: Fifth Ave./ Young Riff, Crazy Crew/ Evona Ave., Queen City Rollers/ Brick Side, Bowery Boys 1/ 2, Puma Crew/ Puma Crew Jr., Funk Mob 1/ 2 and a bunch of others. Since I attended a government sponsored after school program at the "Y" and made friends with a lot of kids in the West End of town, I decided to get down with "Bowery Boys 2".

During this same era, the youth in the community were still being raised in consciousness as many throughout the city began adopting nicknames and Arabic or Muslim names. So I decided to take on the name "Wa'kee" and this is what I became known as in my street organization. I was excited about the name and I would say that my thought process was along the lines of a Black Nationalist with the ambition of becoming something like a "Muslim". My reasons were my love of Black People that was cultivated by my surroundings growing up and because it seemed like the right thing to do or be based on what I saw and wanted. However, I was way too ignorant of what it meant to be Muslim. While it was true that my aunt and cousins were Muslims, it appeared they lived in a very strict household and had different ways I didn't understand. I would later learn that this was the time period that Wallace Deen Muhammad took over the Nation of Islam and converted it over to Sunni Islam. This would explain why my relatives' customs appeared to be strange to me because they embraced the orthodox concept of Islam that had Arab overtones to it. This would explain the image conflict with the other Muslims who joined up with Farrakhan and re-established "Temple #80" a couple of years earlier in the East End of town. The "Temple" as they were called in those days was dedicated to the teachings of The Most Honorable Elijah Muhammad. Now those brothers looked more like the image I could identify with on multiple levels.

The Muslims of the Nation of Islam were strong and growing at a steady pace. Minister Farrakhan successfully reestablished the Temple in Plainfield under "the second resurrection" which was the term referred to the rebuilding of the Nation of Islam after Wallace Deen Muhammad had denounced the teachings of his Father and dismantled the original organization and it's teachings. In its stead, Wallace had christened the organization "The Community of Al-Islam in the West" and referred to his followers as "Bilalians". Wallace made it extremely unpopular for anyone to refer or believe in his Father's teachings. When all appeared lost for those faithful to Elijah's teachings, Farrakhan had decided to rebuild the NOI. This he had to do in the face of opposition by Wallace's group so he was very careful how he maneuvered in those days. I would later hear Farrakhan say at a Saviours' Day speech that he faced too much opposition in the larger cities such as New York, Newark, Philadelphia and Chicago so he started study groups in smaller cities such as Plainfield.

One example of the times is when Minister Farrakhan gave one of his first public lectures under the second resurrection. It was in 1977 at a restaurant called L' Affaire in Plainfield. Finding himself starting all over from scratch, Farrakhan didn't have an entourage to accompany him as he traveled to the venue in a Volkswagen with only his female cousin and her companion. One would imagine that this was a very humble situation for a man who just years earlier seemed to have all of Black America's attention as The National Representative of the Nation of Islam under his benefactor Elijah Muhammad. To make things more complicated, a rumor had surfaced that some Bilalians from Newark were coming down to possibly do harm to the Minister because of his choice to stand back up and reclaim Elijah's version of Islam. This news alerted the militant Muslim diehards in Plainfield who were loyal to Elijah's teachings as they regrouped once more to come and secure Minister Farrakhan who formally was the Minister of Mosque #7 in Harlem. The militants headed by an active community leader formally known as Linward Cathcart showed up in force at the event. Seeing that Brother Farrakhan had no security and was risking his life to resurrect the Teachings of the Most Honorable Elijah Muhammad caused Mr. Cathcart who later became "Minister Karriem" to stand post for the Minister. Other brothers quickly followed. Perhaps surprised by this demonstration of solidarity, the Minister continued his speech. All went well as his newfound security team stared down any potential troublemakers in the audience. Farrakhan later said when he witnessed what the brothers did for him he knew it was possible to rebuild the Nation of Islam. A short time later, the brothers had a greater surprise for the Minister when he was scheduled to speak at Plainfield High School. This time the brothers showed up wearing the FOI uniforms. That was the first time the Minister seen the FOI uniforms since the Nation had fell. It was another sign that "the Black Man would accept his own once again."

The show of solidarity was strong enough for Minister Farrakhan to establish a strong hold in Plainfield while the rebuilding effort of the NOI was underway. It served to send a message to the Muslim community at large that a foundation was being developed to resurrect Elijah's theology. This was evident when the Muslims in Plainfield created the slogan "Hands off Farrakhan" and passed out buttons in the community with the same slogan. The local Plainfield administration was soon rewarded when they were sent to re-establish the Temples in Harlem (#7), Newark (#25) and Philadelphia (#12). After the Temples were re-established, Minister Farrakhan rewarded Minister Karriem by giving him the post as the East Coast Regional Minister and the head of Temple #7 in Harlem. The rest was history and that will have to wait to be told in another book.

Per Farrakhan's success, many elders in the community would go back to The Temple. The youth would be carried down to the Temple, too. One of my earliest experiences with this teaching was when my older brother and his friends decided to go and visit "The Temple" with his friend's mother. My older brother Eddie went to visit the Temple and he came back and told me about it. I remember that he was visibly excited about the whole experience. He was startled by their check procedures and he said the Fruit of Islam (FOI) explained to him that they didn't want a "Malcolm X" situation to happen again. That news strangely enough put me in even more awe of the Muslims. When I seen them on the streets the strength and authority they showed was impressive. I would later see this of the Five Percenters, too, although it was a more youthful expression.

Another major significant cultural change happening during this time was the advent of "Hip Hop." In my neighborhood we were into "emceeing" and "deejaying." This was especially true after The Sugar Hill Gang came out with "Rapper's Delight." Hip Hop put our ear to the street of what was happening in New York City. This phenomenon had everybody's eyes and ears open as we scrambled for cassette tapes of popular DJ's and MC's. Damn near everybody became a DJ or a MC. Hip Hop would play a significant role in spreading the knowledge of the 5% too although it was perfectly camouflaged or undetectable to the untrained ear in its earlier stages. Some of the DJ's in New York had "the knowledge of self," primarily "The World's Famous Supreme Team" that consisted of Just Allah "The Superstar" and See Divine "Master Mind." The two had a radio show in New York City that came on odd days of the week during the wee hours of the morning. Their signature song was an anthem they played called "The Enlightener." It was known to only the initiated few that this song was in fact the Five Percenters anthem written during the days of the founders Allah and Old Man Justice. Thus the lyrics in the anthem belted "Peace to Allah and Justice!" It was a catchy anthem too. You were considered to be cool if you knew the lyrics and could recite it out on the playground or schoolyard.

This brings me back to the conversation I had with the two brothers from the Bronx and their mentioning of the Five Percenters. Although I wasn't familiar with them, little did I know that a couple of years prior some Five Percenters came from Brooklyn a.k.a. "Medina" to Plainfield to spread the message of the Gods. It was three brothers named "Sincere," "Born" and "Mathematics." They began teaching some young teenagers. A few brothers embraced it but it didn't take root or become extremely popular until around 1983. That was the year I heard about them again, although I didn't make the immediate connection because they were being referred to exclusively as "The Gods." A few older brothers in rap crews in town began to take on names like "Righteous," "Freedom," "Supreme" and "Wise." I remember in my eighth-grade homeroom class, a girl classmate, perhaps joking or maybe serious, said they derived their names from food products like "Supreme Cake Frosting" and "Wise Potato Chips." However ludicrous the statement, I was curious and wanted to know more about this latest happening. Over that summer of 1983 more youth in my class began to identify with Islam and the Five Percent was beginning to make its impact. We would really see a boom in its growth after we graduated to the 9th grade.

After summer recess, in the first week of my freshman year, kids from all over the city attended the same high school. The Five Percenters were the talk of the school. I shared a metal shop class with my play cousin "Ty'lee" who lived on the West End and was in Bowery Boys 2 with me a couple of years earlier. He told me not to call him Ty'lee anymore and his name was now "Black Intelligence." He was now in the "Five Percent Nation." He asked me when I was going to get down. He then pulled out a folder and handed me a copy of a newspaper article clipping and pointed to a man's picture and said, "This is Allah right here." I looked at the picture (that appeared to be a mug shot) and soaked in the man's features. He was a dark-skinned man with a short haircut, trimmed moustache and a slight smirk on his face. I read the caption underneath the picture that read, "Allah was shot to death in a Harlem elevator on 112th Street." However the word "death" was crossed out and the word "life" was penciled above it. The article mentioned that this man's name was Clarence 13X Smith and he broke from the NOI to start his own youth movement that he called the Five Percenters. I looked at Black and just nodded my head and he said we could "build" about it later.

Black would continue to share with me the concepts of the Five Percent Nation and I would continue to listen. My experience made me want to learn more about the man in the picture, but it was very limited information about him. I went to the school library to find this knowledge and it was literally nowhere to be found, at least where I checked. However, there was information on other popular NOI figures such as Master Fard Muhammad, the Honorable Elijah Muhammad, Malcolm X, Muhammad Ali and a little on Louis Farrakhan, but nothing on Clarence 13X (Allah). However, all wasn't lost because I became very adept in NOI history, which was of significant value to my studies. Besides, at that time, the Gods never pushed the issue about the history of Allah (Clarence 13X) as a priority. The common response was that Allah didn't want us worshipping him; he left us the lessons so that we could become all that we could be. We already had a very short abbreviated history of the man we called the "Father Allah." The abbreviated version was that Allah joined the Temple in the early 60's under Malcolm X. He "mastered" the NOI "lessons" and left the Temple a few years later to teach the children in the street "the truth" as contained in the lessons. He blessed us with "Supreme Mathematics" to further "breakdown" the "sciences" found in the lessons. Then he was killed in Harlem but the "Nation" never died because "you cannot kill Allah." "Allah-U-Akbar!"

Now the above account may not appear much to some who aren't in the know but to a young impressionable mind that was seeking truth and knowledge of Black History it was captivating. Especially when you seen one of your peers embrace this teaching and then blossom to become very cool with a newly loaded vocabulary that made them appear smarter than the school teachers. Young Black kids contrary to popular opinion really want to "be something in life." I guess the message we received was be all that you can be...you are GOD. It was this notion that made me and many others sign on to this doctrine. A motto of the Plainfield Public School System was that "It was Cool to Be Smart." No one believed that until the Five Percenters came along. The Gods and Earths made that motto a reality. Even their names showed it. If I had to guess, at least 150 brothers in my high school changed their name. My cousin added onto his name "Black Intelligence" and he became "Black Intelligence Divine Star All Complete 360 Degrees God Allah." He used the acronym B.I.D.S.A.C. to shorten it. My best friend and I linked up with an "Enlightener" who was "Righteous So Natural God Allah." My best friend became "Dr. KAOS Born Engenderer P.H.D. God Allah." I became "Wakeel Allah."

My name was a variation of my prior "Muslim" name I had when I was in a street organization. It was actually given to me by my older play brother whose name was "Jamil Ali Quan." He had given me this name in the middle of a street beef that spilled over from a basement party in Roselle, New Jersey. On our way to meet back up with our adversaries he said my new name was "Wakill." The only explanation he gave me for the name change was that "everyone had to put ill in his name because we got to be ill." That little anecdote of his was enough for me to gather courage for the task at hand since I was one of the younger ones in the group who got to tag along that night since my older brother was there. I would later learn what the name meant in one of my trips to the library to study the history of Islam. A god let me do the knowledge to the "book of names." The name happened to be one of the 99 attributes of Allah and it mainly meant one who is trustworthy, advocate of truth and a counselor. Although I got the name under odd circumstances I knew it was meant for me and I have worn it ever since with pride.

With a new name and new identity we adopted a new name for the city and our crew. Each city in the region that had an abundance of Five Percenters was given a name that indicated it was a strong hold for the Gods. In New York City, Manhattan was "Mecca," Brooklyn was "Medina," Queens was "The Desert" and Long Island was "The Oasis" or vice versa depending on who you built with. In New Jersey, the state was called "Now Justice" and each of the cities where the gods resided were given names too. There were a few cities that had a sizeable population of Five Percenters such as Plainfield, Jersey City, Paterson, Elizabeth, Trenton, New Brunswick, Newark, Asbury Park, Atlantic City, Camden, Red Bank and many other cities in Jersey. Each city was given a divine name. For example, Asbury Park was called "Allah's Paradise" and Plainfield became known as "Power Force." Thus we adopted this as our crew name as well. We were the Power Force because the Gods rolled "with Power and Force."

Having the "knowledge of self" made my high school years very interesting and adventurous. It's definitely too much to tell here but some very fond memories nonetheless. It was a great experience to grow up in a community of "A-alikes." After making it through my teenage years and graduating from high school Allah blessed me with the opportunity to attend Morehouse College in Atlanta, Georgia. I owe this to my parents and Allah who made this opportunity possible for me. My mother always told me that I was going to end up going to that college. I used to think it was a joke and I believe she thought it was a joke too until circumstances came into play that allowed it to happen. The institution was a big change for me because it was a different environment from what I was accustomed to but in a good way. Except for the fact that there weren't any Five Percenters and/or any NOI Muslims on campus. Mostly everybody was Christian even though you had a certain level of "consciousness" on the campus. Plus you had some brothers from the tri-state area but they didn't really deal with Five Percenters because of the street reputation it had at that time. But I linked up with some good people from around the way. But it was cool to me because I viewed it as an opportunity to share the positive side of what the Five Percenters represented. I would later see that Islam blessed me to gain friendships in all walks of life and by Allah's permission I was able to have an impact on some of the students and by the time I graduated there was a whole community of Five Percenters on the campus. There is so much to tell about that whole experience and so little time to tell it so I will just leave it be for now.

So here I am after a couple of decades later after first receiving the "knowledge of self" and I'm still true to the same principles I was given as a kid. Many of us are much older and still believe in the same sound doctrinal principles although with a more mature expression. I still am a Five Percenter in a true sense of the word and still a Muslim in a true sense of the word. I pray to Allah that this never changes. But this isn't just my story; my story is one of thousands from young men and women who have been affected by the influential Five Percenters and its founder. *In The Name of Allah: A History of Clarence 13X (Allah) and The Five Percenters.* This is a book I have written and compiled to hopefully give back to my community and brothers and sisters who are traveling down the same path of enlightenment. I guess the God MC AZ put it best when he said in his rap, "we were beginners in the hood as Five Percenters, but something must have got in us cause all of us turned to sinners. Now some, resting in peace and some are sitting in San Quentin, others such as myself are trying to carry on tradition." I'm just trying to do my part and help carry on a tradition that still thrives by Allah's permission. I hope that this book helps to continue the rich tradition of the Five Percenters and Nation of Islam. I hope that this book makes it on the shelf of the libraries so that the next young God or Earth will be able find information on the man called Allah (The Hon. Clarence 13X Smith).

Introduction

Allah is God!" exclaims a young Black man as he stands in the center of his peers. His comrades listen intensely as he rapidly fires out a mini-lecture during the Five Percenter gathering known as the *"Universal Parliament."* The young Five Percenter is currently engaged in a ritual that is called "the cipher" in which he manifests "today's mathematics." His mini-presentation consists of Islamic teachings, life lessons, living clean and civilizing the world. The phalanxes of attentive men and women who surround him are members of the movement known as *"The Five Percenters."*

The origin of the Five Percenters can be traced to its founder, the late Clarence 13X Smith also known as Allah, a former member of the Nation of Islam. Inside the movement, he studied the teachings of the Honorable Elijah Muhammad under the auspices of Minister Malcolm X at the Harlem Mosque from 1960-1963. He eventually parted ways with the mosque and subsequently began to teach the NOI doctrine known as "the lessons" to neighborhood teens that led to him founding a movement he suitably called the Five Percenters.

The name and the ideology of the Five Percenters are based upon the core doctrine of the Nation of Islam (NOI). In NOI teachings it was taught that the population consisted of three types of people referred to as "the 85%, the 10% and the 5%." 85% of the population was ignorant of the truth of God and believed in a mystery spirit or "spook" god as they wandered aimlessly through life. 10% of the population was the ruling elite who duped and deceived the majority by promoting lies of a mystery spirit god in turn benefiting off of the hoodwinked population's ignorance; thus growing rich from their labor (a prime example were preachers and their followers). Alas, 5% of the population was the righteous teachers who knew the truth and had a sworn duty to liberate the rest of the population from their prison of lies into "Freedom, Justice and Equality." Most importantly was their duty to teach the truth of God -- that God was and is "the Black Man of Asia" whose proper name is Allah.

Clarence 13X who changed his name to "Allah" intentionally focused his message of Islam toward disenchanted youth. He was highly successful in attracting large numbers of teens to his movement. So much so that the Five Percenters became the largest youth organization in New York City once its numbers allegedly surpassed the membership of the Boy Scouts of America. These numbers garnered the attention of religious, political and civic leaders. Major political icons such as New York Mayor John V. Lindsay and Governor Nelson A. Rockefeller sought out Allah to help keep peace in New York City streets during the turbulent 60's. Allah advantageously put his political clout to use to foster programs for his movement and further his cause of teaching the youth the principles of his version of Islam.

During his short reign as leader of the Five Percenters, Allah faced many challenges but accomplished many achievements. Unfortunately, in June of 1969, unknown assassins fatally gunned him down. Even after his physical passing, countless youth have embraced the Five Percenters concepts. Throughout America and abroad, you hear young people referring to "Supreme Mathematics" or "120 lessons" (the fundamental teachings of the Five Percenters and the Nation of Islam). Thousands of young Blacks and Latinos have pledged allegiance to the Five Percenters philosophy. The message of the movement has had a profound impact on the subculture we know today as "Hip Hop" which has added to the group's popularity.

Within recent years, adherents have made attempts to chronicle the history of the persons and events that made it all possible. Different accounts have sparingly been made available through various sources. Often the material provided has proven to be contradictory because of conflicting perspectives. Even so, there has yet to be a comprehensive history written in regards to the man called Allah and the Five Percenters.

The Honorable Elijah Muhammad stated that "History is best qualified to reward all our research and it is the most attractive." With this in mind, a history of Allah and the Five Percenters have been compiled and presented as an anthology. The information is a result of numerous interviews, newspaper archives, Five Percenter articles and books that included references to the subject.

"In The Name Of Allah: A History of Clarence 13X and The Five Percenters," is an attempt to provide the reader with a basic comprehension of the origins of Allah (Clarence 13X) and the Five Percenters. The main purpose of this text is to enlighten and inform. May Allah bless you with the light of understanding. Peace.

Chapter 1
Son of Man

"For as the lightning comes from the east and flashes to the
west, so also will the coming of the Son of Man be."
-- Matthew 24:27

"I am the Supreme Ruler of the Universe."
-- Master Fard Muhammad

Master Fard Muhammad

One cannot understand the Five Percenter phenomenon
without first examining the history of its predecessor; the Nation
of Islam and its founders Master Fard Muhammad and The
Honorable Elijah Muhammad. What eventually became known
in American history as "the most powerful Black organization"

had a humble origin. Earlier historians captured the setting of the start of the movement:

> What we now know as "the Nation of Islam" had its beginnings in the ghettos of Detroit. The time was 1930. It was the first year of the Great Depression, a time of hunger, confusion, disillusionment, despair, and discontent. In 1931 shadows hung over the Black ghettoes of the United States. Scattered from East to West, North to South, were 17 million Black people wondering adrift in a veritable wasteland like ships long lost at the bottom of the sea.[1]

This history of the so-called American Negroes prior to and during this time was filled with slavery, suffering and death. It was inevitable given the horrible peculiar institution of slavery and its atrocities. In the early 1900s, with Blacks just recently being declared free by the Emancipation Proclamation, their "freedom" appeared to be more of the same injustice they faced over the centuries. Especially when the Great Depression hit America in 1929. Black people were worse off than all other nationalities and hit hardest by this event.

> Sick on the streets, some were trying to commit suicide. Alleys were ravaged for food. Many people searched high and low for their next meal. Hunger was all about. Evictions were everywhere. People were falling low looking for staple bread, meatless bones, raw potato peelings, or spoiled vegetables from which to make stew or soup, or image of soup. So wretched, filthy and poor were Black communities that in some cities twice as many Black babies as white babies were dying. The Black death rate exceeded the white birth rate. Many suffered from heart trouble, high blood pressure and malnutrition not to mention the day-to-day sicknesses and diseases such as fever, headaches, rheumatism, toothaches, etc.[2]

Throughout their sojourn in North America, Black folks had been waiting for years for some kind of relief from this miserable state of condition. There were noble attempts made by two great Black leaders but by this time both had come and gone. One was the great Marcus Garvey and the other being Noble Drew Ali. Both virtuous and dedicated men tried their best to uplift their people and met with limited success. These two figures were only soon to be toppled by the same injustices and oppressors they fought against. Noble Drew Ali had died under mysterious circumstances while Marcus Garvey was arrested by the United States Government and later deported on some trumped up charges. After the removal of these two Black leaders, only remnants of their movements survived and hope appeared to be lost.

Throughout the annals of history, it is an interesting fact that when a people reach their height of despair, there appears to be a yearning in nature that produces a savior—a messiah to snatch them back from the edge of the abyss. For Black Americans in the Thirties that Saviour was Master Fard Muhammad.

Ironically, Mr. Fard Muhammad chose to make his debut on July 4, 1930, in the midst of the American holiday known as "Independence Day." This day was set aside by America to celebrate its independence from the tyranny of Great Britain. To more conscious Black Americans this day reminded them of the hypocrisy of white America. The famous Black orator and abolitionist Frederick Douglass shared this perspective in his famous speech delivered 80 years earlier on July 4, 1852:

What, to the American slave, is your 4th of July? I answer: a day that reveals to him, more than all other days in the year, the gross injustice and cruelty to which he is the constant victim. To him, your celebration is a sham; your boasted liberty, an unholy license; your national greatness, swelling vanity; your sounds of rejoicing are empty and heartless; your denunciations of tyrants, brass fronted impudence; your shouts of liberty and equality, hollow mockery; your prayers and hymns, your sermons and thanksgivings, with all your religious parade, and solemnity, are, to him, mere bombast, fraud, deception, impiety, and hypocrisy a thin veil to cover up crimes which would disgrace a nation of savages. There is not a nation on the earth guilty of practices, more shocking and bloody, than are the people of this United States, at this very hour.

 Go where you may, search where you will, roam through all the monarchies and despotisms of the old world, travel through South America, search out every abuse, and when you have found the last, lay your facts by the side of the everyday practices of this nation, and you will say with me, that, for revolting barbarity and shameless hypocrisy, America reigns without a rival.[3]

It was in this same vein on a hot summer day on July 4, 1930, that Mr. Fard publicly proclaimed the independence of the Black Man in the midst of white America's Fourth of July celebration. Years later, Elijah Muhammad would share the significance of his teacher selecting that day to start his public ministry:

Who's Independence? Since 1776 you, Black man, have been worshiping the 4th of July along with the real author of the 4th of July...(the white man) as a day of Independence for themselves. It is the white slave-master and his children who enjoy setting forth the 4th of July as a day of rejoicing over achieving this country's Independence from any other foreign source.

Now, the history of the 4th of July shows that it is the Independence Day of the American white man. They wrote the Declaration of Independence for themselves. The white man did not put anything in the Declaration of Independence for the benefit of the Black Man, who was the servitude - slave of the white man at that time. The joy which the black slave experienced on these holidays of the white man was due to the Black man getting a rest from his labor and the days which the white man had set aside for celebration. That is all the Black slave was rejoicing over...that he did not have to work that day. But, you are free now; and you do not need this for an excuse for your worship of the 4th of July. There is no further need for us to worship the gaining of the white man's independence.

Let us look again at our own Black independence and how it came on this same day of the 4th of July....at the Coming of Allah (God) Who came in the Person of Master Fard Muhammad, to Whom praises are due forever, on July 4, 1930.

The significance of His coming to us, on the Independence Day of the white man, is very great. It is their day of great rejoicing. As with former peoples and their governments, their destruction took place when they were at the height of their rejoicing.[4]

Little is known about the kind of reception Fard faced immediately after his proclamation. Some critics advised that perhaps it was a lukewarm reception since he was viewed as a stranger in the very community he selected to address. Only a few things seemed to be clear about the visitor whose mission was "to teach Islam to Black people in America."

Fard began his mission first as a peddler selling among other things, artifacts, beads, Moroccan leather bags and silks on the street corners of Detroit. To attract attention he would tell Black pedestrians as they passed that "these wares are from your home country and that he himself was from there."

At first skeptical Blacks paid scant if any attention to the lanky peddler who claimed to have come from their home country. The sidewalk crowds loitering around the UNIA building on West Lake Street ignored his harangues and dismissed him as just another carpetbagger. Even the presence of African beads and artifacts among Fard's wares failed to arouse more than a casual interest in the peddler.

For one thing, many Black residents of Detroit were leery of the peddler, for he was a man without known friends or relatives and his nationality and racial origin were subject to dispute, all they knew about him is that he called himself Fard Muhammad or Fard Muhammad Ali.[5]

If Fard faced challenges in the community, perhaps this would have been expected. After all, he had two obstacles to overcome in the minds of the people. One was the fact he didn't have any known ties in the community, secondly, was his obscure racial heritage. To many Fard had an Asiatic countenance but it was hard to make out his racial identity. He would be considered by some to be very "light-skinned" in complexion. Perhaps light enough to blend in with Caucasians but swarthy enough to be recognized as a so-called Negro. Perhaps more accurately he could have easily fit in with any mulatto, as Fard himself would later confirm of his mixed parentage. But prior to him revealing his origins, there were speculations about his background.

Inevitably a proliferation of legends developed about so mysterious a person. One legend about Fard is that he was a Jamaican born of a Muslim Syrian father. Another described him as a Palestinian Arab. Still another claims he was a Saudi and a son of wealthy parents of the tribe of Koreish—the tribe of Prophet Mohammad, founder of classical Islam. Even the Detroit police contributed their own to the exercise. Their record claims that Fard himself told them he was "The Supreme Ruler of the Universe."[6]

Others in Fard's circle said he was closely related by blood to the dynasty of the Hashemite sheriffs of Mecca who became kings of the Hejaz. He is said to have been educated at a college in England, in preparation for a diplomatic career in the service of the kingdom of the Hejaz. However, he nobly abandoned his secure future to bring "freedom, justice and equality," to "his uncle" living "in the wilderness of North America, surrounded and robbed completely by the Cave Man." Nevertheless to many he encountered, he appeared to be another very light skinned Black man or perhaps a "mulatto."

Racial origin and divine claims aside, what couldn't be questioned was the timeliness of Fard's message and its specific design to address the situation of Black America. No other place was probably more ideal than Detroit that seemed to be the perfect fit with the right demographic.

> Detroit in 1930 was the logical place to begin any organization of American Blacks. Within the crowded confines of the Black section of the city, a would-be leader could find support for almost any type of movement. A compacted Black ghetto, Detroit at the time had the largest concentration of poor Blacks. Here were to be found representatives of all elements in the Black world: sensitive artists, struggling businessmen, self-anointed preachers, poorly-paid laborers, and ignorant sidewalk loafers.
>
> Among such a desperate people it was easy for an emotional appeal that might otherwise be ignored by a more sophisticated Black community, to find a sympathetic audience any movement that addressed itself to the needs of the Blacks who had been left out or deprived of the gratification of material wealth promised in the American dream would certainly make a strong impact among the lower stratum of the community.[7]

Considering the task at hand, and undeterred by any initial seeming indifferences on the part of his future followers, Fard adopted a more personal approach to gain the confidence of his people. He underwent a door-to-door campaign under the guise of selling his wares with the real intention of getting into their homes to teach Islam. At first, Fard's relationship with the Black community was casual and informal. He went about his business in an unobtrusive way, sharing whatever they had to offer him.

Initially when given the opportunity to speak, Fard confined his discussions to his own personal experiences in foreign countries and suggestions for improving the personal health of his listeners. Soon his discussions escalated to include rigorous Muslim prohibitions against dancing, smoking and adultery. He admonished men and women to live soberly and with dignity, encouraging them to work hard to devote themselves to the welfare of their families and to deal honestly with all including authorities.

"He came first to our houses selling raincoats, and then afterwards, silks. In this way he could get into the people's houses, for every woman was eager to see the nice things the peddlers had for sale. He told us that the silks he carried were the same kind our people used in their home country and that he had come from there. So, we all asked him to tell us about our own country. If we asked him to eat with us, he would eat whatever we had on the table, but after the meal he began to talk: "Now don't eat this food. It is poison for you. The people in your own country do not eat it. Since they eat the right kind of food they have the best health all the time. If you would live just like the people in your home country, you would never be sick anymore." So, we all wanted him to tell us more about ourselves and about our home country and about how we could be free from rheumatism, aches and pains.[8]

At Fard's own suggestion, the small group was invited to a customer's house he frequently visited so they could hear more. The small bunch readily accepted; as they were already accustomed to holding small informal meetings for church gatherings in others homes. As the people cared less about his origin and he drew nearer to his core audience, Fard came out of his true bag. The posing merchant condemned the Judeo-Christianity religion as, *"a contrivance of the white man designed for the enslavement of nonwhite people."* Instead of it responding to the hopes and aspirations of the Black man, Fard declared, *"Christianity helped keep the Black Man doped into subservience to the White Establishment."* It was these types of strong accusations that caused an emotional crisis for some of his listeners. W. D. Fard soon adopted a more tactical approach as he pointed out subtle criticisms of the Bible. An early follower recalls his first experience hearing Fard:

The first time I went to a meeting I heard him say: "The Bible tells you that the Sun rises and sets. That is not so. The Sun stands still. All your lives you have been thinking that the Earth never moved. Stand and look toward the Sun, and know that it is the Earth you are standing on which is moving." Up to that day I always went to the Baptist church. After I heard that sermon from the prophet, I was turned around completely. When I went home and heard that dinner was ready, I said: "I don't want to eat dinner. I just want to go back to the meetings." I wouldn't eat my meals, but I goes back that night, and I goes to every meeting after that. Just to think that the Sun above me never moved at all and that the Earth we are on was doing all the moving. That changed everything for me."[9]

In lieu of Christianity, Fard taught that Blacks true religion was called "Islam" and its adherents are rightfully called "Muslims." Fard supplemented his points with great stories of the Black Man's history and greatness. He imparted to his listeners that there existed a cavalry of "brothers and sisters in the East" waiting for them to claim their true heritage.

As news traveled quickly through Paradise Valley, curious dwellers sought to hear the prophet with their own ears. To meet the demands, tenants set up more group meetings in their homes. Once Fard drew a captive audience he wasn't shy in delivering his teachings. As NOI biographer and author, C. Eric Lincoln explains.

He had come, he told the handful of Blacks who gathered to hear him, from the holy city of Mecca. His mission, as he described it, was "to wake the 'Dead Nation in the West'; to teach [them] the truth about the white man, and to prepare [them] for the Armageddon."...Fard was explicit on the point: In the Book of Revelation it is promised that there will be a final battle between good and evil, and that this decisive battle will take place at Har-Magedon, "the Mountain of Megiddo," in the Great Plain of Esdraelon in Asia Minor. But the Bible has a cryptic message for the initiated of Black Islam...The forces of "good and evil" are the forces of "black and white." "The Valley of Esdraelon" symbolizes "the Wilderness of North America." The Battle of Armageddon is to be the Black Man's final confrontation of the race which has so long oppressed him.[10]

Wallace Fard Muhammad's words reverberated throughout Black Detroit. His fame began to spread far and wide. Impressed by his lectures, His first band of followers bestowed the divine title of "prophet" upon him, although he didn't say it of himself. In fact, Fard just shared little about his own personal background. An early follower who heard some of his first addresses recalls Fard speaking on the subject:

> My name is W. D. Fard and I came from the Holy City of Mecca. More about myself I will not tell you yet, for the time has not yet come. I am your brother. You have not yet seen me in my royal robes."[11]

As He gained ground and his following increased He grew bolder in his attacks on Western society. Specifically He claimed that the Blacks of the United States were not Americans but "Asiatics." For it was their forefathers who had been stolen from the continent by white slave masters who came in the name of Jesus four centuries ago. He condemned the name "Negro" as an invention of the white man designed to separate Blacks on American soil from their Asiatic brothers and sisters.

Fard used the Bible as a textbook to teach so-called Negroes about their true religion—Islam, not Christianity. He advised that Islam was the true religion of the Black Men of Asia. He widely used the Bible because it was the only religious book his followers knew. It was not the proper book for the Black Nation; but carefully interpreted, it could be made to serve until they were introduced to "The Holy Quran."

The prophet also emphasized that the ailments Black people suffered was a direct result of their rearing by the white man. He advised that disobedience to Islam was responsible for the peoples' sickness. In his doctrine he would vividly describe the condition of the Black man in the ghetto:

> "He had fever, headaches, chills, grippe, hay fever, rheumatism, also pains in all joints. He was disturbed with foot ailments and toothaches. His pulse beat more than eighty-eight times per minute: therefore he goes to the doctor every day and gets medicine for every day in the year: one after each meal and three times a day, also one at bedtime."[12]

Part of Fard's lure was his ability to utilize the Black man's environment to illustrate his key points. Both their physical and economic hardships bared witness to his teachings. Fard drew from other references as well. He cited different Bible verses and included some of the teachings of Marcus Garvey and Noble Drew Ali that foretold the coming of a new prophet.

As Fard's star grew, the house-to-house meetings became inadequate to accommodate all those who wished to hear the prophet. The solution was obvious: they would rent out a Hall to hold their meetings. After the Hall was secured, the house-to-house meetings were discontinued and a tightly knit organization replaced the informal gatherings. Potential members were examined before acceptance and were registered by the group; subsequently a hierarchy in the organization was established.

> Maladjusted migrant Blacks came into contact with the prophet at the informal meetings in their homes. With the change to temple services, the movement took on a more formal character. The teaching became more systemized. Membership was recognized and "registered." The movement itself became organized in a hierarchical manner...The rapid increase in membership made necessary the development of a formal organization. Subsidiary organizations had been established as the need for them arose...[13]

At this point many of the old followers of Marcus Garvey and the Late Noble Drew Ali began to pledge themselves to Fard's movement. Fard used other familiar venues that had a history of Black Nationalist speeches where he echoed the same sentiments as his forerunners.

> Early in August 1931 Fard told a crowd of Blacks gathered in the Old Universal Negro Improvement Association (UNIA) Hall at 1841 West Lake Street, that he was a "prophet of Allah from the holy city of Mecca." His mission, as he described it was, "to wake the dead nation in the West, to tell the Black population of the United States the truth about the white man and to help them prepare for an impending Armageddon."
> Often referring to the book of Revelations, Fard reiterated to his listeners that there would be a total war between good and evil and that this battle would occur at a place he called Har-

Magedon in the plains of Esdraelon. The important question was exactly where were these two places located? To this question Fard was very explicit: the valley of Esdraelon represents "the wilderness of North America" and Har-Magedon "the United States."

The battle of Armageddon was to be the Black man's final clash with the white man who had for so long kept him enslaved. To avoid losing the battle, the prophet prescribed Islam as the only solution because "it was the natural religion of the Black man." Only in Islam could he hope to find freedom, justice and equality.[14]

Fard took advantage of his opportunity to address this large audience in the hall. Many were electrified by his words. He had yet to use his magnetic personality on a group of that size, and intended to make the most of it. He carried the audience along with him in an impassioned plea for Blacks to throw off the white man's religion because it had not been of service in making better Black communities. Among the several hundreds of people who eventually heard Fard's message was a young Elijah Poole (soon to be renamed Muhammad), the future Messenger of Allah. Many people familiar with the message had accepted Fard as "the Prophet." However, it would be to one man that He would fully reveal Himself.

Chapter 2
Behold I Will Send you Elijah

The Honorable Elijah Muhammad

"Behold I will send you Elijah the prophet before the coming of the Dreadful day of the Lord; and he will turn the hearts of the fathers to their children, and the hearts of the children to their father, less I come and smite the earth with a curse." Malachi 4:5-6

Thirty-four years after the signing of the Emancipation Proclamation, Elijah Muhammad was born Elijah Poole on October 7, 1897, in rural Sandersville, Georgia. He was the seventh child of thirteen children born to proud parents Willie and Marie Poole. From the very beginning it was sensed that Elijah was extraordinary.

When Elijah was born a perceptive paternal grandfather had given him the name Elijah and always addressed him as "Elijah, the prophet." He often told the boy's parents that one day he would be a prophet of God. The grandfather was correct. His grandson lived to become a prophet and the "Last Messenger of Allah."[15]

From the beginning of his upbringing, Elijah's parents and siblings knew he was special. Elijah was often asked by his brothers and sisters to settle their arguments because of his fair mindedness. In this regard, Elijah took after his father who was a student of the Bible.

Elijah's father was a hardworking sharecropper and a Baptist minister to Black town residents. In addition to giving informative sermons every Sunday, Willie Poole was also known to preach to his family. As little Elijah attended his father's church as well as the family sessions, he grew fond of the prophetic utterances and apocalyptic verses he heard in the sermons.

Unlike the depiction of Christianity's heaven, Elijah's family had it hard like hell along with the rest of the Blacks in the South. To be a southern Black at the turn of the century usually meant a life of hardship, pain and numerous threats to their survival. The lynching of Blacks was the order of the day and hate groups like the Ku Klux Klan ran rampant. Given the times, Elijah learned the harsh reality of murderous racism at a very early age.

Willie Poole had warned his family about the perils of being Black and how to avoid the hanging rope of the white man. One such instruction was for his children to never stray away from the long dirt road that led to their tenant farm. Under no circumstances were the Poole children to ever attempt a shortcut through the woods even if other neighborhood children decided to do so.

Elijah, who typically stayed out of trouble, usually heeded this warning but on one autumn day allowed his curiosity to get the best of him. It was on this day that his older brothers and sisters were working chores on the farm for the upcoming harvest and felt that Elijah at his young age would only get in the way. Dismissed from all duties, Elijah ventured to the path of the long dirt road. Straying far from home Elijah decided it was to time to go back before his family missed him. In an effort to get home quicker, he felt it best to find a shortcut through the forbidden woods his father so tenaciously warned him about.

Elijah speculated that his family's small cabin was just on the other side of the woods. He ventured in and felt a surge of guilt but soon became comfortable with his surroundings. So comfortable that he was confident he'd find his way home too soon and decided to stretch out on the grass and take in the surroundings. While lying on his back studying the tree patterns against the spacious sky Elijah felt this was a place he could come whenever he felt like it. His peace was soon startled by a thump he heard in the woods. Afraid that his brothers came looking for him, Elijah ran and hid behind a nearby thicket to avoid from being punished. What he seen next would change his life forever.

When he saw that the approaching figures were not his brothers, he felt relieved. Then, as the people came closer, his sense of relief turned to a mixture of fear and disbelief. There were four people. At the head of the small party was a white man holding on to a rope. At the other end of the rope was a Black man, who had it tied about his midsection, as though he were a horse or a mule. They were followed by two more white men in work clothes. These two pushed the captured black, whose hands were tied behind his back, to keep him moving. Was this some kind of game? Elijah wondered.[16]

Unable to process what was happening in his young mind, Elijah continued to look on in silence. Witnessing the man forcefully pushed to the ground by his captors, Elijah recognized him as an occasional visitor of his father's church. He wanted to reach out to the man but Elijah was paralyzed as the white men proceeded to kick their victim.

When the whites began kicking their prisoner and insulting him, Elijah buckled as if he, too, had been kicked. Silent tears rolled down his face. The man in front proceeded to untie the rope around the black man's wrists. He took one end of the rope and threw it over a sturdy branch. Leering at his captive, who still lay facedown on the forest floor, he formed the other end into a noose. Then he slipped the hooped rope around the black man's neck. Elijah covered his face with his hands as the victim was hoisted from the ground, sputtering and choking. It only took a matter of minutes. After the lynchers were sure the man was dead, they passed a bottle among themselves and looked up at his body, admiring their handiwork. Then, as though they had just concluded an entire day's work, they strolled away, leaving the strangled black man swinging from the tree.[17]

Shocked by what he saw, Elijah mustered up the courage and came out of hiding. He noticed the victim's shoe on the ground. As in a daze, Elijah crept upon the shoe and was transfixed in awe until his spell was broken by something warm he felt dripping on his face. Seeing tints of red, he realized that he was under the corpse as blood trickled onto his cheek. The horrible images of that day remained with Elijah throughout his life and he drew from this experience as fuel for the prophetic role he assumed in his future.

After witnessing this tragedy Elijah came of age to attend school where he only went up to the 3rd or 4th grade. Due to his family's economic problems, Elijah quit school to work as a sharecropper where he plowed behind a mule and tended to crops during harvest time to help make ends meet. Coming of age, he left his house at sixteen and a couple of years later began courting a young lady named Clara Evans from a neighboring town in Georgia. Two years later, the young couple eloped and married on May 2, 1917. From this union would eventually come eight children —Emmanuel, Ethel, Lottie, Nathaniel, Herbert, Elijah Jr., Wallace and Akbar.

Only having two kids at that time, Elijah got a job with the Southern Railroad Company and the Cherokee Brick Company in Macon, GA. He was a good worker and exemplified the same golden characteristics he shared as a child. Elijah had one main condition of his employer; never disrespect him or curse him. As common in that time, the inevitable would soon happen. One day He was unjustly disrespected by a hostile white employer and decided he had enough. Elijah said, *"I saw enough of the white man's brutality to last me 26,000 years."*

After this incident, Elijah decided it was a good time to leave Georgia and make a move up North to help his family. In those days it was common for Black families to leave the South in pursuit of a better life of economic promise in the North. So in April 1923, he moved his wife and two kids to Detroit, Michigan. The budding auto industry in Detroit made it an upwardly mobile city that held out promise for recent southern migrants. Detroit did initially prove to offer opportunities for Elijah. He landed a job on the assembly line in an auto plant.

> In 1923 my wife and our two children went to Detroit, Michigan and from that year on, to 1929, I worked for various companies in that city, including the Detroit Copper Company, the American Nut Company, Briggs Body and the Chevrolet Axle Company.[18]

Like the other legions of southern Blacks, Elijah soon discovered that the bright promise of the North was a failed lie. To many Blacks, the North was the South all over again minus the white liberal sweet talk about equality. His employers were impressed by his dependability, but the work was backbreaking and offered very little in advancement opportunities. To make things worse, a severe economic crisis was about to hit America and Elijah lost his job.

> In the latter part of 1929, due to the depression, I was out of work but remained in Detroit.[19]

In 1929 the United States was plundered by the New York Stock Exchange crash. This inevitably led to the period of economic misery known as "The Great Depression." This only helped to exasperate racial matters as race relations took another decline. Lynching and race riots continued unabated without any relief in sight. In America, Black people were still on the bottom and were despondently treated as such.

The average wage for Blacks in Detroit was 55 cents an hour and dropped to 10 cents during the lean times of the Depression. Many Blacks were lucky if they had a job at all. Elijah was impacted by the fall.

> Poole was among those who lost their jobs in 1929 and stood on relief lines. He and his family faced extremely lean times. The Pooles often subsisted on such meals as chicken feet and vegetable leaves. Coal for the kitchen stove, which was used to heat the house, was collected from the beds along the railroad tracks. Nothing of even the slightest use was thrown away. The four Poole children wore hand-me-downs given to Clara by the people for whom she cleaned, washed and ironed.

...Poole remained on relief until 1931. He had no other alternative. Every morning, he left home before dawn to join the lines of thousands of unemployed people that formed in front of the gates of the local manufacturing plants. He often waited there all morning, hoping to be hired for a day's work, only to return home empty-handed to his hungry children.[20]

Elijah was of one of those who lost his job and was forced to stand on relief lines that extended for blocks. His family barely could make it by on portions of chicken feet and vegetable leaves. His four children at the time wore hand me downs from the white people whom Clara cleaned for and had to put cardboard in pairs of shoes that they took turns borrowing from each other.

Every morning Elijah sought work in front of the gates of manufacturing plants only to wait hours before being sent home empty handed to a hungry family. In an attempt to drown his woes Elijah turned to drinking. Things became so bad that Clara would have to search for Elijah to bring him home. One day she discovered him passed out on the railroad tracks.

In the midst of this great disillusionment, Elijah was at the crossroads of his destiny. He would soon discover that hope was on the way.

Chapter 3
Al-Najm (The Star)

1. By the Star When it goes down –
2. Your companion is neither
   Astray nor being misled.
3. Nor does he say (aught) Of (his own) Desire.
4. It is no less than Inspiration sent down to him:
5. He was taught by one Mighty in Power,
6. Endued with Wisdom: For he appeared (In stately form)
7. While he was in the highest part of the horizon:
8. Then he approached and came closer,
9. And was at a distance of but two bow-lengths Or even nearer;
10. So did (Allah) convey The inspiration to His Servant—
    (Conveyed) what He (meant) To convey.
11. The (Prophet's) (mind and) heart In no way falsified That which
    he saw.
12. Will ye then dispute With him concerning What he saw?

Holy Quran, Surah 53: 1-12

In the midst of these great trials and tribulations, Elijah's will outlived the negative circumstances surrounding him. Elijah groped to find a way out of the overwhelming hell that engulfed him and his people. His prayers were soon answered with unexpected good news from a family member.

Elijah's brother, Charlie, came to tell him about a man who was speaking in a basement. Charlie was excited as he explained to Elijah some of the things the man was teaching. After his brother described his experience, Elijah was very interested in meeting the heralded man. In his book "This is the One," Mr. Jabril Muhammad writes:

One day, in the early fall of 1931, in Detroit, Michigan, Messenger Muhammad heard from his brother, Charlie, that there was a man teaching things he ought to hear. Charlie was excited. Among the "things" the man was teaching was Islam.

At that time the Messenger had the wrong idea of Islam. He would later say that he thought it was a "heathen religion." However, he was told enough to want to meet the Teacher and hear His teachings. He also felt this was the One he was expecting. He was told that the man's name was Mr. W. D. Fard and that He was teaching a few people in a basement. Elijah rushed to the place but did not see Him. He was told the man was there earlier.[21]

Perhaps disappointed by his near encounter, Elijah didn't let it deter his pursuit of Fard. He relentlessly attended meetings throughout the city in hopes of catching a glimpse of the evasive sage.

He went to other meetings, held there and elsewhere, but continued to miss Him until the night of September 22nd. He (the Messenger) was eager to see and hear Mr. Fard because he had a strong feeling about this man's identity.[22]

Finally getting the opportunity to hear him speak, Elijah hearkened to the words spoken by Fard that night. Many years later Elijah would repeat the contents of the lecture in his future speeches and writings. Elijah recalls his encounter and experience with his teacher Wallace D. Fard:

He began teaching us the knowledge of ourselves, of God and the devil, of the measurement of the earth, of other planets, and of the civilization of some of the planets other than earth.

He measured and weighed the earth and its water; the history of the moon; the history of the two nations, black and white, that dominate the earth. He gave the exact birth of the white race; the name of their God who made them and how; and the end of their time, the judgment, how it will begin and end.

He taught us the truth how we were made "slaves" and how we are kept in slavery by the "slave-masters" children. He declared the doom of America, for her evils to us was past due. And that she is number one to be destroyed. Her judgment could not take place until we hear the truth....[23]

Being quite astute in scripture, Elijah noticed that Fard's words and actions tallied with the Bible's prophetic verses He studied as a child. Stored in Elijah's memory were all the Sunday sermons from his Father that spoke to past and future prophecies. In Elijah's mind, Fard perfectly fit the bill about what the coming one would say and do on his arrival. "This is the One expected by the prophets," Elijah thought while in the audience.

As soon as he saw and heard Mr. Wallace D. Fard he knew Him to be the One the world had been expecting for the last 2000 years. It came to him that the man he beheld was the very man expected by the prophets, and others, Who would come in, or under, many good names: Jesus included.[24]

After analyzing the speaker's words, Elijah collected his thoughts and felt compelled to communicate what was on his mind. When Mr. W. D. Fard concluded his lecture, he offered to shake the hand of all those in attendance. Elijah filed in line and awaited his opportunity to speak to the prophet. When his turn arrived, Elijah expressed his thoughts directly to Fard.

When the meeting was over he got in line with others to shake the Speaker's hand. When his turn came, Elijah told Him that He was the One Whom the Bible's prophets foresaw coming along about that time, about 2,000 years after Jesus, or the Son of Man.
Almost simultaneously Mr. Fard Muhammad looked around to see who else heard that, and then at Elijah a little sternly. His smile followed the look. He bent His head close to him, put one hand on his shoulder, and the other on his forehead. Pressing His mouth against Elijah's ear, He whispered:
"Yes, I am that One. But who else knows that but yourself?"
God continued that he (Elijah) should keep quiet about this. He would let him know when to make that known. Then, gently, He nudged Elijah away and began talking with the others nearby.[25]

Fard's response confirmed Elijah's hunch. Full of excitement, he left the meeting and attempted to explain what he saw to his brother Charlie. His brother couldn't grasp Elijah's claim. Undaunted by his brother's failure to see his point, Elijah put his thoughts on paper. A short time later He wrote W. D. Fard a letter reiterating his belief in his identity. A month went by before Elijah heard anything. Perhaps by a divine appointment, Elijah's wife Clara had attended a meeting where Fard was addressing an audience in another area of town. During the public meeting Fard openly told Clara to advise her husband Elijah that he can start teaching in a section of Detroit called Hamtramck.

After receiving the good news from his wife, Elijah readily accepted and took this as his cue to spread the message of Islam. So he started teaching that W. D. Fard was the answer to the prophecies of the coming of Jesus as outlined in the Bible under the name "Son of Man." Not long afterwards, Fard paid Elijah a special visit at his home. He came to confirm Elijah's acknowledgment of his identity in person. Elijah recalls their conversation on the subject:

> I asked him, "Who are you, and what is your real name?" He said, "I am the one that the world has been expecting for the past 2,000 years." I said to Him again, "What is your name?" He said, "My name is Mahdi; I am God, I came to guide you into the right path that you may be successful and see the hereafter."[26]

After reaffirming his identity to Elijah, Fard addressed his business at hand. He described his mission as it related to freeing the poor so-called Negro from the grips of the white man in North America. He proclaimed that America was to be judged for her mistreatment of the so-called Negroes. Her European sister nations would not be spared either, but America was number one on the record to incur Allah's wrath.

> When God appeared to me in the person of Master Fard Muhammad, to whom praises are due forever, in 1931 in Detroit, He said that America was His number one enemy on His list for destruction. While He mentioned other European whites as getting a little extension of time, He singled America and Germany out as being the two worst vicious, evil, destructive trouble-makers of the entire nation earth. And that America had mistreated us (the so-called Negroes) so much that she cannot be equally paid back for the evils she has done to the poor black slaves.[27]

Recognizing the serious nature of Fard's claim, Elijah seemed to take it all in stride as if he was somehow prepared in advance to receive this revelation. Some would argue that any Black Man's experience liken unto Elijah's had prepared him for this message of retribution against a colonial oppressor. Others might say he was born for the mission and divinely prepared for his destiny. In any sense, Fard and Elijah created a strong bond from their first meeting. Perhaps this was due to Elijah's acknowledgement of Fard's status, even though Fard cautioned Elijah about revealing his true identify before the proper time. Given the magnitude of this assertion, Fard instructed Elijah to stay within limits and to be cautious about this when in public. He instructed him not to talk too much about him while he was present in front of others. Fard used an analogy to justify his tactic. He advised Elijah, referring to the people, "not to give the little baby meat, but milk instead." The two grew very close and Fard would visit Elijah's house almost daily since their first meeting.

In Islam, it was important for the recent convert to receive a "righteous" name. Fard single-handedly was responsible for giving out new names to his followers.

> Those who accepted this teaching became new men and women, or, as the prophet expressed it, were restored to their original true selves. As a mark of this restoration, the prophet gave them back their original names which the Caucasians had taken from them...Each new believer wrote a separate letter asking for his original name, which the prophet was supposed to know through the Spirit of Allah within him.[28]

To reflect his new status, Fard gave Elijah the surname, Karriem, replacing his slave name, Poole. He became known as Elijah Karriem. Later, in the very near future, He would ask Elijah to take on a "bigger" name. For the initiated in Islam, a righteous name wasn't to be taken lightly.

> The people who secured the new names value them as their greatest treasure. "I would not give up my righteous name. That name is my life." The became so ashamed of their old slave names that they considered that they could suffer no greater insult than to be addressed by the old name. They sought to live

in conformity with the Law of Islam as revealed by the prophet, so they might be worthy of their original names. Gluttony, drunkenness, idleness, and extra-marital sex relations, except with ministers of Islam, were prohibited completely. They bathed at least once a day, and kept their houses scrupulously clean, so that they might put away all marks of slavery from which the restoration of the original name had set them free.[29]

Elijah dedicated himself wholeheartedly to Fard and joined the student ministers' class. Though opposed by some moderates in the hierarchy, He became Fard's most trusted lieutenant. This sparked jealousy among others that held certain ranks in the movement. Many of the current ministers in the organization didn't feel Elijah was the most qualified to represent the movement at their level. So when it came to electing ministers from amongst themselves the body never elected Elijah. After all, he wasn't the most charismatic or eloquent as some of the other leaders in the organization. But W. D. Fard had seen something that his ministers didn't see. In an unprecedented move Fard had rewarded Elijah's faith by bestowing upon him the highest honor. This He did publicly in front of the other rival Ministers so there wouldn't be any misunderstanding about his choice.

The Savior, Master Fard Muhammad used a system of permitting the student ministers to select their own minister from among themselves. They would always select the most articulate, smooth-talking one. However, one day the Savior decided to select his own. "I've let you select yours for a while," he told the student ministers. "Now I'll select mine."

"Hey, you over there, Karriem!" Master Fard called out to the humble little man seated in the corner rear of the classroom. "Who me?" The Messenger asked humbly, "Yes, you Elijah Karriem," The Savior commanded. "Come up here with me." The humble little man went to the front of the class and stood beside his master. The Savior put his right arm around the little man's shoulder and said, "From now on this is My Minister." The Savior gave Elijah the name of Muhammad, His name. Muhammad was given the title of "Supreme Minister."[30]

As the Supreme Minister, Elijah began to receive private tutelage from Fard for the next three and a half years; during which time he said he "heard things never revealed to others."

Fard's Teachings

In confidence Fard disclosed to Elijah more information on his personal background. He also revealed to Elijah his identity as his Apostle or Messenger:

> Among the many things Master Fard Muhammad told Messenger Muhammad was His own history. He told him that He came from the Holy City Mecca, Arabia, and began teaching Black people in Detroit July 4, 1930.
>
> He tried to get to Black people by going from door to door taking orders for made to measure clothes. His real aim was to get into their homes. Some of our people got a little suspicious. So later He would get business card orders from office people. After designing the cards, He would have them printed.
>
> This was, as the Messenger put it, a cover up. His real identity and purpose could not be revealed before the proper time. The problems of the Depression also served His purpose of "slipping in" to get to His future Apostle.
>
> ...The Messenger said that his Teacher came from the city of His birth, The Holy City Mecca. He (the Messenger) was given much information of His childhood, and of His life in general right up to the time of their meeting in 1931.[31]

Fard revealed to Elijah intimate details about his birth and childhood including information on his parents. He claimed his birth was rooted in divine prophecy and he was the offspring from a divine lineage for a divine purpose. According to scripture, God's children were to be taken off to a far strange land and made to serve a wicked race of people for a period of 400 years. Then it was written that God himself would come for his people. According to Fard, the Black Man in America best fitted this description.

> He took the Messenger back to what led His (Master Fard Muhammad's) Father to produce him in the first place. That which led to His birth was rooted in prophecy (the foresight and insight of the Gods) written in the Bible and Holy Qur'an concerning a lost people that needed finding, and of the new world that He would produce through them.

This lost people...would be living among the infidels. They would be living in subjection to the infidels...The Father of Master Fard Muhammad and the other wise scientist knew that it was time for them (us) to be found and redeemed. However, the scriptures did not give the location except in symbolic terms. So the Father wanted a Son Who would be able to search the civilizations of the earth to locate that lost member. He wanted a Son capable of getting among the infidels, among whom the lost people lived. This Son would then have to be able to make from among the lost people a disciple for Himself. Through that disciple He would get His people and return them to their own people. He would also destroy those who had deceived and misled his poor people.[32]

Perhaps the most shocking was Fard's revelation of his parents. According to Fard, his Father was an actual God himself and his mother happen to be a woman from "the Caucasus mountains."

This Father was a real Black man. He knew, therefore, that it would not have been wise for Him to come Himself. He knew He had to have a Son Who looked like the wicked infidels among whom He would have to go (and there were other factors in His reasoning). So He went up into the mountains and got a white woman: a Caucasian. He prepared her to give birth to this special Son.[33]

Due to the startling nature of the claim, NOI scholars including Elijah Muhammad, provided reasoning behind Fard's parentage.

This is hinted at in the Bible in the mention of a woman out of whom was drawn seven devils in the "gospels"...Again this Redeemer of those who were lost, had to be prepared in such a way that He could be accepted among the whites and His own people. He had to be able to move among both without being recognized, or discovered until the proper time. This was done. He was also made in such a nature that He would naturally deal justly with both people.[34]

Fard revealed his birth date as February 26, 1877. Fard told Elijah He studied for 42 years to prepare for his assignment. Fard mentioned He came in and out of North America since 1910 studying both people – Black and White. He even enrolled at the University of California at Berkley. In a mighty addition to that, Fard claimed he studied every educational system of the civilized world and traveled all throughout the vast earth. His claim grew grander when he indicated that he studied life on other planets including Mars.

> The Mahdi is a world traveler. He told me that He had traveled the world over and that He had visited North America for 20 years before making himself known to us, His people whom He came for. He had visited the Isle of the Pacific, Japan and China, Canada, Alaska, the North Pole, India, Pakistan, all of the Near East and Africa. He had studied the wild life in the jungles of Africa and learned the language of the birds. He could speak 16 languages and could write 10 of them. He visited every inhabited place on the earth and had pictured and extracted the language of the people on Mars and had knowledge of all life in the universe. He could recite by heart the histories of the world as far back as 150,000 years and knew the beginning and end of all things.[35]

The Teachings

After Elijah was selected as Fard's chief confidant, the two were practically inseparable night and day. Fard established an Islamic curriculum for Elijah to advance in his studies. He gave him his own personal copy of the Holy Quran and provided him a bibliography of 104 books to study. Many of the books were on the life of Prophet Muhammad. Elijah asked if these books were in the library there in Detroit. "No," was the answer.

Still rearing his new Nation, Fard sought to lend more credence to his ideology in the eyes of his followers. An unusually resourceful teacher, he was able to utilize such varied literature from the writing of the leader of Jehovah's Witnesses, Van Loon's Story of Mankind, Breasted's The Conquest of Civilization, the Quran, the Bible and certain literature of Freemasonry to teach his followers. Each contained different pieces of truth and Fard would provide the correct interpretation. However, some of his critics in efforts to understand the teaching often chose to explain it in a sensational way:

The Nation's story of creation had a unique twist, making it markedly different from those of other religious groups. According to Fard, the world was initially ruled by members of a black race who were known as the original men. Theirs was a highly advanced civilization, and their scientists formed mountains and seas, covered the land with animals, and blasted the moon, which had been part of the earth, into the sky. Some of the original men settled in Arabia and became known as the Tribe of Shabazz. They lived in peace, worshiping Allah from the holy city of Mecca, until evil entered the world in the form of a mad scientist named Yacub. Full of pride, Yacub broke the laws of Islam and was exiled from Mecca. His heart set on vengeance, he applied his knowledge of genetics to create a race of immoral men, the white devils.

The white caused endless trouble for the blacks until they were herded together and exiled to the cold wasteland of Europe. Allah then sent his black prophets Moses and Jesus to convert the white devils to Islam. Instead, the whites distorted the prophets' teachings and founded the blasphemous religions of Judaism and Christianity.

Fulfilling an ancient prophecy, the whites gained dominion over the entire world. They transported millions of blacks from Africa to the Americas in slave ships and stripped them of their language and cultural heritage. Along the way, blacks were brainwashed into thinking that whites were their superiors. Fard claimed it was time for the reign of the whites to end.[36]

To supplement the symbolic literature of the white man, Fard himself wrote manuals or "lessons" for the movement. One such manual was entitled *Teachings for the Lost Found Nation of Islam in a Mathematical Way* and was printed and given to registered believers. It was written in Fard's own "symbolic language" and required his interpretation. Following is an example of early NOI teachings:

"The Black man in North America is not a "Negro," but a member of the lost Tribe of Shabazz, tricked by traders 379 years ago into leaving their homes 9,000 miles across the ocean. The prophet came to North America to find and bring back to life his long lost brethren, from whom the Caucasians had taken their language, their nation, and their religion. Here, in North America, they were living other than themselves. They must learn that they are the original people, noblest of the nations of the Earth. The Caucasians are the colored people, and have been grafter away from their original color which was black. The original people must regain their religion, which is Islam, their language which is Arabic, and their culture, which is astronomy and higher mathematics, especially calculus. They must live according to the law of Allah, avoiding all meat of "poison animals," hogs, ducks, geese, possums, and catfish.[37]

Fard and Elijah co-authored another manual known as *The Secret Ritual of the Nation of Islam.* This manual was (and still is) transmitted orally; it is memorized verbatim by the Muslims and has become an oral tradition. These manuals would soon come to be termed as "The Lessons" by NOI registered believers and Five Percenters alike.

The Nation of Islam under Fard continued to grow and he continued to add more structure around the movement. In addition to establishing "Temples of Islam," Fard also established "Universities of Islam" which was a combined elementary and secondary school dedicated to "higher mathematics," astronomy, and the "ending of the spook civilization." The school was primarily for Muslim children but it also had adult classes that taught, among other things, reading and mathematics, to help the poor Negroes quit being duped and deceived by the "tricknology" of "the blue-eyed devil white man."

The rapid increase in membership made necessary the development of a formal organization. Subsidiary organizations had been established as the need for them arose. Chief of these was the University of Islam, to which the children of Muslim families were sent rather than to public schools. Here they were taught the "knowledge of our own," rather than the "civilization of the Caucasian devils." Courses were given in "higher mathematics," astronomy, and the "general knowledge and ending of the spook civilization."[38]

W. D. Fard developed two internal units within the Temple to address the gender needs in Islam. One was "the Muslim Girls Training Class (MGT)", specifically for the women in the movement, and the other was "The Fruit of Islam" specifically for the men in the movement.

That women might keep their houses clean and cook food properly, there was established the Muslim Girl's Training and General Civilization Classes. Fear of trouble with the unbelievers, especially the police, led to the founding of the Fruit of Islam – a military organization for the men who were drilled by captains and taught tactics and the use of firearms. Each of these organizations was under the control of a group of officers trained specially by the prophet for their task. Finally, the entire movement was placed under a Minister of Islam and a corps of assistant ministers, all of whom were selected and trained by the prophet.[39]

The two corps, FOI and MGT, took on a militant presence reminiscent of Marcus Garvey's honor guard. Selected ministers were appointed to run different aspects of Fard's organization as the Nation of Islam enlisted a few thousand Black people in the city of Detroit alone. With things apparently going well for the Muslims, perhaps it looked a bit too well for the Detroit authorities. The absence of the Muslim kids from the public school system appeared to be too noticeable. The city's authorities would plan their move on the Muslims. In opposition to the Muslim school, the state of Michigan ordered the Muslims to send their children back to Detroit Public Schools. The Muslims refused to comply. The Michigan State Board of Education had the Muslim teachers arrested for "contributing to the delinquency of minors." Elijah Muhammad himself was arrested for the same. Highly organized and efficient, the Muslims fought the case in court and the charges were eventually dropped.

Still teeming from their legal loss to the Muslims, the Detroit police were still on a mission to harass the Nation of Islam and its adherents. W. D. Fard himself became a central target for the zealous Detroit Police Department. This inevitably led to his arrest. The Detroit Free Press Newspaper ran a story on the details of Fard's arrest.

Farad was taken into custody Wednesday morning as he was leaving his room in a hotel at 1 W. Jefferson Ave. He did not resist the officers, smiling enigmatically when told he was under arrest.

At Police Headquarters he evaded questions cleverly.

With the complacent smile of the Oriental Fakir, Farad calmly told detectives that he was the "supreme being on earth.".…[40]

This was an interesting claim because at the time Fard's followers (Elijah aside) only thought him out to be a prophet. Little did they know of any claims of Fard claiming to be God incarnate. Obviously his chief confidante Elijah was aware of this and it isn't known what made Fard go on public record with this revelation. One thing for sure is that He identified himself as the sovereign power of the universe when confronted by learned authorities even perhaps to the chagrin of his followers. Yusef Muhammad, an early follower of Fard, witnessed him admit this on another occasion:

> When the police asked him who he was, he said: 'I am the Supreme Ruler of the Universe.' He told those police more about himself then he would ever tell us.[41]

As a result of him proclaiming himself to be God, or perhaps the efforts of the police to silence him, Fard was placed in the psychopathic ward of the Receiving Hospital for observation. As a result, hundreds of Muslims protested in front of the hospital. Fard was released days later.

Until 1933, the NOI leader went by the name Wallace D. Fard, often signing it W. D. Fard. In the third year of his visit, he made known more of his name with an added change perhaps signaling his godhood.

> Allah came to us from the Holy City Mecca, Arabia, in 1930. He used the name Wallace D. Fard, often signing it W. D. Fard. In the third year (1933), He signed his name W.F. Muhammad which stands for Wallace Fard Muhammad.[42]

As things were heating up in Detroit, W. F. Muhammad and Elijah traveled to other Mid-western states and cities to spread the teachings. They left Detroit and went to Chicago, Illinois. The Chicago police must have knew of his plans because He was immediately arrested upon his arrival. Elijah Muhammad explains:

He (Mr. W.F. Muhammad, God in person) chose to suffer 3 ½ years to show his love for his people, who have suffered over 300 years at the hands of a people who by nature are evil and wicked and have no good in them. He was persecuted, sent to jail in 1932, and ordered out of Detroit, on May 26, 1933. He came to Chicago in the same year and was arrested almost immediately on his arrival and placed behind prison bars.

He submitted himself with all humbleness to his persecutors. Each time he was arrested, he sent for me so that I might see and learn the price of Truth for us, the so-called American Negroes (members of the Asiatic Nation).

He was well able to save himself from such suffering, but how else was the scripture to be fulfilled? We followed in his footsteps suffering the same persecution.[43]

Fard was eventually released. In spite of opposition from authorities, Fard and Elijah successfully established Temple #2 in Chicago and amassed a strong following in the city. The two even traveled to Milwaukee, Wisconsin and established the beginnings of Temple #3. Both Fard and Elijah resettled in Detroit to foster the movement's growth. The movement rapidly grew in all three cities. In 1934, the Nation of Islam at its zenith boldly declared a mass following of over 25,000 followers.

The Departure

Within three years, Wallace Fard Muhammad developed an organization so effective he was able to withdraw almost entirely from active leadership and gradually stopped his public appearances.

Master Fard Muhammad would often remind His Apostle, and others, the He would not be long among them. He indicated that He was only to spend a certain amount of time with them.

On His leave he began to emphasize specific things the Messenger could expect to come to pass. He went deeper into what the Messenger should do to try and make Black people qualified to escape the doom of this evil world. The Messenger was taught how to reform us and make us acceptable to the Islamic people. It was made clear to him that we must change completely into righteousness; not the righteousness of this world, nor righteousness according to the standards of this world. No. We would have to get into the righteousness of the God Who would rule the next world; that God being Master Fard Muhammad.[44]

All in all, Fard taught Elijah Muhammad what he needed to know over a period of 40 months. W. F. Muhammad hinted that he completed this chapter of his assignment; and now it was on Elijah to lead his people to Freedom, Justice and Equality in his absence. Fard implied that he was in contact with the "24 scientists" and they were very aware of Elijah's progression in understanding the teachings. Elijah recalls W. F. Muhammad reporting with glee the approval of the 24 scientists with the success of the teachings. As Elijah reports a statement made by Fard on the day of his departure.

"They just waited. They're so glad that the day has come now that they can show you now that the Black Man is God!"[45]

There were actual witnesses who say they were present with Fard on the day he left Detroit never to be heard from again. This is at least by the general public. Elijah Muhammad's oldest son, Emmanuel, describes the last meeting in person between Fard and Elijah with a warm sentiment.

There are, in my mind, many memorable instances of my father's love for Allah, but the one that sticks in me most is of the tears Allah and The Messenger shed the day Allah left us.[46]

In June of 1934, Fard had taken leave from the public as He had appeared without a trace. Upon Fard's departure, schisms broke out within the Nation. Old rivals resurfaced and challenged Fard's command that Elijah was to be the Supreme Minister. As a result, the movement began to decline in size and power due to internal conflicts. Some members even started their own factions or went to the wayside.

At the same time per Fard's directive, Elijah openly started teaching that Fard was more than a prophet; he was in fact God Almighty himself, and that He Elijah Muhammad was his Messenger. Elijah said that attempts were made on his life because the other ministers' jealousy had reached such a pitch. He says that the "hypocrites" forced him to flee to Chicago. Temple #2 became his headquarters until the hypocrites pursued him there, forcing him to flee again. Even Elijah's brother was a part of the scheme:

It was in 1935, that his blood brother, Kalot Muhammad rebelled against him (the Messenger). Not long afterward a group of envious hypocrites, who were formerly his followers, sought his life. With the help of Allah and a little help from a brother named Ali, the Honorable Elijah Muhammad first fled to Milwaukee, Wisconsin. After a short stay, he went by train to Washington, D.C.

He would spend the next seven years on the run, never spending more then two weeks in a city, as Master Fard Muhammad instructed him. Running, or traveling, teaching, praying, suffering and studying what Allah taught him, was an ordeal; but it was necessary for his growth, and for out benefit too.[47]

Elijah said His enemies made serious attempts to track him down. One of his adversaries was so zealous that he offered a bounty on Elijah's life. The Honorable Elijah Muhammad recalls the incident:

"Yes, for 37 years I have been trying to get the truth over to my people. I ran from my people, and other than my people, for about seven years. I went hungry and out of doors to be here today. I served those seven years, just running and dodging from my own people, who were out to kill me for a little sum of money, $500, from a brother in Detroit, Michigan, who said he would get a peck of rice and eat one grain a day, until I was dead. So, now he is dead.[48]

While on the run, Elijah said his rivals made strong efforts to track Him down. Even in the face of adversity, wherever he went He continued to teach and experienced the trials and tribulations of a major prophet.

There were close "shaves" with those who tracked him from city to city. There were the joys of awakening the mind of this or that Black man or woman. Then there were the disappointments over the rejection by others. There was the exhilaration that comes from a clearer perception of some valued truth. There were times when he went hungry. There were nights when his pillow was soaked with his tears.[49]

Whenever able, Elijah slipped back home to see His wife and his eight young children, who were fed by other poor Muslims who shared what little they had. His family kept his visits secret for security reasons. Elijah said the hypocrites made serious efforts to kill him.

Elijah went back out East where He selected to live and spend the majority of His time in the Nation's capital. In Washington, D.C., He started Temple #4. Establishing residence he resumed his studies by researching the books Fard instructed him to read. He would go to the Congressional Library where He studied the 104 books Fard told him contained different pieces of the truth. The white man had recorded this truth but it wasn't in books generally available to the public.

> One day, while in Washington, D.C., it occurred to the Messenger that those 104 books Master Fard Muhammad told him of probably were in the Congressional Library. (He was to experience the shock of seeing a picture of himself in one of them.)[50]

Undergoing an intense study of the bibliography of books given to Him by his teacher, Elijah studied the life of the Prophet Muhammad of Arabia of 1400 years ago, of which was the subject of the majority of the books on His list:

> "While running for seven years, I was going in and out of the Congressional Library daily to hide and study and read books on Islam and Muhammad of 1400 years ago. That is the way I spent a lot of my time."[51]

It was becoming increasingly difficult for Elijah to avoid attention. Wherever He went Elijah made an impression on all those who heard His voice. This sent rumblings up to the authorities who were anxious to be rid of people they considered troublemakers like Elijah. A plot was hatched to remove him off of the streets.

On May 8, 1942, the FBI arrested Elijah Muhammad in Washington D.C. Elijah said, "Uncle Tom Negroes" tipped the white man off to his teachings and he was charged with draft dodging even though he was too old to register for the military.

"After that, I was arrested by the F.B.I. in Washington on the eighth day of May 1942.

"They took me to their jail. First they questioned me all night long in their office, until approximately eight or nine o'clock that morning—it was Friday when I was arrested. And they sent for a doctor to examine me to see if I was getting a little "off", but I was still normal.[52]

Elijah revealed that he had divine insight into what was about to occur. Often claiming to be a guided man, he found solace in the revelation he received by his teacher Master Fard Muhammad.

Nevertheless, Allah revealed to him, one day, as he was traveling on a train, that he would have to give himself up to his enemies and go to prison. He gave him insight into how this imprisonment would ultimately serve the cause for which he was sacrificing. The F.B.I., on the orders of the president and J. Edgar Hoover were seeking him to take him into custody, and worse. Allah showed him why prison was to be his lot, for a while.

He submitted to Allah's will. He indicated to his followers what was coming. He deliberately wrote certain points, of what he was taught, on the blackboard, in the Temple in Washington, D.C., which he wanted the government to study.

They arrested him in a U.S. hat store, a few blocks from the office of the F.B.I. They walked a few blocks to their office...they seized his brief bag and made copies of all that it contained. They kept it for about seven months. Among the things they read—which many years later they saw come to pass—was the future of China.[53]

After interrogating Elijah, the F.B.I. moved forward with their plans to incarcerate him. They would later admit that it was done so under the orders of then President Franklin D. Roosevelt. Elijah was sentenced to five years in prison where he served for 3 ½ years.

"After that they sent me, for five years, to the Federal Correctional Institution. I stayed there approximately three years and five months. That was in Milan, Michigan. And I stayed in jail in Chicago for approximately 11 months. I spent two months and 15 days in Washington before they ever came down to say whether they were going to have a trial or anything—or let me sit there and mold.[54]

Behind bars, Elijah would continue to run the Nation of Islam from prison through his wife, Clara Muhammad. She served as the interim leader while many of Elijah's male followers were arrested for refusing to go the draft.

I was arrested on May 8, 1942, in Washington, D.C., by the F.B.I. for not registering for the draft. When the call was made for all males between 18 and 44, I refused (NOT EVADING) on the grounds that, first, I was a Muslim and would not take part in war and especially not on the side with the infidels. Second, I was 45 years of age and was NOT according to the law required to register...

In 1943, I was sent to the Federal Penitentiary in Milan, Michigan, for nothing other than to be kept out of the public and from teaching my people the truth during the war between America, Germany, and Japan. This war came to a halt in 1945 when America dropped an atomic bomb on Japan. And the following year, in August, 1946, I was released on what the institution called "good time" for being a model prisoner who was obedient to the prison rules and laws...

In the year 1942-1943, according to reports, there were nearly a hundred of my followers sentenced to prison terms of from 1 to 5 years for refusing to take part in the war between America, Japan and Germany because of our peaceful stand and the principle belief and practice in Islam, which is peace.[55]

Elijah's eldest son Emmanuel Muhammad was incarcerated with his Father for refusing to register for the draft. By his Father's side he witnessed his Father teach Islam to prison inmates. Elijah's congregation rapidly grew inside the prison walls. His son Emmanuel recalls their prison experience:

What has impressed me most, I think, was my stay with my father in prison. He set up a Temple in the prison despite the difficulties he experienced with the blackboard and all. He set up classes right there in prison. He would teach on Wednesday and Friday evenings until the bugle was blown for us to go to bed. He also taught on Sunday afternoons at 2:00pm. He made many, many converts in prison. Even the devils who came by to steal an earful wound up bowing in agreement, an unconscious bearing of witness to the truth The Messenger taught.[56]

Muhammad was eventually released from prison in August 1946. He would resume leading the Nation of Islam and wage a campaign in Black communities across America to "restore the Black Man to the top of civilization." Elijah's message captivated his listeners and earned him new converts from the rejected of society.

> Elijah became the only voice in the wilderness. There in the dirty streets and tenements where life was cheap and hope was minimum, where isolation from the common values of society and from the common privilege of citizenship was most acute, the voice of the Messenger did not fall upon deaf ears. So often it was the only message directed to the pimps, the prostitutes, the con men, the prisoners, ex-convicts, the alcoholics, the addicts and the unemployed, whom the responsible society had forgotten.[57]

It was in this same way that the message of Elijah reached a troubled young inmate in a Massachusetts prison who was so notorious that other inmates referred to him as "Satan."

Malcolm X

In 1948, Malcolm X, then known as Malcolm Little, heard Islam for the first time. While serving a bid in prison he received a couple of letters from members of his family. In the letters, Malcolm's brothers urged him "Malcolm, don't eat any more pork, and don't smoke any more cigarettes. I'll show you how to get out of jail." Malcolm was excited about this news. He felt that his brother knew of a con to get him out of prison. But on the contrary, his brother wrote him again telling him that he "found the natural religion of the Black Man." This religion was called "Islam."

Malcolm X was born in Omaha, Nebraska, on February 19, 1925. His father, the Reverend Earl Little, a Baptist preacher, was a dedicated organizer for Marcus Garvey's Universal Negro Improvement Association (U.N.I.A.). The Littles moved to Lansing, Michigan in attempts to one day own their own store, as Marcus Garvey stressed that "Negroes shouldn't seek to depend on the white man." Earl Little preached self help amongst the Black community in Lansing. As a result, Malcolm's mother and father were vilified by the local Klansmen and town folk who sought to stop his father's work amongst the Black community.

In 1929, the Littles home was firebombed by the Ku Klux Klan nightriders. Malcolm's father shot at the Klansmen on their horses as they fled away while hurling threats at his family to move out of the city. Never intimidated by the antics of the local whites, Earl Little met his fate one night when he was found dead on the railroad tracks. Everyone figured it had to be whites following through on their threats to "kill that nigger."

Malcolm's mother wasn't able to take care of her family or stand the pressure and ended up in a state mental hospital. Malcolm and his seven siblings were shipped off to different foster homes as a result. He attended integrated schools but was still discriminated against. When asked by his favorite teacher what he wanted to be when he grew up, Malcolm replied, "I want to be a lawyer." In true Jim Crow fashion his teacher chided Malcolm and told him, "That's not a realistic goal for a nigger." Encountering racism and his attempts to survive out on his own, Malcolm found it hard to stay out of trouble. Moving to bigger cities such as Boston and New York while running with the wrong crowd, he turned to vices such as pimping and robbing. He eventually wounded up in jail.

Malcolm's brothers, Reginald and Philbert, were fortunate enough to find a new way of life. They had dedicated themselves to the cause and were now followers of The Honorable Elijah Muhammad. Malcolm's experiences made him a prime candidate for Elijah Muhammad's teachings too. Remembering his father's stance plus coupled with his own life lessons he realized the truth to what his brothers were telling him. The news hit home and Malcolm took on a new look at life and started on the path to becoming a Muslim.

During his incarceration he utilized his time to gain more knowledge about the teachings of the Honorable Elijah Muhammad. He became a regular at the prison library where his studies consisted of Black history, world events, geography, English and religion.

Malcolm regularly wrote the Honorable Elijah Muhammad from prison and Elijah often wrote him back. Elijah sometimes even sent Malcolm money as he did with other prisoners he corresponded with. Malcolm spent the rest of his prison days studying subjects relevant to NOI teachings. As a result, he became skillful in the art of debate and was respected as such.

In August of 1952, Malcolm was released from prison and moved to Detroit to live closer to his brothers and other family members who were now in the Nation of Islam. This is when Malcolm began to live the daily life of a Muslim. He attended Temple #1 in Detroit and became an active member in the Temple. He earned his "X" and joined the Fruit of Islam (FOI).

Around Labor Day of 1952, Malcolm traveled to Temple #2 in Chicago along with the Muslims from Temple #1 in Detroit. In Chicago he would get the opportunity to see and hear the Honorable Elijah Muhammad in person for the first time. At the end of his speech, Elijah Muhammad praised Malcolm X for being steadfast and true while in prison. The Honorable Elijah Muhammad invited Malcolm X and his brothers to have dinner with him that evening. Malcolm would recall this same evening later in his autobiography.

> I sat thinking of how our Detroit Temple more or less just sat and awaited Allah to bring converts—and, beyond that, of the millions of black people all over America, who never had heard of the teachings that could stir and wake and resurrect the black man...and there at Mr. Muhammad's table, I found my tongue. I have always been one to speak my mind.
> During a conversational lull, I asked Mr. Muhammad how many Muslims were supposed to be in our Temple Number One in Detroit.
> He said, "There are supposed to be thousands."
> "Yes, sir," I said. "Sir, what is your opinion of the best way of getting thousands there?"
> "Go after the young people," he said. "Once you get them, the older ones will follow through shame."[58]

From that point on Malcolm X pursued that mission and became one of the Honorable Elijah Muhammad's student ministers. He was soon promoted to asst. minister in Temple #1 in 1953. He began to devote all of his time recruiting new converts from the streets of Detroit.

That same year in December, the Honorable Elijah Muhammad sent Malcolm to Boston to establish a Temple. In Boston, he had established Temple #11 and then traveled to Philadelphia to restore and strengthen the already existing Temple #12. From there he had traveled up and down the East Coast establishing Temples for the Honorable Elijah Muhammad in Springfield, MA, Hartford, CT, and Atlanta, GA.

In June of 1954 Malcolm went to Harlem where he was appointed Minister of Temple #7, which at that time was a storefront. Malcolm X remained in New York and continued to build up its membership. Soon the Muslims outgrew the storefront and relocated to a much bigger and modern facility at 102 West 116th Street in the heart of Harlem.

A very important incident occurred in 1959 under Malcolm's watch that was consequential to the rise of the NOI presence in Harlem. In that year an FOI was brutally beaten by the police after witnessing an incident of police brutality himself. Malcolm X gathered a great number of the FOI and marched down to the police precinct. While marching down the street, the FOI attracted other brothers and sisters who stood behind them in their defense. When the police witnessed this show of unity they agreed to release the wounded Muslim brother to the Harlem Hospital to be treated.

That incident in Harlem was the kind of power displayed by the Muslims that attracted Harlemites such as Sister Dora and Brother Clarence Smith who entered the Mosque shortly thereafter.

Chapter 4
Clarence 13X

Clarence 13X (background left) selling the Muhammad Speaks Newspaper

Allah was born Clarence Edward Smith on February 22, 1928, in Danville, Virginia. He was the fifth son born to His parents Louis and Mary Smith, who gave birth to seven children, six boys and one girl. As a young boy, Allah's mother affectionately called him "Put" and this is what he was called early in life.

Danville was like any other southern town. The "separate but unequal" Jim Crow laws of the South were its mandate. Black people were subject to an inferior education and second-rate living conditions in comparison to their privileged white counterparts. Blacks were often the victims of random racist attacks including heinous crimes committed by whites. Under the double standards of Jim Crow, whites were almost never prosecuted for any aggressions against Black people.

The Smiths were a proud family and never sought companionship with the racist whites. They preferred to make friends within their own community and stay among their own kind. They did not believe in going where they were not welcome.

The Smith Family lived at 834 Valley Street, six blocks from the heart of downtown Danville. The town had two movie theaters, one was a "Colored Only" theater and the other was a "Whites Only" theater. Black people had the option of going to the Colored only theater or sitting in the balcony of the white theater. Whenever going to the white theater, Clarence along with his brothers and sisters would look down from the balcony and observe the silly and trivial behavior of the whites.

Young Clarence and his siblings spent most of their summers with relatives down in St. Petersburg, Florida. They would swim in a river located behind a slaughterhouse that prepared cows for market. The young children often swam to a landing at the base of a train trestle in the middle of the river. There they would catch candy that was thrown by "whitey" from the windows of passing trains.

Young Clarence was known as a remarkable swimmer and his brothers often joked that "Tarzan" didn't have anything on him. One day while out swimming, Clarence and a friend had reached the landing at the trestle when they noticed his younger brother was drowning in the water. Seeing his brother in danger, Clarence dove back into the river, swam quickly to his brother's rescue and pulled him back to safety, saving his younger brother's life.

Growing up in Virginia in the 30's and 40's, Clarence experienced the typical incidents of racial prejudice and discrimination that occurred in the segregated south. One such incident took place right outside of the Smith's house when his father had a violent altercation with a burly white man. The white man prompted this incident by disrespecting Clarence's mother by using profanity in her presence. Louis, Clarence's father, known to be a courageous man of strong convictions, confronted the man and the two engaged in a physical altercation. In the course of the melee, Mr. Smith knocked the man over the porch banister causing the man's children to attempt to come to their father's aid. Seeing this, the Smith children immediately involved themselves in the battle to defend their family honor. These were the types of incidents that would help shape young Clarence into the man he would become in the future.[59]

As it was with other Black families in the South, the Smith's heard of employment opportunities that existed in the industrial northern cities. In the 1940's, Mrs. Smith moved to New York City to seek employment. She settled in Harlem. In 1946, while still in his early teens, Clarence moved to Harlem along with his brothers John, Louis, Weldon, Ernest, Charles and his sister Bernice.[60]

Harlem was vastly different than the South. Harlem's population had the greatest density of Black People in the USA and was considered to be the Mecca for Black America. While in New York, the nickname "Put" his mother had given him became mistaken for the name "Puddin." Thus, Clarence became known as "Puddin" and this moniker followed him throughout the rest of his years.

In order to make a living, he performed a variety of odd jobs such as shining shoes and working as a shipping clerk. One of his ventures was a fruit stand that he opened up in a hole-in-the-wall in Harlem. It was also in the 1940's that he developed his insatiable love for gambling that would linger with him throughout his life. He spent a lot of time in the pool halls and earned a reputation as a pool shark.

In 1946, Clarence met a young lady named Willeen who became his teenage sweetheart. He wanted to marry her but reportedly her mother did not approve because she felt the couple was too young. Despite the disapproval, the two continued their relationship and she eventually gave birth to two sons who would later become known as A-Allah and B-Allah, respectively born in 1949 and 1951. The couple's relationship would be short-lived and soon ended. Clarence eventually met another young lady who captured his heart named Dora. Clarence and Dora were very fond of one another and he asked for her hand in marriage. Dora accepted and the two became husband and wife. From this union came the birth of their children Christine, Debra, Clarence and Perry.[61]

Joins the Army

During this era, America was on the heels of the Korean War. President Truman had just passed the bill to desegregate the Military in 1948. A new chapter in America race relations was ushered forth. With the onset of the Korean War, the U.S. military could not function without the large-scale recruiting of Blacks. As it was with other young Black men in his era, Clarence joined the Service. At the age of 23, he was inducted into the United States Army on Oct. 30, 1952, and went off to fight in the Korean War where he also spent time in Japan.

The Army demanded that Clarence forego his civilian ways and adopt a new set of principles of a soldier-at-war. While in Korea, he participated in rigorous military training. As part of his military exercises he learned to discipline himself in order to enhance the skills that would increase his chances of survival. He received military instruction in weaponry, judo, karate and war tactics. His title was a Light weapons Infantry Man. When he wasn't training, he would often write his family and send money home that he won from gambling.

Clarence was often on the battlefield and saw plenty of action while in war. In this heartless war, he learned not to befriend anyone because of the uncertainty who would be killed in the line of duty. He too had many near brushes with death. One such incident occurred while he was walking in a field flanked by men from his unit. Gunfire erupted and the men on both sides of him were picked off and killed. Clarence was left unscathed and reportedly felt that his life was being spared because of a "calling" or a mission he had to fulfill back in the States.

Throughout the war Clarence distinguished himself through his brave heroic deeds. His performance earned him medals and awards of honor. Among these medals were the Korean Service Medal, Combat Infantryman's Badge, Presidential Unit Citation (Republic of Korea), United Nations Service Medal and the National Defense Service Medal.[62] His treasured medal was the Bronze Star Medal that he received for his feats and accomplishments during the war.

After his tour of duty in Korea he returned to the United States to fulfill the rest of his time in the Army. He was previously assigned to Company "F," 39th Infantry, Ft. Dix, NJ.

Clarence was honorably released from active duty on 8/22/54 as a PFC at Camp Kilmer, NJ and transferred to the U.S. Army Reserve to complete his military obligation. He served in the U.S. Army Reserve, in active status, from 8/ 22/ 54 to 9/ 30/ 60, at which time he was honorably discharged with his character and efficiency rating as excellent.[63]

Visits NOI Temple #7

After completing his stint in the Army, Clarence returned to Harlem to discover things were different at home. His wife, Dora, had become a Muslim and joined the Nation of Islam (NOI) under the leadership of the Honorable Elijah Muhammad. She attended Temple #7 in Harlem under the local leadership of NOI Spokesman Minister Malcolm X.

The Nation of Islam had a growing presence in Harlem where they had established a mosque, school and a few businesses in the Black community. Sister Dora invited Clarence to attend a meeting at Temple #7 to hear the teachings of the Honorable Elijah Muhammad for himself. Clarence decided to take her up on the offer and went to visit the Mosque.

First time visitors went through the traditional processing at the Temple of Islam. Muslim brothers at the door greeted all visitors and searched the guests for any weapons or contraband. Next the guest was escorted to the Secretary of Islam who recorded their name and address.

After completing the process, the guest was escorted to the main sanctuary of the Mosque where the men were seated to the right and the women sat to the left. In the background of the speakers podium was a red and white flag on the wall that was the Star and the Crescent—the national emblem of the Nation of Islam. Clarence was instructed to sit on the right along with the rest of the men to wait to hear from the speaker.

In the Temple, all Muslim men were clean-shaven and wore dark suits with bow ties or neckties. The modestly dressed Muslim women were adorned with headpieces and long dresses that covered their figures. They greeted each other with the Arabic greeting of, "As Salaam Alaikum," which translated into English means "peace be unto you." The Arabic language they were taught was the language of their Black ancestors from their homeland. They also referred to each other as "brother" and "sister"; a term that wasn't often used at that time but became popular in Black America through its use by the Muslims.

The men and women carried themselves in a dignified manner reminiscent of a militant order. This probably appealed to Clarence who just came out of the United States Military. But instead of the United States Army—this was "the Army of the Black Nation."

While waiting for the main speaker, an assistant minister would take the stage and open up service with a prayer in the Name of Allah. This was the official opening of the Mosque meeting. In synch with NOI custom, the speaker politely explained the search procedures that the visitor had just undergone. In a brief sermon, the orator explained the meaning of the Star and Crescent that decorated the wall. The Minister explained that this insignia was the Sun, Moon and Stars that according to NOI theology symbolized, *"Freedom, Justice and Equality."* Together these three principles represented Islam—the nature of the Original Black Man. The speaker professed that this was the Universal symbol recognized by the entire Islamic World.

After the first speaker concluded his presentation, he'd introduce the main Minister who approached the stage flanked by solemn bodyguards. As the Minister (who was usually Malcolm X) approached the podium, the crowd would stand and applaud. After the ovation, Malcolm would open up in the name of Allah and offer the salutations of peace in the Arabic language, "Salaam Alaikum!" He would then delve into his lecture that consisted of the teachings of the Honorable Elijah Muhammad making an impassionate plea to the audience.

You see my tears, brothers and sisters... Tears haven't been in my eyes since I was a young boy. But I cannot help this when I feel the responsibility I have to help you comprehend for the first time what this white man's religion that we call Christianity has done to us...

"Brothers and sisters here for the first time, please don't let that shock you. I know you didn't expect this. Because almost none of us black people have thought that maybe we were making a mistake not wondering if there wasn't a special religion somewhere for us—a special religion for the black man.

"Well, there is such a religion. It's called Islam. Let me spell it for you, I-s-l-a-m! Islam! But I'm going to tell you about Islam a little later. First, we need to understand some things about this Christianity before we can understand why the answer for us is Islam.[64]

Malcolm X was extremely zealous in his condemnation of "the white man's religion." He savored the moments in his speeches where he ripped holes in the white man's concept of Christianity. Malcolm's exegesis enthralled many of the first time visitors such as Clarence, whose mother raised him to believe in Christianity. Like a skilled artist, Malcolm commenced to destroy what he believed to be a false ideology.

"Brothers and sisters, the white man has brainwashed us black people to fasten our gaze upon a blond-haired, blue-eyed Jesus! We're worshiping a Jesus that doesn't even look like us! Oh, yes! Now just bear with me, listen to the teachings of the Messenger of Allah, The Honorable Elijah Muhammad. Now just think of this. The blond-haired, blue-eyed white man has taught you and me to worship a white Jesus, and to shout and sing and pray to this God that's his God, the white man's God. The white man has taught us to shout and sing and pray until we die, to wait until death, for some dreamy heaven-in-the-hereafter, when we're dead, while this white man has his milk and honey in the streets paved with golden dollars right here on this earth![65]

If any visitors had doubts about Malcolm's assertions, he easily convinced them once he related it his claim to the lives of his listeners. Like the mastery exhibited by Master Fard Muhammad and The Honorable Elijah Muhammad, Malcolm was a skilled craftsman in driving the point home about the Black man's unequal living conditions.

"You don't want to believe what I am telling you, brothers and sisters? Well, I'll tell you what you do. You go out of here, you just take a good look around where you live. Look at not only how you live, but look at how anybody that you know lives— that way, you'll be sure that you're not just a bad-luck accident. And when you get through looking at where you live, then you take you a walk down across Central Park, and start to look at what this white God had brought to the white man. I mean, take yourself a look down there at how the white man is living!

"and don't stop there. In fact, you won't be able to stop for long—his doormen are going to tell you 'Move on!' But catch a subway and keep on downtown. Anywhere you may want to get off, look at the white man's apartments, businesses! Go right on down to the tip of Manhattan Island that this devilish white man stole from the trusting Indians for twenty-four dollars! Look at his City Hall, down there; look at his Wall Street! Look at yourself! Look at his God!"[66]

Malcolm X was a brilliant orator. It was almost impossible not to admire his wit and charisma. Never being one to take the credit for the teachings, Malcolm often referenced the history of the Nation of Islam and its founders giving them the credit for what the audience was hearing. Following would be the typical content found in Malcolm's speeches reiterating the history of the Nation of Islam.

In Detroit in 1931, Mr. Muhammad met Master W. D. Fard. The effects of the depression were bad everywhere, but in the black ghetto they were horrible, Mr. Muhammad told me. A small, light brown-skinned man knocked from door to door at the apartments of the poverty-stricken Negroes. The man offered for sale silks and other yard goods and he identified himself as "a brother from the East."

This man began to tell Negroes how they came from a distant land, in the seeds of their forefathers.

He warned them against eating the "filthy pig" and other "wrong foods" that it was habitual for Negroes to eat.

Among the Negroes whom he found most receptive, he began holding little meetings in their poor homes. The man taught both the Quran and the Bible, and his students included Elijah Poole.

This man said his name was W. D. Fard. He said that he was born in the Koreish tribe of Muhammad ibn Abdullah, the Arabian prophet Himself. This peddler of silks and yard goods, Mr. W. D. Fard, knew the bible better than any of the Christian-bred Negroes.

In the essence, Mr. W. D. Fard taught that God's true name was Allah, that His true religion was Islam, that the true name for the religion's people was Muslims.

Mr. W. D. Fard taught that the Negroes in America were directly descended from Muslims. He taught that Negroes in America were Lost Sheep, lost for four hundred years from the

Nation of Islam, and that he, Mr. Fard, had come to redeem and return the Negro to his true religion.[67]

Undoubtedly, the most startling revelation to first time visitors was Fard's concept of the true identity of God and the Devil. This too was one of Malcolm's favorite subjects. The man who once was called "Satan" had the honor of revealing the true Satan, as so he believed. Malcolm would share the Muslim perspective of God and the devil. Malcolm X:

> No heaven was in the sky, Mr. Fard taught, and no hell was in the ground. Instead, both heaven and hell were conditions in which people lived right here on this planet Earth. Mr. Fard taught that the Negro in America had been for four hundred years in hell, and he, Mr. Fard, had come to return them to where heaven for them was—back home, among their own kind.
>
> Master Fard taught that as hell was on earth, also on earth was the devil—the white race which was bred from black Original Man six thousand years before, purposely to create a hell on earth for the next six thousand years.
>
> The black people, God's children, were Gods themselves, Master Fard taught. And he taught that among them was one, also a human being like the others, who was the God of Gods: The Most, Most High, The Supreme Being, supreme in wisdom and power—and His proper name was Allah.[68]

Next, Malcolm repeated to audiences what Fard told Elijah and other NOI pioneers many years earlier; that these were the last days and called for God to appear in person.

> Among his handful of first converts in 1931 in Detroit, Master W. D. Fard taught that every religion says that near the Last Day, or near the End of Time, God would come, to resurrect the Lost Sheep, to separate them from their enemies, and restore them to their own people. Master Fard taught that Prophecy referred to this Finder and Savior of the Lost Sheep as The Son of Man, or God in Person, or The Lifegiver, The Redeemer, or The Messiah, who would come as lightning from the East and appear in the West. He was the One to whom the Jews referred as The Messiah, the Christians as The Christ, and the Muslims as The Mahdi."[69]

It was with these claims of divinity that, "the Lost-Found Nation of Islam in the West," was born. It was also the inspiration that put Clarence on his destined journey.

Chapter 5
The Mosque

Malcolm X speaking at Harlem Mosque #7

During Clarence's visit to the Temple, the words spoken by
Malcolm X had a spellbinding effect that captivated his
audience. The normal time span for a Muslim lecture often
lasted for two hours. Many of those in attendance agreed more
than not with the ever-so-real truths they heard in the teachings
of the Honorable Elijah Muhammad.

Malcolm spoke about the horrors of slavery inflicted on the
Black Man by the white man and its effect on the psyche of the
Black Man. How he was made to feel inferior because of the
color of his skin and how he came to believe in Christianity that
Elijah Muhammad taught was equivalent to teaching white
supremacy.

Malcolm addressed the economic plight of Black people. He
explained how they were exploited daily by the white man who
robbed them for their resources. Malcolm used Harlem as the

best example to illustrate his point. The fact that Harlem was mostly all Black but yet the majority of the store owners in Harlem were mostly all white. He explained how the white merchants greedily took the money out of the Black community and used it to build up their own communities. Thus the Black ghetto became poorer and the white man became richer.

Malcolm berated the fact that the Black man had fought wars for the white man and when they came back home they were made to feel as second-class citizens in their own country. He revealed the fact that Black soldiers fought and some died to protect the United States. He pointed out the irony of the living soldiers who returned home from the war were not protected from police brutality, mob attacks and other racial injustices practiced here on the so-called Negro in the United States.

Malcolm X emphasized that Christianity was the religion of the slave master and was not fit for the Black Man. Under the cross of Christianity the Black Man received nothing but slavery, suffering and death. But under the Star and Crescent of Islam he would be free, justified and made equal to all other civilized societies. The best solution according to Malcolm X was to come follow the Honorable Elijah Muhammad and reclaim your own heritage. In closing, he would then urge all of the visitors in the Temple to get behind and support the Muslim program.

Clarence Joins the Nation of Islam

After his speech it was common for Min. Malcolm X to ask the audience, "Will all stand who believed what you have heard today is the truth and good for Black People?" Next he followed with the question, "How many of you want to stand behind the truth and come follow the Honorable Elijah Muhammad?" Clarence Smith was one of those amongst the audience who stood up and accepted Islam. This was his first step to obtaining the knowledge of himself and joining the Muslim Brotherhood.

The next step in the joining process for Clarence Smith was to attend orientation classes held at the Temple. This is where he would learn the basic fundamentals of Islam as taught by the Honorable Elijah Muhammad. He was taught what separated the civilized man from the uncivilized man— was that the civilized man lived the laws of Islam. The uncivilized man was a "savage" who needed to be taught the correct way by Allah's Messenger Elijah Muhammad. By joining the ranks of Islam, he would learn civilization and then go back out to the world to pull the rest of his brothers and sisters "out of the mud."

The Muslims taught Clarence what foods to eat and what not to eat. They insisted that he must drop pork from his diet. Muslims railed that the nasty pig was "a grafted animal that was one third rat, one third cat and one third dog." The Muslims also prohibited any of its members from smoking, drinking or using any narcotics that were consumed in the "dead world."

In orientation class, Clarence further reviewed the Muslim Program, *What the Muslims Want* and *What the Muslims Believe*. This list was a chart of Muslim demands and cardinal principles.

"What the Muslims Want" began with three basic ethics:

1. We want freedom. We want a full and complete freedom.
2. We want justice. Equal justice under the law. We want justice applied equally to all, regardless of creed or class or color.
3. We want equality of opportunity. We want equal membership in society with the best in civilized society.[70]

Since the Muslims had little faith in the white man to honor the above basic principles, they felt the answer was separation from their oppressors. The NOI presented the issues as well as their proposed resolution:

4. **We want our people in America whose parents or grandparents were descendants from slaves, to be allowed to establish a separate state or territory of their own—either on this continent or elsewhere. We believe that our former slave masters are obligated to provide such land and that the area must be fertile and minerally rich. We believe that our former slave masters are obligated to maintain and supply our needs in this separate territory for the next 20 to 25 years—until we are able to produce and supply our own needs...**
5. We want freedom for all Believers of Islam now held in federal prisons. We want freedom for all black men and women now under death sentence in innumerable prisons in the North as well as the South.

    We want every black man and woman to have the freedom to accept or reject being separated from the slave master's children and establish a land of their own.

We know that the above plan for the solution of the black and white conflict is the best and only answer to the problem between two people.[71]

The next few demands were more specific to the political climate of America and its effects on Black Americans. Elijah Muhammad addressed the subjects of police brutality, unemployment, taxation without representation, the educational system and the taboo of interracial marriages:

6. We want an immediate end to the police brutality and mob attacks against the so-called Negro throughout the United States.
   We believe that the Federal government should intercede to see that black men and women tried in white courts receive justice in accordance with the laws of the land—or allow us to build a new nation for ourselves, dedicated to justice, freedom and liberty.

7. As long as we are not allowed to establish a state or territory of our own, we demand not only equal justice under the laws of the United States, but equal employment opportunities— **NOW!**
   We do not believe that after 400 years of free or nearly free labor, sweat and blood, which has helped America become rich and powerful, that so many thousands of black people should have to subsist on relief, charity or live in poor houses.

8. We want the government of the United States to exempt our people from ALL taxation as long as we are deprived of equal justice under the laws of the land.

9. We want equal education—but separate schools up to 16 for boys and 18 for girls on the condition that the girls be sent to women's colleges and universities. We want all black children educated, taught and trained by their own teachers...

10. We believe that intermarriage or race mixing should be prohibited. We want the religion of Islam taught without hindrance or oppression.[72]

The Honorable Elijah Muhammad crafted another outline for the general public detailing the NOI belief system entitled *"What The Muslims Believe."* The first few missives were familiar to mainstream Islam and would appear normal to any sect of Muslims:

1. WE BELIEVE in the One God Whose proper Name is Allah.
2. WE BELIEVE in the Holy Qur'an and in the Scriptures of all the prophets of God.
3. WE BELIEVE in the truth of the Bible, but we believe that it has been tampered with and must be reinterpreted so that mankind will not be snared by the falsehoods that have been added to it.
4. WE BELIEVE in Allah's Prophets and the Scriptures they brought to the people.[73]

As it was with the NOI, Elijah personalized the precepts of Islam to the Black Man's experience in America. The language of the NOI was unapologetic in its stance that the Black Man of America was the chosen of Allah and the United States had a responsibility to their ex-slaves:

5. WE BELIEVE in the resurrection of the dead—not in physical resurrection—but in mental resurrection. We believe that the so-called Negroes are most in need of mental resurrection, therefore, they will be resurrected first...
6. WE BELIEVE in the judgment; we believe this first judgment will take place as God revealed, in America.
7. WE BELIEVE this is the time in history for the separation of the so-called Negroes and the so-called white Americans. We believe that the black man should be freed in name as well as in fact. By this we mean that he should be freed from the names imposed upon him by his former slave master's slave. We believe that if we are free indeed, we should go in our own people's names—the black peoples of the Earth.
8. WE BELIEVE in justice for all, whether in God or not; we believe as others, that we are due equal justice as human beings. We believe in equality—as a nation—of equals. We do not believe that we are equal with our slave masters in the status of "freed slaves."
   We recognize and respect American citizens as independent peoples and we respect their laws which govern this nation.[74]

In contrast to the civil rights movement, the NOI strongly dissented from the philosophy of integration. The Muslims viewed the option of integration as a "trick" by the white man to delay the judgment of America:

9. **WE BELIEVE that the offer of integration is hypocritical and is made by those who are trying to deceive the black peoples into believing that their 400-year-old open enemies of freedom, justice and equality are, all of a sudden, their "friends." Furthermore, we believe that such deception is intended to prevent black people from realizing that the time in history has arrived for the separation from the whites of this nation.**

If the white people are truthful about their professed friendship toward the so-called Negro, they can prove it by dividing up America with their slaves.

We do not believe that America will ever be able to furnish enough jobs for her own millions of unemployed, in addition to jobs for the 20,000,000 black people as well.[75]

Obviously undeterred from his time served in prison, Elijah openly stood on his belief that Muslims shouldn't fight in the white man's army. To do so was considered sacrilege, unless the white man agreed to the NOI demand to establish a land for the exclusive use of the Black Nation.

10. WE BELIEVE that we who declare ourselves to be righteous Muslims, should not participate in wars which take the lives of humans. We do not believe this nation should force us to take part in such wars, for we have nothing to gain from it unless America agrees to give us the necessary territory wherein we may have something to fight for.[76]

Probably the most important in the NOI belief system was the necessity for the Black Man to protect his woman. Elijah made it clear that *"the Nation can rise no higher than its woman."* According to Elijah, if there was anything worth dying over, was the effort to protect and defend the Black Woman:

11. WE BELIEVE our women should be respected and protected as the women of other nationalities are respected and protected.[77]

Lastly, Elijah felt if all else failed, it was on Allah whom he could depend. Elijah maintained that He was The Messenger of Allah and his God was more than capable of delivering him and all of Black people.

12. WE BELIEVE that Allah (God) appeared in the Person of Master W. Fard Muhammad, July, 1930; the long-awaited "Messiah" of the Christians and the "Mahdi" of the Muslims. We believe further and lastly that Allah is God and besides HIM there is no God and He will bring about a universal government of peace wherein we all can live in peace together.[78]

These were the type of teachings that stirred the souls of Black people as they lined up to become "Registered Muslims" in the Nation of Islam.

In order to become a registered Muslim and receive his "X", Clarence had to hand write a letter of intent to the NOI National Headquarters, Temple #2 located in Chicago, IL. First, he was given a copy of the following letter, which he had to copy himself exactly (in the original handwriting of its original author) by hand without any errors or mistakes:

Mr. W.F. Muhammad
4847 So. Woodlawn Ave.
Chicago, Illinois 60015

Dear Savior Allah, Our Deliverer:

I have been attending the teachings of Islam by one of your Ministers, two or three times. I believe in It, and I bear witness that there is no God but Thee, and that Muhammad is Thy Servant and Apostle. I desire to reclaim my Own. Please give me my Original Name. My slave name is as follows:

Name
Address
City and State[79]

Upon finishing his letter he mailed it to Chicago to be scrutinized and approved by the proper NOI authorities. In turn they mailed him back a certified letter of approval and confirmation that he was on his way to "earning his X." But before he could do so, there was one more step in the process.

The teachings of the Nation of Islam were presented to its members in a catechism (question and answer) format; the grouped sets of questions and answers were designated as a lesson. There existed several lesson sets representing about a hundred or more catechism questions and answers that constituted the core doctrine of the Nation of Islam. NOI founders Master Fard Muhammad and the Honorable Elijah Muhammad authored these lessons themselves and made it mandatory for all Muslims to learn and recite them by heart.

The first ten questions and answers were known as the **Student Enrollment**. Clarence had to memorize and recite this lesson 100% right and exact without slightest error in front of a mosque authority before he could earn his "X".

The NOI Student Enrollment Lesson began thus:

1. Who is the Original Man? The Original Man is the Asiatic Black Man, the Maker, the Owner, the Cream of the Planet Earth, the Father of Civilization, and the God of the Universe.
2. Who is the Colored Man? The Colored Man is the Caucasian (white man), or Yakub's grafted devil, the Skunk of the Planet Earth.
3. What is the population of the Original Nation in the Wilderness of North America, and all over the Planet Earth? The population of the Original Nation in the Wilderness of North America is 17,000,000, with the 2,000,000 Indians makes it 19,000,000; All over the Planet Earth is 4,400,000,000.[80]

After studying it and memorizing it word-for-word, he would recite it to the proper Mosque authority. Clarence successfully recited the Student Enrollment and had earned his "X"; he was now officially registered into the Nation of Islam and his name was written in the *"Lamb's Book of Life."*

As it was in NOI tradition, to commemorate his rebirth, Clarence would drop his last name and be known simply by his first name and the letter X. To facilitate identification among Muslims having the same first name and belonging to the same temple, numbers were prefixed to the X. Thus the first man named Clarence to join Temple #7 is named Clarence X; the second becomes Clarence 2X and so on. Since Clarence Smith was the thirteenth Clarence to join Temple #7 he had the number 13 prefixed to the X, thus he became known as Clarence "13X."

As taught in the NOI, the symbol X has a double meaning: implying "ex," it signifies that the Muslim is no longer what he was; and as "X," it signifies an unknown quality or quantity. It at once repudiates the white man's name and announces the rebirth of the Black Man, endowed with a set of qualities the white man does not have and does not know. In short, Minister Malcolm X would explain:

> X is for mystery. The mystery confronting the Negro as to who he was before the white man made him a slave and put a European label on him. That mystery is now resolved. But X is also for the mystery confronting the white man as to what the Negro has become. That mystery will be resolved only when the teachings of Elijah Muhammad has been received by enough of the "Lost Nation" to counter "three hundred years of systematic brainwashing by the white man.[81]

Eventually, at a later date, the Muslim with an "X" as a surname would replace it with an "original" or Arabic name. This honor was totally dependent upon the Muslim proving themselves worthy by their works, accomplishments and moral standards. Once they were deemed as the said person of that ability the "X" was replaced with either the name of Allah or one of his righteous attributes, which he would receive from the Honorable Elijah Muhammad himself. Thus the Honorable Elijah Muhammad elaborates.

> He (W.F. Muhammad) told us that we must give up our slave names (of our slave masters) and accept only the name of Allah (Himself) or one of the Divine attributes. We (the so-called Negroes) must also give up all evil doings and practices and do (only) righteousness or we shall be destroyed from the face of the earth. [82]

> Examples of the changed names are:
> Joseph Shepard became Jam Sharrief
> Lindsay Garret became Hazziez Allah
> Henry Wells became Anwar Pasha
> William Blunt became Sharrief Allah

As it was in the same sense of the Korean War, Clarence 13X had to prepare his self to accept a new set of values never before asked of him-- only this time it would be of a high moral obligation to himself and the Nation of Islam. The Honorable Elijah Muhammad's teachings provided a spiritual transformation for Clarence that opened up a new chapter in his life and changed him forever.

The Muslims were known for their high degree of refinement and their outstanding discipline. This creed was accompanied by a very strict code of ethics known as "the restricted laws of Islam." By adhering to the law 100% at all times ensured that all its members were lived the civilized codes of conduct. If they failed to adhere to the Islamic Laws, it resulted in suspension, or in some cases lifetime banishment from the NOI. It was a challenge Clarence readily accepted and he became a full-fledged member of the Nation of Islam. The Muslims gave him a new identity, newfound pride and employment. Clarence 13X took a job with the Muslim owned *"Earth Painters Improvement Company"* based out of Brooklyn, New York. Clarence's position as a painter within the Temple granted him more access to Mosque officials:

> When He was in the Mosque He was a "Painter" this was Temple #7 and He was around the Temple all day working, He was able to study His lessons and speak to the "Top Ministers, Captains and Lieutenants such as Malcolm X and Captain Joseph, just to name a few..[83]

Brother Clarence 13X and his wife Dora were regulars at the mosque. The Muslims of the Nation of Islam had a weekly schedule of events that were usually held at the mosque. The two integrated into the Muslim way of life as described by Minister Malcolm X:

> I ought to explain that each week night a different Muslim class, or event, is scheduled. Monday night, every temple's Fruit of Islam trains. People think this is just military drill, judo, karate, things like that—which is part of the F.O.I. training, but only one part. The F.O.I. spends a lot more time in lectures and discussions on men learning to be men. They deal with the responsibilities of a husband and a father; what to expect of

women; the rights of women which are not to be abrogated by the husband; the importance of the father-male image in the strong household; current events; why honesty, and chastity, are vital in a person, a home, a community, a nation, and a civilization; why one should bathe at least once each twenty-four hours; business principles; and things of that nature.

Then, Tuesday night in every Muslim temple is Unity Night, where the brothers and sisters enjoy each other's conversational company and refreshments, such as cookies and sweet and sour fruit punches. Wednesday nights, at eight P.M., is what is called Student Enrollment, where Islam's basic issues are discussed; it is about the equivalent of catechism class in the Catholic religion.

Thursday nights there are the M.G.T. (Muslim Girl's Training) and the G.C.C. (General Civilization Class), where the women and girls of Islam are taught how to keep homes, how to rear children, how to care for husbands, how to cook, sew, how to act at home and abroad, and other things that are important to being a good Muslim sister and mother and wife.

Fridays are devoted to Civilization Night, when classes are held for brothers and sisters in the area of the domestic relations, emphasizing how both husbands and wives must understand and respect each other's true natures. Then Saturday night is for all Muslims a free night, when, usually, they visit at each other's homes. And, of course, on Sundays, every Muslim temple holds its services.[84]

Mosque #7 became a haven for Clarence and Dora. The two were very active in the Temple and established many friendships throughout its ranks.

Chapter 6
Fruit of Islam

12. What is the meaning of FOI?
Ans. Fruit of Islam. This is the name given to the military training of Men that belong to Islam in North America.

Captain Joseph (left) and Malcolm X surrounded by FOI

As time passed and Clarence 13X matriculated in the ranks of the NOI, he was required to memorize several other lesson sets. Among these included: Original Instructions to the Laborers (1-13), English Lesson C-1 (1-36), Lost-Found Muslim Lesson no. 1 (1-14), Lost-Found Muslim Lesson no. 2 (1-40), The Actual Facts (1-20), The Problem Book (1-34), General Orders (1-12) and the Restricted Laws of Islam. It was required of Clarence 13X to know all of the said above lessons in order to receive an honorable place amongst the Fruit of Islam. C. Eric Lincoln in his book, "The Black Muslims of North America," notes this tradition:

> Recruits to the FOI are carefully screened before admission, for they are expected to set the highest possible standards of character and dedication. Each candidate is required to pass oral examinations on certain levels of knowledge about the Movement and its history—examinations in which the candidates must recite long memorized passages verbatim, without a single error. Candidates are also required to take a secret oath on admission.[85]

Clarence, as an aspiring FOI, took a strong interest in learning the NOI lessons. He was fascinated with the life-giving teachings of the Honorable Elijah Muhammad and the powerful wisdom contained within the lessons. It developed in him a fiery wisdom that later became referred to as his own "self-styled wisdom." He often conversed about the lessons with his peers whom were on the same mission as he—to be fully ratified as a Fruit of Islam. In order to be considered you had to learn all of your lessons and be able to recite them verbatim without error when called upon by a peer or a mosque authority.

There was pressure on the FOI to know the lessons because they could be called to recite any lesson at anytime in front of the FOI in their meetings. Minister Malcolm and Captain Joseph (who were over the FOI) were very stern about making the FOI learn their lessons. It was their responsibility to keep the FOI on point about the teachings of Elijah Muhammad.

Minister Benjamin Karim, assistant minister to Malcolm X at the same time Clarence 13X was at Temple #7, reminisces of Malcolm's methodology in teaching the Lessons to the FOI.

> Had Malcolm started a Friday meeting by asking who was the Father of Civilization, any member of the FOI would have responded without blinking, and probably without comprehending the full significance of his reply, that it was the Asiatic Black Man. Malcolm, however, was not looking for rote replies. He wanted us to think; he taught us to reason out how abstract ideas applied to our daily lives. The FOI, on the other hand, required us to memorize, and in the first of five NOI lesson plans, which all FOI members had to learn word for word, appeared the question "Who Is the Original Man?" Its

answer was "The Asiatic Black Man, Owner, Maker, Cream of the Planet Earth, Father of Civilization, God of the Universe." Not until we had proved our mastery of the NOI catechism by memorizing and reciting perfectly every question and answer, every statement, proposition, and problem in all five of the lesson plans was our membership in the Fruit of Islam fully ratified."[86]

Upon successfully passing this oral examination, Clarence 13X was now considered to be a full-fledged member of the FOI. He became part of a circle of brothers of whom he had grown close. One of his best friends in the Mosque was a brother by the name James 109X Howard who became his right-hand man. James 109X was also known in the Mosque as "Four-Cipher Akbar" a.k.a. "Free Cipher Akbar" and eventually became known by the Five Percenters as "Old Man Justice." There was another brother who was one of Allah's chief confidants in the Mosque named John 37X; he later became known as Abu Shahid by the Five Percenters. Since Clarence conversed about the lessons daily, he earned a reputation as being a part of the "High Scientists" (a circle of Muslims who often delved into the Lessons) in the Mosque.

Clarence sought out other learned teachers in the Temple. One was Brother James 7X, who was a student minister and eventually ended up as the Minister over the Bronx Temple. Although he recalls some initial reservations he had about Clarence, he remembered the fond memories as well:

"Clarence didn't come out to the Mosque as much as some of the other Fruit (of Islam) did. I remember that he was kind of like a natty dresser, he was a good brother but still had some street in him. I remember he used to wear white suits sometimes. He would always ask a lot of questions during class. He confided in me to teach him about the history of the Nation. He often asked questions about the lessons. He didn't like to do too much work (laughs). I always thought he wanted to be a leader. But he ended up doing a good job. He did a good job. He was a very good talker. I admire Clarence because he started from a mustard seed to a tree."[87]

Outside of philosophical point of views, the Fruit of Islam focused on enhancing the physical attributes of themselves and their communities. This required a lot of training and adhering to certain protocols. As it was described in the lessons, The Fruit of Islam were extremely regimental:

> 12. What is the meaning of FOI?
> **Ans**. Fruit of Islam. This is the name given to the military training of Men that belong to Islam in North America.
> 13. What is the meaning of Captain and Lieutenant?
> **Ans**. Captain and Lieutenant. The duty of the Captain is to give orders to the lieutenant and the lieutenant's duty is to teach the private soldiers, also train them.[88]

As indicated in the Lessons, the FOI was a military structure that consisted of Captains, Lieutenants and Private Soldiers. The Captain or the head of the FOI in the Harlem Mosque was a man named "Captain Joseph." His name later became Captain Yusef Shah. He was one of Elijah Muhammad's top Captains in the Nation. If it was Minister Malcolm who preached the law in the Mosque— it was Captain Joseph who was responsible as the enforcer of the law. He was left in charge of the task to train the men who wanted to be in the Fruit of Islam. He was a very security-minded man and was knowledgeable in NOI teachings especially as it pertained to the military structure. He had a reputation as being a no-nonsense type of man. He had trained many men and often traveled with the Messenger to serve as one of Elijah Muhammad's personal vanguards on his security force.

Part of Captain Joseph's training techniques included a rigorous physical program for the FOI in Mosque #7. Assistant Minister Benjamin Karim recalls:

> Without exception, all Muslim men were required to participate in the FOI, which included Captain Joseph's program in martial arts. Captain Joseph, who headed the FOI at Number Seven, conducted our military drills and calisthenics. He also trained us in martial arts. Though military in its organization and discipline, the FOI instructed us only in combat techniques that did not employ weapons. It developed our instincts, our pride, our stamina. It taught us to rely upon our own individual strength; strength multiplied a thousand fold inside an Islamic regiment. Captain Joseph was making sure that we'd be ready for the War of Armageddon. He made better men of lesser men. He took the new brothers—men who had just left a secular

community where they may have been abusing their minds and bodies with drugs or alcohol—and indefatigably he reformed them. He made of them the Fruit of Islam.[89]

Clarence 13X participated in Captain Joseph's program along with the rest of the FOI. He learned a lot from his Captain as well as helped contribute to the class by sharing his expertise and experience as a war veteran. Because of his experiences he was able to fit right in with "God's Army." He assumed the regular duties and responsibilities of an FOI as described by a researcher of the Nation of Islam:

> The FOI's duties fall under two broad headings, security and discipline. As a security force, the FOI stands guard in the temples, checks visitors at all Muslim meetings, and provides a personal guard for all ministers and traveling officials, including the Messenger and Louis Farrakhan. As a disciplinary force, its supervises the "trials" of Muslims charged with such offenses as adultery, the use of narcotics, misuse of temple funds, not attending meetings, sleeping during meetings, failing to bring "Lost-Founds" (visitors) to meetings, reporting temple activities to outsiders, using unbecoming language before female Muslims, eating or selling pork, failing to pay extra dues for being overweight, allowing anyone to enter the temple under the influence of liquor, or stating an unwillingness to die for Allah."[90]

Clarence 13X was able to make all adjustments necessary and made it within the ranks and added to the camaraderie of the Fruit of Islam.

The Ranks

The FOI was a highly organized corps divided into groups called "squads." Each squad consisted of private soldiers that had a squad leader who reported to a Lieutenant. The Lieutenant reported to the First Officer who reported to the Captain. These squads routinely went on missions called "pushes" or "soldiering" which mostly consisted of "fishing" (an NOI term for recruiting people) for new converts and selling the NOI newspaper *Muhammad Speaks* on street corners.

As it was with the rest of the FOI, Clarence 13X was required to sell his quota of 50 papers a week. This he did by going back to the same streets he once hustled on. While selling the paper, he would speak with brothers and sisters in the community and tell them about the teachings of The Honorable Elijah Muhammad. Reportedly at first, according to some FOI in the mosque, Clarence experienced slight difficulty selling the paper because of his slow methodical cadence of speech. However, the more experience he gained selling the paper he honed his skills and became proficient at it. He noticed while teaching the "Lost-Founds" that many of them bore witness in agreement with the teachings, however some were still apprehensive about attending the Mosque for whatever reasons.

While out on pushes, it wasn't unusual for the FOI to converse or test each other in the teachings. Clarence 13X sometimes participated in these debates with his FOI peers on key points in the lessons. Abu Shahid (John 37X) recalls his first encounter with the "Father" Clarence 13X during one of these sessions:

> I met the Father in our Universal Womb, (Temple #7), the mosque on 116th and Lennox Ave. It was in 1960, if my memory serves me correct, sometimes in the spring. We were out selling 'Muhammad Speaks' Newspapers and we were on that mission out in the Desert, on Strong Island. We were a couple of a squads of Brothers, (FOI) and on our way back home. We were up on the 'El' platform when I heard "Puddin", the Father, Clarence 13X, Jowars Smith arguing with another Brother and I went to check it out. I was not a Lieut. and neither was the Father. Neither of us ever was. We were in a 'Special Class', the A.F.O.I., (Advanced Fruit of Islam) we had Lieut. status but were not officially classified as Lieutenants. We, (Temple#7), were in charge of Security wherever Malcolm X went, inside or outside of New York City.
>
> The Father was arguing with a Brother who had challenged the Father for 'identifying' himself as Allah. The Brother only recognized Master Fard Muhammad as Allah. I will never forget it. The Father said, "I'm Master Fard Muhammad's Uncle, that means that I'm his Father, Alphonse Shabazz's Brother and Alphonso was Allah before Fard." Then the Father took him to the Student Enrollment question number one. "Who is the Original Man?" ans. The Original Man is the Asiatic Blackman, the Maker, the Owner, Cream of the Planet Earth, Father of Civilization, God of the Universe. Then the Father said, "I am an Original Man and The Original Man is God and that makes me Allah." [91]

These kinds of "builds" were commonplace amongst the FOI. In some cases, the FOI in the ranks had their unique perspective of the lessons. Some were more open-minded than others. Clarence always had an open mind and looked for the deeper meanings in the teachings. This attracted others of like minds. Abu Shahid describes his involvement in the discussion and how he came to be close friends with the Father Clarence 13X:

> I had been standing by and listening and at that point I joined in on to the Father who was my own kind. We squashed the beef as the train pulled into the station. The Father and I built all the way home and we became fast friends and Brothers for sure. We sought each other out and became a force to be reckoned with because of our perspective of the 'Lessons'. We were opening a lot of eyes. The Father was never no 'elevator operator'. We were inseparable on a daily basis. I was living in the Bronx, (which later was named Pelan after me) and he was living in Harlem, (which later he named Mecca). We built on the 'Lessons' daily and were called the 'High Scientists', by the Brothers that knew us.[92]

Needless to say, the two along with other brothers in the mosque, formed a bond. They would always link up for future squad assignments when the troops went out on the streets to sell the paper and fish for converts. Clarence 13X pressed on working the streets of New York City, along with his Muslim brothers recruiting for the NOI. He participated in Muslim Bazaars sponsored by the NOI and was active holding security posts at large NOI events where the Hon. Elijah Muhammad or Min. Malcolm X would speak.

As part of his FOI duties, he traveled to Chicago and to other cities to hear the Honorable Elijah Muhammad address audiences across the country and to work security. It is even rumored that during the annual Muslim Celebration known as Saviour's Day held in Chicago, the Honorable Elijah Muhammad recognized Clarence in a private meeting. He allegedly rewarded Clarence with the name "Abdullah" for his hard work in pushing the Muslim Program. However, Elders in Temple #7 have vehemently denied this rumor. Abu Shahid:

"Temple #7 always did security for The Messenger when we traveled to see him or when he came to town. That was our job whenever we was on the scene. We held down the front rostrum when he spoke. We traveled all over the place doing security sometimes. We went everywhere, Detroit, DC, New York all over. We held down the rostrum during Savior's Day too. That was all Temple #7. We always did Minister detail for Malcolm X wherever he went."[93]

When asked if Clarence 13X received the name Abdullah from the Messenger during a Saviour's Day celebration, Abu Shahid strongly denies this:

"No! The Father didn't have a name like that when he was in the Mosque. His name was Brother Clarence 13X and I was Brother John 37X. Some brothers had names like that in the mosque. I was known as Shahid back then too. Everybody didn't get his name from The Messenger. I chose my name from the Quran. I was with my Lieutenant Clarence 7X. We both were looking in the Quran for names. He said he was going to choose first because he was the Lieutenant. So he chose the name "Sideeq" and I ended up getting the name "Shahid." I'm happy I got the name because that name belongs to me. But some brothers had names. Justice was recognized as "4 Cipher Akbar" in the mosque. But Allah didn't have a name then, we called him Brother Clarence or Puddin'.[94]

During the course over the next three years, Clarence 13X remained on his post as a dedicated soldier in the ranks of the NOI. The Nation grew in presence and in stature. The Nation was receiving national exposure in the media along with the Honorable Elijah Muhammad and his National Spokesman Min. Malcolm X. Of course with the Nation's growth and added exposure came extra duties, responsibilities--and problems.

Counter-Intelligence Program

The Nation of Islam's rise in power and influence didn't go unnoticed by the United States Government. Thousands of Black People were becoming Muslims as the NOI grew in numbers and developed into a strong financial empire. This resurgence in the Black community alarmed and captured the attention of the Federal Bureau of Investigation (FBI) as well as other government agencies.

The Government began to work against the NOI using the directives known as the "Counter-Intelligence Program" or "COINTELPRO" for short. This governmental program was established under FBI director J. Edgar Hoover to neutralize and destroy progressive Black movements by any means necessary. The Government placed handpicked agents in the Mosque to disrupt and cause dissension amongst the ranks. Since the FOI was highly organized and secretive, it aroused the menacing government agencies. C. Eric Lincoln expounds:

> This virtually autonomous body is an elite group, carefully chosen, rigorously trained, aware of its own distinction and responsibilities, admired and feared by the people within as well as outside of the movement. The FOI are entrusted with top security assignments and remains on constant alert. Most ominous of all, it shrouds its activities in nearly absolute secrecy—a tactic that has aroused the deepest suspicions of observers like the FBI.[95]

Mr. Lincoln's assessment would prove to be exactly true. The FBI through its spy intelligence had NOI membership under constant surveillance. In fact, NOI officials claimed that the FBI had personal dossiers on all of its registered members. Minister Farrakhan explains:

> But their best-trained agents are among us. And these agents who are among us are taught and trained to do the same thing they did among other groups. That is to provoke incidents within the movement; to provoke division; to sow the seeds of dissention. And to work against the element in the Nation which has come out from a life of crime, which has been reformed from its former habits. These wicked provocateurs work among those brothers, knowing who they are because they have a dossier on every one of us...[96]

Both, C. Eric Lincoln and Minister Farrakhan accusations proved to be truth. Brother Clarence 13X was not excluded from the FBI's list. In fact, the FBI had a personal dossier on him as well. Following are actual excerpts from authentic FBI documents pertaining to Clarence 13X's activity in the Nation of Islam as secured through the FBI's "Freedom Of Information Act."

At an NOI meeting held on [word redacted] at Mosque #7, 102 West 116th Street, New York, New York, in which CLARENCE 13X was in attendance, MALCOLM X said that the white man have proven themselves to be devils as the Honorable ELIJAH MUHAMMAD has taught that they were. He said he was tired of this devil and he hoped that Allah would take the so-called Negroes away from this earth.

At an NOI meeting held on [word redacted] at Mosque #7, 102 West 116th Street, New York, New York, in which CLARENCE 13X was in attendance, MALCOLM X said that the courts would like to throw all the Muslims in jail, but he does not think the courts can. He said the Muslims are taught not to be the aggressor, but if an adversary aggresses on the Muslims, then the Muslims should kill the aggressor. He said the Muslim Mosque is a place of worship, not fighting, but if the Muslim Mosque is attacked then the attacker should be killed.

At an NOI meeting held on [word redacted] at NOI Mosque #7, 102 West 116th Street, New York, New York, in which CLARENCE 13X was in attendance, [word redacted] said that the white man, with all the soldiers, guns, tanks, rockets, bombs, police, FBI and Uncle Toms, are worried about the Muslims because the Muslims pray five times a day. He said that today the Muslim God has the devil, the white man, in a deep freeze.[97]

The FBI did more than observe. Their handpicked Black agents infiltrated the Mosque with the sole intent on destroying the movement by employing underhanded tactics to sabotage efforts of the organization. As a combination of agent provocateurs fostering in-house rivalries, it led way to factions in the Mosque. Minister Malcolm developed a strained relationship with NOI officials in Chicago. This led to him ultimately rebelling against the authorities at the NOI headquarters. It even leaked over to him rebelling subtly then overtly against his benefactor—the Honorable Elijah Muhammad.

Most noticeable was the transition of Malcolm's disposition in regards to teaching the Lessons of the Honorable Elijah Muhammad. In his lectures, Malcolm would fail to mention the name of Elijah and his teachings less and less. Instead of teaching the lessons, Malcolm began to teach a more political doctrine while in the pulpit. Malcolm's transgressions were noticed by the Mosque administration including the rank and file. Malcolm's omission of the Teachings didn't go unchallenged. There was Captain Joseph who would call Chicago and report Malcolm to NOI authorities whenever he observed it. Then you had the private soldiers such as Clarence 13X who were proficient at the lessons and remained loyal to "the teachings."

> Malcolm's camp, of which included Benjamin and Sidney, tried to poison others. They were telling people in the mosque that "the Messenger didn't treat Malcolm fairly." Malcolm went as far to write letters to other ministers. That's what led up to him being kicked out of the Temple, although there were many NOI members that were jealous of Malcolm X. I remember that Malcolm had literally cried one day from the rostrum as a result of the jealous reaction of some brothers. I think he said he wouldn't teach in the mosque because of it. Farrakhan from Boston, Sidney, Thomas, Jay from Hartford and George from Camden were invited to come and speak in his stead sometimes.[98]

Malcolm X's distractions caused only minor rumblings in the Temple but yet had their impact. Muslims began to whisper about the hypocrisy of Malcolm X. His dissatisfaction soon was made apparent, as he would disobey a direct order from the Honorable Elijah Muhammad when he made his infamous "chickens coming home to roost" comment after the JFK assassination. His reckless boast earned him a 90-day gag order from the NOI.

Chapter 7
Expelled

Clarence 13X (Allah)

"He refuses to abide by the rules and we gave him many chances. I think he would fare better out of the Mosque."
-- Malcolm X on the expulsion of Clarence 13X.

Prior to Malcolm being suspended, Brother Clarence 13X, after 3 ½ years, would end his tenure at the Mosque. As to exactly why—various theories and accounts have emerged. With the passing of time, there are a few speculations and claims as to why he left or was expelled. It is only appropriate that we observe some of the theories, assumptions and statements that suggest why Clarence 13X came out of the Mosque.

One source claims that Clarence 13X was put out of the Mosque by Minister Malcolm X as a result of not complying with the rules of the Mosque (which some speculate was drinking and gambling). Les Matthews, a well-known Harlem news reporter for the *The Amsterdam Newspaper* said:

...he was expelled from the Muslims by the late Malcolm X who said Clarence Smith was a rebel. 'He refuses to abide by the rules and we gave him many chances. I think he would fare better out of the Mosque,' Malcolm said.[99]

There existed another rumor that suggested Clarence 13X was expelled from the Mosque because of gambling habits. There wasn't any secret that prior to joining the Temple, "Puddin" was known to take in a good dice game or two. He was a very passionate gambler and often traveled in those circles. "Puddin" never hid his passion for the game. Besides, since he came into the knowledge of himself Clarence applied what he learned in Islam to the game of chance.

The leading rumor of the cause of Clarence's expulsion was his admitted love for playing craps. Dice playing, it was claimed, was a way of demonstrating the probabilities inherent in the nature of the universe. By contrast to Einstein's famous dictum, "God doesn't play dice," the former Clarence 13X Smith, who took on the attribute (or name) Allah, did claim, "I am going to shoot dice until I die. And he did.[100]

Two Muslims in Temple #7 during the same time as Clarence 13X give another account. They allege that Clarence 13X was part of a group of brothers and sisters who although in the mosque, regressed or indulged in worldly vices on occasion. It is claimed that this circle of Muslims held private parties every other Friday only soon to be exposed by a disgruntled sister who was a former participant. Subsequently she informed Captain Joseph of the events and as the story goes, he busted the party as well as those in attendance--among them Clarence 13X. According to this story, Clarence along with the others came to trial in the mosque and was suspended for a period of 90 days. The alleged charges were for "smoking reefer and drinking."

Clarence had joined the ministers' class since he was heavy into the lessons. But he never became a Minister. He ran with a group in the mosque that was still "hip" and "street." It was said that this group still wanted some parts of the world, so they had parties every other Friday. A few people knew about it since they were attending the parties themselves but nothing ever was reported because they kept it quiet.

But there was a sister in particular that was a part of that group, and it wasn't just Clarence it was a whole group of them. But they must have made this one sister mad because for whatever reasons she ended up reporting this to Captain Joseph. So when he heard this, and Captain Joseph was no nonsense. He went to bust all of those in attendance at the party where it was reported that they were "smoking reefer and drinking" which wasn't tolerated in the Nation.

No matter what they tell you, you couldn't get any time out the mosque unless The Messenger approved it. No minister could kick you out. Malcolm had investigated these claims about what happened at these events. He surveyed those in attendance, individually, including Brother Clarence. I wasn't involved but I think he didn't fare too well in his interview. Malcolm had called the Messenger and told him what happened, including the reports that they "were smoking reefer." The Messenger said to put them out.[101]

Some dismiss the allegations of immorality and say it was theological differences that caused Clarence 13X to leave the Temple. One story produced by the Nation of Gods and Earths says Clarence 13X was told to leave the Mosque by Captain Joseph because he taught and insisted that the Black Man was God as stated in the lessons of the NOI.

One day in 1963, Allah was addressing the student ministers class. He was speaking about one of the lessons which dealt with what makes rain, hail, snow and earthquakes? He was manifesting his self style, literal interpretation that "all the above is caused by...man.

The head of the FOI, Captain Joseph, walked into the room and heard what Allah was teaching. He stopped the meeting, dismissed the men, and spoke with Allah. He told Allah that he couldn't teach what he was teaching there.[102]

Some tenured Muslims and Five Percenters deem this theory unlikely since it was Captain Joseph's job to ensure that the FOI knew their lessons. So it wouldn't seem appropriate or likely that he would punish someone for teaching the NOI lessons verbatim. This is besides the fact that one of the fundamental teachings of the NOI is that the Black Man is God.

Another story suggest Clarence 13X left the Mosque on his own accord because he allegedly began to question and eventually doubt the NOI teaching that Master Fard Muhammad was God in person.

> In the early 60's he began to encounter troubles in the NOI when he started to doubt, and eventually rejected, the doctrine that W. D. Fard was Allah. He reasoned that Fard could not be God because the NOI lessons stated the Original Man or Black man was God and by appearances Fard was not Black. He reinterpreted the lessons and began to teach that it was not Fard, but the black man collectively, who was God.[103]

Another account speaks to Allah not necessarily downplaying the fact that Fard was viewed as God in person. The main issue appeared to be some in the Temple only limiting godhood to Master Fard Muhammad and denying this same right to other Black men. This account emphasizes Clarence claim that it was ok to view yourself under the title "God" even in the mosque. Clarence 13X allegedly caught some flap about this from his peers who decided to single him out one day—among them Malcolm X. A Five Percenter recalls Clarence "The Father" explaining this to him one day. Um Allah expounds:

> The Father taught us that when he was in the Mosque that he was an FOI and that they played with him. He was working on the elevator and Captain Joseph and them said, "Yeah, brother Minister." So they brought him up to the podium. Now, if you know anything about the Father, you know anything about the mosque. As a brother teach-- you say- you got to show, and everybody say, "peace, you got to manifest yourself." So Malcolm and them was in the back and they heard the commotion. They ran out there. In the mosque is a little bell, which you cling one time, and it's a chrome-like-- a little school bell. It goes 'cling' and everybody pays attention. All the FOI, Captain and Lieutenants, they come to attention and then they start responding. Well, the Father was teaching. He said that, "Fard gave it to Elijah, Elijah gave it to him." And as they were coming towards him he said, "And I'm Allah." He said the Half Original Man gave it to the Brown Man, the Brown Man gave it

to the Black Man and that made him understand that he was Allah. And how he came at that is that everyday he would question the lessons.[104]

Some Five Percenter historians question the theological rift theories because of accepted knowledge that Clarence 13X was well aware Fard taught collectively the Black Man was God. Their primary defense is that Fard and Elijah repeated this throughout the NOI lessons. The Honorable Elijah Muhammad made many statements before the public that the Black Man collectively was Allah so it would not have been anything new for Clarence 13X to restate this—let alone leave the mosque because of this "discovery." A Five Percenter notes why the theological theory would be incorrect:

As mentioned earlier, the concept of the Blackman being god did not start with Allah in 1964. This concept had been taught in the Nation of Islam of which Allah, as Clarence 13X, had been a part. Neither was this some esoteric doctrine reserved for an inner cipher, but was clearly made manifest in publicly broadcast interview. When the historian Louis Lomax interviewed the Messenger Elijah Muhammad in the Mike Wallace documentary "The Hate That Hate Produced," he asked: "Now, if I'm to understand you correctly, you teach that all the members of the Nation of Islam are God, and that one of you is supreme and that one is Allah. Now, have I understood you correctly?" Elijah answered: "That's right." That was in 1959.(cf. C. Eric Lincoln, Black Muslims in America, 1991, pp 75).[105]

Other rumors say Clarence 13X left the mosque because of alleged marital problems with his wife he felt were caused by the Temple. Perhaps a main concern could have been that it appeared women in the mosque placed Elijah Muhammad in a superior position versus their husbands. Years later after he left the Temple, Clarence voiced a similar concern:

Now, if you have to go to church for someone to teach your women, I'm not saying nothing about the Reverend or trying to make you feel bad or nothing like that, because I'm only going to tell the truth. My wife wanted to teach me Elijah Muhammad. She tried to put my mind under the capture of that man. I said, 'woman you crazy.' She said, 'what, what, what,' I said 'what,

what.' I'm not going to let my woman go up under this man when I'm a man myself and if I fall for that my children can never respect me.[106]

An even heavier accusation of alleged marital problems between Clarence 13X and sister Dora have come from other sources in the mosque. According to one source, it was reported that there was a domestic violence situation that caused Clarence's expulsion by the mosque administration.

Clarence 13X and Caldune, we used to soldier together and sell papers. But you have to know the history of what happened to him. And it's the history of him being put out of the mosque for hitting his wife...and Shah was death on wife beaters. Now sister if your husband is beating you at home, in those days if you keep it to yourself and take that kind of abuse, then that's your business. But the minute you come and make it known to Yusef Shah he was up out of here. He'd get 30 days the first time, and then if he came back he'd get 90 days, because he didn't tolerate it, it was not in here and Shah almost had a case on him himself...

But Clarence got put out the mosque. But he got put out the mosque at a time that Malcolm had left the mosque in early '64 and he became confused. We used to see him on 125th street with his old Muhammad Speaks, but he had all this in his brain, and he had other kind of problems I won't talk about them now...[107]

Other theories or accounts are based on "factional" disputes that Clarence 13X had with his personal adversaries in the mosque; which included Malcolm X. Minister Farrakhan, who replaced Malcolm X as Minister of Temple #7 shortly after Clarence 13X left, touched on the topic about possible strained relationships in a brief discussion with a Five Percenter. During a Q&A session before an audience, Farrakhan addresses the subject:

There was a brother who was in Temple #7 in New York City under the name of Clarence 13X. (Farrakhan addresses a heckler in the audience) 'No, don't do that, don't do that.' The Holy Quran says evil is a bad name after faith. You may not like Clarence 13X and what he did— but brother and sister if you don't have any works that you can show for your faith, why would you knock a man who you don't think have faith? A lot of people inside the house who didn't agree with the way the house was being run and they left the house.[108]

Another former NOI spokesman says Clarence 13X left because he was the first to see and detect the hypocrisy in Minister Malcolm X himself. According to this account, Clarence 13X recognized that the 10% (corrupt leaders) had taken over Mosque #7 and infiltrated the Nation of Islam, so he left to continue teaching the truth and subsequently founded the Five Percenters. Dr. Khallid Abdul Muhammad (then Minister Farrakhan's National Assistant) stated during his speech called the "Hypocrisy of Malcolm X," states Clarence 13X's reason for leaving the Mosque:

"That's why Brother Clarence 13X left the Nation of Islam and started the Five Percent Nation of Islam. Peace Gods! And started the Five Percent Nation of Islam because he knew there were hypocrites and agent provocateurs all around honeycombing the ranks of the Hon. Elijah Muhammad. So he left the Nation of Islam. He left the Ten Percenters, who were the bloodsuckers of the poor— all around the good and the righteous man the Honorable Elijah Muhammad, with just one or two or a few other good ones on his staff, and many other Eighty-Five Percenters who were good, the masses of the movement, but who were direction followers who had to follow the FBI agents and the others who were envious hypocrites and jealous hearted hypocrites around the Honorable Elijah Muhammad. And he started the Five Percent Nation of Islam-- but it was a move based on something that he thought at that time. That's why I respect the Five Percent Nation of Islam. Hell, I'm a Five Percenter myself. I'm not 10%. And Allah did not make me to be 85%. I'm Five Percent..."[109]

A Five Percent author noted that Clarence 13X left -- not due to theological differences— but rather because of factional disputes that existed within the Mosque. As pointed out in a Five Percent Publication:

It would do well to remember that both Malcolm and Clarence did not leave the Nation of Islam because of ideological differences; neither rejected the basic tenets of the organization, but that factional struggles played their part in the expulsion of both men.[110]

Abu Shahid (John 37X) who left the mosque a couple of weeks after Clarence 13X gives another version. When asked about the circumstances under which they left he replied, "He left for his reasons, I left for mine." When asked about any theological differences he vehemently denied any existed at that time.

No! No! No! That's not true. Whoever told you that doesn't know. I don't ever recall that being the case and I was there with the Father. Whoever said we left for theological differences don't know because they wasn't there. And they know the lessons say that "the dead has never been known to return from the grave to tell the living whether they lied or not." So that's a lie.[111]

When warming to the subject and asked specifically if Clarence was expelled he remarked, *"If you were put out the mosque for 90 days and never returned, it's the same as leaving."* In one of his earlier writings he cites the main cause for "leaving" was due to financial reasons. It did not appear to have anything to do with theological or factional differences. Shahid recalls:

We, the Father and I, were working for the "Earth's Painters", a couple of Brothers named George X and Ben X, when we came out of the Mosque for "Economical" reasons. We weren't making enough money to take care of our families, so we went for ourselves...[112]

Whatever the case may have been, the one fact stands that Clarence 13X departed ways with the mosque and entered into another stage in his life. He was back on the Harlem streets without the strict confines imposed by the Muslims. If you believe the expulsion account, the reference to time out of the Mosque was referred to as "C" time. Some NOI officials perhaps in jest say it's called "C" time to "see" what you do during your time out. Clarence 13X was now free to make a way for himself but he wasn't alone. Due to attrition in the mosque there was an entire host of FOI before and after him in who were in the same boat. They too were on the outside and traditionally kept their bonds with each other in the streets. Some became reacquainted with the street life. Some founded other militant factions. Clarence 13X was no exception. In order to make ends meet it is alleged he worked and hustled here and there for financial income. Abu Shahid recalls his and Clarence 13X (referred to as "The Father") experiences at that time:

> The Adventures we had are "legendary". We worked together and hustled together. I had a number business in Pelan and came up with a Hashish connection. The Father gambled a lot. Whatever else he was doing, that he wasn't doing with me, I can't speak on. Some brothers say I shouldn't tell about the "negativity" of the "Life" we were living but we were in "The Life" and every Nation starts out down and dirty. This is an actual and factual account of what was. I'm "Keeping it simple" and "Teaching it real". I caught a pistol beef and was sent away for six months. When I came back, 4 cipher Justice, who was James 109X, who was then called Akbar, had become the Fathers right hand man, we were still tight but I had to handle my business. I would come out of Pelan and hang with Pop and the Father. Since Justice was hanging with the Father I would "hit the Father off" and roll with Pop.[113]

Over the next few months Clarence 13X would keep company with his comrades. He returned to many of his old haunts and carried his Islam with him. Not much on the streets had changed but things were just starting to heat up.

Chapter 8
Hell Up In Harlem

Allah (Clarence 13X) and 4-Cipher Akbar "Justice" (James 109X)

It was the spring of 1964. While Clarence 13X was fresh on the grind, all hell was about to break loose in Harlem. Conflict had taken its toll on the people. The white police was viewed as the most oppressive force in Harlem because of their repeated acts of police brutality. Black youth were not spared their wrath either and often fell victim to the jaws of the police. Many cases resulted in black fatalities. These vicious acts caused rising tensions in Black America to finally reach its boiling point. The atmosphere served as the precursor to what historians now refer to as the riotous "long hot summers."

The Blood Brothers

Malcolm X often used an analogy that compared the Black community to "a powder keg ready to explode." His analogy proved to be accurate. His message gained favor with the fearless youth who embraced his concepts. One cannot underestimate the impact Malcolm X had on the youth in New York City. It was Malcolm's apparent fearlessness and the manhood demonstrated by Elijah Muhammad's FOI that attracted the youth in New York, in particularly Harlem. This led to many youth wanting to join the ranks of the Nation of Islam but many of them were just too young or not ready to lead the disciplinary life of a Muslim. Some of those who were of age would get their "X" but leave soon afterwards and were back out on the street. Others just chose to attend mosque or hear Malcolm and other NOI speakers at different events held throughout the city. This caused the youth to emulate the Muslims by embracing the little terminology they were aware of and they acted out on this information they way they saw fit. Different youth began to make their own organizations based upon Black Nationalism and Muslim ideology. Eye God a.k.a. Amin was amongst the first waves of youth to go down this path. He lived off of 129th street in Harlem and was an acquaintance of Clarence 13X's niece and nephew. On occasion he saw Clarence 13X and the other FOI on the streets selling the Muhammad Speaks Newspaper. This was before Clarence assumed his role as leader of the Five Percenters.

There were no Five Percenters at that time. This was before the time of The Five Percenters. We would always go hear Malcolm X speak. I knew the Father because I was friends with his niece and his nephew Dale. But that was before he started manifesting himself as Allah. We knew him as Brother Clarence or Puddin'.

We had a group of about six brothers. Two brothers had wrote their letter to Elijah Muhammad and got their "X's". That was Malik and Walik around 1962. They didn't stay in the mosque, they just wrote their letters and got their "X", they was out on the streets with us. They shared what they knew with us and we learned a little karate from some of the Muslim brothers in the Temple and just worked with it.[114]

The youth in the community were rising up with the tides of the times. As Eye God would put it they were already "thirsty for Islam." They were starting to rebel against "the system." A showdown was inevitable when you coupled a violent abusive police force and a group of tough street kids defiant of an oppressive authority. It made for an explosive mix. One that would eventually blow up and land right in Allah's lap, although no one knew it at the time. Although he didn't initiate what was about to come; Clarence would assume the responsibilities. Prior to Clarence 13X leaving the Mosque, there existed a youth group who later became referred to as "the Blood Brothers." The group was heavily influenced by NOI ministers' speeches and their railings against "the blue-eyed devils." Historically speaking, the Blood Brothers served as the forerunners to the Five Percenters. A former Blood Brother turned Five Percenter named Um Allah talks about the transition:

> My name is Um Allah and I'm from Mecca. I'm not really one of the first borns but I've been in Mecca and in the Nation before it was called the Five Percent Nation, it was called the Blood Brothers. The Father wasn't teaching at that time. A little bit later as a grew up and I'm saying during that period of time it was something that you couldn't say it was a month or two months, it was like six months to a year. All of a sudden the nation changed to the nation of the sons of Almighty God Allah. And we taught. We went to the streets. As a young man, I was sixteen and I met Brothers who was younger than me, and Earths who were younger than me, that knew 120. I never got it that way. Until 1965 is when I started getting all the lessons, before that time we was being taught by mouth. We wasn't getting the whole script. We were getting what you call taught by word of mouth.[115]

The youth of Harlem began receiving NOI teachings orally from current and ex-members. It became part of the culture in their attempts to become acquainted with the "life-giving" teachings. Many of the youth sought out adults and peers who were willing to share any information or teach them self-defense.

Mr. Allah speaks about his experiences with the Blood Brothers and how he first discovered the youth organization:

When it was the Blood Brothers that was 1964. Let me tell you how I found out about the Blood Brothers. I was working as a young man, I walked by the "Y", I was working at the YMCA as a [sic]. And I walked by the precinct on 135th street and I saw some young people, some males and females, talking about "Come on out we'll kick your ass." I never seen anybody threaten the police. Young people, threatening the police? So I went to the "Y" trying to learn karate. I had two people, one was Donald Washington whose name is Hassan, and I asked Curtis Gordon who is now Shaka Zulu. He told me, "If you want to know karate why don't you go down there and learn it from the Blood Brothers, go on 127th street." And I went down there that Saturday, walked into the block and I saw-- I was looking and I saw some brothers in the school and a brother outside shaving heads and I walked up to him and he said, "Salaam Alaikum!" And I said, "huh"? I didn't know that, and I was a pig eater. I used to eat ham and all that stuff, so I ain't know you know. I wanted to learn karate. The brother said, "You want your haircut?" And I said, "Uh huh." You know, being a gopher. So I sat down, he cut my hair and I went home.
  And I started hanging out with these brothers. The things they taught me both physically was self defense and the things they taught me mentally...like the brother said, "How old are you?" And I said I was sixteen. Then he said, (referring to another person) "How old are you?" He said, "fifteen." "Then you held responsible for this brother." He said, "Have you not heard your word is bond regardless to whom or what?" I said, "huh"? I said, "Naw, I don't know the degree." He said, "Well your word is bond and your bond is your life and you give your life before your word will fail." I said, "Yeah, I'll do that." He said, "You held responsible for the young brother."[116]

The above was the ideal example of how youth initially came in contact with "the teachings." Blood Brothers members also used to visit Temple #7 where they listened to Elijah Muhammad's ministers. These visits were most impressive to the teens who were attracted to the Muslims and their personalities. Um Allah:

I went to the mosque one time, and we used to go the mosque and as young men we mimicked the Muslims but we wasn't Muslims. Like, we didn't go through all of that you know. I wrote to Elijah but my mother caught my letter and told me I had to get her permission --and she took me to a priest and all that. But the point is as that as young men we used to go to the mosque and we used to listen at all the ministers teach. And one of the things while I was there, they brought in one of the ministers, he got up and said, 'I want to introduce in our audience one of the greatest fighters in the USA,' and he said Cassius Clay, And that's before he changed his name to Muhammad Ali.[117]

The contact between the Muslims and Black youth were most impressive. Many other youth in this era experienced the same types of occurrences. If you were to interview the youth in the neighborhood in that time period, perhaps everyone would have a story to tell. Another Blood Brother turned Five Percenter named Dawud Allah gives his account of his experiences:

For me it was in 1964. But prior to that I used to live at 111 Lenox Avenue. And Minister Thomas, Minister Louis, the ones accused of killing Malcolm...Scar face Oscar, who made the recipe for the Bean pies for the Messenger. Oh, Captain Joseph. All of them used to be out there trying to pull us into the Mosque and a lot of us went in there. You know you sit on the right, the Earths were on this side and we were on this side.[118]

As with any other adolescent movement, the Blood Brothers who later morphed into Five Percenters experienced its growing pains. Trouble soon appeared in the early horizons for the adolescent organization as it faced the scrutiny of the media and police authorities. No one knows this better than the six young men who later became known as "The Harlem Six." Through a set of dire circumstances, they became the poster children for the entire youth movement happening in Harlem.

Harlem Six

Eye-God (Amin) of "The Harlem Six" recalls the beginnings of this dramatic experience:

April 29, 1964, was a turning of my life. Along with five other brothers. Our names were and are (were because a few have passed on) and are because there's four of us left. Jahad passed and Justice passed. Amin (aka Eye-God)-Rahim-Malik and Latif. We were known as THE HARLEM 6. Six young black men within this discombobulated system of so-called Justice for all, HA!

1964 was a time when you just didn't call another blackman brother, because he'd say, "I'm not your brother!" or you wouldn't call a black woman sister because of the same reactions. Knowledge of self was not heard of at that point of time. Sure there were Muslims but during that date and time they were souley house (Mosque) people. We began to hear things from the older brothers in the block about the white people doing this, and white people being of such a negative nature. At this point in our lives this kind of information was right on time. Cause we just came out of the gang type mentality. So this was right down our line. It wasn't until much later that we found out that this was the opening of one door that would change our lives, even to this very day.

However, after hearing these things from the older brothers on the block we (the younger brothers) went to a meeting where they learned all this. It was Mosque #7 on 116th Street and Lenox Avenue. This was 1963. The man we heard speak that night was Malcolm X. The knowledge and wisdom that the whiteman is the devil was so thick in the atmosphere, we left the meeting feeling completely different about ourselves. And with a dislike for white people.

Our young minds were being molded for things we'd later come to know that could only result in being locked up for nine years of our lives. And no relief came to us until the Son of Man (The Father) came to our aid.[119]

From all appearances the die had been set with the teenagers. Their minds were still grasping the hardcore concepts of what happened to Black people during their sojourn in America. Hearing all of these different vivid accounts of what happened to their people during slavery incited them to want revenge on whites. When one received any information about some history, it became infectious and was taught to everyone they came in contact with. On the other hand, anyone who appeared to go against it received a meted out punishment. Eye God:

Those of us that were still in school took those ideas into our schools and on our block, 129th St. between 7th and Lenox Ave.

This was ours to rule, run, govern or whatever came into our young, unknowing minds. Older brothers that had knowledge of karate came around and showed us how to use it.

We took up the art because the police had started messing with us. At one point only to show off. Also to beat up homos and drug dealers, also our young friends that were still eating pork.

This was what we thought was right, we kept going to the mosque and all of the time we would come out with more hate than with the knowledge of ourselves, as taught by the Father.

Our soul reason on the planet was to do the 10th degree in the 1-14. Hate had taken it's root within our minds, and nothing anyone said could change that (at that point in time). We would go to school and beat up the white boys. We would stop welfare workers from coming on the block.[120]

At the time, a lot of the actions of the young group (including violent acts) were not necessarily viewed as negative. After all, they felt they were on a mission to make things even. The young bunch thought they committed noble acts whenever helping out each other or even families as a result of any loot they acquired. In their mind they became "Little Robin Hoods" of sorts.

We would go to stores and actually fill bags with food, and give some of it to poor mothers on the block. No! we would not pay for the food. We would take it in the name of Allah-U-Akbar! These were white-owned stores.

Sometimes we would place some food in front of "not doing so good" black family's door, ring the bell and hide until they took the food. We call this "Making the white man pay for the poor rate."[121]

Needless to say, the authorities didn't share their point of view. The police didn't find their acts to be so noble. The police viewed the bunch as a menace that needed to be dealt with the old fashioned way. Perhaps a good beating by New York's finest. Their ages notwithstanding, the police made efforts to stop the band of teens. Police trailers were put on the groups to thwart their efforts:

Sometimes the police would follow us around, saying things like "Go back to where you came from!" We'd say "Give us carfare and we'll go!"

They would get mad, and jump out of their cars, with their nightsticks and guns. We would jump into our stances and yell at them, "Allah is God! C'mon suckers!" People would gather around, and start yelling for them to stop bothering us. Most of the time they would jump back into their cars and drive off. To us, this was a sign of them being punks. Not knowing that they had a plan for our behinds.[122]

Being able to evade the police for a period of time, gave the group confidence. This probably led to even more carelessness on their part. Full of spunk and feeling like they just got started on their quest, they searched for their next mark. After all, 400 years of slavery had earned the white man a good deal of retribution. Perhaps more than what they could accomplish in their lifetime. They would at least get their shot when an opportunity presented itself to have an all out brawl with a group of white kids.

One day on our way from Cooper J.H.S. we all got together, and started talking to our friends. As we walked and talked from school, people were adding on to our little group. By the time we got to 125th St. and Lenox Ave. (from 119th St. and 5th Ave.) there were at least 75-80 young people; hot headed, and wanting to destroy whitefolks.

It started on 125th St. and Lenox Ave. where a white man was getting a shoe-shine. Someone jumped up and hit the man in the face. Then it was on! There was a school on 124th St. and Lenox Ave. called Rice; a mostly white school. While all of this was going on their school bell rang, and look who came out of the door...white people. All hell broke.

People were yelling, and trying to get away from the so-called gang of blacks. Whites were running into the train station, onto the tracks yelling for help. While up on the street the bus wasn't moving fast enough for them, so they ran all over the place. We moved on uptown to 129th St. where there was a fruit stand.[123]

Perhaps feeling invincible at this time or just caught up in the euphoria of the moment. Nothing could stand in their way. On this day they were going to vent all their frustrations as they pleased. Not considering that the police was on their way to finally have the confrontation they so ever looked forward to.

The police were well prepared. The same could not be said of the young mob.

> Being that this was a nice day, we just helped ourselves to all we wanted. This turned into what was called Harlem Fruit Stand Riot. Police seemed like they were waiting for this day. They came out of everywhere. We started fighting, and it went into our block; there we thought we had it made. People started yelling and throwing stuff. A little old man came out and said, "Stop beating those boys!" The police jumped on him, and he lost an eye.[124]

On April 17, 1964 it was reported in the New York Times that: "75 IN HARLEM THROW FRUIT AT POLICEMAN".... "Four Policemen and a social worker were injured in a free-for-all with an unruly crowd of youths and adults in Harlem yesterday afternoon." According to the New York Police Department (NYPD), four youths and two adults overturned a fruit stand and attacked its owner. Then afterwards, the incident supposedly escalated into a "free-for-all in which about 75 Negroes clashed with the police after a group of boys overturned a fruit stand at 368 Lenox Avenue, near 128th Street. Fists, flying fruit, rocks and garbage cans were used in the melee. As a result of the altercation 3 teenagers and two adults were arrested." The three youths arrested were later accused of being part of a youth gang called the Blood Brothers.

However, the three along with the witnesses present gave a different version of the event. These testimonies were captured in a movie documentary made in 1980 that detailed the events of the Harlem Six from the perspectives of the teens. The movie was entitled "Torture of Mothers," which included famous African American actress Ruby Dee. As detailed in the movie narrative:

> On April 17th about 15 Negro children on their way home from school overturned some cartons at a Harlem fruit and vegetable stand and what might have been a minor incident grew into a riot.
>
> On April 19th the Times carried this story slightly different. 'The defendants four youth and a man was involved in a free-for-all on Friday afternoon after they allegedly overturned a fruit stand at 368 Lenox Ave. near 128th street.'

The truth was that there were three boys and two men. The men, a Puerto Rican seaman, 47 years old, and a Black salesman had no conceivable reason for overturning a fruit stand and pelting the proprietor with fruit as they were charged with doing. The three boys Wallace Baker 19, Daniel Hamm 18, and Frederick Frazier 16, was definitely cleared by the proprietor who told the police that they were not at his store.[125]

The fruit stand owner wasn't the only one who allegedly cleared the three young men. Other witnesses present at the scene stepped forth to testify. According to one witness:

I saw the cops running behind a couple of kids, they snatched at one of the kids and reached and grabbed at the other. So the kids were trying to find out what was going on. So the cops asked why they went and bothered this man fruit stand. So the kid said, 'Listen, I don't know nothing about it,' and they started shaking the kid around smashing him around. The kid said, 'Wait a minute, listen, don't shake me like this I don't know nothing about it.' So the kid got mad and dropped his books and the kid tried to get away from the cop. So the three cops teamed up on this one kid and just beat him down until he couldn't take it anymore. All he could do is just lay there, he couldn't throw another lick and then the cops had messed up his eyes. They was all bloody, his nose, his mouth, his head. This was a kid who couldn't be no older than seventeen. I saw the kid myself trying to fight this cop with his fist trying to get away because he said he didn't do nothing. So the three cops jumped on him and they beat him down with this stick and he couldn't move...[126]

According to the teens, they became involved after they feared for the safety of the children being accosted by the police. Following is the testimony of one of the three young men:

We got half way up the block and we heard a police siren and we didn't pay much attention to it. Then we heard these children scream. So we went back down the block to see what happened and we seen this policeman with his gun out and he had his billy in his hand and he was shaking it. So I like put myself in front of the kids because I thought he might shoot them because he was shaking like a leaf and jumping all over the place...[127]

After the teens attempted to stop the police officer, the police attacked them. Two adult bystanders witnessed the incident and were also arrested at the scene. The two adults claimed their only crime was inquiring with the police about their rough treatment of the children. After their inquiry, they too were beaten and harangued by the over zealous policemen. Following is the testimony of the 47-year-old black salesman arrested at the scene:

So I stood up and said why you all beating on him like that, huh? You going to take him to jail? You know there's no reason why you all should beat up on him like that. Then one cop he jumped up and start swinging on me, you know. Then he took out his gun and said get up over there. I said, for what? Then another cop hit me on the head from behind, you know. Hit me right upside my eye man and then there was nothing I could do then but just fall on the ground and try to cover up and protect myself. They snatched me up and practically dragged me over to the detective car...[128]

The three young men and the two adult bystanders paid dearly for their bold stance against police brutality. All five were arrested and taken to the police precinct. All five claimed to be savagely beaten while in police custody. As relayed by one of the young men Daniel Hamm who repeated it in a May 2nd New York Times article:

We went to the precinct and that's when they beat us for nothing. They like took shifts on us 6 and 12 at a time. They just beat me until I couldn't barely walk and my back was hurting and all this time they never took the handcuffs off.
    They got so tired of beating us; they just started spitting on us. Made us crawl all over the floors like animals and crap like that...[129]

The older man was beaten so severely he lost one of his eyes in the fierce altercations. Afterwards all the parties were taken to Bellevue hospital to receive medical treatment and were later released.

This vintage case of police brutality infuriated the people of Harlem. The Black Community had seen its share of police brutality and opted to take a stand. There was open protest in front of the police precinct and the Black Community organized an appeal against the NYPD for police brutality on behalf of the elderly man and the 3 young men. Even Malcolm X got involved. Hearing about the melee he rushed down to the precinct in attempts to calm things down.

Two brothers got picked off in the whole thing, Justice Allah (Walik) and Latik were beaten as we'd never seen anyone beaten in our lives. So we took to the streets once more, and marched to the 82nd precinct.

Busloads of police blocked our way, but we still got there and stood outside crying and yelling that, "We want our Brothers!" The police would not allow anyone in or out. Just then a brother showed up, and it was Malcolm X. He went inside, and came out a little while later.

He told us that the brothers were all right, and for us to be cool. Then they brought the brothers out, and I'll be damned if they were all right.

Justice couldn't hold his head up because he was out cold, beat real bad. Latik couldn't walk because they beat his legs and spit all over him. The police put them in cars and took them to Harlem Hospital.

We went there, and demanded to see them but the police were all over the place. They were eventually locked up for causing a riot. Shortly after that happened our parents got in touch with Malcolm X to tell him what the police had been doing us.

Also about the phone calls they were receiving, like "Tell those nigger kids of yours to go back to Africa!" Also, "Death to all those Muslims and Muhammadans!" So Malcolm X gave our parents a phone number to call if anything happened to us.[130]

Witnessing their peers coming out of the police station smoldering and bloody outraged the Harlem youth. How dare the police beat up on children in that manner? The community was outraged and the story had hit the news. Youth in Harlem wanted to do something about it and was angry as hell.

Murder was the Case

What the community failed to realize was this was just the lull before the storm. Less than a few days later, the police went on an all-out manhunt for the same three teens. This time for an alleged connection to a murder of a white woman shopkeeper that took place on April 29, 1964, in an unrelated case separate of the fruit stand incident. The NYPD also had an all points bulletin out on an additional three other young men that they linked to the same homicide. Using 30 men per squad the police raided three of the boys' homes and apprehended them one-by-one.

Oh yeah, the devil had a plan; but Allah (the Father) is and was the best planner. A lot of things happened to us between that time, and the time we got picked up on April 29, 1964. It was raining on that day, and we all just came home from school or wherever...We planned to go the night center at P.S. 144. A fellow by the name of Akbar (Robert Barnes) was with us. First Born Prince Allah was with us also.

We all met at the center and had our Karate class. Then we played music and danced. Robert Barnes left, and later we all started being picked up by the police. We were told that we were being held for the murder of a store owner on 125th St. We later learned that Barnes had warrants and got picked up. He gave up his freedom and changed the lives of six blackmen.[131]

One of their associates, Robert Barnes who went by the name of "Akbar" was picked up on a probationary warrant. While in custody, in an effort to negotiate his freedom, Barnes claimed he had information on a murder that took place that day. Robert Barnes, knowing the police were seeking revenge against his associates, provided information against the teens involved in the previous fruit stand riot. After picking up the teens based on the police informant's testimony, the NYPD claimed the teenagers reluctantly admitted to not only the murder of the shopkeeper --but also of three other white persons. Later the teens contested they were forced and coerced into a confession and maintained their innocence. As a result from police pressure, two other suspected teens eventually turned themselves in. As recorded in the New York Times:

Two youths arrested yesterday in the slaying of a woman shopkeeper in Harlem admitted having stabbed another woman to death on a Harlem street on April 11, the police reported.

Altogether, five teenagers have been arrested in the shopkeeper's murder and a sixth is being sought. All will be questioned about the slaying of the two women and also about the slaying of two men.

One of the men was...a 29-year-old blue-eyed blond man from Idaho who went to Harlem several years ago to live like a missionary and conduct Bible studies. He was slain March 23rd.

The other, Jules Bulgach, 71, was stabbed to death last Oct. 21 while selling fruit from a wagon.

All the teen-agers involved are Negroes. The four murdered victims, all attacked for no apparent reason, were white.

The police are investigating the possibility that some Negro youths have been carrying out a campaign of attacks on white people.

They said that several of the arrested youths were members of the Black Muslims but that the crimes had not been done at the behest of the Muslims. This sect has it as an article of faith that the white man is evil and violent, but it has not gone beyond preaching that the Negro should defend himself from this "white violence."[132]

A couple of days later, the sixth young suspect turned himself in. As in the first case, the police beat the boys severely until they got a forced confession. The police identified the teens as "Black Muslims" because of their affiliation with some of the Fruit of Islam that were outside the Temple. Although the teens professed to have Islamic ties, the police claimed they were really part of a vicious street gang that directed violence at whites. This was also the genesis of how after the Blood Brothers joined onto the Five Percenters, Allah's organization became labeled as an "anti-white gang" by the media.

The NYPD leaked this information to journalists and reporters hungry for a news story. The news rapidly broke out in the media. For the next few days it gave way to a media frenzy. On May 3, 1964, read the sensationalized headline and article: "Whites Are Target of Harlem Gang."

A gang of about 60 young Negroes who call themselves "Blood Brothers" is roaming the streets of Harlem with the avowed intention of attacking white people. They are trained to maim and kill.

Confirmation of the group's existence was given yesterday by a high-ranking police official in Harlem...when asked about the anti-white gang, said only, "We hope to have something for the press within the next two or three days."

The police already suspect that members of the gang are responsible for four Harlem murders, all of white persons.

The gang members range in age from 12 to the twenties and usually attack without provocation.

Training sessions in karate, an Oriental system of fighting, take place on roofs and in tenements around 135th Street and Lenox Avenue.   The instructors have not been identified by authorities...

Although they do not admit being affiliated with the Black Muslim sect, they greet one another with "Salaam alekim" – peace be with you—the traditional greeting of Muslims.

Their idol is Malcolm X, the Negro leader who broke away from the Black Muslims and formed the Black Nationalist group. Blood Brothers attend Malcolm's meetings and rallies on Harlem street corners or at Rockland Palace Ballroom...

The Blood Brothers are making traditional street warfare in Harlem obsolete. The members are recruited from the ranks of the old-line gangs, with the blessings of their leaders.

The new gang has no turf—no territory—to protect, and its target knows no geographic limitations: It is the white man.[133]

The sensational story startled white people who were accustomed to being perpetrators of racial attacks rather than the victims.   One noticeable thing was that the article lay the forming of the "Blood Brothers" at the feet of Malcolm X (who had recently left the NOI and was on tour visiting Africa). While visiting in Africa, when Malcolm was first questioned about the Blood Brothers, he denied any knowledge of such a movement. In his autobiography, Malcolm recalls the first time he heard of the shopkeeper incident while dining in Lagos, Nigeria. Malcolm X:

As we ate, a young doctor asked me if I knew that New York City's press was highly upset about a recent killing in Harlem of a white woman—for which, according to the press, many were blaming me at least indirectly. An elderly white couple who owned a Harlem clothing store had been attacked by several young Negroes, and the wife was stabbed to death. Some of these young Negroes, apprehended by the police, had described themselves as belonging to an organization they called "Blood Brothers." These youths, allegedly, had said or implied that they were affiliated with "Black Muslims" who had split away from the Nation of Islam to join up with me.

I told the dinner guests that it was my first word of any of it, but that I was not surprised when violence happened in any of

America's ghettoes where black men had been living packed like animals and treated like lepers. I said that the charge against me was typical white man scapegoat-seeking—that whenever something white men dislike happened in the black community, typically white public attention was directed not at the cause, but at a selected scapegoat.

As for the "Blood Brothers," I said I considered all Negroes to be my blood brothers. I said that the white man's efforts to make my name poison actually succeeded only in making millions of black people regard me like Joe Louis.[134]

Naturally, the New York Times article wasn't totally accurate. Though Malcolm was telling the truth that he wasn't directly responsible for organizing any such "gang"—there was a subtle affiliation. Although at that time it was not known possibly to even Malcolm or the general public that these teens were admittedly influenced by him and his former protégés. Or Malcolm could have feigned ignorance because he was already in hot water with the Nation of Islam. In any case, parents of the young teens and the kids themselves felt betrayed by Malcolm X who claimed they could call on him in their time of need. Eye God:

> Malcolm was called, and stated that he had no knowledge of us; that we were not part of his movement. This blew our parents' minds because now they had no one to turn to for help with their children.[135]

The NYPD would quickly piecemeal together some half-truths to fulfill their promise to the press when they said, *"we hope to have something for the press within the next two or three days."* This time it was a story worthy of making the cover of The New York Times Newspaper. The May 6, 1964 headline read: "Anti-White Harlem Gang Reported to Number 400: Social Worker Says Its Members Are Trained in Crime and Fighting by Defectors From Black Muslims."

> About 400 youths are now members of a Harlem gang whose indoctrination and training come from dissident members of the Black Muslim sect.
>
> This was disclosed yesterday by a researcher for Harlem Youth Opportunities Unlimited (HARYOU), an organization financed

partly by the city and partly by the Federal Government to diagnose the social, economic and educational ills of Harlem.

The police already suspect that members of the gang are responsible for four Harlem murders, all of white persons. The gang members range in age from 12 to the 20's.

The group's researcher said that his information had been obtained in taped interviews with hundreds of youths in Harlem. He said that the rebel Black Muslims indoctrinating the youth gang had left the parent Black Muslim group when Malcolm X did, but that they later left Malcolm because they considered him too mild in his denunciation of whites.

Most of the rebel Muslims, the researcher said, belonged to the Fruit of Islam, the security arm of the Black Muslim organization, whose members are trained in karate and judo fighting techniques...the rebel Black Muslims are believed to be using the youth gang to build up a strong force to oppose the police if trouble should develop in Harlem.[136]

If white New Yorkers were worried a few days ago—this most recent information left them terrified. The article struck fear into the hearts of white merchants whose stores were checkered throughout Harlem. As a result of white outcry, the NYPD chose to wage an all-out investigation into the young movement. The NYPD dispersed 40 Black detectives into Harlem to gather information on the "Blood Brothers."

The New York Times carried a 2nd article on the next day detailing the investigation. The headlines read: "40 Negro Detectives Investigate Anti-White Gang."

More than 40 Negro police undercover men moved into Harlem yesterday to investigate an anti-white gang, six of whose members are suspected of the murders of four white persons.

The police in mufti fanned out into community centers, restaurants, bars and other haunts where members of the gang are reported to gather during and after school hours. The police are also questioning social workers from city and independent agencies responsible for the organization and supervision of youth activities in the area.

The police have leads on two adults, whom they suspect might be responsible for organizing and teaching hatred to members of the gangs, whose members refer to themselves as "Blood Brothers."[137]

During the ongoing investigations, the police finally obtained the information they were looking for. They discovered that it wasn't Malcolm X who was organizing Black youth. Malcolm had just returned from his trip in the East and gave a press conference on his birthday May 19, 1964 in which the subject came up.

In Harlem especially, and also in some other U.S. cities, the 1964 long, hot summer's predicted explosions had begun. Article after article in the white man's press had cast me as a symbol—if not a causative agent—of the "revolt" and of the "violence" of the American black man, wherever it had sprung up.

In the biggest press conference that I had ever experienced anywhere, the camera bulbs flashed, and the reporters fired questions. "Mr. Malcolm X, what about those 'Blood Brothers,' reportedly affiliated with your organization, reportedly trained for violence, who have killed innocent white people?"...

I answered the questions. I knew I was back in America again, hearing the subjective, scapegoat-seeking questions of the white man...[138]

Malcolm denied any part in forming the Blood Brothers although he acknowledged the complicity of perhaps an indirect role. It was understood that former members of Temple #7 were involved with the Blood Brothers. It could have been any number of FOI who were no longer active in the Temple. As to specifically whom, charges were never filed against any of the Muslim trainers. However, the six teenagers were all booked and arraigned. Three were charged with felonious assault and the other three were charged with homicide. The six young men became known as "The Harlem Six."

The roots of the movement began to grow as other interested youth began to meet and connect under similar circumstances. Dawud Allah who was amongst and knew the Harlem Six provides his testament about their conversion:

My name is Dawud also known us Understanding Supreme Allah. I go back to 1964 on the 8th floor 275 Atlantic Ave which was the Brooklyn House of Detention. The Harlem Six and myself we were all on the 8th floor. Eye God, Walik, Malik, Percy, you know all of them from that day. As Um Allah said it was related to that article, that was the Life Magazine or the

Look Magazine. It was on the front page it said the Blood Brothers, that's what they was calling us back then. So I always had a good memory so I would write and print the Lessons out. So in 1965, the Harlem Six and I were sent up to Elmira Reformatory. I was only 18 years old then. And I was writing all the degrees, all the degrees, and remember we had one of the biggest riots in the country in 1965 in Elmira. Since we advocated that we were God they "bugged us out" which is to certify you as criminally insane and they sent us to Dannemora State Hospital for the Criminally Insane. It was illegal to send a 17 year old, 18 year old kid because back then it was a state prison. But I continued to teach.[139]

Pretty soon there were multiple encounters of youth coming together after being placed in these situations. It was inevitable that some kind of movement was going to happen. All of the dynamics of urban youth began to tie itself together as these teens shared the same experiences. Allah B, who was on the scene at that time, talks about his development on his path to getting knowledge of self:

I became interested in Islam at about thirteen. I liked what I heard of the Honorable Elijah Muhammad's teachings. I had an older brother who was an orthodox Muslim. He took me to their services and the only thing I really looked forward to was learning some karate. But the teaching didn't grab me. I wanted to learn about what I read in the Honorable Elijah Muhammad newspaper "The Muhammad Speaks." Where it mentioned "Who Is The Original Man?" and things like that.

I knew two FOI named Melvin Taylor and the other one was Donald Craig. Another brother named Linwood Smalls or Abdullah got a copy of the lessons. A group of us would get together to study lessons every Saturday. By this time I had broke off from the orthodox Muslims but retained the name I was given "Hakiem."

I had seen the courageousness of Malcolm X and was attracted to that kind of message. He seemed like he was, you know, a stand up guy. A lot of the youth in the community began to become islamicly inclined. Malcolm was like the main guide for many of us. We would go to the Temple and after the meeting Malcolm would shake your hand. I had gotten a copy of "my letter."

The Harlem 6 had gotten arrested. All the youth looked up to the Harlem 6 and The Blood Brothers. The Harlem 6 and Blood Brothers had more recognition of the Muslims.

In the process, I was arrested for armed robbery. I was in jail at the Brooklyn House of Detention for 11 days with the Harlem 6 from 9/7/64 – 9/18/64.[140]

At the same time Allah began to raise his first Five Percenters out in the Harlem streets. Only later for the rest of the Blood Brothers organization to soon follow. The Blood Brothers became known as the Five Percenters in latter 1964 and early 1965. The "anti-white" label followed the Blood Brothers over to the Five Percenters by the Police and Media.

However defiant the stand taking by the Harlem Six, it didn't slow down or decrease police brutality. A couple of months later on July 15, 1964 a white off-duty police officer was hosing down a sidewalk in Harlem and doused three young boys with water. When the boys complained, the officer fatally shot 15-year-old James Powell to death. This triggered a crowd protest that escalated to a full-scale riot. Rocks, bricks and bottles were thrown. The crowd lit garbage cans on fire and looted stores. The riot left 520 people arrested, 100 people injured and 1 dead. The "long hot summers" had officially begun.

Chapter 9
The Five Percenters

L-R, Uhuru, Allah and Black Messiah.

In the midst of the turbulence of the long hot summer, a nucleus was being formed that evolved into the head of the Five Percent Nation. This circle consisted of mainly Muslims (FOI) who was no longer active in the Mosque. Among them were:

1. Clarence 13X (Allah)
2. James 109X (4 Cipher Akbar, Justice)
3. John 37X (Abu Shahid)
4. Eugene 32X (Hebekha, Rasul)
5. Raa'jab
6. Walik
7. William 16X (Abdullah Shabazz)

This group included many others as well as some local teens that became their proteges. As Abu Shahid explains:

Our inner circle was the Father, Justice, Poppa Daddy (Pop) a giant and he was to me as Justice was to the Father and then there was Me. Hebekha and his brother Saladin, both Angel Babies. Just to name a few. Saladin stuck up Gladys Knight and the Pips in the back of the Apollo, with a plastic toy gun. Oyami and Oscar, Murphy, Sportcoat and Gilocki. Little Oscar was so tough that he broke the handcuffs, when the Police shackled him, with a burst of incredible energy and the cry Allah-U-Akbar screaming from his lungs. But that is another story. Little Oscar used to sell "Bean Pies." Then there were the two first born cremators, Uhuru and Messiah, not to mention a host of others...[141]

Some of the older brothers such as Allah, Justice, Shahid and Hebekha eventually became known as the Elders of The Five Percent Nation. They could always be spotted out and about in the byways of Harlem. They frequented the same haunts they did before joining the Temple and becoming registered believers. This time they had hordes of other brothers that shared their same experiences. Many of them began to balance Islam with what they were exposed to in the streets.

Albeit Clarence 13X and his comrades were no longer active in the mosque, they still reviewed their NOI lessons with each other. Clarence 13X and company continued to share the "knowledge of self" with their peers and identified themselves in the NOI lessons as "the Five Percent in the poor part of the Planet Earth." Just because they were not active in the mosque—this did not mean that they would not teach. After all Clarence 13X would recall, *"Elijah said we had to stand on our own two feet."* Shahid notes the thinking that Clarence 13X adopted during this time period:

He knew that if we were to take our rightful place as, Righteous Rulers, we had to stop squabbling over petty things, like "crabs in a barrel" and rise as a Nation and be recognized for our contributions to 'Society as a whole. God is God, to the Good and the evil alike. Salvation can only be found in God, the Devil the Arch Deceiver and the Adversary, there is no salvation there, only Slavery, Suffering, and Death.[142]

It was obvious that Clarence 13X maintained his strong interest in the lessons. It was written in his lessons that *"the duty of the civilized is to civilize the uncivilized."* As an FOI, he was instructed by his first General Order to *"take charge of this post and all temple property in view."* This post is the assignment given by Allah clearly stated and defined in the NOI Lessons and *all temple property in view* had a two-fold meaning to it. Captain Joseph on occasion in FOI class explained that the Messenger meant this in a dual sense. On one hand, it meant literally to safeguard the Mosque or Temple of Islam where meetings are held. On the other hand, he said the Messenger taught him that the whole earth was a Mosque and it was their job to civilize the human families of the entire earth.

The other key teaching of the General Orders was *to quit your post only when properly relieved.* NOI folklore has it when the Honorable Elijah Muhammad was asked what could properly relieve you from your post; his response was, *"only death could properly relieve you from your post."* This was an indication that the righteous had a duty to teach wherever they went. And this is exactly what Clarence 13X would take it upon himself to do.

What Clarence 13X now realized was that this mission applied to him as an individual. That he, as an individual, was responsible and therefore could not sit by idle and depend on a "mystery God" to do what he himself was blessed with the innate abilities to do. For a brief period of time Clarence 13X wrestled with this idea but soon realized that this was indeed his calling. Born Allah elaborates:

> Many think it's easy being God, however, there aren't many showing and proving that they are God. Allah, the Father had his second thoughts, until he finally realized that it was no mistake that he, in fact, was the One. The Father used to look at himself in the mirror and attempt to persuade himself that he was not Allah. However, he could never deny this unmistakable fact—the Original Man is God! So the Father decided to accept this knowledge of himself and began to teach it as he saw to add it—Positively![143]

As a result, in 1964, he changed his name from Clarence 13X to "Allah" and went to the streets of Harlem to continue God's job. God's duty as he saw it would be to teach his blind, deaf and dumb people and from them raise "The Five Percenters."

At first he took the message of Islam to the adults but it appeared that the older people were already set in their ways and were stubborn to change. As it is relayed in the "Greatest Story Ever Told":

> Allah began teaching Islam to the people in the community. The message he carried to them was that they had to clean themselves up in order to regain their long lost stature of prominence in this world. That they should abstain from smoking cigarettes, drinking alcohol, and eating pork. However, it was not long before he recognized their reluctance to change their way of life and thinking.[144]

A year's time had elapsed since Allah's departure from the Mosque. The current events at the time mostly featured youth organizations or "gangs" who were getting in trouble with the law. Many of these youths admitted they were influenced and attracted to the message of the Nation of Islam. Allah eventually took the same advice that the Honorable Elijah Muhammad gave to Malcolm X a few years earlier, *"Go after the young people."* He realized that it was the children who were the link to the future. All along it was the children who were suffering because of the lack of knowledge. How could the children know the truth, unless they had a teacher? How could they have a teacher, except that teacher was sent? He recalled a book that he once read that said the wealth of any Nation is not money—but it is the children. He realized that the children needed a teacher and he had to be that teacher. Allah spoke on the subject years later:

> To hold any nation together I read in a book one time--and I take all book knowledge and use it to benefit myself. I don't care who I heard it from. He said the wealth of a country is the children-- not the money. Once upon a time there was no money. The wealth of any country is the children. And if you don't keep the young people strong; how you going to win?[145]

- 128 -

One of Allah's early converts, recalls when Allah was asked later in his career by authorities why he specifically targeted the children:

I have not come to the churches because they have their religions, I have not come to the 10%'ers because they have their riches, I have come to the Children because they have nothing, the Truth has been concealed from them and theirs is the Kingdom that is to come![146]

So Allah and his comrades would embark on a mission—to teach Islam to the masses of Black youth that had not been reached by the Muslims. Since members of the NOI were forbidden to frequent certain venues of ill repute this made them inaccessible to some potential converts. Allah and his cohorts filled this void. A Five Percenter addresses the need for this strategy:

You couldn't go to the movies and see a Muslim. Muslims didn't go to the movies. They didn't go to discotheques. That's where our people who had need knowledge of self is. They in the movies, they in the discotheques, you see what I'm saying? They in the dice holes, they in the drug dens. Who's going to teach them people? Who's gonna teach them? He was a leader who made leaders, he wouldn't make no followers. He told us to be leaders who make leaders because if you got to stand out and be the Arm, Leg, Leg, Arm, Head. That's nothing but A-L-L-A-H.[147]

Other Five Percenter scholars touch on the necessity and further explain Allah's purpose. That purpose would be to reach the youth who were looking to be taught but didn't have the resources to get the information.

During that period in history VCRs were non-existant; and audio tapes of lectures produced by the Hon. Elijah Muhammad or any of His ministers was indeed a rarity. The Muhammad Speaks newspaper was the major media vehicle of the muslims. And there were no Nation Of Islam flash cards being printed, to be circulated through out the community, so that little Black children could become familiarized with the Life-Giving teachings of the Most Honorable Elijah Muhammad. Thus, in short, the most vital, vibrant part of the Black community was not receiving THE FINAL CALL: THE BABIES! Now since our Universe which is 76 quintillion miles in diameter, is a JUST Universe no need goes unfulfilled. It is the yearning and desire of the people that have always called forth the necessity for prophets, messengers, apostles, warners, etcetera. And at this particular period in the history of the planet Earth ALLAH was called forth himself![148]

In addition, there were swarms of young people searching for FOI to teach them bits and pieces of the lessons. Perhaps the most adamant of the youth on a quest to learn more about Islam was a local teen that became Allah's "First Born." This youth whose given name was Matthew Johnson had a run in with Clarence 13X the year before in 1963.

According to Black Messiah, he first met ALLAH in 1963, on 116th Street and Lenox Avenue. Black Messiah stated to me that he first observed ALLAH trying to get into Temple Number Seven, while he was dressed in short pants (cut-off pants). Muslims held fast to a strict code of dressing. Men were not permitted to wear short pants. At the time of their first encounter, ALLAH was a registered Muslim with the name Clarence 13X, under the teachings of The Honorable Elijah Muhammad, with Malcolm X, serving as the National Spokesman and Minister of Temple Number Seven, in Harlem, New York.[149]

Black Messiah's passion for Islam wasn't a secret in his circle. He shared what he knew with his peers and family members. So much so that one day his older brother Jimmy approached him with some news. This news led to him receiving the name "Karriem" and eventually the name "Black Messiah" after he crossed paths again with Clarence 13X, who by that time, started assuming the name of "Allah." Allah B explains:

Black Messiah lived on 127th street. It was on October 7, 1964, that "Karriem" brought knowledge of Math from Allah. It was relayed to me that it was Messiah's older brother Jimmy who had approached him about a man who was down in a basement on 127th street. Jimmy had said to Messiah, "You all say you all believe in Allah?" He then added, "Well, there is a man down in the basement saying He is Allah." Messiah had hurried down to the basement to see what his brother was talking about. From what I understand he wanted to kill Allah for even making this kind of claim. But after he had met Allah in person he ended up coming out baring witness. So you see, you could say the Nation was born then. It was on the Honorable Elijah Muhammad's birthday that the Five Percenters was born.[150]

Excited about his encounter, Karriem ran to tell the other brothers in his crew. Among them was his cousin who became known as "First Born Prince." The next day Prince went down to the basement to meet the man who called himself "Allah." Prince too ended up learning more about Islam and he became a student of Allah. The two would pull others to be taught by Allah. These youth started as the protégés for the Elders of The Five Percent Nation. Every now and then the Elders shared the lessons with them such as in this example with Messiah and Uhuru. Shahid speaks of this period:

Messiah and Uhuru were like my babysitters. They used to come to my rest, in Pelan, and if we were not home, they would go next door, to our Puerto Rican Babysitter, who lived on the same floor, in the next building. They would get my son, Shaheed and pass him, across the air-shaft, into my rest. They would then cross over, put a "Pot" on, get my lessons out and be studying and jammin when we came home. Messiah was Karriem then and Uhuru had a Queen named Makeba.[151]

Teach The Babies

In order for Allah to be successful with the youth he had to develop an effective way of communicating with them. With Four Cipher Akbar (Justice), Abu Shahid, Hebekha and others, Allah devised a plan to go out into the streets to teach and organize the masses of Black Youth who had never been reached by the Nation of Islam.

Inside the Mosque, the Fruit of Islam (FOI) studied a lesson written by Master Fard Muhammad called, *"The Problem Book."* This lesson consisted of 34 mathematical mind-boggling word problems. Each problem contained an esoteric meaning for the student to decipher. From this book would come the genesis of Supreme Mathematics and Supreme Alphabets that would become a staple teaching of the Five Percenters. Abu Shahid explains:

When last we were building together, I spoke of how I was in an "Elite group of brothers known as the A.F.O.I., the advanced Fruit of Islam. It was then that the "Problem Book" came into my hands. It was while I was studying this precious Book that I came across the thirteenth (13th) problem, or those of you that don't have access to it, you can find it in "Theology of Time", by the Hon. Elijah Muhammad, in the prefix....

Well, I had been studying the "Problem Book", and was all caught up in it's science. I had offered it to the Father, but He said that He didn't have any problems. I had been fasting for about three (3) days when I came across the thirteenth (13th) problem. I science it up for the whole day and twisted and turned with it until it began to come into focus. So this then is how I developed my concept of the "Living Mathematics". First I had to identify the actual facts to build on. Mathematics is Islam and Islam is Mathematics, a right and exact science that can be proven in no limit of time.[152]

The Problem Book was a book that many of the "scientists" in the Nation of Islam reviewed to attempt to break its different codes. According to NOI legend, not too many people understood or were able to decipher Master Fard Muhammad's riddles. Among the different problems in "The Problem Book," Fard expressed a simpler but yet a most important one called Problem #13.

Problem No. 13

After learning Mathematics, which is Islam, and Islam is Mathematics, it stands true. You can always prove it at no limit of time. Then you must learn to use it and secure some benefits while you are living—that is luxury, money, good homes, friendships in all walks of life.

Sit yourself in Heaven at once! That is the greatest desire of your Brother and Teachers.

Now you must speak the Language so you can use your mathematical Theology in the proper term, otherwise you will not be successful unless you do speak well, for she knows all about you.

The Secretary of Islam offers a reward to the best and neatest worker of this problem.

There are twenty-six letters in the Language and if a Student learns one letter per day, then how long will it take him to learn the twenty-six letters?

There are ten numbers in the Mathematical Language. Then how long will it take a Student to learn the whole ten numbers (at the above rate)?

The average man speaks four hundred words; well.[153]

The Elders of The Five Percent Nation began to dissect this problem. Each appeared to add their input as a result of their own study of problem #13 and began to pen their own lesson as parts of the answer. Shahid explained his approach to this process:

What was the specific relationship between the Alphabets and the Mathematics. I had to find the Alphabets computation of the Mathematical evaluation in order to be successful and work my mathematic theology right and exact. You must remember that I was fresh out of the Mosque and that, that information was foremost in my mind. The first thought that came to my mind as I re-collect, was "Belief in the Seen and the Unseen"...So the Knowledge supercedes belief. Therefore, knowledge assumes a Mathematical Evaluation Equal to the number One.
1...Knowledge
What could I relate to knowledge to from what we were taught in the Mosque? We were always taught knowledge, wisdom and understanding, which I then preceded to break down. When you know the Edge, you have the advantage. You must then ACT, the knowledge, which is called acknowledging the knowledge. How I would manifest this showed my wisdom. The results of which, if I could stand under them, I then would understand them...[154]

Together, Allah and the Elders invented the beginnings of the system called the *"Supreme Mathematics"* and *"Supreme Alphabets."* They introduced this system along with the Nation of Islam Lessons (also known as 120 degrees) to a group of Black Youth. Abu Shahid explains:

The foundation of our Nation is the lessons (120*), given to Us, the Nation of the Gods and Earths (formally known as the Five Percent) by the Father with his understanding. We received it and accepted it as knowledge and processed it and developed it until it evolved to the high degree of understanding we do have today. We are a people, the very people whose very nature is rooted in our culture, which is Islam. Islam: I Self Lord And Master. I S (I+S=IS) is what's happening NOW. In Self Lay All Mathematics. Mathematics is Islam and Islam is Mathematics, a right and exact science that can be proven in no limit of time. "If it ain't right it don't add up, if it don't add up, it ain't right." There are ten numbers in the Language of Mathematics. The Supreme Mathematics are a result of the 13th problem in "The Problem Book", given to the Hon. Elijah Muhammad by Master W. D. Fard. It is a language and you must speak your Mathematics right and exact, because She knows all about you."[155]

Allah went on to develop the science of Supreme Mathematics as the basis of his teachings and the key to unlock the minds of Black youth. This lesson *Supreme Mathematics* is a corresponding numerological system which has meanings applied to each number of the numerical system. The Supreme Mathematics:

Supreme Mathematics
(1) Knowledge
(2) Wisdom
(3) Understanding
(4) Culture or Freedom
(5) Power or Refinement
(6) Equality
(7) God
(8) Build or Destroy
(9) Born
(0) Knowledge Add a Cipher

Each number has a moral definition applied to it. For example Allah taught the first principle was Knowledge- *"Knowledge is to know, look, listen, observe and respect. Knowledge is the key to all aspects of life. Knowledge is the foundation of all things in existence."*

Allah taught that the second principle is Wisdom- *"Wisdom is the manifestation of one's knowledge. The ways and actions one uses to make his knowledge known. Such as speaking wise words to wise the dome or through your purified ways and actions to show and prove God exist."*

Allah's third principle was Understanding- *"Understanding is the mental picture one draws up in the mind of knowledge and wisdom.*

- 134 -

To Understand is to see all things clearly with the Third Eye which is the Mind, the All Seeing-Eye. Understanding is the best part- the Cream that rises to the top."

In addition, Allah and the Elders added the **Supreme Alphabets** as well. The Supreme Alphabet is a system in which every letter of the alphabets is given a mystical meaning: *A* stands for Allah, *B* is Be or Born, *C* is See, and so forth on down to *X* which is Unknown, *Y* which is "Why?" ("the question most asked by the Eighty-Five Percent") and *Z*, which is Zig Zag Zig.

Supreme Alphabets

1. A- Allah
2. B- Be or Born
3. C- See
4. D- Divine
5. E- Equality
6. F- Father
7. G- God
8. H- He or Her
9. I- I, Islam
10. J- Justice
11. K- King
12. L- Love, Hell or Right
13. M- Master
14. N- Now, Nation or End
15. O- Cipher
16. P- Power
17. Q- Queen
18. R- Rule, Righteous
19. S- Self, Saviour
20. T- Truth or Square
21. U- You or Universe
22. V- Victory
23. W- Wisdom, Woman
24. X- Unknown
25. Y- Why
26. Z- Zig Zag Zig

Each mystical meaning of a letter has a moral or parable connected to it. For example, the fourteenth letter in the alphabet is *N*. In the Supreme Alphabets *N* stands for *Now, Nation or End* which is defined:

Now, Nation or End- *Now is the time for the Black man to wake up and come into the realization of Islam, which is his true and righteous Self, which is his true Nature and his true Nation or End in the pit of the devils civilization. Fourteen is the "Knowledge-Culture degree," "when a man ac-knowledges his culture he is going to see the Power. And the Power is the Truth and the Truth is the Light. Before a man can see the Light he must find the switch and before we put on Our Light we must find our switch—we must acknowledge Our Culture."*

The Supreme Mathematics and Supreme Alphabets were the building blocks that enabled Allah and Justice to attract the children and effectively spread the message of Islam to the youth. Many of the youth were attracted to the "smooth rap" maintained by these two gifted conversationalists. [156]

The First Nine Born

Allah took his message to poor, delinquent and hard-core street youth. Many of them were drug addicts, dropouts, and incorrigible black youth that society had long since failed and given up on. As described by one of Allah's early students Universal Shaamguadd:

> Brothers and Sisters, before ALLAH came to us (His First Borns), we were the most savage things in the streets, some of us were members of the Chaplains and Sportsmen youth gangs. We had little respect for our parents and no respect for anything else, the elderly, women, police, society or the clergy. Black or white, we were looking for some ghost so we could take them off! So for someone to come and show and prove to us that He was the Supreme Being and turn us from our wicked ways was no small miracle (we weren't dumb, just savage!).[157]

Since Black Messiah was the first one to accept Allah's teachings he is recorded as being the first Five Percenter. Allah actually gave him the Muslim name Karriem (later he became known as Black Messiah). According to some, it wasn't a coincidence that he received the name Karriem on the Honorable Elijah Muhammad's birthday. As it was Fard who first gave Elijah the name Karriem when they first met. Like Elijah, Karriem turned out to be a wise choice because of his ability to attract the other youth in the community. Karriem made good by bringing other Black youth to be taught by Allah.

Allah started out by teaching nine Black youth. In Five Percenter ideology, the number nine represents the principle of *"Born"* in the Supreme Mathematics. Nine is the highest number in the numerical system thus it means to be complete, just as it takes nine months for a baby to be birthed into this world. Thus this early core of nine Black youth later came to be known as the *"First Nine Born."*

As it was with the Nation of Islam, Allah taught the young men to drop their "slave" names (also referred to as government names) and wear one of the righteous names of Allah. Hence, his first followers adopted Muslim names in lieu of their "government" names. The First Nine Born took on the following names: Karriem, Uhuru, Niheem, Al-Jabbar, Al-Jamel, Kihiem, Bilal, Akbar and Al-Salaam.

Allah taught them the understanding behind their names, age and why life was so hard and cold for the Black Man. The children affectionately referred to Allah as *"The Father"* because many of them were the products of broken homes and this was the only father they knew. Thus the Father taught his First Nine Born.

Besides Allah, the first Nine Born had a host of other "Elders" to confer with for guidance. Among the most notable was James 109X who was known as "Free Cipher Akbar" or "Old Man Justice", John 37X who was known as "Abu Shahid", Eugene 32X who was known as "Hebekha" and others who had left the mosque with Allah.

Five Percenter Teachings

Allah utilized his Muslim training and lessons to begin and guide the group of youth. The concept and identity of the Five Percenters is directly taken from the NOI Lesson known as *"Lost Found Muslim Lesson no. 2."* Author Yusef Nuruddin elaborates:

Within the Lost-Found Muslim Lesson no.2 (1-40) it teaches a naturalist theory of the universe which denies the idea of life after death as well as the existence of a "mystery god." The only resurrection possible is a revival from "mental death" (ignorance and superstition). Those who believe in a mystery god are mentally dead. The only "god" is man himself; it is the "devil" (white man) who has tricked 85 percent of humanity into believing in a god whom they cannot see, so that he can "make slaves [of them]... rob them and live in luxury." This exposition leads into a series of three important questions from which the Five Percenters draw their self-conception:

14. Who are the 85%? The uncivilized people; poison animal eaters; slaves from mental death and power; people who do not know who the living God is, or their origin in this world and who worship that which they know not. Easily led in the wrong direction but hard to lead in the right direction.

15. Who are the 10%? The rich slave-makers of the poor, who teach the poor lies to believe that the Almighty True and Living

God is a spook and cannot be seen by the physical eye; otherwise known as bloodsuckers of the poor.

16. Who are the 5% in this poor part of the Planet Earth? They are the poor righteous teachers who do not believe in the teachings of the 10% and are all-wise and know who the true and living God is and teach that the true and living God is the Son of Man, the Supreme Being, the Black Man of Asia; and teach Freedom, Justice and Equality to all the human families of the Planet Earth; otherwise known as Civilized People, Also is Muslim and Muslim Sons.[158]

It was through this decree the Five Percenters found its ideology. Allah explained this same concept to others in much simpler terms. Barry Gottehrer:

He explained his religion to me at some length. The world, he believed, was inhabited by three kinds of people: 85 per cent of the world are cattle; 10 per cent are the devils who mislead the cattle, and the 5 per cent, with Allah at its head, had become the Five Percenters. Much of the theology was similar to Muslim teachings; when Allah left the mosque, he took a good number of books and pamphlets with him to guide his new sect.[159]

After becoming well versed in the teachings, a Five Percenter was required to recruit others. As a result the teachings began to spread throughout Harlem. Manhattan (especially Harlem) became known as *"Mecca,"* named after the center of ancient Islam and birthplace of prophet Muhammad; thus Harlem was the birthplace and center of Allah's brand of Islam. Allah eventually renamed the boroughs using Islamic geographical names. Each borough has a "history" as to how Islam (via the 5%) was established in that territory. Allah gave his first adherents timely dictates to ensure their success. Among them were matters of how to approach security and self-defense:

The Father taught us that because we were the Most High that we would be considered by some Most Low in the Wilderness of North America. However, that we should fear nothing of this World, that even the Devil did not fear Death. His only fear was of ALLAH because he knew not when or how He would come! And if we were on with Allah, there should be no reason to fear anything in this world. He told us that we did not need Guns unless we had Legal Papers for them because our Tongue was our Sword and that we could slay more with the word than any army or machine gun could ever do. And that he who must live by the Gun shall surely Die by the Gun!!! Now don't take me wrong. He didn't teach us to fight fire with Tulips, however, he taught us not to try to put out a fire with Gasoline!!![160]

A main directive from Allah was to ensure that all of his Five Percenters were healthy, strong and good breeders. A goal was given to each Five Percenter to teach other children and bring them into the fold. Allah instructed each of them to take precautionary measures when teaching others:

He taught us that we were each required to teach at least 10 children or people who were younger than ourselves and they shall be our Fruit. Just like a Farmer, we would be held responsible for the actions of our crops and that we should do all within our power to keep the snakes out of our gardens. We should watch and see what things tried to infect or poison our fruits and then weed them out. This would insure us a Righteous Harvest. He taught us that some of us and our Fruit may have to Die to show the rest of us that everything is for Real and that we should hold fast and pray to the Allah that is within, and that each of us will be rewarded according to his individual works because the future of the Human Families of the Planet Earth and Mankind in general depends on the success of ALLAH's Nation of Islam, A/K/A The 5% Nation!!![161]

Allah taught that the culture of the original man was Islam. Islam, according to the lessons was Freedom, Justice and Equality. Like Malcolm did in FOI class, Allah expounded on the different lessons. In this particular example, he showed his Five Percenters how to view "Equality":

The Father taught us that Equality means to be equal in everything. This does not mean that if one brother is working, he must support those who are not working with his paycheck...or if one brother has a sister or an Earth that he must share her with brothers who do not have their own women...it means the Exact Opposite...that if one brother has a job if you are his EQUAL, you should HAVE YOUR OWN JOB OR YOUR OWN WOMAN!!! If he has been successful in Building in His community, or in Business or in Education, if you are his equal, his alike, YOU should have the same success in your endeavors, whatever they shall be. Because a brother may have a beautiful home, apartment, car, clothing, this does not mean this is OUR HOME, OUR APARTMENT, OUR CAR, OUR CLOTHING, He is under NO OBLIGATION TO MOVE YOU IN, GIVE YOU HIS CAR OR LET YOU WEAR HIS CLOTHING...UNLESS THIS IS HIS WILL! Remember, "THOU SHALT NOT BE A LEECH!!!" God is Independent. He is not even dependent on his woman!![162]

Allah had a unique way of addressing a taboo caste system in the Black community that was perhaps more prevalent in the earlier part of the century but still lingered somewhat in the 60s. This was the matter of different skin complexions within the Black community. To battle that old slave mentality, Allah made it so each Five Percenter had to partner with two others of different skin complexions. The three would serve as a unit and look out for each other in times of need.

Almighty God Allah taught us that the Devil using our knowledge had learned to separate the Seeds of the Original Man and Weaken Him and with this in mind, He, ALLAH, was going to show us how to Reunite these seeds, for this reason every brother who was of the Black Seed (in complexion), must have a Brown or Yellow Seed Brother. Every Brown Seed must have a Yellow or Black Seed. Every Yellow Seed must have a Black or Brown Seed. The purpose of having a Seed was so that when we went out to teach on could do the knowledge while the other would do the Wisdom (or watch each other's back). Also, if one Seed took a fall, or had to go through trials and tribulations in prison or wherever for the cause, your seed would keep the Buzzards, Snakes, Vultures and Devils out of the Nest!!! (And when properly done, it works). Your seed also would keep you from slipping or falling too deep into the traps of Society. After all, six eyes are better than three when they are all Righteous.[163]

Allah's words served as inspiration for the young men to move forward with their mission. The First Borns started multiplying their numbers. Many of the Blood Brothers began to join onto the Five Percent Nation. The knowledge soon spread up to the Bronx. Allah renamed the Bronx "Pelan" in honor of his brown seed John 37X (Shahid) who lived there. This honor was in parallel to the NOI lessons that specifically mentioned the prophet John who *"was a witness on the island of Patmos or Pelan for the testimony of his brother."*

Gods and Earths

According to the Lessons, the original Black man was *"the Supreme Being, God of the Universe."* In Five Percenter nomenclature, Supreme is defined as *"the most high"*; Being is defined as *"to exist."* Five Percenter rationale dictates that according to physics, anything that exists can only exist in three stages or forms – liquids, gases or solids. God therefore is the apt title given to the highest form of mental, spiritual and physical existence; the Black Man. This supreme form of life is the vehicle through which Allah's will is made manifest. The underlying principle is there is no substance in the universe that the Original Black man's body does not contain. All forces around him, above him and below him all have their beginning with him. This anthropomorphic understanding did away with any concept of *"a spook god,"* that NOI literature described as a spirit or *"mystery god that does not exist."* Thus, Allah taught that all Black male Five Percenters were "Gods" by birthright. His astral twin in nature was the Sun, *"Such as the Sun is the foundation to the Solar System so must the Black Man be the foundation to his family."* In the Supreme Mathematics he was symbolized as "Knowledge."

Allah taught his Five Percenters that the Black woman is the *"mother of civilization."* He taught that her rightful place was to be a Queen at the side of Allah. He explained to his followers that the Planet Earth symbolizes the Black Woman and is her twin in nature. As the Earth produces life, so does the Black woman produce life and she *"is the field from which the Black Nation is produced."* Another similarity was that ¾ of the Planet Earth's surface is covered under water; so in parallel, the Black woman in Islam must cover up ¾ of her body with clothing for *"protection from the devil's civilization."* In this sense, Five Percenter women are called *"Earths."* Her astral twin in nature is the *"Moon."* *"As the Moon reflects the light of the Sun, so does the Black Woman reflect the truth given to her by the Black Man."* In Supreme Mathematics, she was symbolized by the principle *"Wisdom."* Because of her nature, Allah stressed that Five

Percenters should treat their women right but they shouldn't lose focus of their roles. Shaamguadd explains:

> Our Father (Allah) taught us that not only should we teach and educate our women, we should treat them right, to love them, respect them and protect them, even pamper them when possible, However that we should always stand fast as Lord and Master of that universe.[164]

At the core of Allah's teachings was his strong love for *"the Babies."* He often remarked, *"The Babies are the Greatest."* Part of his philosophy was that the Black Nation should have as many babies as possible, *"because the only way you will find God is by reproducing."* Allah affectionately referred to the children as *"Understanding,"* and their astral twin in nature was the *"Star."* As denoted in Five Percenter philosophy, *"Understanding is also the Black Child. As the Stars justify the light of the Sun, so does the Black Child justify the truth (light) of the Father (Sun) and the Mother (Moon)."*

Allah and the Elders even shared this philosophy with many of their brethren still in the Temple. Abu Shahid recalls one of these instances when after they left the mosque, him and Allah went to go hear the Honorable Elijah Muhammad speak at an arena in New Jersey. Upon them attempting to enter the arena they were stopped by the Fruit of Islam who denied them entrance because of their status:

> They didn't want to let us in the arena in New Jersey because they thought we was "out of pocket." The FOI made a big fuss about it because we was out the mosque. They called for the Captain to come talk to us. Captain Joseph came outside and approached us and said "Brother John, Brother Clarence." I said, "Brother Captain, How are you going to have all those MOONS and STARS in there to see The Messenger but you going to leave the SUN outside?" Brother Captain knew what we was talking about and he let us in to see The Messenger. And he knew our love for The Messenger because that's how we started...We didn't have a "beef" with anyone in the mosque. It was between Malcolm and Elijah. We loved Elijah. It was Malcolm who told the lie and got killed. But we loved them both. But we was with Elijah.[165]

Prophets, Messengers and Gods

Allah gave the Five Percenters the Star and Crescent of the Nation of Islam to wear as the official emblem for his movement. He gave them the history on the *"National"* and taught them that this Flag was *"the greatest and only flag known in the universe--the Sun, Moon and Stars."* He taught that the National Flag represented Islam— *"Freedom, Justice and Equality"* as well as *"Man, Woman and Child."* On occasion young Five Percenters wore this emblem on their person to facilitate identification amongst themselves and to others.

Allah didn't leave his Five Percenters to guess about their origin. He taught them the history of the Nation of Islam and his connection to its founders. According to Allah's teachings, Master W. F. Muhammad represented "Knowledge" because he was the foundation upon which he stood. As explained by Universal Shaamguadd:

> Allah taught us that in this 50-year period a mental seed was planted in the mind of W. F. Muhammad. He was chosen for many reasons, one being because he was a Holy Man who was pure in mind and body. Another was because he was a man of Knowledge and Wisdom, a Master of Supreme Knowledge. Also because of the complexion of his skin and the texture of his hair—this allowed him to move and speak relatively free among both types of people, Black and Coloreds—while a man of darker complexion would have been put to death without hesitation for teaching what W.F. Muhammad was teaching. On February 8, 1930, he announced the Birth of the Nation of Islam in Detroit, Michigan. The rest is a matter of History...[166]

In succession, the Honorable Elijah Muhammad played an inherent role in Allah's teachings. To him, Elijah Muhammad represented "Wisdom" because he was the one who received the knowledge from W. F. Muhammad and then manifested this knowledge to the so-called American Negro. He recognized Elijah as the *"Last Greatest Messenger of Allah."* As detailed in a Five Percent article written circa 1982:

> Was Master Fard Muhammad successful in raising the dead, deaf, dumb and blind so-called American Negro? Yes! How did he raise the dead, deaf, dumb, and blind so-called American Negro? By giving them knowledge of self and the devil. Can

there be any seen proof of the above? Yes! By looking at god (Allah), the Muslims and their divine Messenger the Honorable Elijah Muhammad. The Last Messenger of Allah, and that is an actual fact, for God (referring to Clarence 13X) himself said so.[167]

Shaamguadd cosigns the same:

Now the Nation of Islam (or Black Muslims Nation) was under the Divine Leadership of the Honorable Elijah Muhammad, the Messenger of Allah (May The Peace And Blessings Of Allah Be Upon Him), successor to W. F. Muhammad.[168]

Another Five Percenter article written in 1974 makes the same claim and places a connection between the movements and its founders:

Is there any chance of the Muslims and Five Percenters uniting together for one common cause? Yes! This unity will come about when the understanding is born about Master Fard Muhammad and his Uncle. The Honorable Elijah Muhammad has this understanding and bears witness to the Five Percenters but very few of his followers are ready for this Supreme Understanding. The Five Percenters are not opposed to the Muslims and bear witness to the Honorable Elijah Muhammad as being the Messenger of Allah. The Five Percenters are actually advanced Muslims and perform the duty of ministers which is to teach freedom, justice and equality. Islam is the nature of the Blackman and all must return to the ONE who is ALLAH.[169]

Consequently, Allah placed himself within this paradigm by defining his connection to Fard and Elijah. As their offspring, he was looked at as the third in succession; therefore he served as the one to bring the "Understanding" or reveal the teachings to the babies. Universal Shaamguadd:

The Father explained that he was born in Danville, Virginia which represents the Divine Virgin of Allah (the Supreme Alphabets Un-like the Supreme Mathematics are flexible) not Georgia like some plus lessons would have you believe.

He then came North where he was baptized by the Wisdom of the Honorable Elijah Muhammad, (similar) to the way Jesus was baptized, by the wisdom of John the Baptist or like the Honorable Elijah Muhammad was baptized by W.F.

- 144 -

Muhammad. Now don't take me wrong. This is not the dipping of one's body in physical water. It is the purification of one body and mind through divine teachings. It is also called the tilling of the mental soil. This is done so that the Body and Mind of a said person of that ability will be both physically and mentally prepared for the mission which Allah has planned for that individual.[170]

This intricate philosophical relationship between the three (Fard, Elijah and Allah) became a part of Five Percenter theology. Allah taught his Five Percenters that they should respect and revere the two pioneers, as it was the foundation upon which he stood and to deny them would be to deny him. As evident in a Five Percenter article:

Brothers ask was Master Fard Muhammad Allah? If THIS Nation is real, then Allah had to be present in the Union of Master Fard Muhammad and the Honorable Elijah Muhammad. If Allah wasn't the maker and owner of that Union, then everything coming from that Union is Non Cipher. To deny the presence of Allah in that Union is to deny the presence of Allah in the Unions which followed that Union (Namely our Union). For if that Union was NOT right and exact, then all which came from it is NOT right and exact.

Allah said, 'If it wasn't for Elijah Muhammad...I wouldn't know who I was.., and if it wasn't for Master Fard Muhammad., Elijah Muhammad wouldn't know who he was.' We are the descendants of the event that took place between Master Fard Muhammad and Elijah Muhammad.

The knowledge had to come back from the understanding seed (Master Fard Muhammad) to the wisdom seed (the Honorable Elijah Muhammad) to the knowledge seed (Allah). If A=B and B=C, then A=C. If their union was fake then so is ours. Allah always has been and always will be. Master Fard Muhammad was taught by the Wise Man of The East, Black Man! To deny Master Fard Muhammad is to deny the Father.[171]

Another Five Percenter Scholar, True Islam, goes even further in explaining Allah's relationship with Fard and Elijah. True Islam:

The Lessons are the words of Master Fard Muhammad and the Honorable Elijah Muhammad. This is what the Father brought for us. And these three men, Master Fard Muhammad, the Honorable Elijah Muhammad, and the Father Allah, represent the Divine Trinity of Knowledge, Wisdom and Understanding. Master Fard Muhammad is the Knowledge, the foundation upon which the Father stood and upon which we stand today. It was He who brought the full Knowledge of God to these shores in 1930 and made it accessible to the Black Man and Woman in the wilderness of North America. This knowledge was made manifest to us through the Wisdom, the Honorable Elijah Muhammad. Everything that we know of Islam was brought by Master Fard Muhammad and taught to us by the Honorable Elijah Muhammad. These two men, the Knowledge and the Wisdom, gave mental birth to the Understanding, the Father Allah. These three exist as a tri-unit. To separate the Father from this unit in order to give him a different teaching from what Master Fard Muhammad and the Honorable Elijah Muhammad taught, is tantamount to separating the Understanding from the Knowledge and Wisdom, or the seed from its parents. The Father, as the Understanding, is indeed for us the Best Part. But Understanding is understood only in the context of the Knowledge and Wisdom which borned it. Zig, Zag, Zig teaches us that Knowledge and Understanding are alike, THUS MASTER FARD MUHAMMAD AND THE FATHER ALLAH ARE ALIKE. To separate them is to violate the Laws of Supreme Mathematics. THERE IS NO INCONSISTENCIES IN ALLAH'S MATHEMATICS. The Honorable Elijah Muhammad, as the Wisdom, is the bridge between the Knowledge and the Understanding. MASTER FARD MUHAMMAD, THE HONORABLE ELIJAH MUHAMMAD, AND THE FATHER ALLAH CANNOT BE SEPERATED, FOR KNOWLEDGE, WISDOM AND UNDERSTANDING CANNOT BE SEPERATED. He who claims that the Father taught something different from what the Knowledge and the Wisdom taught are setting up an inconsistency in Allah's Mathematics. THAT IS AN EMPHATIC NOW CIPHER.[172]

Other Five Percenter accounts depict that Allah made it clear his coming out of the mosque was not in opposition to Master Fard Muhammad or the Honorable Elijah Muhammad; rather it was to fulfill divine prophecy. As an FOI, he was given the assignment of delivering the word of Allah to "the 17,000,000 Original people in the Wilderness of North America." He set out to do that by loosening the seals of the Lost-Found Muslim lessons and revealing them to "the babies." He saw this as his personal assignment in the "resurrection of the mentally dead." Even though some of his FOI peers still in the mosque didn't quite understand his reasoning, he emphasized he was not rebelling against the law of Islam but rather upholding the laws of Islam. This he would do by fulfilling his divine mission: to teach Islam to the Babies. As told by one 5% historian:

> But one important fact should be made clear, and he himself made it clear, as have earlier prophets: he did not come to refute or dispute the message of Allah (Master Fard Muhammad) or his prophet Elijah, but to add to, and fulfill, the earlier scriptures (writings) of the Nation of Islam. He performed this service in bringing those Lost-Found Muslim Lessons out of the Temple and putting them out into the streets...Everything that Allah taught was consistent with the scriptures of 120 degrees and the Nation of Islam.[173]

Dietary Laws

Allah kept his strict Muslim diet he practiced while in the mosque. Always the health conscious individual he taught the same to his followers. He placed a strong emphasis on eating the right foods to stay healthy and adamantly taught on what foods not to eat. On top of his list, was his strong prohibition against eating pork.

Allah: Don't eat the swine![174]

Allah taught the same as Elijah, that the pig was a grafted animal never intended for food. Elijah Muhammad said it was a mixture of rat, cat and dog. He taught that the prophet Moses (Musa) originally used the pig to clean up the refuse in the caves of the Caucuses Mountains so he could civilize the white man. Barry Gottehrer recalls Allah mentioning this point about the pig being a grafted animal:

> Allah once told me that the Five Percenters, like the Muslims, would eat no product of the pig. He described the pig as one-third dog, one-third rat, and one-third cat. "Now," he wound up with a flourish, "would you eat dog, rat, or cat?"[175]

As it was with one of his mentors, Malcolm X, Allah broached this subject often with people he came in contact with.

Malcolm X used to mention this subject in the majority of his speeches at the Temple. He always warned the "lost-founds" about "eating that filthy hog." Allah did the same with his Five Percenters as he made it a first priority to get people "off that swine." Universal Shaamguadd recalls Allah speaking on the subject:

> The first thing ALMIGHTY GOD ALLAH taught was how to Clean Up Ourselves. He taught us that the pig was forbidden, that it was the lowest form of Life Form on the Planet, and was never meant for Human Consumption, rather it is a Natural Garbage Disposal System which originated during the period of the caveman in Europe. He taught us that any person of any religion who consumed this animal was as wrong as an Eight dollar Bill!! We were not allowed to have it in our homes or to be given to our children. For this reason, He taught us to maintain our own households rather than hassle our parents if they refused to stop cooking or eating the Swine.[176]

Allah taught them about other permissible as well as unacceptable foods for the civilized to eat. In particular he described the different kinds of seafood that were either good or taboo. Shaamguadd explains:

> He taught us that we should avoid scavengers, such as tuna fish. He explained that these were fish that were the Pigs of the Sea, while they were nowhere near as bad as the Pig itself. They lived off the waste of other fish in the oceans and garbage that was dumped into it. He told us that it was not forbidden to eat it, however, we should not eat it more than twice a year, when in the streets. He made it clear that brothers who were going through trials and tribulations in Prison were exempt from the "No Tuna Laws" and if we sent tuna fish to them it should be Chicken of the Sea. At the time, this was the only tuna that was Government Inspected and less likely to be tampered with. He further explained that the tuna was one of the few fish that absorbed chemical waste into it's system such as Mercury, which causes baldness, also rapid graying of the hair and other dangerous chemicals that are dumped into the sea by Industry. This is why in periods of High Sea Pollution we can find tuna fish on sale at reasonable prices in our communities. The Father did not eat tuna fish at all. He also taught us to avoid other small scavengers such as shrimps which are the worms of the

sea. Also, lobsters, crabs, clams and oysters. All fish over 50 pounds in weight...As an alternative, He recommended that we eat better quality fish such as Rainbow and Salt Water Trout, Salmon, Portuguese Sardines to name a few...[177]

Allah taught his young followers to adhere to the Muslim dietary laws. The Muslims had a strong regimental diet. Not only did it include prescriptions for what to eat but when to eat as well. Muslims were known to limit their meals to one time a day, every other day, or once every three days. Elijah Muhammad speaks to this rational in his books "How to Eat to Live." Elijah Muhammad:

Allah (God) said to me, in the Person of Master Fard Muhammad (to whom praises is due forever) that we who believe in Him as our God and Saviour should eat but one meal a day (once every 24 hours). Eat nothing between meals, not even candy, fruit, or anything which would start the stomach, digestive processes. In this way, our eating of the proper foods and drinks--- at the proper time –would extend our life to 140 years. This would protect us from sickness. He said if we start our infants eating one meal a day, as soon as they are able to partake of solid foods, it would enable them to live at an age of 240 years. I then asked Him, "How about eating once every 48 hours?" He said to me, "You would be ill only one day out of four or five years." I asked Him what was the cure for that one day of illness? He said, "Fast three days and you will be alright." I asked Him, "What about eating one meal every three days?" He said, "You will never be sick if you eat once every 72 hours." This is about two meals every six days, which would extend our lives to a span of 1,000 years – for there is no poison from the previous meal three days ago which has enough power to do you any harm. The fast destroys the accumulation of food poison.[178]

Allah suggested to the Five Percenters that they should adhere to eating one meal a day, every other day or every third day as prescribed in the Nation of Islam. He even took it a step further and emphasized that the Five Percenters should fast on occasion as prescribed. In an interview, Allah speaks to this principle:

Allah: ...the United States are the most easiest people in the world because they live in luxury. Where other people eat one day and can last three. The Muslims taught me the same way. Eat one meal a day, one every other day or one every three days. And they can do it! They eat the proper foods to keep them strong.

Interviewer: Who does this? The Muslims?

Allah: I'm trying to teach those Five Percenters to do it. I do it, because I go on a six to seven day fast. I don't eat nothing but drink water.[179]

Allah advised his young organization on the proper way to approach this subject and the benefit of adhering to the dietary laws. Universal Shaamguadd recalls Allah specifically addressing this concept with his Five Percenters:

ALLAH taught us that we should eat only one meal a day, or one meal every two days and better still, one meal every three days. He explained that this did not apply to the babies who need more because their bodies were still developing, and that the less we ate, the more acute our learning abilities would be. This would keep the mind and body alert. It would also help in hard times when funds were short. As the head of your household, you would not have to spend as much on meats, etc. Since your consumption would be less, leaving more for the children and women, and that we should adhere to the Dietary Laws of the Honorable Elijah Muhammad, the Messenger of Allah (M.T.P.A.B.O.A.B.U.H.) (How to Eat To Live) and that we should eat from public restaurants as seldom as possible because they were unclean for us, with the exception of Muslim establishments and some strict Hebrew establishments, and when shopping for foods we should not just shop to eat, but shop to preserve. This means that we should always buy some items that we could store away for a "Rain Day", such as Navy Beans, Powdered milks, dehydrated fruits, juices and canned goods. This way you are always prepared for depressions or inflations and there will always be something for the babies to eat.[180]

Surprisingly enough, many of the youth bonded to the concept of NOI dietary laws and fasting as prescribed in Islam. This provided them with a discipline that made for a cohesive group. They looked to each other for moral support and developed a bond amongst themselves. Gykee Mathematics recalls when the firstborns of Medina fasted after six days of first receiving Allah's teachings from ABG#7:

> Those six (6) days and six (6) nights are unforgettable and shouldn't never be allowed too. Shortly after that we went on a three (3) day fast, which was just water and black coffee without sugar. We did a lot of fasting and we ate only one meal a day when we did eat.[181]

Fasting was later suggested to be part of an induction process for new adherents. Earnest Five Percenters who partook in fasting were promised to achieve good results. This concept is further explained by the Five Percenters:

> When entering the Nation of Gods and Earths, it is highly recommended that you go on a THREE DAY FAST. This Fast should be a liquid fast (which is done by only consuming liquids for a period of three days). Fasting is good for your body and your mind. The first day of the fast is strictly PHYSICAL. During this time it is a matter of mind over matter. The body will crave for solid food and the mind must resist this craving and feed the body water, juices, or other liquids. The second day of Fasting is a MENTAL journey, where the mind slowly becomes (OMNIPRESENT) and there is a lightness about the head. For the CONSCIOUS AND SUBCONSCIOUS mind meld. Sporadic thoughts of solid foods converge on the brain. The third day of Fasting overwhelms the physical and mental aspects of the body and mind with a presence of righteous (aka Spiritual) well being of body and mind (OMNIFICIENT), as the SUPERCONSCIOUS mind blooms or evolves and merges with the conscious and subconscious mind. Intense serenity and healing is evoked, as the body and mind are cleansed. You will find that you learn your lessons rapidly, when fasting and those who already know their lessons will find that a clearer understanding (OMNISCIENT) OF THE LESSONS OCCUR WHEN YOU FAST. Although fasting is good, too long a fast is not. Fasting for long periods (7 & up) can cause insanity. For your mind will be at the MAGNETIC AND INFINITIVE stage. It's like your mind will be on Pluto while your feet are on Earth, and relating to people on Earth will be somewhat tedious for you. Your thoughts will be above their heads (OMNIPOTENT). That is why it is suggested that

you only fast three (3) days. UNDERSTAND? When you break the fast (breakfast) you should eat lightly and eat light foods (salads, fish, etc.). As soon as you bite into solid food and digest it you will feel the return to the lower planes of thought, and you will know (from experience) the flight of the mind, caused by fasting.[182]

The same article acknowledged fasting during the Muslim holy month called *"Ramadan."* Ramadan is a fast between sunrise and sunset practiced during the ninth month of the lunar calendar. In addition or in lieu of, Elijah Muhammad directed his followers to observe Ramadan every December (as the NOI and some 5%) still do as evident in the article:

Other types of Fasts are: 1. Ramadan Fast- Where you DON'T EAT UNTIL THE SUN GOES DOWN. 2. Dry fast- Where you ABSTAIN FROM BOTH LIQUIDS AND SOLIDS. Those experienced in FASTING, can LIQUID FAST day one (1) and two (2) and DRY FAST day three (3).[183]

Revealing of The Lessons

Bringing an older tradition to a young audience, Allah made it mandatory for his Five Percenters to study, memorize and recite by heart the Lessons of Master Fard Muhammad and the Honorable Elijah Muhammad (coupled with his own lessons Supreme Mathematics and Supreme Alphabets).

Prior to the advent of Allah, the lessons were never shared with believers outside of the Temple. The lessons were previously intended for Registered Muslims only, hence the name "Lost-Found Muslim Lessons." However Allah advocated that being a Black man or woman qualified you as a Muslim by nature. Shaamguadd explains:

He taught us that a Muslim is only someone who submits to the will of Allah so that by Nature, we are all Muslims.[184]

It was in this justification that Allah shared the once secret ritual with the young cadets. He took some of the lessons from the Mosque arranged them in a specific order for his faction. He provided them with 8 lesson sets in the following order:

(1) Supreme Mathematics (1-10)
(2) Supreme Alphabets (1-26)
(3) Student Enrollment (1-10)
(4) English Lesson C-1 (1-36)
(5) Lost-Found Muslim Lesson #1 (1-14)
(6) Lost-Found Muslim Lesson #2 (1-40)
(7) Actual Facts (13)
(8) Solar Facts (9)

In the same sense as an FOI, the Five Percenter was required to completely "master" (recite verbatim by memory) one lesson set before graduating to the next lesson. In all, his goal was to master all eight lesson sets and be able to recite it word-for-word without error. After a Five Percenter advanced through all the lessons, he was then qualified to teach other students as an "Enlightener."

Allah had a special way of distributing the lessons to his young organization. On occasion he would reveal certain parts of the lessons to the young and have them write it down and memorize it verbatim. However, just like how Malcolm X taught him in FOI class, Allah wouldn't just look for rote replies from his Five Percenters. He wanted them to think and reason by forming profound relationships between the lessons and significant experiences within life. Allah often demonstrated this quality his self.

Allah would spend days, hours on a lesson with us breaking it down, when a brother quoted a lesson, it was required of him to break it down, or we invalidated his statement, it was just that simple. And it was difficult for those who could not or did not speak the language of Alphabets and Mathematics. All breakdowns were valid because it demonstrated that person's level of understanding.[185]

By Allah combining the lessons made for a dynamic teaching. One Five Percenter phrased it this way:

"He put the icing on the cake of the teachings of the Most Honorable Elijah Muhammad, after he sprung off of the tree of the Nation of Islam in 1963 and put the cap stone on the pyramid of the life giving teachings of Master Fard Muhammad...."[186]

Allah encouraged his Five Percenters to always seek knowledge. In Islam, knowledge was infinite. It is reported by Shaamguadd that Allah even mentioned the study of the Quran to some of his followers. Shaamguadd:

> That if we were going to study the Holy Koran, the only one to study was The Holy QUR'AN with the translations and commentary by A. Yusuf Ali, he explained that it is the closest you can get to the Original Qur'an without being able to read Arabic, also because A. Yusuf Ali gave the purest and indepth study and explanation of the creation of the Qur'an and the Revelations of the Prophet Muhammad.[187]

Allah was preparing his Five Percenters with the tools necessary to live a righteous life. However, Allah and the Five Percenters would have to face even more trials and tribulations during these perilous times. The next time Allah himself would be the victim of wayward assailants and would literally face the barrel of a gun—and take the bullets.

Chapter 10
The Assassination Attempt

"I had been shot with a double-barreled shotgun and a high powered rifle."[188]
-- Allah

It was on December 9, 1964 that the first assassination attempt was made on the life of Allah. A group of henchman consecutively shot him in a basement (that moonlighted as a gambling den) on 127th Street in Harlem. The bullet wounds were near fatal and Allah suffered broken bones and barely survived the attack.

> December 9th, 1964, comes to mind, the last supper when they came to assassinate Allah, the first time. And upon their arrival asked Allah did he know the meaning of the picture of the last supper? His response was "Come on with it lollipop." And they did first with a shotgun blast followed with a 30-06 rifle.[189]

As to why Allah was shot, there appears to be extenuating circumstances surrounding his near death experience. As the years have passed different recollections of this event have emerged as to why and what happened that night.

One source says Allah was in a gambling den he often frequented and was shot as a result of a crap game gone sour. Barry Gottehrer:

> Bit by bit Allah opened up with me, although most stories emerged with many variations and some events were left shrouded in mystery. Much of what he told me he made up on the spot. He had been shot in the chest in 1965 during a crap game, staggered outside, and fell in the street more then dead than alive. (I could believe that, for Allah was constantly gambling and he was not a good loser. He kept himself surrounded by Five Percenters, and when he lost they would gorilla the winners and get Allah's money back for him. Most people who gambled with Allah sooner or later had it in for him.[190]

Another source provides a different version. This source claims that it wasn't Allah who was gambling in the basement. This account says Allah went to the basement that night in a noble attempt to rescue other Five Percenters that were held hostage by a group of stick-up men. Allah B:

> I remember quite vividly when the forces of evil with its attencant weak and wicked mentality, attempted the first assassination on Allah, the Father's life. The dastardly deed unfolded about three months after Al Fatir (The Originator) began enlightening "The First Nine Born" in Mecca.
>
> It was in 1964, on a cold dark Winter night in early December. The Father was on God (7) Avenue between Knowledge Wisdom Equality (126th) and Knowledge Wisdom God (127th) Streets. A woman named Mary approached Him and said, some men was holding guns on Four-Cipher Akbar (His Brown-Seed Justice) in the Hole and they were demanding that Allah come and save his Brother!
>
> The Hole was a gambling spot in the basement of a building at the corner on Knowledge Wisdom God Street and God Avenue. After Mary told Al Fatir what was happening with Justice, she begged Him not to go down in the basement to save him. However, Justice was not the only person the wicked held in the

basement. First Borns Kareem (The Black Messiah), Uhura, Bilal (ABG), Ebeka, Shahid and maybe some other young brothers whose names I can't recall was there, and a host of 85% (Build Powers) were in the basement shooting dice before the wicked men came with the guns.

The Father went in the basement to save Justice and the First Borns, then he was shot with all sorts of high-powered weapons and left for dead.[191]

This same version reports that Allah miraculously saved his own life through an out-of-body experience. The account attributes Allah's metaphysical powers for his recovery from the grips of death. Allah B continues his recollection of that night as he adds:

However, Allah couldn't return to "The Essence" then because "His First Fruit" were not yet ripe! So Al Fatir Allah revived Himself after laying consciously out of His Body in Harlem Hospital's morgue for Understanding (3) hours and observing all that transpired after being shot in the basement. Then He startled the lone janitor there by freeing the dam in His sinuses and letting the Wisdom of His Tears freely flow. The janitor realized that "dead men don't cry" as he astounishedly revealed the matter of the Father's miraculous return from the dead to inquiring New York City reporters...[192]

A Five Percenter who alleges Black Messiah told him what happened that night gives another account. The following report is his version of what occurred. Beautiful Life Allah:

There was even an assassination attempt on the life of the Father (Allah) in December 1964. As it was reported to me. Karriem was in a second floor apartment on 126th Street between 6th and 7th Avenue. As he had prepared to go out into the Harlem winter night, he sense that the rest of the day held tremendous trials. In the early days of establishing Allah's Nation, there were many problems, trials and tribulations. As Karriem approached 7th Avenue (later called Adam Clayton Powell Jr. Blvd.) he became cautious for 7th Avenue was a very busy avenue in those days. As he turned the corner on 7th avenue he bumped into Allah (the Father). Karriem immediately jumped into a martial arts stand, ready to defend himself against any and all possible attackers. Realizing that it was Allah who he bumped into Karriem said Peace. Allah responded in likeness, Peace.

Karriem fell in step with Allah and Abu Shahid. Allah explained to Karriem that he was going into the basement and that he did not want Karriem to come down there. As they approached the steps that lead to the Basement, Allah again admonished Karriem, "Do not come down." Karriem stopped at the top of the step and slowly began to count to ten. 1,2,3,4,5,6,7,8,9,10. At the count of ten Karriem then went into the Basement himself. Before anyone could get to the area where the hustlers, gamblers and other people who frequent the Basement hung out at. You had to walk down a slight hallway, then it opened up into a bigger area. As Karriem approached the inner part of the Basement, he noticed that a few of the brothers were on one side of the Basement. As he got closer, out of the corner of his eye he saw Allah and Abu Shahid confronting the gunmen. He (Karriem) then tried to break a pipe off the furnace to use as a weapon. All of a sudden the shooting started. People began to dive for cover. Karriem laid on the floor and began to count the shots. 1,2,3 etc., at the sixth shot he jumped up ready to take action, at that point Ebeka grabbed and pulled him back to the floor and yell into his ear, "Karriem, they got more guns then you think, stay down." As people began to run out of the Basement it was discovered that Allah had been shot by a negro named Carlos. Karriem and the other brothers accompanied Allah to Harlem Hospital, where it was learned that Allah had been shot with a high-powered rifle. The wound was serious enough for the Father (Allah) to have to be hospitalized, but it was not fatal.[193]

John, I'm Hit!

In contrast, a different account of the shooting is reported from Allah's longtime friend Abu Shahid. According to Shahid, his association with Allah directly involved him in the incident. In fact, he says he was present that night at Allah's side and claims he was the very reason Allah went to the basement in the first place. Shahid cites this as an incident he vividly remembers as he relays the chain of events. The following is part of a memoir written by Mr. Shahid aptly entitled *"Let's Straighten It,"* in which he reveals very intimate details of why and what caused the incident. Shahid:

We were hanging out on 7th Ave. between 126th and 127th streets. We hung out in Big Walter's basement, known as "The Hole", it was in 3 dungeon like chambers, entered from 127th St...

The assassination attempt came about when I had run out of "Hash" and some guys came around saying that they had it. It was like they were moving in on us. It was about business with us and probably was with them. They, however took it to another level. "Or it could very well have been a direct "Hit," in which they used the Hash as a front." There are those who say that the Father told them that the "HIT" came as a result of an "Unpaid Bar Tab" that the Father owed the Barmaid in the "Glamour Inn" that is NOT my recollection. If such were the case, I do not believe that I would have been involved. There is no doubt in my mind as the reason that Pop and I were in the basement that night and it goes as follows.

I don't recall what night it was as the Father and I chilled out, with Justice, in the "Wellsworths" bar on the corner of 126th St., on our block of 7th Ave. When Big Pop came in and told us that, "them guys were down in the hole talkin about the Hash." The Father came with us when we went to see what was up. He didn't have to. Mary, who used to be a waitress in the Chinese joint on the corner of 127th and 7th Ave., didn't have anything to do with it. It was strictly me and Pop's business. The Father and Justice came along and we were alright with that. There was nobody being held "Hostage" in the basement. ABG and Born Allah weren't even there.[194]

Mr. Shahid then describes the moments leading up to the episode. He recalls the importance of this night because it was when Clarence 13X begin to crystallize his thoughts that he was Allah.

That night is forever etched in my memory and I remember it as clear as day. It was the night that the Father manifested the reality of his being Allah. He was always clean, he stayed sharp. He used to say, "Cleanliness is Godliness for the Blackman." He had on a grey plaid trenchcoat, kangaroo dress shoes with white stitches.

Anyway as we made our way into the gloom of the Hole, people loafin' around cleared a way through for us. As we approached the men, that we came to see, (there were 3 of them), I spoke to the one that I recognized, "What's up?," I said. He was a Black Seed, the other two were Brown Seeds. "We come to see about the discrepancies," he replied, "Man, whatchu talkin' bout." I said, "There ain't no discrepancies, you got Hash and we got bizness, let's take care of bizness," I said. [195]

At this point is where the argument escalated. Father Allah, Abu Shahid, Old Man Justice, Pop, Hebekha and Messiah faced their foes in a battle like a posse from a scene in the "Wild West". Shahid vividly recalls this experience:

At that moment someone burst into the chamber shouting, "John one of them got a gun." Instant pandemonium. Niggaz was breaking as the Father and I began frisking the two in front of us. They were clean and as we turned towards the one that was left the Father was a step in front of me as the gunman backed into the darkness of the coal room behind him. The Father and I rushed in behind him when a 'boom' resounded in the narrow chamber. The Father was flung back into me, "John I'm hit" he shouted as he bounced off of me and rushed back into the darkness. Another shot rang out, this time it was the crack of a 30.06. The assassin had both a sawed off shotgun and a sawed off rifle on slings under his short car coat. He was a short, wiry, brown skin man. Again the Father was flung back into my arms. This time with a broken collarbone.

It was his superb conditioning that saved his life, along with the "Power of Allah". He was as hard as concrete, he would knock-out 100 push-ups at the drop of a hat. I backed off with him in my arms and set him down to one side as our assailant came bursting out of the darkness of the coal room.

There was alot of scampering as Niggaz fled for their lives. Hebekha and Messiah were on the opposite side of the room as the gunman came out, Messiah reached for the jack handle on the furnace and as he did so Hebekha grabbed him by the back of his neck and flung him down out of the line of fire, saving his life, as the gunman moved towards the door. The Black Seed got behind the gunman and with his hand on the gunman's shoulder he road the gunman's coat tail, pointing at Pop, as they charged pass Hebekha and Messiah, he cried, "Get that one" and the assassin shot Pop. The bullet went through Pop and through the steel basement door behind him. Billy was pulling on the light chain and the gunman shot him then paused spinning in the doorway to fire at me. All praises are forever due to Almighty God Allah, the gun jammed and with a curse they fled, through the door and into the night. The basement was in an uproar. Someone called the 'Cops', I don't think they had 911 in those days.[196]

Shahid recalls the aftermath of the shooting incident. He relays the chain of events that happened afterwards. His version verifies that Allah recovered from the attack but as to how; he tends to strongly disagree with the previous miraculous recover story.

The paramedics showed up, sirens wailing, lights flashing and scooped up the Father, Pop and Billy and sped off with them to Harlem Hospital. It was a ball of confusion as we desperately waited for word from the "Operating Room". Me and Justice walked 7th Ave. inviting further attacks. I got news, 3 days later, that they had all survived and the word in Harlem and throughout the Nation of 5% and the Nation of Islam, was that Allah was still the God. Always was and Always will be. We were all relieved.

That's a crock of bullshit about the Father being left for "DEAD" in the Morgue and the Janitor coming by and seeing him shed a tear, after he had been left for dead and calling for help and thereby saving the Father's life. It didn't go down like that. Ask his wife Sister Dora, his sister Bernice and/or his daughter Christine. Believe me when I tell you everything is real, take nothing at face value. Examine the facts and "Show and Prove." Don't let mystery Gods and jive percenters mis-guide, mis-direct and mis-educate you. If you want to know what happened at the "Hospital" that night ask "First Born Prince Allah, because by that time, I was near out of my mind. Justice and I returned to the Wellsworth Bar and got "Stoned" and I got in a fight with someone Justice said was "laffin at us." Now you can ask Ms. Mary about that, she was there and that's the Truth. Keep it simple and Teach it Real. The Truth is easy to tell. Allah is the God. Always was and Always will be.[197]

Stay at Harlem Hospital

Severely injured from the shooting, Allah was taken to Harlem Hospital to recover from his wounds. During his hospital stay, the Five Percenters frequently visited him in his room. One of Allah's First Nine Born named BILAL, now known as ABG#7, recalled his first face-to-face meeting with Allah at Harlem Hospital after the shooting:

In a most delicate period of my life, adolescence, on a cold December evening, the year 1964, I came face to face with the man who would change, mold, and ground my superego. The mystery surrounding that day and the events leading up to that day manifested to me in Harlem Hospital...

I felt a sense of belonging because I was chosen to accompany Al Jabbar on this journey... We made the Hospital less than five minutes... The floor we ascended to I do not remember, except that it was higher than the 5th floor. We entered the room, Al Jabbar giving the greetings, then introduced me, "this is Bilal", I spoke then, the greetings. And the man said how do you spell that?, my reply was B-I-L-A-L. He then stated, "I am ALLAH". And as I hung onto that, he proceeded to tell me of the men who had shot him with a high-powered rifle, and a shotgun point blank. The hush conversations, the mystery was now clearing up. Allah and Al Jabbar begin to speak, about what?, I just caught bits and pieces. I was fixated on the man, and attempting to justify what I had just heard. The name screamed in my head. "ALLAH" – "ALLAH"- "ALLAH" it rang over and over again.[198]

These visits proved to be advantageous for Allah and his students as he took the liberty to teach Five Percenters right from his hospital bed. ABG#7 carries on with his account:

I was pulled back into the conversation by Al Jabbar statement "He has a better handwriting." We were given the UNDERSTAND CULTURE DEGREE. ALLAH quoted it from his bed, and I wrote it down, word for word. The question was "And can you reform devil?", The answer is, "NO!" all the prophets have tried to reform him devil but was unable. So they agreed that it could not be done, unless they graft him back to the original, which would take six hundred years. So instead of losing time grafting him back, they decided to take him off the planet. Who only number (1), to every eleven (11) original people." This was given in the year one. (1), Equality Culture. Knowledge add a Cipher. I did not know how many constraints nor restraints we faced. Allah stated, "I am giving you the meat..."

Yes!, the Understanding Culture. We were told by the Father, ALLAH, "make sure all the brothers get this lesson." As siblings we were always quoting lessons, sharpening our skills with one another, and now Al Jabbar and I had the thirty fourth degree. The thoughts I had, (laughter) ALLAH knew, and Al Jabbar and I shared the lesson as soon as we returned.[199]

Allah shared another mandate with the youth during one of these visits. Allah decided to change the traditional greetings of the Five Percenters which at time was the same as the Muslims of The Nation of Islam. He explained his reasons why:

In December, late December, 1964, one afternoon, while visiting Allah during his recovery from the assault on his person in "Big Walters establishment", He stated, "I am going to stop saying "I-Salaam A-lakuim and start saying Peace". The reason and logic he gave us was "We walk this Earth in humility, and when we approach the ignorant we say Peace", and he continue to break this statement down even further, as he did with everything, especially the Lessons. He also stated during one of these many visits, that we, [The First Born], would not be together as we were at that present time. That we would go our separate ways. Each one of us would have to swim his own nine thousand miles (9,000 miles).

He further stated that there would be stumbling blocks or the roads we chose, and that there would be peoples there to guide us. How would we know, who they are?, was one of the questions ask, and his reply was, "you will know". For me he was speaking of life, and, life's journey that we would undertake.[200]

Teachings Spread to Brooklyn (Medina)

Allah's command registered fervently with his disciples. They were very enthusiastic about spreading his message. A few days later young Bilal (ABG#7) traveled to the borough of Brooklyn to spread Allah's teachings there. Upon his arrival he met two young men named Gypsy and Geno. After successfully converting the two, Gypsy became Gykee Mathematics and Geno became Universal Shaamguadd. The borough of Brooklyn was renamed Medina. Gykee recalls the experience:

We would also like to dedicate this History to the brothers that brought the knowledge of self to Medina, to Gypsy and Geno on the 19th day of December, of the year 1, 1964 (December 19, 1964). The locale was 203 Carlton Avenue, which could have easily found quite a few brothers there that Saturday evening, it just so happen that the only brother's who were there was Gypsy and Geno and they was present when Bilal arrived. Yes, then Bilal later changed his name to Jihad and now known as ABG#7

Allah, who holds the dubious distinction of bringing the knowledge to Medina and making it born.

The divine equality was ceen when the knowledge was born from the seventh born, when he walked into the house immediately there was something entirely different about him.

First of all he wasn't dressed like how we use to dress and when He took off his hat, his bald head shined and glittered. This was no large El-Roy and when he open his mouth that really did it. While some of the brothers cracked on his boots, he must slayed them with the words coming out of his mouth. We all took turns trying to trip him up in what he was saying, to no avail we even went at him all at once, the same results was nobody could get around Allah being God, which had held the test of all times, always has, always was, and always will be God is Allah by nature.

So after six (6) days and six (6) nights the brother return back to Mecca, where the borns and four elders were. The borns were mostly in Akbar's and Al-Salam's old earth's house. The elders were down in the hole, at the time Allah was at his wife Dora's house recuperating from the near fatal gunshot wound...[201]

In classical Islam, Mecca's sister city is Medina and is revered as the second place to embrace the prophet Muhammad and his teachings. Thus, Brooklyn became known as *"Medina,"* as it became a stronghold for the Five Percenters and Allah's teachings. A new crop of first borns hatched in Brooklyn with names like: Gykee Mathematics, Universal Shaamguadd, Hasheem, Byheem, Uhuso Lakee, Sha Sha, Gamal, Waleak, Ahmad, Raleak, Akim, Bali, Ali and Siheem.

The Five Percent in Medina was born out of a warrior like mentality because they hailed from "the land of the warriors." Gang problems was of epic proportion in Brooklyn and many of the teens lived a hard knock life.

I would like to start this by saying that in 1964, I could only imagine the Medina being vast, united, speaking many dialects, and only one language, the language of alphabets and mathematics as taught by Allah, as we understood him. I could only imagine, and plant the seed of the knowledge, wisdom of the brotherhood grounded in Islam. Islam meaning, "I, Self, Lord, and Master". I taught the basic knowledge of the 23 black scientists. Brother had to, no, it was critical that brother STOP KILLING BROTHER. The time was the roaring 60s, and

Bishops, Killers, El-kovons, Hobo Lords, Chaplins, Buccaneers, Roman Lords, Latin Kings, Diplomats, Mau Mau, Students, Gowanus, and others held court... most arsenals were truly man made, and lethal. If you traveled five or ten blocks in any direction you were off your turf, in most likely in hostile territory...The land was filled with chieftains, Vice-Presidents, and War Counselors, and War Lords...[202]

In spite of the hostile environment, the Five Percenter ideology went over well with the youth who were influenced by the teachings of Allah and Elijah Muhammad:

Through this the first-born Medians traveled carrying the words of peace, because the Honorable Elijah Muhammad had already brought the message to Allah. "As we understood him." They, The Medina walked giving the greetings of peace, these men who was well known for their ferociousness, and tenaciousness in combat against their rivals. Some groups were sworn enemies, trapped in generational feuds so old no one could even remember when they started or what they were about. Their peers stood witness, there was something different about them all right, they had found religion was the first assumption, and this new religion was Islam because they spoke of Allah.

Six days and six nights, and Medina were born unto Allah, the Father, and they carried the teachings of the Five Percent Nation throughout all of Medina...they taught with the same fierceness that they displayed in confrontation with others...[203]

This was the first time the Five Percenters did not have Allah on the streets with them. They seemed to take his orders in stride and still taught in his absence. Perhaps this was the first test and a sign of what Allah could accomplish with the youth.

Allah had even claimed a bigger miracle. Reportedly, while still in the hospital Allah informed the Five Percenters that God *"brought me back to life to show you the way."* It was alleged that as a result of his surviving the gun attack, Clarence 13X boasted that he was immortal proving that he was Allah. The New York Daily News cited this report:

Jowars had been attacked once before. In 1965, two years after he was expelled from the Black Muslims, he was gunned down on a Harlem street and left for dead. But he survived, and reportedly told his young followers that God "brought me back to life to show you the way." From then on he was known among the Five Percenters as Allah, investigators said, and boasted, "I cannot be killed.[204]

Nevertheless, during Allah's convalescence he had time to think and calculate plans of action to guide his young group. Given the recent turbulent times that engaged him and his baby organization, he was preparing a way for his young adherents to excel in other directions. In early 1965, he proceeded with his mission.

Chapter 11
Allah The Educator

First Born of Medina: From Left to Right - Siheem, Bali, Akim, Knowledge God, Sha Sha, Hasheem, and Casheem

Medina's 1stborn: From Left to Right - Siheem, Bali, Akim, Knowledge God, Sha Sha, Hasheem, and Casheem

Out in the streets of New York City, things were the same and in some cases worse. On February 24, 1965, even Malcolm X was brutally assassinated in the Audubon Ball room in Harlem. The temperament in New York was one of gangland violence but there were signs of progress to come. The youth were slowly coming out of a gangland mentality to grow into Black conscious street organizations. Allah recognized that the only way to successfully do this was to "show and prove" through ways and actions:

> **Allah:** Now this is the way it is. You can't do the wisdom until you have the knowledge, right? Right? When you go to school

you got to have the knowledge before you could come out and put that into practice. And they don't know you got it until you go out and put it into practice. This is why I teach the child go out and get the knowledge, come back and put it into practice, then the people will get the (what) understanding.[205]

Either Go Back To School Or Get a Job

In addressing the times, Allah gave important instructions to all his Five Percenters. In his message he stressed the significance of getting an education. He knew some of the children had dropped out of school prior to becoming Five Percenters. So Allah prepared three options for all his followers. He advised them, *"To go back to school, or get a trade, or get a job!"* So Allah commanded that everyone had to adhere to these options if they wanted to remain in the fold. He encouraged them to take advantage of training programs that offered courses in vocational trades. He informed everyone who already graduated school to either seek further education or secure employment. Allah insisted upon this as recalled by Shaamguadd:

In 1965 ALLAH instructed all the First Borns to either go back to school or get a job. This, the First Borns of Medina did without hesitation while the majority of us enrolled in Youth Leadership and Training Programs, (at that time sponsored by the Office of Economic Opportunity). Some of us enrolled in Vocational and Cultural programs. We received $38.63 a week, the Leadership program paid slightly more, believe it or not, back then this was enough for us to rent a furnished room, buy food, a few pieces of clothing and still take a sister to the Show if we wanted to. Anyway, I managed to enroll in both programs (don't ask how). The Leadership program for the money, however I have always had a genuine love for Art even while in the Grave, but I was too foolish and too busy seeking a degree in Streetology to pursue it while in public school. The Art program gave us all the material that we needed before long my little furnished room seemed to have more Art material than the Art Dept. itself. This allowed me to work on subjects that related to our teachings such as portraits of W.D. Fard Muhammad, The Honorable Elijah Muhammad and the Father.[206]

Education became a huge priority on Allah's agenda, and he passed it on to all his young followers. Allah praised the Five

- 168 -

Percenters who took his advice and commended them by referring to them as his *"righteous gods."* Many of them took advantage of the youth training programs while some went back to school and others found jobs.

Righteous Ethics

It was in these turbulent times that Allah chose to address the issue of violence head on. He shared ethical guidance and values with the street kids by placing an emphasis on certain ethics to be observed. One being tolerance of one another. Although a staunch advocate for self-defense and belief in the Law of Moses, "an eye for an eye and a tooth for a tooth," Allah took steps in his messages to curtail any possible violence amongst his followers. Shaamguadd explains:

> Almighty God Allah taught us that when a Brother attacked another Brother or lifted his hand to him that he was dead wrong and should be punished by the **NATION OF ISLAM**, let alone pull a knife or gun. He taught me that to even speak against your Brother was a form of attacking him, and when people outside of your Family saw that you would attack your own kind, this would make them attack them even quicker.[207]

In the same manner Elijah Muhammad forbade the use of guns for the Muslims, Allah did the same for the Five Percenters. Perhaps using savvy, he prohibited the use of guns unless they obtained it legally and for legal purposes.

> He told us that we did not need guns unless we had the legal papers for them because our tongues was our swords and that we could win more battles with that sword than any army with machine guns could ever do. And that he who must live by the gun shall surely die by the gun![208]

This mandate if taken seriously by the Five Percenters would have disarmed anyone who had firearms. As the majority of the Five Percenters were underage and others had previous records that definitely would have barred them from legal possession of firearms.

One of Allah's main purposes was to ensure that all his Five Percenters become achievers in society. He knew that prior to joining the Five Percenters many of the youth were juvenile delinquents who had been in trouble with the law at one time or another. In order to correct this pattern he remained proactive in encouraging corrective behavior or what he referred to as "righteousness."

One of his first moves was to encourage all of his followers who had outstanding legal warrants to turn themselves in to the proper authorities. This Allah advised would "wipe their slates clean" and give them a fresh start at life. Allah did not want any of his Five Percenters to be in trouble with the law. As relayed by Shaamguadd:

> When one of us had a warrant out for our arrest, He told us to go to court and take care of it if we wanted to be one of his Righteous Gods. He explained that to say you were God and have a warrant on you was to have a Sword above your head and that when it was time for us to stand tall and do our jobs if we were not Honorable, that the Sword would fall and the Government would scoop you right up and cast you into Prison to silence you. Now this may sound strange to you, however, I assure you it's the Truth. I wish you could have seen the look on some of the Judge's faces when we walked into court with our towels, toothbrushes, toothpowder, etc. and told them that we were there to surrender because we wanted to be Righteous and clear our Records. Nine times out of Ten they dismissed the charges because they saw that our Intentions were Honorable.[209]

Another Five Percenter recalls this same directive given by Allah. He too was present when Allah made this command of all the young Gods and Earths. Gykee Mathematics recalls this time period:

> The discipline were ingrained into us as we walked along the path of righteousness. Allah made it easy for us to admit promptly when we were wrong. He sent us to the people and institutions, we may have wronged and made us correct the injustice and apologize for our wrongs. You see he was that kind of man. Many of us didn't like it, however, we adhered to his principles, which was made better men out of many of us, today.[210]

In another article, Mr. Mathematics reiterated the value system Allah established with his young organization:

One of the main principles and values that was given and ingrained into me from Allah is the principle of amends, this is when He, Allah sent us to make amends with all the people and institutions we had harmed, many were surprised and overwhelm when we did it. Many didn't and to this day many still don't make amends and that can account for a lot of the discord in your life today. Allah had us digest many of his values, many peoples couldn't digest them then and still to this very day many can't digest or comprehend his values.[211]

The Authorities themselves were shocked that a leader such as Allah (who was initially viewed as a threat to society) gave such a directive to his followers to comply with the law. But Allah on the other hand reinforced that the culture of Islam teaches to obey the laws of the land and those in authority over you as long as it does not conflict with Islam. In an interview with the authorities, Allah touched on his position:

It's up to you. If you don't teach the young right, you not hurting me, you hurting yourself. Now, I can gain power by even not turning them over to the law. Couldn't I? When they come to me about this stuff I can say, 'No, I don't know nothing about these gangs and eighty-fivers, right'? I don't want that kind of power. That's not power. Power comes through the truth. That's what power comes through. I don't want that kind of power that these other so-called American Negroes are trying to gain. I don't want that kind of power.[212]

Allah's moral stance had additional benefits to his organization as well. Five Percenters who were incarcerated now had the opportunity to teach within the penal institution and add new converts. Although, their true test of faith came when they were released back to society. Allah explains:

Never let it be said that I taught the children to do wrong. When the knowledge was first born in the wilderness of North America some of my young Five Percenters had to take this knowledge into the prisons to teach those who had not heard the teachings, and these were my first borns. And the only reason they were imprisoned was for teaching the truth on the streets or defending themselves. It's much easier to be righteous in jail than it is in the streets. There is no temptations, no responsibilities. They tell you when to get up, when to eat, where you can or cannot go, what you must wear, and what you must hear! The true test of a God is in the streets, showing and proving, taking care of what is his and showing others the proper way, and that's merciful because Yacub didn't play those type of games. When one fell victim the penalty was death and was enforced on all who did not hold fast." (The FATHER)[213]

Although Allah instilled in the Five Percenters the moral value to obey the laws of the land and to respect those in authority—it was the authorities themselves that still considered him and his group undesirables. Reminiscent of the days of the Blood Brothers, the police and Five Percenters would clash again.

Chapter 12
Incarcerated

"I could have sued New York City for putting seven charges against me and I hadn't did any of them. I didn't do a thing."
-- Allah

Many of Allah's youngsters enrolled in government sponsored programs throughout the city. However, one problem facing the young group is that they didn't have their own edifice to hold Five Percenter meetings. So Allah had to improvise and set-up meeting places on the streets, schoolyards and public parks. He often taught the youth while standing on Harlem street corners in small congregations. These street gatherings became known as "ciphers." In Five Percenter ideology, a cipher represented a circle consisting of 360 degrees in which the Five Percenters would form a circle and "build" or discourse about the lessons of Allah and Elijah Muhammad.

These impromptu gatherings caught the attention of a special division of the New York City Police Department called the Bureau of Special Services (BOSS). The BOSS agency was a local counter-intelligence program that operated under the same guidelines as their federal advisors, the Federal Bureau of Investigation (FBI). Among their goals were "to prevent the long-range growth of militant Black organizations, especially amongst the youth." In fact, it must be noted that the FBI had the Five Percenters under constant surveillance during this time period. FBI agents were actively monitoring and keeping files on Allah and any Five Percenter activity.

The NYCPD didn't take kindly to the Five Percenter street gatherings. The local police dreaded the control and influence Allah exercised over the youth. The police often attempted to break up these ciphers that inevitably led to a confrontation between the Five Percenters and the NYCPD. As documented in an FBI file:

It was reported that on June 1, 1965 by the Bureau of Special Services (B.O.S.S.) of the New York City Police Dept (NYCPD), that at 9:15 PM, May 31, 1965, six Negro males were blocking the sidewalk and interfering with street traffic in front of the Hotel Theresa, 2090 Seventh Avenue, New York City. When told to move on by two police officers these six supposedly turned on the officers, called on bystanders to attack the officers, and shouted anti-white and anti-police invectives. All six were arrested. One of whom was subject who identified himself as "Allah". He was charged with felonious assault, conspiracy to commit same, resisting arrest, assault with a deadly weapon, disorderly conduct, possession of a marijuana cigarette, and malicious mischief.[214]

Allah disavowed the police allegations. In his defense, he categorically denied all seven charges and claimed innocence. He addressed the subject in an interview a couple of years later:

I could have sued New York City for putting seven charges against me and I hadn't did any of them. I didn't do a thing.[215]

Per the FBI files, the arrest followed an earlier public disturbance that took place at 116th Street and Lenox Avenue across from Nation of Islam's Mosque #7. It is reported that Allah had a physical confrontation with a courier messenger named Wilbert Lee earlier that day.

On June one instant, BSS, NYCPD, advised that at approximately six thirty pm, Negro NYCPD Patrolman observed a group of Negroes creating a disturbance at One Hundred Sixteenth St., and Lenox Ave, NYC, and told them to cease their activity. Group berated and cursed patrolman and continued on Seventh Ave. Patrolman did not attempt to arrest them.

At approximately six fifty pm, cab driver informed same Patrolman that mob of Negroes had two policemen pinned up in Hotel Theresa, One Hundred Twenty Fifth St. and Seventh Avenue, NYC, and were threatening them.

Police reinforcements arrived at Hotel Theresa, NYC, and arrested following individuals on charges of felonious assault, resisting arrest, and conspiracy to commit a felony.

A male Negro, thirty five years old, who stated his name was Allah and that he was born in Mecca and that he resided at Harlem Hospital, NYC. No previous record for him located...[next few sentences are partially redacted that contains information for the other 5 defendants who were with Allah].

All six above Negroes are employed and state they are members of organization called "Five Percenters" which means, according to them, the Five Percent of the Muslims who smoke and drink. [Name redacted] stated they have no headquarters and "hang out" on the street corners of Harlem.

According to a Negro named Wilbert Lee, filed a complaint of felonious assault against the Negro named Allah, who is self-proclaimed leader of "Five Percenters." Lee charged he was struck on head by stick wielded by Allah. Allah in turn states he was acting in self-defense because he saw gun in Lee's possession.[216]

According to some Five Percenters, there wasn't any actual public disturbance until the police had arrived at the scene. This source advises that Allah was speaking at a peaceful rally. When the police arrived, they felt the need to break it up and rough up those in attendance. Upon seeing this, it is said that Allah flung himself in front of his Five Percenters to protect them from the police.

Al-Jamal said the police showed up with their guns drawn. When Allah seen this he jumped in front of the young gods and screamed out to the police, "Don't shoot my sons!"[217]

As Allah was attempting to keep the police from harassing his young followers, he urged some of them to leave the scene to avoid confrontation with the police.

On May 31, 1965, Allah was speaking at a community rally in front of the Hotel Theresa at 125th Street on 7th Avenue, when two police officers attempted to break up the peaceful community rally, this produced a disturbance and as the police became more and more physically aggressive Allah began to instruct Karriem again. "Karriem get away" He yelled. "Get away." Reluctantly Karriem ran around the corner and down 124th Street. As Karriem would later tell me. "Allah knew that I wasn't going to leave him, so he gave me an order to get away. The cee-cipher-powers were no match for my arts."[218]

Even so, some Five Percenters felt the need to attempt to defend their leader and went down with him to the police precinct.

In the year two=1965, when many of us took on the Father's name and carried it after The Father was taken off the streets that "Memorial Day" weekend, an appropriate memorial memory. Al Raheem and Hasan Jamel went up against the 28th Precinct, in their effects to prevent the Father from being harmed. These two brothers put up a helluva fight, they accompanied the Father to the precinct and were later released.[219]

You Can't Charge Allah

Overall, six people including Allah and 4 Cipher Akbar (Justice) were arrested at the event. After the group's arrest, Allah and Akbar (Justice), along with four other Five Percenters; Gumeal, Uhuru, Arrasan Jamal and Raheem were arraigned to appear in court on June 1, 1965, "under the tightest security measures seen in the Criminal Courts Building for the last 10 years."

The court case became a media spectacle as police beefed up security and Five Percenters showed up in force. Several instances prior, previous court dates were adjourned in hopes that Five Percenter attendance would dwindle. The efforts didn't help the purpose. The Newspapers recorded the event. The article's headlines read: "POLICE FILL COURT FOR

MUSLIM CASE, Security Tightened as 6 Are Arraigned in Assault."

> Six Black Muslims accused of assaulting a messenger and biting two patrolmen were arraigned under the tightest security measures seen in the Criminal Courts Building for at least 10 years. Fifty uniformed patrolmen and 30 detectives were stationed at Adolescent Court to prevent any disturbances as 150 young Negroes, many of them wearing fezzes, milled about outside the court. The patrolmen lined up the Negroes near the entrance to the courtroom where Judge Francis X. O'Brien was presiding. During a recess they entered the court, where patrolmen and officers lined the walls and guard rail. The court was cleared of all spectators before the six defendants appeared. The defendants identified themselves as Allah, 35 years old, who gave his address as Harlem Hospital; Akbar, 37, of 1274 Fifth Avenue; Gumeal, 21, of 2 East 129th Street; Leon (Uhuru) McCray, 16, of 105 West 127th Street; Arrasan Jamal, 16, of 141 West 127th Street; and Ronald (Rahim) Perry, 16, of 369 Lenox Avenue.[220]

During this arraignment, the judge and prosecution cited the accusations for the arrest of the six. In hindsight, many wonder as to whether or not this was a police provoked incident consistent with the counter intelligence program of the FBI. Regardless of the provocation, it showed that the Five Percenters were a force to be reckoned with.

> The six were accused of beating Wilbert Lee, a 37-year-old Negro messenger, of 309 West 119th street, shortly after 6 P.M. Monday. Patrolman H.T. Webb, a Negro, said he rescued Mr. Lee and the six escaped. At 9:15 PM, three white policemen, Jerome McGuire, James McClafferty and Joseph McCullah, went to 126th St and Seventh Ave. to question the six about reports of broken bar windows. In the ensuing melee, Mr. McGuire and Mr. McCullagh were bitten. Patrolman Webb arrived and helped make the arrests. A hundred or more sympathizers then gathered at the West 123rd St. station house, and the defendants were taken to the East 51st St station house, where they were booked.[221]

Not willing to let these accusations go unchallenged, Allah vocally hurled objections throughout the court hearing. The article captured his remarks:

As the charges were read yesterday, Allah, wearing a black fur hat, a gray windbreaker and tan pants, began mumbling, "Lie, lie, lie." He told Judge O' Brien, who remained silent. "You're wrong for accusing righteous people. The city will blow up. We're going to cause much trouble, you watch. We're not charged with nothing. You can't charge Allah." At one point when a patrolman's name was mentioned in the reading of the charges, he said, "He's not a patrolman. He's a bum! You have no right to come to Harlem and ask us to move. We don't come to your city. We could have killed many officers." And then in reference to Mr. Lee, he said: "If he tells the lie we hit him he'll never see the street no more." Then when Judge O'Brien began to speak of legal representation, Allah, who is known to the Harlem Hospital as Clarence 13X, said: "I'm the lawyer. We don't want your people to do nothing for us. They called me to stop fighting. They attacked me."

At the request of the prosecution the case was adjourned to June 18th. Judge O'Brien set bail of $9,500 for Allah; $9,000 for Akbar; $3,000 for Gumeal and $2,000 each for the other defendants.

All were charged with felonious assault, conspiracy, disorderly conduct and resisting arrest. Allah, in addition, was charged with violating the weapons law and possession of a marijuana cigarette.[222]

Allah fervently denied the charges. He maintained this was a conspiracy of the NYCPD to eliminate the Five Percenters through trumped up charges.

Further Investigations and Occurrences

The long hand of the law saw fit to keep the six in police custody. A bail was set but due to a lack of funds, none of the six were bailed out. On June 18, 1965, Allah and the other Five Percenters had another hearing. This time the Five Percenters showed up in force again at the courthouse. The judge decided to clear the courtroom and continue the hearing. This upset the courts and law enforcement as they decided to go on the offensive and seek out additional arrests in a hunt for the Five Percenters. With Allah still detained, the NYCPD and FBI initiated a full-blown investigation into the Five Percenters that started this same day and resulted in further arrests.

This month bring to mind when eight of us five from Mecca and three from Medina were wrongly arrested and charged as conspirators, saboteurs, and espionage agents in a plot to over throw the government and burn down the city to the ground. That Friday morning we left Medina early and converged on the Supreme Court House, Allah came out and we all said "Peace Allah" he responded "Peace" and the whole courtroom went in an uproar. The judge cleared the courtroom and held the preliminary hearing without our presence. This all transpired on Just-U-N-Equal / knowledge build or destroy day, the year two knowledge born equality power=June 18th, 1965.

After that we all came back up-town to Mecca and as my beloved brown-seed Sihiem reminded me. Big brother Hebeca [Ebeca] a.k.a. Rasul led us in salat in the schoolyard of P.S. 68, which is now known as Oberia Dempsey located between 7th and Lenox Avenues, on 127th and 128th streets, the horse sables was located across the street on 128th street. We went up on the roof where the pigeon coop was and it was there shortly afterwards we were detained.[223]

Pretty soon the jails begin to swell with the ranks of Five Percenters as a result of these kind of arrests. Many of them began to teach in the jail system and were successful at reaching other inmates. Allah himself taught while incarcerated. It was at this time He asked to be placed in the same cell with members of the Harlem Six. Eye God recalls their meeting in prison:

All was lost as far as they could see. But, there was a much greater plan in store for us that we didn't even know about until one day while in the "bull-pen" (jail). The Father came through and asked to be placed in our cell. From then on we received a whole new look at life, white folks, and ourselves.

But, it didn't set in right then and there. It took Gods like Prince, Dubar, Bismi Allah, Kalim, Um Allah, Kareem, Aliem, and Knowledge Allah, plus many more to show us just how it is, how it always will be; to live Allah's Mathematics and not just sit around. Some of these brothers came from the belly of the beast, and overcame the hate, and lack of understanding. They went to school and mastered it. This and much more came into being;

We are neither anti-white, nor pro-black. Our duty as civilized people is to teach all nations of people of the planet Earth.[224]

With its leadership in custody made the group susceptible thought the authorities. On the contrary, with its ardent creed of "each one, teach one," made it difficult to spur its development. As if following protocol, Hebekha, a senior member within the organization temporarily assumed a leadership role in Allah and Justice's absence.

That summer, police authorities made every effort to pin any juvenile crimes on the Five Percenters. In many instances, Five Percenters were hauled to the police precinct to be interrogated. One such occurrence happened on July 29, 1965, when 17 Five Percenters were arrested for "disorderly conduct" and assault on a police officer. The NYCPD claimed two white patrolmen took preemptive measures to stop 30 Five Percenters from molesting a Black woman; in turn the group allegedly attacked the policemen. An article covered the story:

> The next public incident occurred in July with the arrests of 10 youths who allegedly hurled garbage can covers, rocks and bottles at two white policemen who had stopped them from molesting a Negro woman.
> The youths, who ranged in age from 16 to 18, were charged with riot, unlawful assembly, resisting arrest and disorderly conduct. Seven other youths, also involved in the incident were booked as juvenile delinquents.[225]

After examination of the case, the assault charges were dropped due to lack of evidence. The youth involved were all charged with disorderly conduct, a lesser offense. The police leaked the story to the newspaper agencies and the clash became public.

Some initial reports questioned if it was a serious issue. As Allah was a mainstay in the Harlem community some felt they knew him and doubted the impact he could make. The July 30, 1965, edition of the "New York World Telegram", a daily newspaper published in New York City, contained an article entitled "Harlem Knows 'Allah' as Puddin". The article read as follows:

"Allah claims he is God – but other Harlemites have different ideas".

"God? A barmaid once exclaimed."

"That ain't God. That's Puddin. That's what we always called him –Puddin."

"Allah is Clarence 13X Smith, 35, leader of a group of youths called the Five Percenters, 17 of whom were arrested last night."

"A man who knew him for 20 years, described him as a 'nice friendly guy, who used to work pushing trucks down in the garment district."

"But Allah hasn't worked since he formed his Muslim sect, which he claims has some 200 followers.

"That claim – as Allah's claim to divinity—is also questioned."

"That cat ain't got nothing but the blues, said another Harlem resident."[226]

A media blitz ensued as they sought to uncover the real happenings behind Allah and his movement. News journalists made it habit to report every accusation circulating in the rumor mill about the Five Percenters, no matter how outrageous. One far-fetched rumor was plans to assassinate the Pope during an NYC visit; another equally ludicrous hearsay was plans for an "armed revolt." Many Harlemites didn't buy the sensational rumors. A youth worker was quoted in an article speaking his peace about the situation.

Very few persons in Harlem believed that the Five Percenters could themselves precipitate an armed revolt in the community. Several leaders, however, feel that the group could and would be used by other hate and disruptive elements if they were not contained.

"These kids don't go around armed, and anyone who says that doesn't know what he's talking about," one youth worker said.

"The cops have been picking these kids up left and right and not once have they been charged with a violation of the Sullivan Law. They know they can be arrested if they have a penknife on them.

"Our greatest fear now is that, with all this publicity, many of the youth who identify with some of the beliefs of the group but are not yet members might be enticed now to join. When you get a place like Harlem and the deprivations that exist, then you're going to get youth gangs like this until something is done to solve the basic problems.[227]

Whether New York's juvenile problems stemmed from valid social issues was of little importance to the NYCPD. They were more concerned with dismantling these youth organizations or "gangs" as they called them. Authorities targeted potential Five Percenter leaders such as Hebekha a.k.a. Eugene 32X White, who was apprehended by police on petty criminal offenses. As indicated in a FBI report.

> Following the jailing of Jowars and Howell one Eugene White, aka "Hebeka", a Negro male age 22, assumed a leadership position with the "Five Percenters". However, on August 29, 1965, White was arrested for selling marijuana to one of the gang members and is currently awaiting sentencing after having entered a guilty plea.[228]

With most of its leadership incarcerated, the Five Percenters refused to die. In an unusual sense, the organization became more active. Perhaps curious youth were attracted to the publicity and reputation oft spoken about in newspaper clippings. The admiration traveled to other boroughs. Harlem wasn't the only hotbed of issues. Brooklyn was seeing it's fair share of racial problems. Many instances occurred where young Black youth were attacked by hostile white mobs. The Five Percenters emerged on the scene in Brooklyn and was at the forefront to fight against white racist attacks. The group developed a stronghold in the borough. One Five Percenter cites his memory of the early beginnings of Medina (Brooklyn):

> A brother by the name of Sha-Sha, he was a wisdom seed that could pass as a understanding seed, he came to Amboy Street between Pitkins Ave., and Sutter Ave., in the summer of 1965, from being up state incarcerated in a correctional facility for 3 years, he had mastered 120 lessons. In this same year another brother by the name of Akbar, who was a cold knowledge-seed moved to Amboy Street between Sutter Ave., and Blake Ave., with his two brothers and his old Earth, one of his brother's was named Charlie and the other was named Fruit Koran; Akbar mastered a set of 120 lessons also!

The two brothers came together and began teaching Islam to the brothers and sisters and babies within the community; they taught to all that wanted the knowledge of themselves. The teachings began on the street corner and in the block during the summer of 1965. Then the teachings were moved to Akbar's house on Saturdays for one hour, and then to Sha Sha's house. Sha-Sha had a brother-in-law, sister and nephew. During the weekends we would meet on Sutter Ave., and Hopkinson Ave., at the Good Shepard Center, where we would go inside or into the yard and or the basketball court. Akbar or Sha-Sha would tell the people who were not interested in learning that was playing basketball, that they had to leave the yard after their game was over, then Akbar and Sha-Sha would start the civilization class.[229]

The FBI carefully monitored Five Percenter activity in Brooklyn. The Feds interviewed potential converts who admitted their willingness to take directions from Five Percenters to safeguard their neighborhoods from white adversaries. As seen in the following FBI report.

[Name redacted] advised that he first heard the term Five Percenters on the night [Sentence redacted]. He has, however, heard the terms Brothers and Sisters used when talking about young Negroes in the Brooklyn Bedford Stuyvesant area. He stated that on several occasions in a local park near Tompkins and Lafayette Avenues, many young Negroes would gather and openly discuss the tense racial situation throughout Bedford Stuyvesant and the rest of the US. [Name redacted] mentioned that on two occasions a young Negro approximately 19 years of age who calls himself ALLAH, who stands approximately 5'11" and weighs 170 pounds, dark brown skin and wears his hair in an Afro, has spoken about the fact that the devils, meaning white man, will not allow young Negroes to have anything and that you are supposed to beat them up when they come around. ALLAH mentioned the fact that these young Negroes were brothers and sisters since ALLAH was their father.

These types of gatherings in the park are not necessarily planned but take place at any given hour when someone decides to discuss anything at the park. The audience, which is composed of over 80 teenagers, may simply be sitting in the park awaiting a turn on the basketball court, a deal at cards or simply a game of softball. At these various gatherings no individual is considered the floor chairman and that anyone who desires to discuss anything simply stands and can be heard...

[Name redacted] indicated that white youngsters in the Bedford Stuyvesant area were not safe while walking the streets at night nor were young Negroes safe while walking the white sections of Brooklyn.

[Name redacted] mentioned many things which indicated that some of the ideas and statements made at the various gatherings were actually things which could have been heard at Black Muslim Meetings but that no black muslims nor anyone believed to be a part of the Nation of Islam have ever been present at any of these gatherings.[230]

Besides increase of new membership, the Five Percenters would suffer a few casualties. One such case was with a young 15-year-old actor from the popular play "Porgy and Bess" who recently became a Five Percenter. The young kid was playing in the playground of Nicholas Garden Housing Projects where he lived. Excited about his conversion it is alleged that the young boy was boasting to a 21-year-old discharged war veteran about his Five Percenter affiliation. The older man insulted the Five Percenters and the two got into a fight in which the 15-year-old kid was fatally stabbed to death.

On Sept. 18, Cedric Avery, 15, who had appeared in "Porgy and Bess" at the City Center shortly before, was stabbed to death on a playground at 221 W. 129th St., in the St. Nicholas Houses, where he lived. Police who charged Earl Green, 21, of 277 W. 127th St., in the slaying said Green told them he had stabbed young Avery after he was attacked by the youth and a gang of other boys.

The dead boy's chest was covered with Muslim medals. Two youths who said they were Five Percenters later told a Herald Tribune reporter that young Avery was a member of their group.[231]

Another article made a more melodramatic attempt to show fanaticism amongst the young group. It pointed to Allah as the ringleader and his enormous influence on the group.

The Five Percenters are followers of a man named Clarence (Puddin') Smith, who calls himself "Allah." They are said to believe he is God. He has been in jail since he was arrested in a disturbance in early June, but the members insist that he still is God and that, as his followers, they cannot be killed.

The report said that when a 15-year-old student and member of the Five Percenters was killed as he and other members fought with an adult on a playground in St. Nicholas Homes, his friends shouted: "Get up. You're not dead. We can't die."

The boy was dead, however, and his friends gave his Muslim name to a recruit in order to continue his life, the report stated.[232]

This terrible news disturbed folks. The tragic incident left bitterness in some Five Percenters. School faculty staffs began to report disruptive behavior by some of the young adherents in Middle School.

Mr. Frey's report said that, on the first day of school, classes were repeatedly disrupted by boys who stood at unexpected moments and shouted at teachers: "You blue-eyed white devil! You'll burn!" If the teacher was Negro, the boys shouted, "You slave! You'll die!"

The disorder spread throughout the school, according to the report, with gangs of the boys roaming halls, insulting and threatening teachers and assistants who were patrolling the halls and beating non-Five Percenters outside the school. They added to the general disorder in classes by refusing to answer to their names and demanding to be addressed by Muslim names.[233]

Many felt the institutions or programs designed to help the kids had failed them. One such example was the Harlem anti-poverty program known as Harlem Youth Opportunities Unlimited Associated Community Teams (HARYOU-ACT). Livingston Wingate, Executive Director of HARYOU-ACT, was criticized for alleged negligence of the program. The Manhattan District Attorney's office and Federal authorities subsequently investigated him for purported mismanagement of program's finances.

Mr. Wingate gave an impromptu press conference on October 14, 1965, in front of the eastern regional conference of the Urban League at the Belmont Plaza Hotel in Manhattan. In his statements, the Director implied that desperate times caused for desperate measures and hinted that the real issue was the Five Percenters. The press covered the event and the following information was contained in FBI files.

WINGATE is the Executive Director of the Harlem anti-poverty program known as Harlem Youth Opportunities Unlimited – Associated Community Teams (HARYOU-ACT). Both articles point out that WINGATE has been criticized for his handling of the program and that he is currently under investigation by the Manhattan District Attorney's Office and the Federal authorities following charges of fiscal mismanagement.

In his speech and press conference, according to these articles, WINGATE denied any fiscal wrongdoing and claimed the spending of certain monies on his part was necessary to avert racial violence in Harlem during the past summer. His main theme was that if anything happened to HARYOU-ACT there would definitely be racial violence. ON this latter point, WINGATE referred to a mysterious "armed" group of Negro youth who are "prepared to die" in a struggle against white people. He refused to identify by name this group stating he feared for his life if he talked too much. He further implied that only HARYOU-ACT was stopping this group from acting.

Both articles indicated that WINGATE was apparently speaking of a black Muslim-oriented extremist youth group known as the "Five Percenters." The "Tribute" article then set forth observations on this group which this paper developed in an "independent investigation" during the past three weeks.[234]

The conference gave more ammunition to the press and the smear campaign against the Five Percenters continued unabated. Two articles carried the amazing headlines *"Wingate Warns of Negro Revolt If Haryou's Program Is Curbed,"* and *"Harlem's '5 Percenters' Terror Group Revealed."* Within the article were direct quotes from Wingate inferring the youngsters had a stockpile of weaponry and would have ransacked the city long ago if not for his intervention.

Dramatic pleas and all, Wingate's performance didn't convince the legal and police authorities. Although his statements made for great tabloid news, the Feds chalked it up as an attempt by Wingate to avoid convictions. As observed in the FBI files:

In regard to the remarks of WINGATE, it appears that he is attempting to utilize the "Five Percenters" and the threat of past and future potential racial violence to neutralize criticism and possible criminal proceedings against him for his administration of HARYOU-ACT.[235]

In follow up to the press conference, media correspondents sought indoctrinated youth concerning Five Percenter beliefs. In many cases the teens deferred to their confidence in the group's leader Allah. Such was the case in an interview conducted by the Herald Tribune. Within the article, the teens pledged total allegiance to Allah and his teachings plus his claim that he is God.

> The two 17-year-olds who described themselves to the Herald Tribune as Five Percenters declared that Allah (Clarence Smith) is God.
>
> "Even if he is in jail, he is still God," said one of them. "The Christians say that Christ was God, but, when he was dying on the cross, he said, 'Father, forgive them, for they know not what they do.' This means that he was not God; his Father was. Christ was a prophet and the son of God Only Allah is God."
>
> The boys denied that they were taught karate or judo in their Five Percenter courses. They said the classes were restricted to Muslim teachings but indicated there also was intensive Black Nationalist training.
>
> One of them had told another Herald Tribune reporter several weeks earlier that he had been a member of the Blood Brothers.[236]

Still incarcerated, it was these very claims of divinity that subjected Allah to his predestined jail sentence. However, instead of keeping Allah in jail—the judicial and federal authorities had different plans. In a strange twist-- the courts placed him in a psychiatric ward at the hospital. Shahid M. Allah elaborates:

> When you bind something you confine, restrain, or restrict as if with bounds. It also means to put under an obligation. The devil attempted to confine Allah in Mattawan, a prison for the criminally insane. It all started on May 31, 1965 when Allah was speaking at a rally in front of the Hotel Theresa, located at 2098 7th Ave., NY, NY. Two police officers attempted to break up the rally; and as a result a disturbance was ignited. Allah, along with several other men were arrested for unlawful assembly and disorderly conduct. At the arraignment in criminal court before

Judge Francis X O'Brien, He told the judge that He was wrong for accusing the righteous people, and that the city would blow up! When offered a lawyer, He told the judge that He was Allah and that He would represent himself. The judge ordered that He be taken and held in custody on a $9,500 bond. That September the judge in Supreme Court part thirty ordered Him to be placed in the custody of the psychiatric Unit at Bellevue Hospital for psychiatric treatment. Again, this was as a result of Him proclaiming Himself to be Allah (GOD). While at Bellevue Allah continued to teach the youth, showing forth His power of freedom of speech. Perplexed by the whole ordeal, the authorities transferred Him to Mattawan. Nevertheless, Allah's teachings continued to spread like wild fire! The White man was learning that you could place the physical Person of Allah in a prison cell. BUT in no way could you confine his Divine Mind![237]

Allah soon was confined in Matteawan State Prison *"For The Criminally Insane."* It was there that He and the Five Percenters would see if they could stand the test of time.

Chapter 13
Matteawan

Five Percenters from Brooklyn would visit Allah in Matteawan.

"I didn't want for a thing in Matteawan. I didn't protest
what they gave me to eat. If they gave me that meat, I
didn't eat it. I had money and everything I want in
Matteawan. I wouldn't buy no food. I wanted to show
them exactly who I said I was and I was going to prove it."
-- Allah

As a result of proclaiming himself to be Allah (and the
authorities relentless pursuit to take Allah off the streets),
Clarence 13X was confined to the custody of the Psychiatric Unit
at Bellevue State Hospital and held on a $9,500 bond. There he
underwent psychiatric treatment to determine whether or not he
was "criminally insane." As described in the related FBI memo:

BSS, NYCPD, advised SA [Name redacted] in November 2, 1965,
CLARENCE 13X SMITH had appeared in New York Supreme
Court, Part 30 (Felony), New York City, on various dates from
June 24, 1965 through October 27, 1965. At each appearance

SMITH was remanded to the custody of Bellevue Hospital, New York City, for additional psychiatric examinations. [Name redacted] further advised that SMITH was next scheduled to appear in the above court on November 16, 1965, and that the judge of the above court had stated that in all probability, SMITH would be adjudged criminally insane and would be committed to a mental institution.

On November 16, 1965 [Name redacted] BSS, NYCPD, advised SA [Name redacted] that on November 16, 1965 CLARENCE 13X SMITH appeared in New York Supreme Court, Part 30 (Felony), New York, New York, and was found "unable to understand the charges against him". On the same date, SMITH was remanded to the custody of the New York State Department of Mental Hygiene for an indefinite confinement.[238]

While detained in Bellevue Hospital, Allah still had tabs on his growing following. It wasn't unusual for the Elders or the First Borns to consult with him about issues they were experiencing on the outside. One such situation presented itself when it was alleged that the local Muslim administration at Mosque #7 wanted to put an end to all the bad publicity it started to get because of the antics of the Five Percenters. It is said that the message from the mosque was to either get down with the program (meaning join the mosque) or leave the lessons alone. A Five Percenter recalls the alleged incident that was brought to Allah's attention while in Bellevue.

In early July of 1965, Karriem came uptown in Manhattan and a few of the brothers told him that Captain Joseph of Temple Number Seven and his Doom Squad had told the brothers that everyone that knew the lessons (120 degrees) better join the Temple. Karriem told them not to worry about it. Karriem then went downtown to Belleview Hospital in Manhattan and called Allah to the second floor window. Allah asked him what was the problem. Karriem told Allah what the brothers told him that Captain Joseph put out on the street. Allah instructed Karriem to go to Temple Number Seven and see Captain Joseph, use his real name which is Captain Yusef, he will be waiting for you, and you tell him that Allah said "I know who I am and he know who I am. My Five Percenters are not Muslims and they never will be Muslims. And he better leave my Five Percenters alone." Karriem, got back on the train and took it uptown to the 116th Street station, departed and walked to Temple Number Seven, which was located 116th street on Lenox Avenue. When he got to the Temple, Captain Joseph and the Fruit of Islam (Muslim Security Men) were in the restaurant part of the Temple. Karriem entered and the Muslims greeted him. As-Salaam Alaikum, Karriem responded wa-laikum As-Salaam. I am here to see Captain Yusef. Some of the newer Fruit of Islam did not know whom Karriem was referring to. One of the Fruit of Islam walked over to Captain Joseph and said, "A young brother is here asking for Captain Yusef?. Captain Yusef said to send him to me. As Karriem approached they greeted each other and Karriem delivered to Captain Yusef what Allah had instructed him to say. Before Karriem left the Temple, Captain Yusef told Karriem to tell brother Clarence, at this point Karriem interrupted Captain Yusef, and said "You mean Allah?" Captain Yusef looked at Karriem for a few seconds and said "Yes, Allah. Tell Allah that I will pull back my people." As Karriem was leaving Temple Number Seven, Captain Yusef asked him, "What is your name?" Karriem answered "Karriem, Karriem Allah."[239]

The alleged incident indicates the access Five Percenters had to their leader. In an effort to stop this relationship, the authorities decided to transfer Allah to Matteawan State Hospital located upstate in Beacon, New York. This happened without many of the Five Percenters knowledge. There initially was some confusion around where Allah was relocated.

Now we in Medina had heard where Allah the Father was at just like so many of us at the time and this time we didn't believe what we heard. This has been written about us before, when we came over to Mecca from Medina to see Bilal, He told us that Allah was in Mattawan. We were told by Old Man Justice and a few other brothers that Allah was in Pilgrim State Hospital. Needless to say who turned out to be correct.[240]

On November 26, 1965, Allah was admitted to Matteawan State Hospital for the Criminally Insane. Upon his arrival, the hospital staff conducted an entrance examination and interviewed Allah. The interrogation was documented by the Matteawan State Hospital and included in the FBI files.

A review of this file by SA [Name redacted] reflected that the subject, under the name of ALLAH aka Clarence Smith, was committed from NY County on 11/ 16/ 65, and admitted to

Mattawan State Hospital on 11/26/65. His crime was described as assault, second degree.

Subject has been assigned Mattawan State Hospital Number E12915 and the file reflects that there are four warrants on file against him.

Subject indicated that he had never worked productively and had described himself as a master gambler and that he had been a student of Muhammad ever since 1960. At the time of the subject's arrest on 5/31/65, he was in the possession of marijuana.

The file reflects that the subject's original diagnosis was described as schizophrenic reaction, paranoid type. He expressed delusions of grandeur of a religious nature and of persecution.

A stop was placed with [Name redacted] requesting that this office be notified when the subject is to be released.[241]

Per the FBI directive, they requested to be notified upon Allah's eventual release from the hospital. That way they could put a "tail" on him once released to see if he resumes any activity amongst his young organization. Following is another related FBI memo addressing the same concern:

In view of the subject's background and his current mental condition, the Bureau feels that upon release from his incarceration at the Mattawan State Hospital for the Criminally Insane, Beacon, New York, you should determine his whereabouts and ascertain whether he resumes his participation in Black Nationalist activities. Therefore, New York should place a stop with appropriate officials at the above hospital, in order that you will be promptly advised of any action indicating that the subject may be released from confinement. Furnish any pertinent information received to the Bureau promptly in a form suitable for dissemination.[242]

The FBI files depicted the standard modus operandi of the FBI, which was to monitor Black leadership to "decentralize and neutralize" the subject. Already aware of these tactics, Allah maintained it was a conspiracy to stop him and his crusade to save the children. Perhaps this is why when asked by the Matteawan authorities if he was the leader of the Five Percenters, he denied for the same reasons. Allah later addressed this issue in an interview conducted a couple of years later:

> They put on my paper that I was a leader and I said, "No, I'm not a leader." Because if I said, "I was a leader," then they would hold records of you. And they would come and ask for my records one day. So I don't have records. So that's when they come—if come ask me and they let me show no records of you. You understand that?[243]

In spite of his tact, Allah was undeniably a leader, especially in the eyes his young followers. In the manner of a true leader Allah sought to combat the negative publicity and the bad rap he was getting in the press. In an attempt to defuse the negativity he reached out to Les Matthews, a news reporter and associate of his. Allah wanted to make clear his aspirations and the steps made in the way of education for the Five Percenters. Most of all, he abhorred that his followers were referred to as a "hate group." He stressed the Five Percenters should not be associated with that kind of a label. Les Matthews recalls.

> It was while he was in the hospital that he changed the thinking of his group. He taught them not to hate, impressed upon them to go to school, work, learn a trade or profession. He sent them lessons from the hospital and sent me word that he had a new look at life.[244]

Allah would share this outlook with some of the Young Five Percenters from Medina (Brooklyn). During a visit, He reminded them of his precepts.

> We went up state and the points that Allah stressed was working and getting an education. Complying and abiding by the laws of this government this is when the problems started for many of the brothers and Gods.
>
> He, Allah taught us that if a man doesn't work he will steal or do other underhanded things that will land him in jail, and when a man goes to jail he loses his worldly possessions. Yes, there is human rights, however when you are suppose to be a righteous God, you can't do wrong and expect to be treated right, that is a direct violation in regards to your natural [nature of being] state of being. And if you are being punished for doing

wrong then it seems to me some one is doing their job and you are providing the fuel for them to do it.

Allah constantly stressed education and work, you mustn't just talk the talk, you have to show that you are working and prove that you are educating yourself as well as others through demonstration.[245]

Of course it was easy to give this kind of advice but it was another thing for his young followers to comply. Although many gave it their best efforts, some were successful and others faced challenges. Allah wanted to avoid any of his young followers from being hurt. He used to attempt to take them through trials to show them what was expected in life. A major blow that had occurred of course was the murder of young Cedric Avery. Allah knew he was at risk and attempted to help him but to no avail. He discussed what happened to Cedric with a group of Five Percenters who visited him in Matteawan. Allah B. recalls this experience.

Allah said while he was in Matteawan that he knew Cedric was going to be killed. The Father gave him the name Al-Hambra. That was the same name of the barbershop where the Allah School stands now. Allah had recalled an incident when he was approached by Al-Hambra about a dispute he had with his father about eating pork. Cedric said he wanted to kill his father and he wanted Allah's help. Allah conceded that he would help if Cedric "threw the first blow." So some Gods actually went with Cedric and by the time they were approaching the door Cedric stopped at the end of the stairs not going through with it. Allah said he knew Cedric would be one of the first to be killed because of faint heart, besides the fact that he even thought of killing his own father. Allah knew he wasn't going to go through with it. But it was a test. He was faint of heart and that's what led to his ending.[246]

In many different ways, Allah truly was a father figure for his Five Percenters. He was always there to give them fatherly advice and attempting to steer their lives in the right direction. It wasn't an easy task. Many things happened with Allah since the short time he left the mosque. He had stepped into the role of Father for many young men. Entrusted with the responsibility of leading hundreds of ghetto youth was a huge responsibility. One could imagine the hardships he endured during this time.

Experiences

Throughout his time served at Matteawan, Allah maintained he was totally innocent and sane. He vehemently denied the initial charges filed against him by the police. He did admit that he believed he was Allah and informed the hospital staff that he would prove it during his stay. Allah often carried on enlightening conversations with the Doctors and Nurses who were amused by his remarks and charm. The hospital staff grew fond of Allah and enjoyed his company. Allah spoke so much about Islam that the psychiatrists described him as a "very religious man," an allegation that he himself denied. He informed them he did not have a religion because Islam (at least the way he practiced it) was not a religion.

> They didn't force me to go to church in Matteawan. They said Allah we don't have your service here. I said if you did—we don't have Muslim service here. I said if you did have Muslim service that is not my service. Because I don't have no religion. And they didn't force me to go. They put on my paper "very religious man" and I said, "No, I don't have no religion."[247]

During an interview conducted with Allah in 1967, he gave an account of his experience at Matteawan. He rarely experienced any trouble there except for one occasion involving an officer. Allah spoke of a confrontation with the hospital guard and how he handled the situation. Allah recalls the issue at hand:

> I went through Matteawan and nobody did nothing. One Officer hit me one time. The Doctor, if I would have told that Doctor that the Officer hit me and I didn't do nothing to him-- they would have fired that sucker. They tried. They said, "Where is he Allah? Let me know who he is,"— I wouldn't tell them. And the Officer know he was wrong because I ain't do nothing to him. Just enlightened him. And when he found out who I was he didn't do that no more. I didn't do nothing to him and no one was supposed to be able to get me out of there because I was the law there.
>
> I was under the Doctor and they had some very intelligent Doctors there. Especially, Dr. David P. Johnson, the Director.

Because if I was to protest -- I couldn't protest because they would send me to the court and the Deacon. And boy, whatever the Doctor say--that Judge do not go against it.

And I didn't have to go too sad. I didn't want for a thing in Matteawan. I didn't protest what they gave me to eat. If they gave me that meat, I didn't eat it. I had money and everything I want in Matteawan. I wouldn't buy no food. I wanted to show them exactly who I said I was and I was going to prove it. All I wanted them to do is ask the questions. And I know I was the only one that could give it to them. And they let me out of there. I could have sued New York City for putting seven charges against me and I hadn't did any of them. I didn't do a thing.

...And them Doctors let me right out of there. And now the Officers are so friendly and intelligent and love me they expressed to me that I can go out by myself. And Matteawan is a place when you go there, they say you a criminal insane. Meaning that you cannot control your emotions. And I had just been--I hadn't been in the hospital too long."[248]

Suns Visit The Father

Although his initial transfer from Bellevue to Matteawan was made to destroy his influence, the Five Percenters membership increased. With only limited access to his followers, he still managed to teach from Matteawan. Five Percenters began to trek upstate New York to visit their leader. During these visits they would ask Allah questions about the lessons as well as listen to whatever information he offered them.

Many didn't survive until the year three=1966 in the summer when we started visiting him the Father in Mattawan. A time comes to mind while on our way up to see him, Waleak, Sha Sha and myself, all the way up there Waleak and Sha Sha asked the Father, "which was right, what or why?" With that in mind the Father proceeded to break the lesson down to us completely, giving us the understanding that it was not so much as what or why as to the understanding the "nature of God."

The reason he can be seen and heard everywhere, sight and sound, just and true, no Unrighteousness in him and can understand everything and everyone [All Eye Seeing], he understands all. The very point of the matter is that God has never been easily Understood. One of the reasons many are grounded in knowledge and wisdom is because The true understanding hasn't been properly grasped.[249]

On this particular day it was said to have been raining outside. Noticing the weather patterns Allah revealed to his young followers its spiritual meaning and related it to their development as Five Percenters or "Gods." After the meeting, feeling re-energized, the teens taught some children in a local township by the hospital.

That same day being a knowledge born day = 19. It rained all the way up there and for the life of us we couldn't figure out why. The Father again took the reins and broke down The birth of a baby, pointing out when one is born the water breaks. This immediately set Us straight and cleared up the atmosphere he also told us that we were not yet strong enough to carry his name and what was to come at anyone who did...

Upon returning to the train station we were all very charged up with the visit. Waleak whom is now known as Knowledge God and his brown-seed Sha Sha set their sights on the nearby town of Newburgh and went into the town and started teaching. I stayed at the train station alone with the thoughts that had just been given to us by the Father. Some years later brother emerged from Newburgh, I can't help to think this all came about as a result of my beloved brothers who planted the seed that summer day in Newburgh in the year three=1966.[250]

Other Five Percenters made the hajj from the city to upstate to visit Allah. During these visits, Allah tutored them about Islam and shared the most effective ways to spread the teachings. As a result, Allah's teachings spread to that county and neighboring communities as Five Percenters from New York City frequented those areas. As recalled by a Five Percenter who went to visit Allah in Matteawan. U-Allah:

In 1966, the Father, Allah was still in Mattawan State Hospital for the criminal insane. By calling himself God Allah, He was deem crazy by the Devil's court.

In the summer of 1966, some Gods manage to get a pass, that would allow 3 to 5 Gods to visit the "Father." The Father used to work for the railroad, so our fare there and back was free. The morning I went to visit "The Father", I was met by a few Gods, Al-Jabbar, Dubar, Akbar Islam and Hakiem (later he changed his name to Born Allah). They took me to the Metro North Train Line.

There we met some more Gods. I said Peace to the Gods I came with, and got on the train with Akbar Islam and four other Gods, that I didn't know at that time. I was sixteen years old at that time, I was on my way to marriage with Almighty God, Allah.

Akbar Islam was the most wisest God among us, so he did most of the wisdom as he was talking, I seen smoke rising from his head, it was as if he was a piece of Hot Ice. He went around asking questions of all of us. When he got to me, I told him "My name is Shameik," which means "The Most Significant" my degree is Knowledge Equality. "Who are the Five Percenters on this poor part of the Planet Earth?"[251]

As the Five Percenters reached their destination, at least one of them encountered difficulties with the hospital staff. This prevented him from seeing the Father. The others were allowed to have their visit with Allah.

The ride was pleasant enough. We pulled into Beacon N.Y., and caught a cab to the Prison. The authorities let us in. These Devils told us we all can wait in the next room, all except Akbar Islam can go in and wait. Akbar Islam could not go in. "The Father" would explain to us later, that in order to see him, you must be right and exact. I believe that Akbar Islam's pants had gotten ripped on the way there, and this was the reason why he was not allowed entrance.

Akbar Islam was pissed, he was bombing the hell out of them Devils. After a while he cooled down and got a chair, and sat directly in front of this devil and stared him down. At this time another Devil came in, and directed us into another room. The last picture I seen of Akbar Islam and this old Devil staring at each other, unblinking, unwavering pure unadulterated hatred.

We were taken to a very large visiting room, we waited for about 15 minutes. A door open, a Devil came through, then a Blackman around 5"9", about 150 lbs and dark in complexion, smiling from ear to ear, I knew instantly that this man was "The Father." This was the first time I had seen "The Father" physically, he was not big, but he had an overwhelming present, He stood smiling and shining, with an aura so thick it seem to float through the atmosphere with scintillating colors.[252]

In the same manner as his stay in Harlem Hospital, Allah utilized these visits at Matteawan by taking the liberty to instruct the youth with more of his teachings. U-Allah continues:

> He seated himself and said, "Peace Suns" and we said "Peace Allah!" For the next few hours he talked of many things. He talked of "The Clock", he said, "Suns the people's minds are on the clock, they wake up at a certain time, they go to sleep at a certain time, they work at a certain time." He was teaching us that if we master the clock, we will be able to master the minds of the people. He taught us, to look at the people and see what they are doing, and you will be able to know what time it is without looking at the clock. After a while, he looked at us and said, "Now I want to hear you speak." When it came my time to speak, I was trying to impress him, I was a talker. I knew my Islam, but I was quiet most of the time.
>
> I said to myself, how in the hell he knew that. He went on to explain, that I was a knowledge-seed, and that I would do the knowledge, he said just as the Brown-seed would do the wisdom, and the understanding-seed would bring the understanding, the Half-original-seed would either have a good or bad equality, the Red-seed will have an equality. I said to myself the Indians did share with the whiteman, when he came to the wilderness of North America.
>
> At the ending of our visit with "the Father" a brother came a little late, this was Uhuru, one of the doctors (Examiners) of the Nation. The last thing "The Father" talked to us about was the magnetic (Truth). He told us to come back and get some more magnetic. Then the Devil informed us that the visit was over.[253]

After the meeting, Allah advised the youngsters to spread the teachings to other youth while on the way back to New York City.

> Before we left "The Father" said don't take a cab back to the train, you walk and teach on the way back. We said, "Peace Allah!", He said "Peace Suns!"
>
> When we were led back to the other room Akbar Islam was still staring at that old Devil, who was asleep now. On the way back to the train we told Akbar Islam about our visit with "The Father", there were tears in his eyes. On our way back to the station, Uhuru seen about ten young brothers and sisters playing, he called them over, and said, Peace! They all said, "Peace", these youngsters were Five Percenters, who the Gods

taught after their visit with "The Father." I thought that was
great to have Five Percenters way up here...On the way back to
New York City, my head was reeling. This was my first, I would
visit him once more before he came home.[254]

Perhaps it was this kind of instruction that allowed his
organization to flourish in his absence. In addition to his
instructions he made sure that the Five Percenters kept in touch
with his right hand man 4 Cipher Akbar a.k.a. "Old Man
Justice." Allah B. remembers these times Old Man Justice served
as the surrogate father in Allah's absence.

> Justice would hold everything together. He was the oldest one
> on the set at the time. Justice gave us orders. Allah always sent
> us to Justice. Justice used to cook for the Gods a real big pot of
> navy beans. He used to put "hashish" in the Navy Beans. It
> took all day for him to cook the bean soup. He'd put "a moon
> of hash" in it.
> But Justice used to eat right, live right and looked like he was
> sixteen. Justice was a merchant marine. He had been all over
> the world. He had a lot of things to talk about.
> Justice would give you anything at "the poor rate." He'd say
> what you got in your pocket, son? You could get anything you
> wanted from Justice at the poor rate. His name in the mosque
> was James 103X. He looked just like a Muslim. Justice used to
> wear bowties and he was real clean-shaven. He had a son
> named Elijah. He named him after the Honorable Elijah
> Muhammad. We used to all go to Justice house for the rally and
> once we got finished with that bean soup everybody would be
> knocked out.[255]

Teaches Matteawan Inmates
When not tending to matters on the outside, Allah stayed
busy in Matteawan. He just didn't teach his visiting Five
Percenters; he taught all who listened amongst the Matteawan
inmates. He taught one inmate by the name of Robert Walker
who became known as "Allah the Sun aka Great God Allah in
the Wisdom Body." Some believe that he was previously a
registered member in the NOI or at least he received knowledge
of self while living in Medina (Brooklyn).

> The First Born Muslims was started by a brother who was taught
> by our Father, who is Allah in Matawan State Hospital for

Criminally Insane. He did receive the knowledge of himself on the streets of Brooklyn N.Y. [Medina] before he was incarcerated. This brother's name was Robert Walker, around February 4th, 1968, He came in the name of Allah the Sun while in Matawan, when He came back to the so-called free world, He changed his name to Great God Allah in the Wisdom Body, when he came home in 1968.

Robert Walker, while incarcerated taught 13 brothers, who he called his Ark-Angels, they would say this statement: "My wings are 4 feet wide and 7 feet long", showing and proving that their word was Bond; and if I remember some of their names were: 1. ..Lord Eternal Allah, 2...Lord God Allah, 3...Mallah God Allah, 4...Infinite God Allah, 5...Eminent God Allah, 6...Lord Allah, 7...Lord Blesseth Allah, 8...Gallah, 9...Boundest God Allah, 10...Organic Allah, 11...Glorious God Allah, 12...Exziel Allah, and 13...Victorious God Allah[256]

Not only did Allah impact the Black and Puerto Rican inmates, in an unprecedented move, He taught a white inmate named John Kennedy. A New York Times article noted this newsworthy information:

John Kennedy, who is known as Azreal in the group and who said he is the only white enrollee, said he had first met Mr. Smith during his confinement at the Matteawan State Hospital for the Criminally Insane. "He gave me knowledge of myself," Mr. Kennedy said, adding that Mr. Smith never preached hatred of whites.[257]

John would become the first white Five Percenter. Allah taught him the lessons and all. However, Allah provided him with a specific teaching and mission to accommodate his nature as a Caucasian. Allah gave him the name of "Azreal" to indicate his status as a white Five Percenter and his mission to other Caucasians. Allah took this name from Islamic mythology that was a name of an angel who watched over the dying in Hell and separated the souls from the bodies. Azreal went deeper into his experience at Mattawan and how he first met Allah and under what circumstances:

My name is Azreal, I am the First Born-Caucasian-Five Percenter. I met the Father, Allah in Matawan State Hospital for the criminally insane on December 31, 1965. My Honorable name is John Kennedy, I was knowledge equality [16] at the time, the correction officers who worked there were all Klu, Klux, Klan or America Nazi Party members.

Because they didn't like my given name, after just being there for 24 hours, they rush in with batons, and started beating and kicking me. They tried to put fear in me, but only anger came out. I told them they were a bunch of punks who needed to bond together to fight a real man. They then sent the inmates, two at a time to fight me and this continued for two (2) weeks. The very last time they piled on top of me and they injected me with 500mg of Theorozine and 500mg of Melaral, that put me in a coma for 8 weeks.

When I awoke, I was in a new ward and I was sitting in a chair and Allah, the Father walked up to me and said, "You are a righteous man." Then He asked me if I knew who he was and I answered, "You must be God." From then on I was getting the Supreme Mathematics, Alphabets and all the lessons. I had been searching for the truth most of my life when I met the Father, and I knew that is all he was about. I want the Gods and Earths, who never met Allah, the Father to know he did not teach a Devil in Matawan, he taught a righteous man.

He gave me my name Azreal "The death Angel" in charge of inhabitants of Hell, the only one with the key to Heaven and Hell, who can come and go as he pleases, who's job it is to get the wrong doers to reveal who they are. So when I see a "God", who calls me a Devil based on seeing me on face value, they are just telling me what they are.[258]

There were also brothers who had knowledge of self on the tier with Allah. One was a fellow Muslim of the Nation of Islam who shared the same ward. Omar Allahkhan, an FOI who was a patient in Matteawan the same time Allah was there, recalls some of his experiences with Allah in a correspondence with 5% author Shahid M. Allah. As mentioned in Shahid's book entitled, "Open It Up Yo!; The Plot to Kill Clarence 13X."

For several years I have been in correspondence with a very good brother by the name of Omar Allahkhan of Salt Lake City, Utah. Brother Omar came into the ranks of the Nation of Islam back in 1962 in the state of Pennsylvania. In September of 1991 he wrote me a very intriguing letter concerning his brief period of incarceration in Matteawan State Hospital while Allah was there: "I was in Mattawan State Hospital with one who was called 'Father Allah,' known in the Nation of Islam as Clarence

13X. I was placed on the same ward with, and was seated six chairs from him, he was impressive and in control of what he was doing...Father Allah, He didn't show any fear of the white man. He would demand respect for him and the brothers. Each day he would teach the brothers that was there. Only three or four was with him on the ward...They (prison authorities) marked the Father's clothes with 'Allah' on them. There's something you got to understand—These men were members of the Masonic Order, Elks, Brothers of the Lodge. They knew he had the Knowledge. But, they didn't test him.[259]

On the contrary, according to Five Percenter legend, Allah was the subject of medical experimentation while at Matteawan. The allegation implies that Matteawan Doctors exhausted all means and resources to attempt "to tamper with the mind of Allah." It is alleged that a battery of tests were conducted on Allah to see if they could "master his mind." Part of the process was through injecting him with mind-altering controlled substances. Legend has it that Allah's mind was so strong that the drugs had no effect on him. Thus further proving Clarence 13X's claim to be "Allah."

During another particular visit by a group of Five Percenters, Allah was in a different mood. He was upset with the present condition of some of his followers. He didn't like the notion that one could quote all this knowledge and wisdom but not live according to its principles. First Born ABG#7 recalls:

When we visited Allah in Matawan in the year three meaning 1966, our firsts were in the cafeteria with the population. Our next visit was in a little room, Allah told us, "The reason why, was because we were savage." Yeah, and we were capable and able to quote all the lessons. We had even learned to quote the so-called plus lessons too. Allah set us straight and put us on the righteous path. He planted into us giving us the understanding "that we were made and grown from his beginning." He told us "that when we revealed this understanding the born would grasp it being masters of knowledge and wisdom."[260]

Allah had received word on the outside that many of his Five Percenters took to "drinking and drugging" on a consistent basis. While in the inside he attempted to remedy the situation by delivering a message to his Five Percenters.

Hasheem and I, went to visit Allah in Mattawan and it was at that particular time he told us to abstain from getting high off of Alcohol and Substances. From Newburgh all through Mecca back to Medina, Hasheem was lightening up everything and everybody we encountered. It was so mathematical that what ever you may be abstaining from, at that precise time the temptation is intensified in your presence.[261]

In an attempt to enforce this new directive in the absence of Allah, the young Five Percenters went to go visit their peers to deliver the message of abstinence from smoking and drinking. Their first stop was Uptown to Mecca (Harlem).

When we stepped off the train at 125th street and Park Avenue there were some brothers drinking and smoking and offering us some. We in turn told them what Allah had just told us which in our standing and presence of mind was binding and bonding. They were reluctant about what we were telling them not hearing it themselves, they continued while Hasheem soared in his deliverance.

We went by one of the hangouts and Akim was there waiting on us, it was Young Allah's house on 134th street and 7th Avenue. Inside the brothers had ounces of smoke and bottles of wine along with, only Young Allah knew what. When we delivered what Allah the Father had told us they just listen and disregarded what we said. I remember when leaving the household was still indulging and Young Allah came and put several joints and bags in my hand to roll with. I returned them to him and reminded him of what and our Father Allah had just said, we left and returned to Medina.[262]

After delivering the message in Mecca, the young comrades traveled back home to Medina (Brooklyn). There they communicated the latest word from Allah.

On the way home on the train Hasheem and I, told Akim just about everything that Allah the Father had told us, by the time we got back home in Medina, Akim was no longer high and he adhered to everything just as we did. I see and hear plenty of talk about Suv's, meaning Sport Utility Vans that was one of Hasheem's concept back in the sixties. He would rent a U-Haul Van or a Ryder Van to do a moving job after the job was done before returning it, he would put sofas and couches in the back of the vans and all of us Gods would pile in and ride around all over Medina.[263]

Eventually some of the Five Percenters began to kick this habit. Although they transferred the stress of abstaining from a youthful pastime off to the people they encountered. Some of the Five Percenters became real rough around the edges and weren't the friendliest people to get along with at that time. After receiving the reports of the behavior of some of his young gods, he decided to lift the ban.

By this time Allah told us to resume smoking and drinking because we were too hard on the people and had started to let them distill continuously.[264]

Leaves Matteawan

Allah would soon get the opportunity to return home after serving his time in Matteawan. Allah stayed in Matteawan for a total of 22 months. After serving his time, he was certified out of the Hospital as a free and sane man. Several years later, Barry Gotteherer, an aide for then NYC Mayor John Lindsay called the Hospital to verify Allah's status when he was there. Barry Gottehrer:

After he told me this story, I called Matteawan and spoke to a doctor who remembered Allah well, even though he had been released several years before. The doctor had a heavy European accent. He said, "Oh, Allah! A fascinating case!" I said, "He told me that you support the fact that he's Allah, since you let him out." The doctor burst out laughing. He thought Allah was very funny, and along the way he indicated that he also thought he was crazy.[265]

On the other hand, Allah believed Matteawan proved his claim when they certified him out of the hospital. Barry Gottehrer recalls a conversation he had with Allah on the subject:

They know I'm Allah," he told me. "They gave me proof." He pulled out the waistband of his prison underwear to show the name Allah inked on it. "This was my name in the hospital," he said. "If they didn't believe I was Allah, why did they let me out? Would they let out a crazy person?"[266]

On March 6, 1967, Allah was released from Matteawan and returned to the Manhattan House of Detention and stood trial on criminal charges against him. On April 5, 1967, Allah stood trial in Criminal Court, NYC where he received a three-month suspended sentence.

FBI Surveillance

Allah was free to go back to New York City where he could resume teaching his followers in person. Still on the job, the FBI monitored Allah closely after his release from the hospital. According to a FBI report:

> On May 4, 1967, [name redacted] advised that he has been familiar with subject's activities since his release from the hospital. He stated subject is unemployed and has no permanent residence, but can almost always be located on 127th Street off Seventh Avenue, New York City.
>
> [Name redacted] advised that since his release from the hospital, subject has not been in any difficulty with the police.
>
> On March 28, 1967, [name redacted] advised that on March 27, 1967, subject was in the Hotel Theresa Coffee Shop, 125th Street and Seventh Avenue, New York.
>
> New York Sources familiar with many phases of "Black Nationalist" activity have not reported any additional activity on subject's part.[267]

According to the above report (per an FBI informant), the FBI alleges that there wasn't "any additional activity" on Allah's part—but nothing could be further from the truth. Even another FBI memo advises to remove Allah off of their security index as a result of his "inactivity":

> My letter dated 1/16/67 [name redacted] advised that the subject's name should be removed from the Security Index. This action has been taken at the Bureau and you should take similar action with respect to the subject's Security Index cards maintained in your office.[268]

It is an historical fact that Allah continued his activity of teaching the youth in his organization. The natural question by

Five Percenters is why would the FBI deny any further activity on the part of Allah. Prince Allah Cuba suggests that the FBI had an ulterior motive:

> Of course the above is only the cut-off date for the open file. This is usually done by the police agencies when they plan to neutralize the subject; it allows them "plausible denial" after the fact. Neutralization can take many forms: prison, exile, or death. Death is the optimum method of neutralization.[269]

Whether the above conspiracy theory is true or not, the Five Percenters was about to face its toughest foe yet. Ironically, at the hands of what many believed to be a conspiracy.

Chapter 14
1967

Allah addresses The Five Percenters at The Universal Parliament.

After his release, Allah set out to do the work of teaching Islam to the children. He was anxious to carry on his mission and was ecstatic to see the young Gods and Earths again. However, when Allah returned to Harlem, he witnessed some disturbing sights. Seeing the heroin epidemic up close and personal, Allah shook his head at what he seen in Harlem. There were junkies throughout the city and it seemed as if everyone was looking for a fix. One day, while watching the drug fiends on the street, Allah made the following remarks to ABG#7:

When ALLAH came home from Matawan State Institution for the Criminally Insane, I met up with him on 125th street & 6th Avenue, (Lenox Avenue or Malcolm X Blvd), as he gazed across the avenue, my eyes followed his to the mass of people waiting to score (Heroin was King), and his statement was, "Yall Have a Hard Job"[270]

This epidemic seemed to impact a large part of the Black community including Five Percenters. Allah discovered that while he was away in Matteawan, agent provocateurs had come amongst the young Five Percenters promoting the use of strong narcotics. Attempts were even made to change the teachings of the Five Percenters. The agents accentuated to the youth that they did not need the standard NOI lessons and promoted another doctrine in which they wrote their own lessons. Many young Five Percenters fell a victim to these wayward teachings. Shaamguadd reminisces:

Now right after his (Allah) departure, we, his sons, were set upon by the doctors and nurses of deception. They came from out of nowhere talking about they had been down since 1960, and 1961, talking about they Allah the Sun, and Abdu, Allah Born to destroy you. They brought with them, their own personnel snow, (dope, LSD, Coke, DMT, PCP, mescaline just to name a few.)

After getting us under the influence of their annestisia they started injecting us with needles in the brain by telling us that the father had sent us these lessons. Allah World Manifest, General Monk-Monk, Islam in 90 degrees, magnetic analysis, the magnetic field, the magnetic flux and countless others, while at the same time they blood sucked us for all the knowledge that Allah had taught us. They had us all high up walking around quoting these other lessons, taking our mind off of what was our original teachings and jobs. All they had to do was add fire water, and shake well, then most of us would wake up the next morning in jail or half dead not remembering what had happened the night before, and they had disappeared to sell the knowledge that they stole from us to the highest bidder. Those of us who knew better had already been set up and were in jail on chumped up charges. This had always been the way of the devil, black or white, to divide and conquer.

When the Father heard of this he told us to burn these lessons, that they were not our lessons that we should not study them, quote them or give or teach them to anyone, because they would make us other than our ownself. He taught us that all we needed were our 120 degrees of knowledge and to be able to quote them would give us 120 degrees of wisdom and that when we were old enough we would have 120 degrees of supreme understanding which would give us 360 degrees...[271]

Another Five Percenter recalls this same event and advised that Allah mentioned the detractors by name and warned his Five Percenters to stay away from these types. Infinite Al' Jaa'maar –U-Allah:

> Now in the "Fall of 1967", when Allah returned to the streets of Mecca from Mattawan State Hospital, He told us at a Rally held in Mecca about a brother that he taught while He was in Mattawan. He told us to stay away from this brother. The Father said his name was Robert Walker known as Allah the Sun (aka) Great God Allah in the Wisdom Body, this brother's name was originally Al-lakarzar, when he was in Ft. Greene, which is known as the head of Medina. Allah told us that this brother was a 1st Born Muslim and don't get caught up in his wisdom and that his teachings was right and exact, and that we the Gods were not yet ready for him.[272]

In another account, some Five Percenters recall the time period and how it was addressed. Old Man Justice and other Elders were cited as helpers to combat the epidemic. Universal Shaamguadd:

> Many of the Elders will remember that when the Father first went away, some brothers came from nowhere and were advocating a change in our Original teachings and many of us fell for it, fortunately for us we had Akbar (Justice) and some first Borns who knew better, JUSTICE taught us that this was just needles and that those brothers were just nurses doing their job as is told in the 28th degree in the one to forty, this is one of the oldest methods of weakening a new nation, other teachings are first injected into your head thus making you a nurse yourself and then you go out injecting these needles into the mind of others then the new name is added to show that you all are different, thus the separating of the seeds is now in play, now the next move is to come among those who have held fast and attempt to degrade the and create confusion among them (sound like anybody you know?)
> As I said this happened to some of us back in 1966 so it can happen to anyone, without their even knowing that it's

happening we had the Father and Justice to help us pull needle and pins out today it's up to the First Borns and Elders because we've been there before.[273]

Not only did the agents say Allah sent the Five Percenters bogus lessons but claimed Allah said it was OK for them to use narcotics. Upon hearing this Allah zealously denied it and said he never made such a statement.

My brother asked me to buy the 120 degrees that he had on cassette tape also the Manifestation of the Mind, Allah's World Manifest, Allah's 360, etc. My mind went back to Allah immediately and his words rang in my ears, stick within the realm of 120 degrees, especially being a young God of 18 years of age.

That was his reply to many brothers when they brought him all these new found lessons that showed up after he had been gone. Many of them were not numerically numbered and therefore mathematically unbalanced they served a purpose however not in mud reality of life, been there, done that. We must always remember our past as to never repeat it, we were to reflect in our past, not dwell in it.[274]

Moreover, he exclaimed that narcotics were forbidden to the Five Percenters. Allah always advised the children in America and in general to stay away from narcotics because he believed it led to the destruction of a society. He is recorded saying in an interview:

Because the children here use drugs, they're going back to sleep. And now it's getting to your people. So they're using it. Sooner or later you're going to see the downfall.[275]

Allah had additional harsh comments about drugs as relayed by US Shaamguadd:

And to always remember that Heroin, Dope, Smack, Speedball, King He, King Kong, Scrabble or whatever one wishes to call it is forbidden to us, it is the Swine of All Drugs, and we shall not handle, use, mix, tough, help carry, advocate or endorse it's use in any way, fashion or form!!! The only way it can be mastered is to leave it alone. When one falls victim to the Pig of Stimulations he is being a Devil!!! It is poison to the System, the Family, the

Community, State, the Nation, the World and the Universe! It has no place among the righteous. So my beloved Brothers and Sisters, if someone tells you that he is Allah or / God and you know he is dealing with Heroin in any way, fashion or form, and he tries to Justify it by saying it s all right of god to deal with it because God can master it, I assure you he sure as Hell ain't Allah, even though he might be God, a God-Damn-Fool, that is!!! And there are no exceptions.[276]

To Allah's dismay, the agents ensnared many of his young followers to fall victim to drug abuse. He admonished everyone who became a user and immediately set out to remedy the situation. An article that appeared in *the Five Percenter Newspaper* recalls this time period:

When Allah was in Matteawan State Hospital for the Criminally Insane, word came to us (5%) on the street, that it was okay to sniff Heroin. The justification was that "we had to be lord of all the worlds". Needless to say, many of us began sniffing dope under this presupposition. Many of us were wine drinking pot smokers already. Now we added Dope (Heroin) to our using. We thought that we could master dope.

By the time Allah came out of that institution, many of his 5% were fully addicted to Dope. It was like a pox. Allah vehemently denied that he had said it was okay to use dope. "DOPE IS FOR DOPES", he exclaimed. "THE ONLY WAY TO MASTER IT IS TO LEAVE IT ALONE", he told us. But by this time so many of his 5% had become enslaved to the effects of the drug, that they couldn't leave it alone, no matter how hard they tried.

Even when Allah stood up at the Universal Parliament and said, "DOPE IS FORBIDDEN TO THE 5%", many brothers who were addicted to it STILL used it. While some brothers who did not USE DOPE chose to SELL DOPE instead.

You see certain substances are put amongst us to retard, stop, prevent, impede and cease the growth of our Nation. Back then HEROIN was the culprit. We thought that COCAINE/ ALCOHOL/ REEFER and the other stuff was okay, AS LONG AS WE DIDN'T USE DOPE! **HOW WRONG WE WERE is seen today in EVERY ALWAYS DRUNK GOD; EVERY CRACK SMOKING GOD; EVERY ALWAYS PUFFING HERB GOD...**

Not to say that every God who Drinks Alcohol will be ALCOHOLIC but EVERY GOD WHO DOES NOT DRINK

ALCOHOL WILL <u>NOT</u> BE ALCOHOLICS. ALCOHOLIC, CRACKHEAD, POTHEAD, DOPEFIEND are all on the same TITANIC because A DRUG IS A DRUG IS A DRUG, and ALCOHOL is the BIGGEST DRUG, because it is LEGAL and promoted. You don't have to duck dodge and hide to buy it. Society accepts it and so do you. Whereas, Crack is another story it is the DOPE (HEROIN) of today but it is EVEN MORE devastating to our Nation than HEROIN was. CRACK has emptied more seats in the Parliament than all of the GANGSTERS, GUNS, GIRLS, AGENTS, TRICKS, LIES, etc that the devil has sent to STOP THE NATION OF GODS AND EARTHS. Not only does it dominate, degrade and destroy those Gods & Earths who use it, it dominates, degrades and destroys those Gods & Earths who SELL it...[277]

The Five Percenters faced its most formidable foe, perhaps the greatest of all vices – drug addiction. Allah rose to the challenge to attempt to defeat this scourge.

The Universal Parliament

Soon after realizing the effect the agents had on his young movement, Allah called for a mass gathering of Five Percenters to deliver an important message. All the young Gods and Earths from all five boroughs were summoned and told to attend. This mass gathering was the first of its kind for the Five Percenters and became known as "The Universal Parliament." The first one took place in Mount Morris Park in New York City, April of 1967.

In a coronation like fashion, hundreds of Five Percenters attended the Universal Parliament to welcome Allah home. Allah spoke and there was a thunderous response that reciprocated his greeting of peace. Allah expressed his gratitude to all who remained strong and steadfast in Islam. He was exceedingly glad to see that the Five Percenters had continued to grow in his absence. He knew they had been building because of all the young he saw.

Allah spoke on the process of refinement and the importance of living a clean life. He reminded the young Gods and Earths that drugs were the root and downfall of every nation. He exclaimed that, *"Dope was forbidden to the 5%."* Allah gave a combination speech and sermon about their mission to take care of their own, live clean, and civilize the world.

"You are all pace setters of the world, you are Guardian Angels. Keep teaching and you will take over the world." Furthermore he said, "Learn One Hundred and Twenty Degrees. Put them (The Lost-Found Muslim Lessons) in your head, because the devil can't take that regardless of what he does. The devil is destroying himself because his children are turning against him. He doesn't let them grow with him. You see how they are going back to the way they used to live in the caves of Europe? Look at the hippies! They didn't teach them the laws of Moses (Musa). But, we are going to let our children grow up with us because we know that the 'cream' must rise to the top, you understand?...."[278]

At this point it was reported that there was a disturbance in the audience by a group of Muslims from the Nation of Islam that came to contest Clarence 13X's claim that he was Allah. Beloved Allah, from the article "The Bomb: The Greatest Story Never Told":

At one point in the parliament there was a disturbance caused by some Muslim followers of the Honorable Elijah Muhammad who were members of Temple No 7 when Allah was there. They had come to question him as to why he was teaching the youth of the nation that he was Allah. Allah responded that "the muslims of the Nation of Islam have never seen W.D. Fard and they worship him as Allah. But they say they don't worship a mystery god. So you are worshipping in blind faith. Elijah said we had to stand on our own two feet. You can bring Elijah, and any of his minister to Rockland Palace and he will tell you that I am Allah. You or any muslims can't judge me or my sons and your lessons say that anything made weak and wicked from the Original Man is devil, and you are running around worshipping a Half Original Man and not the Blackman." The muslims departed as the Five Percenters celebrated a moral victory with thunderous cries of "All praise are due to Allah!"[279]

In a speech given in New York City at Mosque #7, Minister Akbar Muhammad, the International Representative of The Honorable Louis Farrakhan, says he remembers this event. In fact, he says it was he who was in attendance at the rally by himself, not with any other Muslims. He has a different version as to what happened on that day. Known as Brother Larry 4X back then, he spoke of how he ended up in the park. According to Minister Akbar, Captain Yusef Shah had given him an ultimatum. He could choose to either run the Muslim restaurant or be Minister Farrakhan's assistant in the mosque. According to Akbar, he wanted to take a little time to make his decision so he walked down to the park to think about it. It was there he noticed Clarence 13X holding a rally. Minister Akbar Muhammad:

> The last time I saw Clarence was a little before he got killed at Marcus Garvey Park in 1967 that Sunday. I remember because I was in a dilemma because Shah told me that I was either going to manage the restaurant, or assist Minister Farrakhan, but for him I couldn't do both. I had to make a decision, so I walked up to the park and they were having a parliament. And at the parliament there were about 1000 Five Percenters. And Clarence had just came home from somewhere, maybe Matteawan again...He was naming a baby, because the sisters are the queens and you plant your seed in the queen...and he was naming a baby. And I just so happen to walk up there and I had my FOI uniform on and when I walked up to the top of the hill in Mount Morris Park, it's called now Marcus Garvey Park, the whole crowd just opened up. And when I looked down there was Clarence. And being that we knew each other I said to him, I said, "Clarence, what is this that you are teaching the brothers that you are Allah?" And he said that, "Because I am Allah." And the whole crowd said, "ALL PRAISES ARE DUE TO ALLAH!" Now imagine 1000 young brothers and sisters saying that. Then I said, "Well, how could you teach that brother and you standing there with a cigarette in your hand?" Because he had a cigarette in his hand, ok. Then he said, "Allah is not bound by anything, Allah must master all things." And the whole crowd said, "ALL PRAISES IS DUE TO ALLAH!" So I gave him my favorite axiom that you probably have heard me say it, "Time is a test for man and all ideas," and no he said something else before that, he said, "I've been shot through the heart with an Elephant gun...and I lived"...[280]

Whatever happened or was said, the Universal Parliament was a success and everyone was happy that Allah was home. The Five Percenters celebrated a moral victory on that day. The event was so successful that it was agreed that the Universal Parliaments would become an institution to be held monthly on the last Sunday of the month. The Five Percenters from Medina

(Brooklyn) approached Allah about holding Universal Parliaments out there. Allah conceded and took the Parliament to Brooklyn during the summer months to appease a demand from The Five Percenters of that borough.

> He commenced with the "Sermons" on the Mount in April=Allah's Power and Righteousness, I live. He then brought the "Sermon" to the Mount in Medina in June=Just-U-N-Equal on the knowledge build or destroy day [18].
> This was due to my beloved brother Hasheem, may the blessings be with him always and Siheem also Sha Sha constantly asking the Father "when are you coming out to Medina?" along with our beloved brother Bilal had just about practically held the "Nation" together. We cannot and must not ever forget this part of the "History" for the most part all of the first born and elders at the time was locked up in jail or else where....
> The very first "Parliament" held on April 30th, the year four=1967, also the very first one held in Medina on June 18th, the year four=1967, brought out the brothers and sisters from everywhere, places where we hand't even known the seed of the teachings had reached. The Father was pleased with what we had been doing with the teachings for the vast numbers made it evident. We had taken the basics and made them flourish...[281]

Although Allah was visibly pleased with the numbers, he wanted to make sure the young Gods and Earths knew that it wasn't just "WHAT you teach as much as HOW you teach it." Black Seed Gykee recalls an experience with Allah about this topic:

> I can recollect his primary concern was with getting the basic knowledge out to the young brothers and sisters. He started exhibiting his culture more and more. Saying things like "know who you are and what and how everything was made," Like "Teach this where ever you go." Once when I was about to go on a trip to "Expo 67" in Montreal, Canada, the Canadian World's Fair, when I told the Father he asked me "Are you going to teach son?" I answered "Yes Allah" it struck me strange that he would ask me this. However, today it's understood thoroughly yes, I would teach not so much what, I was teaching as opposed to what was being advocated and the method that

was used to convey the teachings. Sending the signal that it was "O.K. to "Drink and Drug" while teaching.

Those of you that knew me know exactly what I'm talking about, he would tell me "Son", I'm trying to make you my "KEE," you just keep [F___] up Son." He could detect my troubles and woes along with my "Drinking and Drugging" back then, when I couldn't....When sober my method of teaching was some what persuasive or to say the least it left one questioning themselves about their own values. After a "Drink and Drug" or a couple of both, all bets were now off and I would become very rude, loud and obnoxious to any and everyone.[282]

Whenever encountering excess on any level, Allah addressed these types of situations, especially with his young Five Percenters. Seeing excessive behavior on a young man's part, Allah instructed what he needed to do and what was coming.

Then he said things like "one day you will have to stop "Drinking and Drugging." When I speak nobody needs to come behind me and speak on anything. No the Father never told us to drink or drug he let us surmise and come to our own conclusion. He told us that we would have to abide and obey the laws of this country and that we could do no wrong. We misconstrued that and thought that everything we did was right, a big mistake. He then told us that "we could no longer be right, we had to be right and exact." This would be achieved by telling the truth and living mathematics.[283]

Knowing in many cases that information is better received when coming from peers, Allah sent other Five Percenters to deliver messages for him. In this particular case, Allah wanted to make sure his seeds were looking out for each other.

A time comes to mind when Sihiem came back from Mecca, having just visited with Allah the Father he had a message to convey unto us, especially me. He found us in our usual spots. I can remember him in I was really drunk and giddy after my brother started revealing what Allah wanted us to hear, specially me. It was a knowledge power day which if not mistaken was his degree at the time, he drew up all the alcohol out of me after he finished I was no longer drunk, just hung over bearing witness to the "Power of Allah" through little brother and brown-seed. These things took place during the years three and four of our nation, which is equivalent to = 1966 and 1967.[284]

Name Changes

During this critical time period, Allah had to make wise decisions in guiding his Five Percenters. Allah knew adolescents were prone to trouble oft times, this included his followers as well. Because of the common and past mistakes made by some of the young gods, not only would the image of the Five Percenters suffer but it would also tarnish the image of the NOI. Muslims were concerned about the negative publicity because of some youths who were giving the police Muslim names when arrested. Shahid recalls this period when NOI officials Captain Joseph and First Officer Lieutenant Clarence 7X from Temple #7 addressed the subject with Allah:

> I was with the Father when Captain Joseph and Lieutenant Clarence 7X came to the Street Academy to speak with us about the warfare that was going on in the streets. They asked about some of the kids who was going around shanking people and stuff and calling themselves "the Tribe of Shabazz." Whenever one of them got caught by the police they would say they was "so and so Shabazz" and this was making the Muslims look bad. The Father told them he was going to check into it and take care of it. The Father put the word out that anybody involved in that kind of stuff better stop. That's when he decided to change the names.[285]

Many times when young Five Percenters got in trouble with the law, the newspapers, authorities and people described them as "Black Muslims," as it was in the case of the Blood Brothers and the Harlem Six. At that time, the term Black Muslims was used to describe the Muslim followers of the Hon. Elijah Muhammad who had a sterling reputation for being well refined and disciplined. So this would surprise the Black community who seen or heard about Black Muslims or "their children" getting in trouble. People often confuse the two and the Islamic community began to draw negative criticism as a result of the actions of a few.

This concerned Allah who respected the fact that he as well as his Muslim brothers and sisters worked long and hard to earn a good name for themselves in the community. Allah decided for obvious reasons he would take action to distinguish his Five Percenters from the Muslims. He decided it best to take away their Muslim names and give them new names made up from the Supreme Mathematics and Alphabets. Shaamguadd explains:

> Brothers and Sisters, this is one of the reasons the Father told us we could not have Muslim names so that they would not have to take the weight for the unrighteous actions of our fruit. He taught us that a Muslim is only someone who submits to the will of Allah so that by Nature, we are all Muslims, and that it's hard enough being righteous or a Muslim in Hell without a bunch of knuckleheads running around on the warpath causing confusion.[286]

Um Allah makes a similar point in his recollection of why Allah instructed the Five Percenters to change their names.

> My name was Kareem Akbar. And when the Father came home he said he went to the Mosque and they made an agreement because the Muslims were getting arrested, we were getting arrested and it was in the papers that the Five Percent, Blood Brothers, Muslim renegade such and such. So the Father said I'll change my nation. And what he did he came back to us and changed lessons, Elijah's lessons, instead of "what" he put "but"; instead of skunk he said we'll take skunk out. He took a lot of lessons and changed them around to fit his nation. And then in 68 and 69 he said next year yall going to be sons of Almighty—yall going to be Allah's, not the son of Almighty God Allah but you going to be Allahs. And what he did the first one he changed his name he called him Allah Man. When he told us to change our names and from there we all started to change our names.[287]

In fact, Shaamguadd would recall a personal conversation he had with Allah in regards to his own name:

> The name Shaamguadd (pronounced- SHAMGOD) is one which I designed myself. In 1965 I went by the complete name of SHAAMGOD, ABDULE, ALLAH, MALIK, JABBAR. However on my first private talk with the Father, he asked me my name. So I ran it off like a little poem. I knew right away that I had

made a mistake. The Father smiled and almost laughed then he said "Son you don't need all those names. A man should carry his name; the name should never have to carry the man. A name that heavy could weigh a young man down, don't make your job any harder than it already is, your job is to help people to find themselves, with a name that long they'll get lost in your name. You'll be trying to teach them about the science of everything in life and they'll be trying to remember what you said your name was. ALLAH is the family name and always follows the attribute of a God. JABBAR is a tribal name and is automatic, and includes all women and children, and this is an understanding within the family. A great name won't make you great; you have to bring greatness to the name. Think about it MUHAMMAD, BUDDA, MUSA, JESUS. SINGLE NAMES MADE great by single men. That's why we have given you'll the Supreme Alphabets and Mathematics by using them properly you can create your own attribute that says the same things all those other names say, and after you have completed the Birth record you can add a name or change yours, however only after you have mastered that name for 10 years can you add or change the cipher!!!"[288]

So in 1967, Allah had many of the Five Percenters change their names from Muslim names to come in the name of Allah as their family name and take a name from Supreme Mathematics or Supreme Alphabets to go with it. Thus, for example, Karriem became Black Messiah. Bilal became ABG7. Al-Jabbar became Prince Allah. Perhaps a little known history fact, this very concept of having the last name Allah, originated with Master Fard Muhammad who taught that all Muslims should wear the last name of Allah or one of his attributes. Elijah Muhammad:

> He (W.F. Muhammad) told us that we must give up our slave names (of our slave masters) and accept only the name of Allah (Himself) or one of his divine attributes.[289]

Ironically, many years later, some Five Percenters would confuse Allah's reasoning behind taking Muslim names away from some of the Five Percenters. Many thought that Allah did this to spite the Muslims, but on the contrary, Universal Shaamguadd stated that Allah had an even deeper reason for doing this. Shaamguadd expounds on Allah's rationale:

I even heard brothers speak against True Moslems here in America without trying to see past their Knowledge and Wisdom and show them your Understanding.

You must always remember that Moslems are lovers of their religion, their QUR'AN, their Prophet Muhammad, their Truth and Allah and because of their Knowledge and Wisdom of the Holy Qu'ran they will refuse to understand you, if all you are able to speak is Knowledge and Wisdom of the Truth.

Like our Righteous names, Our Father, Almighty God Allah, knew that some would try to take his teachings and run wild with them, however, he knew that you couldn't run forth with this if you were not right.

You see to (orthodox) Moslems, our names appear to be a blasphemy to Allah according to their Knowledge and Wisdom, that is why we were taught that Allah shall be our last names.

However, when one takes the time to give the Understanding to a Moslem he will learn that if they were to read our names from right to left, as they were originally taught, that our names become a Blessing and a praise to Allah and his Glory and more times than not they will see it. Because they were taught from right to left and to study from right to left, and they think of Western Society as backward.[290]

The reason for Allah changing the names amounted to two purposes. First, was to distinguish his Five Percenters from the Muslims for the obvious reasons although he did allow some Five Percenters to retain their Muslim names. Second, was to give the Five Percenters a brand new start and opportunity to live up to their new noble names. Allah encouraged his young followers to grow into their names per righteous ways and actions and always remember that they weren't just representing themselves but they were representing for ISLAM.

Since many of the youth were being exposed to more Black militant factions in the city. Allah advised his Five Percenters to be cautious of other militant factions that promoted violence such as the Black Panther Party. Shaamguadd wrote:

BROTHERS and SISTERS when they were first trying to form the original Black Panther Party, they came to some of the First Borns and took us up on the Mountain by offering us Homes, Cars and Unlimited Expense Accounts if we would accept the Leadership positions and teach and train their Troops. I'm glad to be able to say that none of us accepted. The Father told me to observe closely what was about to happen to the B.P.P and I would get a Lesson in how a NATION could be Destroyed by Infiltration and the Seperation of the SEEDS and how just one Infiltrator or Snake in the right place giving out false information could not only cause them to fight and kill one another, it could also destroy a NATION that thrived on Violence. He said that they would try this method against His NATION. However, it would be unsuccessful as long as there was one Righteous God to uphold his Teachings.[291]

The Universal Flag of Islam

Another significant change was a new addition to the Five Percenters insignia. Prior to this time the Five Percenters exclusively used and wore the Nation of Islam (star and crescent) flag on their lapel. In April of 1967, Universal Shaamguadd (who also was an artist), presented Allah with an emblem he designed and said was originally inspired by a conversation he had with Allah about the universe a year earlier. Shaamguadd recalls the conversation:

What amazed me most was the Universe and its relations to us here on the Planet. So the majority of my oils and drawings were of the Sun, Moon, and Stars. One which I considered my masterpiece was of our Solar System, with a mathematical breakdown of all the Planets...

One day I decided to take this picture to the Father. He had always showed an interest in our works and achievements, and I knew I would receive some constructive criticism.

This day I met the Father and Justice on 126th Street. The Father complimented the picture and then asked me to walk with them. As we walked He began to explain the errors that I had made and what was the proper order of the Universe. Brothers and sisters do not ask where we walked because I do not know. I do know that as I walked, He taught, I recall feeling as though we were walking through the Universe itself. All I recall seeing was the things he spoke about, the Sun, the Planets, the Stars, Haley's Comet, other Comets, shooting stars, falling stars, Space Voids (now called Black Holes).

After what seemed like a personal tour of the Universe, I recall Him saying "And remember Equality can never get above ALLAH. Six, when drawn up to its fullest Equality, shall distill back to whence she came, to her 7 is an impossibility!!!" With this I realized that we were at the train station. While the conversation seemed to have lasted only a short period of time when we began it had been broad daylight and now it was pitch dark. The Father told me that I would understand everything that he told me, only that I would see it in what—Time! With that I said Peace and I got on the train to Medina.[292]

It would be a couple of years later before Allah saw the effect he had on Shaamguadd that day. Shaamguadd would present Allah with a painting of the "Universal Flag of Islam."

Now if you think I was in Love with the Universe before, you can imagine what my experience with the Father did to encourage the Love. I decided then that I would make a picture for the Father's Birthday, February 22 to show him what I had seen and learned from the experience, as well as it's relationship to us as a Nation. Now you must remember that at this time we used the Crescent Star as our Flag, so when some of my brothers saw me adding the 7 and points, they thought I was flaking out (Bugging Out nowadays).

The Flag was completed in May of 1966. It was one of three. (Considered the best of 3). Black Seed Gykee ALLAH and myself went to visit Him and we took the Flag. However, the Authorities would not allow us to take it in, so the Father did not receive the Flag until April of 1967 when he came home. I took it to Him in Mecca. He took one look at it and said, "That's it! That's Our Universal Flag!"[293]

The Universal Flag of Islam emblem was an eight-pointed black and gold star. Within the eight-pointed star were a smaller five-pointed star, crescent moon and the number seven fixed in the center. The emblem was ordained as the *Universal Flag of Islam* and became the official insignia of the Five Percenters.

After divulging his supreme understanding to us, we began to set all the things right with the people and the brothers and sisters who was awaiting his return. A point of clarification on who was present when we took the flag to the Father upstate also in the Year three = 1966. There were only three of us at the time, Shaamgaudd, Gamal who is now Goddef and I, all it wrote. For the life and love of me, I don't know why. Although that's who was there and anyone saying any different is completely false. Once before for we took the flag up to the

Father that same year, we brought a drawing of a flag over to Mecca for Four Cipher Akbar to see. He told us that it wasn't appropriate for our flag, yet it was enough to take the head off of the Messenger. Many of the Medina born had seen the flag in the making not knowing what Shaamgaudd had in mind.

With what Four Cipher Akbar told him my brother Shaamgaudd went back to the drawing board and after three different flags the last one was accepted by the Father when he came home in March the year four=1967.[294]

After the creation of the Universal Flag of Islam, the Five Percenters continued to grow into their identities. This time under their own universal emblem that distinguished them amongst the crowd.

Chapter 15
The Mayor's Man

Allah talking to Barry Gottehrer on a Harlem street

It was in May of 1967 when New York City Mayor John Lindsay began to show interest in Allah and his organization. Mayor Lindsay during his term saw the eruption of Crown Heights, Brooklyn as a result of racial turmoil between the Blacks and Jews. In his efforts to influence and settle the situation, Mayor Lindsay realized that the city administration was not in touch with the true leaders of the people in the communities.

This prompted Mayor Lindsay to create a Task Force designed to develop ties with community leaders. The Mayor assigned one of his personal aides, Barry Gottehrer, over the Task Force. One of the main purposes of Mr. Gottehrer was to develop a rapport with the most sought out "Black Militants" in New York. High on that list was Allah. This impelled Mr.

Gottehrer to arrange a meeting. In his book, called *The Mayor's Man*, Mr. Gottehrer explained his purpose to meet with Allah:

> Not all the men I was going to be dealing with would come down to City Hall and walk into my office. Some of the people we wanted were so inaccessible local task force offices weren't getting through to them. Some of these leaders had given up on city government altogether, and some had grand ideas—they would talk to Mayor Lindsay directly, or to no one. I set out to convince them that I spoke for the mayor, and that it was worth their while to deal with me. High on the list of priorities was Clarence Smith Jowars, born in Danville, Virginia, forty-one years before, whose police record included time for gambling, felonious assault, narcotics, resisting arrest, weapons, and one charge I never did get the straight story on, "turning over a garbage can." After leaving the Harlem Mosque during Malcolm X's period of leadership there, Clarence 13X Smith surfaced once again as the head of a sect similar to the Muslims which he named the Five Percenters, and he renamed himself Allah. In 1964, a white shopkeeper and his wife had been murdered in their store on 125th Street, and a group of young men identified as Five Percenters had been arrested and charged with the brutal slayings. In these pre-Panther days, no group struck fear into whites more than the Five Percenters. Allah and his group had a reputation for being unreachable, anti-white criminals, and these qualities were exactly the ones that interested me. The police had told us that if we could reach him, we really would be doing something." [295]

Meets Allah

As fate would have it, Barry Gottehrer knew an associate of Allah named Jim Lawson who arranged a meeting between the two. On May 12th, Barry Gottehrer met Allah and Justice at a bar in Harlem called *The Glamour Inn*. In his book, Gottehrer recalls the meeting that took place:

> The bar was virtually deserted except for a couple of men, one of them answering Allah's description, seated several barstools from me. I picked up my drink, a rum-and-Coke, and moved over to introduce myself. Allah was with his main man, James Howard, who was at that time calling himself Jesus. There I was, a white man, overdressed in a jacket, and tie, sitting having a drink between Allah and Jesus...

Allah's speech pattern was uniquely his own, with its own pitch and rhythm. He would start a sentence, "I am neither pro black or anti-" and then he would pause. He'd add, "whi-i-ite," stretching the emphasis on that last syllable. He explained his religion to me at some length. The world, he believed, was inhabited by three kinds of people: 85 per cent of the world are cattle; 10 per cent are the devils who mislead the cattle, and the 5 per cent, with Allah at its head, had become the Five Percenters.

Much of the theology was similar to Muslim teachings; when Allah left the mosque, he took a good number of books and pamphlets with him to guide his new sect. (I never found out why he split with the Muslims, as former members are never discussed. From what I learned later, it was likely he violated the rules against drinking and gambling.)

At the time I met Allah, his followers numbered either from two to five hundred, if you believed the police reports; or eight hundred, if you believed Allah. I've been told that sooner or later he could try to start some kind of armed revolution, and that the Five Percenters would try to take over Harlem.[296]

Initially Gottehrer's biased perception was based upon information he received from the NYPD. One thing that should be noticed is when he finally met Allah—he didn't agree with their report. Mr. Gottehrer elaborates:

But Allah wasn't sounding like a revolutionary. He was asking me if the city could provide enough buses to take the Five Percenters on a picnic. I said I thought it would be possible. Then he asked about school facilities. The Urban League, which used corporate funding to staff store-front street academies, for dropouts with teachers who were former dropouts themselves, told Allah they weren't willing to give over a street academy for the exclusive use of Five Percenters. Allah wanted the city to do better by him.[297]

Some Five Percenters recall Allah asking for a little more for his movement. Allah wanted to push his agenda of placing the Five Percenters back on the path to getting an education, vocational trades or jobs. He also wanted them to have fun on the way.

Allah didn't ask for much, He asked for a Street Academy for the children to learn the basics of education to prepare for college.

Trips to state parks outside of the city, airplanes rides, to be able to attend rock and roll shows, Broadway plays and shows, and Museums.[298]

After their conversation, Allah felt confident enough to extend Barry Gottehrer an invitation to the Five Percenters Universal Parliament. There Gottehrer could be heard out by the Five Percenters.

> ...Allah invited me to visit the monthly gathering of the Five Percenters, which they called their Parliament, to explain about the proposed picnic and the possibilities for the school, and I accepted for the last Sunday in May. All the time we talked, my mind kept drifting back to the police report on Allah. It didn't go together. I began to wonder if I was talking to the right man. Allah's sidekick, Jesus, who for some unexplained reason later changed his name to Justice, was a fine looking man with white hair. He didn't fit either. When I asked how we'd get in touch, Allah gave me the numbers of the two pay phones at the Glamour Inn and I wrote them on a matchbook, promising I'd call him with the week. Then we ended our conversation as Allah had begun it, with a handshake and the assurance, "Peace!"[299]

Attends Universal Parliament

During the next few days Mr. Gottehrer made good on his promise. He discovered the city owned a closed storefront (which they had taken over in a tax case) located only a few doors down from the Glamour Inn.

Mr. Gottehrer called Eugene Callender (the Black Director of the Urban League) who was previously working with Allah to try to secure a building for the exclusive use of the Five Percenters. Together, Mr. Callender and Mr. Gottehrer arranged for the Urban League to run a street academy for the Five Percenters. The arrangement was that the city would turn over the store front to the League for a dollar a year with a 20-year lease if the Urban League supplied two teachers. Both mutually agreed to the conditions and it was a done deal.

On the last Sunday of May, Barry Gottehrer attended the Five Percenters Parliament at Mount Morris Park to share the good news. He recalls this event:

When I went to the park, which interrupts Fifth Avenue between 120[h] and 124th Streets, and walked up the long, winding circular steps to a clear area at the very top around an old landmark lookout tower, where Five Percenters from all the five boroughs were now assembling...

Allah was up there with his friend Jesus, or Justice; Al Murphy, another man who hung out at the Glamour Inn; and almost 200 young Five Percenters, all of them Black. The meeting opened with ritual greeting, "Peace" and Allah gave a combination speech and sermon about their mission to take care of their own, live clean, and civilize the world. It wasn't a new speech, for the Five Percenters would chime in with key words or phrases. The young people, who ranged in age from eight or nine years old to twenty-five, with a handful of older people, stood in a circle and took turns stepping forward to make a short speech. Most of the boys wore small African hats that looked like square Jewish yarmulkes. There were a great many young girls, most with small babies pulling at their skirts or held in their arms. Few were married. Allah believed that one way for Five Percenters to inherit the earth was to produce more children than any other group and outpopulate the competition.

I was introduced and stepped into the center of the circle to speak my piece. Lieutenant Boxley and the plainclothesman, whose identity was no secret from the Five Percenters, faded to the periphery. I explained that the mayor was interested in working with their organization and that we would be able to get them buses to go to the beach in Long Island, at one of the state parks. We settled on a 8 A.M. departure time the following Sunday.[300]

Barry Gottehrer broke the news about the plans to secure the long awaited street academy during the Parliament.

I told them some of the plans for the street academy. When I was finished, there was silence. No one believed a thing I said. When I went back to the Glamour Inn with Allah, he was polite but I could see he didn't believe me either.[301]

Contrary to Barry's thoughts, Allah did believe it. At least enough to conveyed this to the Five Percenters at a Parliament. A Five Percenter recalls Allah speaking on the topic with his followers that sparked a controversy. ABG#7 elaborates:

Everything ALLAH taught us was toward change, from what the processes of dehumanization had made us, to what we would choose to be.

Just to present my reader with an example where we were at. Allah informed the sisters, and the Brothers on the Mountain that they could wear anything they desired. That the sisters should keep themselves beautiful and attractive in order to maintain the brothers. He spoke of how he would slick his hair down, smell good, dress correctly himself. The sisters ask that summer if they could wear pants to the first Bus Ride, His Answer, Yes!, they then ask could they wear bathing suits, his Answer, Yes!, shorts etc. The sisters being elated over this begin to speak about the attire they would wear, bikini, two pieces swim wear. The Brothers begin to talk about how they wanted to see, and attract (for lack of a better term) the women of others (their brothers). This led to hostility within the Nation. So ALLAH called the wearing of bathing attire off. Because the brothers were not ready. (savages). I am more than sure many brothers remember that. This allowed many of us to witness first hand the imposters, they had no discipline, they professed one thing, and thought and did another. In otherwords they could not walk the walk........Our disciplines had to be established, achieved, and maintained by us. OUR WOMEN MUST BE RESPECTED AND PROTECTED, AT ALL TIMES.[302]

Bus Trips and Picnics

Whether Barry's suspicion was real or imagined, his word in regards to the buses and picnic came through the following week. That Sunday the buses arrived early that morning. The Five Percenters filled six buses and went to a Long Island State Park. Mr. Gottehrer:

The next Sunday morning I was at 127th Street an hour ahead of time. Although I had reconfirmed all the arrangements myself, I was very relieved when, at ten minutes to eight, the first buses pulled around the corner from Seventh Avenue.

We filled six buses and headed for the beach at a Long Island State Park. The Citizen's Summer Committee had a commitment from Restaurant Associates, one of the better chains in the city, to provide us with free food for different poverty groups over the summer. I filled my city car with their sandwiches and followed the buses to the picnic grounds.

Allah once told me that the Five Percenters, like the Muslims, would eat no product of the pig. He described the pig as one-third dog, one-third rat, and one-third cat. "Now," he wound up with a flourish, "would you eat dog, rat, or cat?" With this in mind, when we were almost at the picnic grounds I pulled over to take a look at those lunches in the back of my car. I opened up one sandwich bag—American cheese and sliced ham. I took out the ham and rewrapped the sandwich. I checked another bag and found more ham. Three hundred bags, each with two sandwiches per child, meant six hundred sandwiches. The job took two hours; by the end of it, I was fast enough to work for a McDonald's.[303]

Despite the lunch mishap that was unknown to the Five Percenters, they enjoyed themselves and the field trip. However, Allah informed Barry Gottehrer the buses really weren't that important to him. Gottehrer recalls their conversation.

Allah told me later that the buses for the picnic weren't so important to him; he was more interested in learning whether I would keep my word. On the street, that was all that mattered. You might be a pimp, a thief, out on bail or hiding from the police, but you would still deal straight in the community if you wanted to keep your self-respect, and if you wanted others to respect you. "Word," said Allah, pausing for his followers to add the last phrase with him, "is—bond."[304]

Barry Gottehrer passed his first test and gained the confidence of Allah. From that point on he started spending more time in Harlem. He seemed to be fascinated and taken by the "street life" and spent the majority of his time in neighborhood bars around Allah and his comrades. Gottehrer:

Passing the street test with the buses gained me Allah's confidence, although most of his friends still had some doubts about me. I took to spending three or four nights a week at the Glamour Inn. I'd leave word that I could be reached on those two pay phones. Although I like to drink, I cut down to a few rum-and-Cokes each night to keep my mind clear in case of trouble. So we would drink for a while, and then Allah and Justice would move outside on the streets to gamble while I stood around and watched or talked with people. I'm not a gambler myself; I shot craps once or twice in the streets to see what it was like. Allah would go home to his wife or to one of his more recently acquired common-law wives, and I would hang out with Al Murphy, a street hustler and gambler five or six years younger than I. He had been in and out of trouble, mostly for gambling. The first time Allah had introduced us at the bar, we happened to discover that we shared the same birthday, and that was the beginning of a strong bond between us. He was easygoing, a good-looking man with a mustache and a beard and a ready smile.

Murphy and I used to spend time at the after-hours joints in the neighborhood, drinking, watching, talking, meeting people, trying to convince them that Lindsay cared, that riots would hurt the poor far more than the rich, seeking their help should we ever need it to restore order.[305]

Totally immersed by his surroundings, Barry Gottehrer became a permanent fixture on the Harlem scene. He boastfully thought himself to be at "home."

It became my block. There was a bar on the corner, the Wellsworth, that I didn't patronize often; it was a rough bar several notches below the Glamour Inn. Right next to it was the empty store front that would become the Five Percenters street academy. There were a couple of shops---a hairdresser, a fish place. The Glamour Inn was in the middle of the block.[306]

Now that Allah had the Mayor's man in his corner, he gained more political clout to obtain benefits for his young organization. Allah made use of this working relationship and the two developed what appeared to be a genuine friendship.

Chapter 16
Allah's Street Academy

**L-R: Knowledge God, Akim, Hashim and Gy'kee
in front of the Urban League Street Academy circa 1967.**

Early in the summer of 1967, a storefront named the Urban
League Street Academy opened at 2122 7th Avenue, Harlem,
New York. The Urban League sponsored the Street Academy for
the exclusive use of the Five Percenters. A Director and two
teachers were provided and the academy took in its first
students.

Perhaps anxious to mark their territory, on the first day
someone painted the number 7 on the door, symbolizing God in
Five Percenter numerology. The two Urban League teachers
came with a proposed academic curriculum but unfortunately
their set of courses wasn't able to match the zeal of the young
Five Percenters. Because of the inability to connect with Five
Percenters and their ideology, the teachers and curriculum took
a pounding from the start. As a consequence, the young Five

Percenters felt free to challenge some of the information given from the teachers the Urban League hired.

Within the Street Academy most of the kids were called by their Five Percenter names out of respect for their culture and to reflect their "universality of godliness." Many students had their own predetermined ideas and believed that the most important thing was to have knowledge of self and recognize their godhood. So that meant everybody is God; (except when Father Allah was present then no one pressed the point). Witnesses say at those times there was only one Allah.

The Urban League and the mayor's aide realized that the Five Percenters were no more dogmatic than any other religious organization, but no less so, and eventually a different solution was found to the problem of their education. It was decided that the kids could attend different street academies, a few to each school, for their more conventional education, while Allah kept his store front open as a place for kids to study Five Percenter philosophy or just hang out. Barry Gottehrer remarked that they were fairly successful at keeping drugs away from the place for the first few summers. As this was a difficult task considering the drug dilemma that plagued some of the youth just months earlier. A Five Percenter recalls how Allah consistently addressed this issue:

> There were times when Allah put everybody out of the School, and let us come back in one by one. Some were into Heroin (including some of the First Born). The Father didn't want us using Heroin and announced that, "DOPE IS FORBIDDEN TO THE 5%", at a Parliament. So some who were disobedient and continued to use Heroin would try to fool the Father about what they were high off. Allah would go off on them. Allah would go off on us for our other iniquities too, in order to straighten us out. HOWEVER, he loved us dearly in spite of our transgressions.[307]

Minus the challenges, the Street Academy became a haven for the young organization. Allah utilized the building as his headquarters in hopes of one day making it an institution. It became a neighborhood clubhouse for Five Percenters, and sometimes a place for young people to sleep. In the daytime different classes were held in relevant subjects pertaining to Five Percenter teachings.

After securing the Street Academy, the Five Percenters approached Mr. Gottehrer about having the Universal Flag of Islam made up as pins or chains to wear. By this time, the Five Percenters already painted a picture of the Universal Flag of Islam on the front window of the Street Academy. Mr. Gottehrer recalls:

> The Five Percenters designed their own insignia: a black numeral 7 and a star within a larger black and gold star. They asked me to get the design made up into small pins to wear on their shirts or hand on a chain around their necks. There was resistance to this at City Hall. With an official medallion, who knows, they might start a recruitment drive, they might start a war. A medallion would give them legitimacy, the argument ran. I wasn't sure how one defined a group or how you took away that sense of themselves if they already had it, or whether it was useful to try. I got the pins made up and the Five Percenters did not start a war. As a matter of fact, some of the kids did commit crimes and some went to jail, but some got through school—the most successful went through Harlem Prep—right now there are twenty or thirty Five Percenters enrolled in college. The first graduated in June.[308]

Universal Flag Pin

After having the Universal Flag pins made, Allah instructed all the Five Percenters who received one to write their names on the roster. This ritual would take on a spiritual meaning.

> And our flags which was made up for us, first compliments of the Mayor of New York City, brother John V. Lindsay, which by the way everyone signed their full righteous and honorable names and addresses, righteous because we live righteously and

honorably because we bring honor to the name by living righteously.[309]

The city continued to subsidize more picnics and field trips for the Five Percenters. Allah's organization participated in additional summer programs, one of the better ones allowed the Five Percenters to receive free plane rides. Barry Gottehrer recalls:

> One excellent program the Five Percenters took advantage of that summer was offered by different airlines: they took kids from poor neighborhoods up on hour-long plane rides. Their route covered the five boroughs, Westchester County, up into Connecticut and back. It was the first time the Five Percenters had ever been on a plane. They were ecstatic. American Airlines ran some flights, and had different Black and Puerto Rican personnel describe their jobs and offer assurances that there was a future in working for the airlines. Word of the plane trips and picnics spread. Young people came from all over to become Five Percenters. By the end of the summer, Allah's Parliament had an attendance of eight or nine hundred. Allah was delighted, the police were delighted, and the kids got plane rides.[310]

Plane Rides

Allah took advantage of another government program that provided free plane rides to city youth. This was one of the highlights of the different activities offered to the Five Percenters. Allah boarded at least one of these plane rides along with Mayor Lindsay and the Five Percenters. The plane ride made the newspapers in an article that appeared in the New York Times on August 6, 1967.

> A 12-year-old boy from Harlem looked down 2,000 feet from his airplane seat beside Mayor Lindsay yesterday and said excitingly:
> "Man! We've seen it on TV and in the movies, and now we're doing it – we're flyin'!
> He was one of 86 youngsters from Central Harlem who went aloft for an hour yesterday in a four-engined Eastern Airlines Constellation. As the guests of the airline, they flew over the Hudson River as far as West Point, then back and over parts of Brooklyn, Staten Island and New Jersey.

Two buses took the youngsters to La Guardia Airport from 126th Street and Seventh Avenue shortly after 9:30.

Seated well up front of the first bus was Mayor Lindsay, who joined them after an hour-long walking tour of Harlem that began shortly after 7:30A.M.

Herbert Miller, an official of the Urban League of Greater New York, who also accompanied the group, said that while most of the children on the flight were of grade-school age, there were "Five Percenters among them." He described them as "a militant group of teen-agers, mostly school drop-outs, who have chips on their shoulders which we are trying to remove."

The Five Percenters took their name from their contention that only 5 per cent of all Negroes are militant enough to redress their grievance against what they felt was ill treatment by whites. However, according to Barry Gottehrer, assistant to the Mayor and head of the Summer Task Force, about a year ago they abandoned their militance.

Mr. Gottehrer said, "They now believe that everyone—whites and Negroes—should learn to live together in harmony and understanding, and that is precisely why we are working with them in every way to help themselves."

The free airplane ride, Mr. Miller said, is part of a program intended to "ease them back to school and to steady employment."

And although there was an atmosphere of gaiety in the 95-seat aircraft, some of the older teen-agers reacted glumly to the hospitality of Eastern's personnel.

Many of the older youths accepted soft drinks from stewardesses but without so much as a nod of thanks.

When asked how they were enjoying the flight, a group exchanged affected quizzical looks and then laughed loudly. Asked for their names, most of them offered two first names. One name, they said, was their "righteous" name, and the other was their "honorable" name. The "righteous" name was always a Mohammedan name.

The idea of the free airplane rides was the Mayor's, who inaugurated it late in the spring as one approach to forestalling trouble in slum areas.[311]

The city officials and programs had come through for the Five Percenters. Allah showed true appreciation for what the city did and the fact Mayor Lindsay and his administration at least appeared to be interested in the welfare of the children.

Allah established a relationship with Mayor Lindsay that lasted throughout his career.

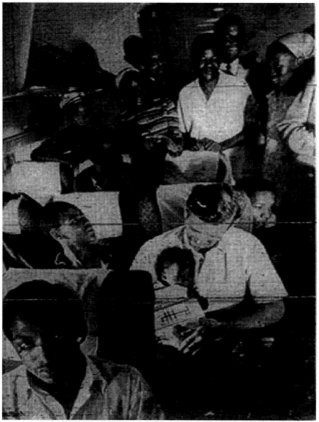

Allah (in background) along with Mayor Lindsay (holding baby) on airplane ride with Five Percenters.

Outside of government-assisted programs, Allah persisted to host his own programs as well. Most noticeable were the monthly Universal Parliaments that swelled in attendance. The Parliaments expanded throughout the boroughs of Manhattan (Mecca), the Bronx (Pelan) and Brooklyn (Medina). Making progress, another Street Academy opened in Brooklyn. Infinite Al'jaa'maar U-Allah expounds:

In 1967-68, our first Street Academy was opened on Jerome Street and Sutter Ave., in the East New York Section of Medina and it was ran by the Gods, Barmeen, Ubeca Islam, Cream-Allah, Doctor God Latik, A-Islam, Spanish Wise-Allah and Janai-Allah from East New York, also the half-original Monik Allah.

These brothers used to hold Rallies in Miller Park, which was located on Bradford st. and Blake Ave, in East New York, also at the Good Shepherd Center located on Hopkinson Ave and Sutter in Brownsville. These were very good brothers, who were teaching Islam in that day and time, the way they receive the knowledge from Allah, because these brothers spent a lot of quality time with Allah, when they went to Mecca, to see the Father.[312]

The Bronx wasn't to be outdone. A Five Percenter recalls when one such Parliament was held in the Bronx the same year and different Five Percenter institutions began to sprout. Shabazz Adew Allah:

One of the first Parliaments that was held in Pelan (The Bronx) was in 1967 at 173rd Street in the Crotona Park right off the Fulton Avenue entrance.

As a young Five Percenter from Pelan, I felt very proud and energized that Allah (The Father) would come to build with Us.

There was many things that He taught on that day, for it was a time when the Nation was rapidly growing throughout the borough of the Bronx.

As early as 1966, brothers and sisters from the Bronx area had started converting Club Houses into Learning Houses. At one time these "Club Houses" was used soly for gang meeting places to lay plans to rob, cheat, do drugs and steal.

Now these same wayward kids was being converted and the Club Houses was being used by the Five Percenters to teach and educate young brothers and sisters into the knowledge of self as propagated in the lessons, and teachings of Allah (The Father) in person to Us.

The Father praised Us on the good job that we were doing in Pelan (The Bronx), however the Father also gave warning to Us regarding the infiltration into our Nation by a people whose only desire is to cause disagreement and confusion amongst His Five Percenters.

The Father manifested that the C.I.A., the F.B.I., and other agencies of the State and Federal Law Enforcement Units are watching and planning against Us, for they do not understand."[313]

Allah was wise in his endeavors. Although he recognized and appreciated the mayor's help, he was fully aware of the Government's overall agenda to thwart his plans. Abu Shahid recalls a conversation he had with Allah about this concern. Allah had already expressed that they tried to "pay him off."

> When I had got out I met with Allah and he said, "John, they offered me a whole lot of money but I wouldn't take their money." I asked The Father about it and he said, "Because if I would have taken that money they would own me."[314]

Allah persisted to teach Islam to all children he came in contact with. He took even greater strides to strengthen the Five Percenters presence in the communities. His work soon paid off as the community and government officials began to recognize him for his efforts.

Through perseverance and hard work, the Five Percenters began to receive positive publicity from their one-time adversaries. Their earnest efforts prompted Senator Edward Brooke to visit the Urban League Street Academy to see the Five Percenters at work. Bayard Rustin, a civil rights activist and Director of the A. Phillip Randolph Institute accompanied the Senator. The two were impressed by what they saw. Mr. Rustin wrote about the details of the visit. The result was positive press lauding the endeavors of Allah and Justice (Akbar). The article entitled "The Five Percenters" appeared in the Amsterdam Newspaper on September 9, 1967, captured the moment:

> At one time, the word Five Percenters used to be feared in New York. In fact, in 1964, New York Newspapers ran stories to the effect that the Five Percenters were one of the most violent youth groups in the city, But these could not have been the same young men I saw two Fridays ago, shortly after they had been visited and interviewed by Senator Edward Brooke, in his capacity as a member of the President's anti-riot investigating commission.
> The young men Senator Brooke and I saw were a quiet, earnest, and disciplined group of students hard at work in the Street Academy at 2122 Seventh Avenue, a school they had

helped create for themselves – an experience they had never seen before.

They seemed interested in nothing than, in learning English, Mathematics, Arabic, Hygiene, and Science. And from what I was told of their extra curricular activities – United Nations field trips, Swimming, Film Discussions, and Track and Field Athletics – they seemed anything but potential recruits for urban street violence.[315]

The article went on to extol the virtues exemplified by the young Five Percenters at the Street Academy. Allah and Justice (Akbar) were commended for their roles. Mr. Rustin continues:

We might all applaud the Street Academy as one of the most constructive contributions to the maintenance of stability in the Harlem Community, as well as creating an effective instrument for the rehabilitation of young men who might otherwise have no choice but the streets.

Chief credit for the founding of this institution goes to two young ministers (Allah and Akbar) and to the Rev. Eugene Callender of the New York Urban League. Several months ago, the two young ministers, approached Howard Bennett, a Harlem community worker, with the idea of establishing a school to help the Five Percenters. Some of them had been expelled from school, some of them were dropouts, some hadn't gone to school at all, and some had had trouble with the police.

Bennett suggested a meeting with other Harlem community leaders, but, as he said, "none of them got the message." In disappointment, Allah and Akbar turned to the Rev. Callender who liked the idea and gave it the financial support of the Urban League. They financed the rental and refurbishing of a storefront at Seventh Avenue, installed school furniture, and hired and paid Herbert Miller to serve as its educational director.

Besides their academic and social activities, the Five Percenters told me that they pursue a spiritual ideal of "helping others discover a true knowledge of themselves." They said they are "neither anti-white nor pro-black," and are convinced that they "possess the power to be perfect in all our ways and actions."[316]

Senator Edward Brooke and Bayard Rustin appeared to be extremely impressed by the conduct displayed by the group. So much so that the academy received their stamp of approval as an institution in synch with the Anti-Riot Commission's aims and objectives. The two shared an admiration for Allah and Justice (Akbar) future plans for the organization. Mr. Rustin:

> Allah and Akbar are so proud of the success of the school that they are thinking of throwing its doors open to any young person between the ages of 14 and 19, whether or not he or she is a member of the Five Percenters. Plans are also underway to open a similar school in Brooklyn.
>
> One of the finer tributes I can pay to the establishment and success of the Street Academy is to say that should trouble break out on the streets of Harlem, I am convinced that the Five Percenters certainly won't be available.
>
> As one of them told me, "we are definitely not interested in rioting; the education we are getting is far more important to us."[317]

The words spoken by the young Five Percenter would one day soon be put to the test during the long hot summer years.

Chapter 17
Otisville

RALLY in Medina
circa 1968 Gods
DID THE
KNOWLEDGE
ONLY socializing
AFTER Rallies NOT
DURING

Young Five Percenters at a Rally in Brooklyn in 1968.

Riding the waves of public accolades for his Street Academy, Allah didn't confine himself or his work to one building. He reached out and made personal appearances at other institutions that had a sizable enrollment of Five Percenters. One such surfacing was at a correctional facility called the Otisville Training School for Boys. On November 15, 1967, Allah held an audience with the Otisville staff that included a Reverend, other counselors and Five Percenter enrollees.

Speaks at Otisville Training School For Boys

The Otisville authorities recorded the interview. It is speculated that this is one of the rare if not only audio recordings of Allah. The now historical interview was very candid as Allah honestly answered the interviewers questions and didn't shy from any subjects. He expressed his views on religion, politics, war, education, health, male-female relationships, drug abuse and his teachings. He talked about his experiences as a war veteran and his stay at Matteawan. While many points made were amicable, just as many appeared controversial. Some more complicated answers required deciphering as interviewers pressed for clarification.

Amid the more affable topics included Allah's method for jail prevention for children, *"Protect the child, show him if he doesn't do right he is going to jail,"* he remarked. Along the same lines he mentioned his goal to stop crime. *"I'm going to stop crime. Do you hear me? The houses and buildings you all are in-- you going to have to give these to children as dormitories for the children. I'm going to stop crime. Hitting people in the head, killing people, that's a shame,"* he exclaimed.

He broached the subject of health as he shared part of his litany of acceptable and non-acceptable foods to eat. *"Don't eat butterbeans. Don't eat collard greens because it belongs to the weed family. Eat the white cauliflower because it melts in your mouth. The spinach, you eat that. The broccoli, you eat that. Cauliflower, you eat that. There are certain foods you have to eat. You've got to save your own (what) self! No medication can save you,"* he admonished.

On Armed Forces

Allah spoke quite a bit about his experiences in the Army and related it to America's current situation, which at that time was engulfed in the Vietnam War. In surprising instances he seemed patriotic, especially in the case when he appeared to favor the United States role in the Vietnam War.

> I'm not against the United States for sitting over there in Vietnam. They should kill all of those people who do not want to build and become civilized and have a sanitary country. Because the earth is supposed to be built on. I'm not against it. Your people protesting against it...[318]

It's easy to imagine this opinion was an affront to other Black Nationalists and to anti-war movements popular in the 60's. Many would perceive the statement to clash with his former organization, the Nation of Islam. But perhaps this is where Allah formed his opinion. The Honorable Elijah Muhammad took an even harder stance on the war and wasn't sympathetic to either Vietnam or the United States. In his "Theology of Time" lecture series, The Honorable Elijah Muhammad explains the NOI stance on the Vietnam War.

There have been wars that you have gone into with the devil wholeheartedly because you don't know yourself. You are blind, deaf and dumb to the knowledge of self. Therefore you say, "Come on come on. Let's go to Vietnam and kill them so that America can rule." You didn't know what you were saying because you didn't know yourself. The root of the Vietnam War with America is to let these two countries fight. They both are enemies of God.

Let them fight and let them kill each other off as many of each other as they can. The Christian and the Hindu. Vietnamese people are Hindu and you have no right whatsoever to try to make yourself a Hindu by trying to defend them. But you did not know that. Now I am telling you that they are no kin to us...The Hindu people are not any brothers of ours, just because they have black eyes or because you see some nature part of the man looking like you. They are not for us at all...

That old Hinduism has been taught by them, so God taught Me, for 35,000 years...They have been on this planet for 35,000 years trying to destroy God's own Religion, Islam. He is an old enemy of God. God lets him and the Christian fight each other because He intends to get both of them...Allah put them to fighting because He doesn't want either one. He lets American Christians kill Hindus, and the Hindu is killing American Christians too...[319]

The Honorable Elijah Muhammad pressed even further as he made clear his personal desires were one with the God he represented.

I wish that my God would allow Me to get one of these nuclear bombs and one of these planes, to fly over their territory. I would show you how long they would be here. I don't love you (Hindus) myself. I don't care if you kill Americans and they kill you too. I don't love either one of you.

The fight over in Vietnam is not a fight of yours. It is not a fight of mine. My God is not trying to save the Vietnamese people nor the white Americans who are fighting them. We have nothing to do with that. I will tell anyone regardless to who it is, or regardless to how wise he is, that he is not wise enough yet to tell Me to go to Vietnam to fight. When it is over, America will be running.[320]

Perhaps not as adamant on the subject as his mentor, Allah took what seemed at first to be a favorable approach to participation in war. Maybe this was due to his personal experience as a war veteran. He made clear he didn't have any restrictions against Five Percenters joining the Army. In fact some of his statements appeared to champion the suggestion. As evident in these three Otisville interview excerpts used as references. Allah:

(1)"Now I was in the Army. I don't teach them not to go in the Army. I went and I came back. I saw action. I got the Bronze Star. I got all these medals. Now I came back home. I didn't benefit from it as by such as luxury, but I did benefit by knowing how to teach a man. To teach a man--to make a boy a man. This is what I did"...

(2)"I don't tell them not to fight for the country. They can. Fight! Now by me telling them children that, all my people are against me because they thought that I was suppose to came out when I come from Matteawan to join them and I haven't joined any of them yet...

(3)"If United States don't wake up, then they going to lose. Because you got babies in the Army now and that's what you need in the Army, those seventeen and eighteen year old boys. That's what you need in the Army. They got to be well qualified though. They got to be more tougher than they are...[321]

The puzzling aspect of Allah's statements is its apparent conflict with the traditional perspectives of Black Nationalists and/ or Black Muslims. It has never been popular for Black extremists to encourage Blacks to join the Service or to fight wars for white America. Albeit, Allah was his own man and stood on his convictions, the difficulty for the observer was trying to identify those convictions. His unorthodox approach made it difficult but in many cases he chose the side of the Black militant perspective too. The Nation of Islam, of which Allah received the basis of his teachings, presented their outlook in their mandate entitled "What The Muslims Believe."

> WE BELIEVE that we who declare ourselves to be righteous
> Muslims, should not participate in wars which takes the lives
> of humans. We do not believe this nation (USA) should force
> us to take part in such wars, for we have nothing to gain from
> it unless America agrees to give us the necessary territory
> wherein we may have something to fight for.[322]

One could possibly find Allah's statement below in reference
to this subject to be in harmony with the said above NOI
mandate. Toward the end of the Otisville interview Allah
addressed the subject again perhaps clarifying his earlier
statements.

> I want them to live in America and help protect their country--
> if the government does right by them. The ones that help
> protect the country-- the government should do right by these.
> The ones that don't-- the government should do away with
> them.[323]

Perhaps "if the government does right by them" was the
qualifying factor and the challenge to the Government to gain
Allah's consent for a Five Percenter to join the Service. In that
case some could argue it a long time coming. Those who shun
going to war for America point out another example in which
Allah praises the Muslims who refused to fight in the war. In
the same interview Allah praised perhaps the most famous
Muslim militant of them all Muhammad Ali for not going to
Vietnam.

> And Muhammad Ali is sure showing a good example. Here is
> what he's fighting. Don't want to go to the Army. He is a very
> intelligent man. There are many Muslims who went onto jail.
> He's fighting it. He's fighting to show the world that he gets
> not only recognition from the Muslim World but from your
> people too from all over the country.[324]

During the time of this interview, Muhammad Ali was the
Heavy Weight Champion of the World and a Muslim follower of
the Hon. Elijah Muhammad. At the height of his boxing career,
Muhammad Ali was drafted to fight in the Vietnam War and
refused to enter the draft based upon his Islamic beliefs. As a

result he was stripped of his title, banned from boxing and possibly facing a jail sentence. At that time Muhammad Ali was appealing the government's decision. Later he took it to court and won. His boxing status was reinstated and he went on to reclaim his title once again. Per his Islamic guidance from Elijah Muhammad, public battles and his own sport acumen, Muhammad Ali eventually became the most recognized man in the world.

As Allah referenced, many Muslims in fact went to jail rather than registering for the draft or joining the "white man's army." The Honorable Elijah Muhammad was even arrested along with his son Emmanuel Muhammad and other loyal followers for refusing to go to war. Elijah Muhammad says of his arrest:

> I was arrested on May 8, 1942, in Washington, D.C., by the F.B.I. for not registering for the draft. When the call was made for all males between 18 and 44, I refused (NOT EVADING) on the grounds that, first, I was a Muslim and would not take part in war and especially not on the side with the infidels. Second, I was 45 years of age and was NOT according to the law required to register...
>
> In 1943, I was sent to the Federal Penitentiary in Milan, Michigan, for nothing other than to be kept out of the public and from teaching my people the truth during the war between America, Germany, and Japan. This war came to a halt in 1945 when America dropped an atomic bomb on Japan. And the following year, in August, 1946, I was released on what the institution called "good time" for being a model prisoner who was obedient to the prison rules and laws...
>
> In the year 1942-1943, according to reports, there were nearly a hundred of my followers sentenced to prison terms of from 1 to 5 years for refusing to take part in the war between America, Japan and Germany because of our peaceful stand and the principle belief and practice in Islam, which is peace.[325]

Child Ethics

In other more revealing moments Allah revealed his methodology of providing the children choices in controversial life decisions. In the interview Allah suggested radical and unorthodox approaches to drug prevention and other vices for young teens. Perhaps this radical suggestion was due to his recent struggles to curtail drug use amongst his group. Allah compared his methodology in contrast to that of the Muslims.

> Protect the child. Show him where if he doesn't do right he is going to go to jail. Just like the Muslims, I'm not against anyone but they are really teaching their children not to smoke, drink or do anything to inquire other people to follow their standards. Now, I don't teach the child not to smoke— I teach him to get the understanding (what) of it.[326]

The Muslims of the Nation of Islam (NOI) are well known for their high standards of refinement and discipline. This included abstinence from pork, alcohol, tobacco and drugs. Muslim children are also taught this at home, mosque and in their schools. If a Muslim child were caught smoking or drinking it would result in direct disciplinary action. The results are evident in a Malcolm X quote, *"we don't have any delinquency, either juvenile or adult"*... Allah used a different approach to get across to the children than that of the Muslims. Realizing in many cases, when a child is told, "not to do", it usually sparks his curiosity and pushes the child to "want to do". So Allah preferred to "teach" rather than "preach" to the children. If the child were given the knowledge (actual facts) and wisdom (information) about smoking and drinking, he would gain an understanding on the matter, enabling the child to use his own intelligence to make the wise decision.

Delving deeper into the subject, Allah spoke about stronger vices. Another controversial perspective was his statement on narcotics and its purveyors:

> I am not against narcotics--because the only way to stop a narcotics pusher from bringing it into this country he must start using it his (what) self. Sending a person away that doesn't cure him. I used it. That didn't cure me. I stopped my (what) self![327]

Allah implied that justice for the narcotics pusher would be to make him taste his own medicine. This way he would suffer first-hand what his victims suffered, learn his lesson and stop selling narcotics. This coincides with the biblical teaching "An eye for an eye, and a tooth for a tooth," a standard teaching in

Judaism and Islam. Allah confessed to having used narcotics in the past. One would naturally assume that he experimented with narcotics prior to joining the NOI in 1960 as narcotics are forbidden to its members. Allah goes on to say that he stopped himself from using narcotics. Allah taught a philosophical concept aptly called *"Self-Saviour,"* which means that ultimately an individual is responsible for saving himself. Many Five Percenters refer to this concept as "external refinement vs. internal refinement". External refinement is when you are compelled or coerced to become refined through an authoritative figure over you such as a captain or lieutenant. Internal refinement is when you are refined through your own will and desire. The latter is considered to be the greatest in the eye of a Five Percenter. The reason being if you have external refinement and the authoritative figure is removed, the subject tends to go back to their former vices per lack of supervision. This could be why Allah says, "sending a person away doesn't cure him". On the other hand, when one has internal refinement he has empowered himself through his own will and desire to master self. Therefore, he becomes sole controller of his own destiny, thus he becomes a "Self-Saviour". This is perhaps what Allah meant when he says "I stopped my (what) self". The Honorable Elijah Muhammad taught this same concept. In his writing Elijah Muhammad said in reference to Master Fard Muhammad, *"A Saviour is Born to teach us the knowledge of how to become self-saviours. When a man has the knowledge of himself, he's a self-saviour."*[328]

In order to make his point, Allah wasn't apprehensive about using himself as an example of overcoming drug addiction. In the interview he admitted his use of cocaine while fighting in the United States Army.

The United States of America taught me to be disciplined. They also done taught me how to raise me an Army. They self educated me to lessen all my trials and tribulations. I have done messed with cocaine. I have done messed with everything but LSD and I'm not going to take any of those trips. Did I gain from using cocaine? Yes. I know what it do for me. I start bringing it on my ownself because I just had it because it freezed me. So, by you going to all these other countries getting all these results and bringing it back in. I know this because they made me [sic] a doctor. No harm did it to me. Every doctor talking about that 'that's no understanding'. So, so it helped me in the Army.[329]

Allah's detractors subordinate him as a mere mortal because of admitted drug use and other vices not usually attributed to those who claim divinity. Whether he still actively indulged has been debated amongst critics and supporters. Shahid M. Allah addressed Allah's critics:

Almighty God Allah came and put His Five Percent in tune with Allah's Mathematics! He did this so that we could chart our own destiny, as a navigator uses the science of astronomy to guide his ship at sea. When a ship is at sea there are all sorts of debris floating around in the water, which the ship will pass over. Some of the debris may stick to the ships sides. However, the ship will still reach its destination. There are those who continue to remark that "Brother Clarence 13X smoked cigarettes, marijuana, sniffed cocaine and gambled. Therefore, He could not have been Allah!" To this I say emphatically now-cipher (no)! Allah had to pass through many "waters" in order to see His Five Percent safely to the other side of living mathematics.[330]

Arguably, Allah's most contentious method was the suggestion to subject children to vices as a means to justify an end, as evident in the following statement.

I don't teach them not to drink, I teach them to keep their mouth (what) shut! And listen and learn. Because I might tell them to drink to do exactly what I want them to do-- to get to that man I want to get to. Just like the United States teach the FBI. I might make one a dope addict--if he strong he'll come out of it. Because there are many dope addicts that come amongst the people to catch who they want and not to use it. I know this.[331]

Some Five Percenters who were a part of this process bear witness to its end result. To many they would have never got involved with anything positive if it had condemned their juvenile lifestyle. Allah in befriending the youth and participating in certain activities caused the youth to gravitate toward him.

> Yes the Father waddled in the mud with the lot of us. So true, it was the only way to get his point across to many of us, had he not utilized that means of facilitation there might have possibly been no "Five Percent Nation." He, however didn't intend for us to stay waddling the mud when he lifted us and himself out of it, that was to be the end of it. We choose to fall back into the mud and continued to waddle and many still do to this day[332]

Shaamguadd elaborates on a similar point in his Sun of Man publication. In speaking of Allah's methodologies relating to alcohol and drug reform he says they were notified of these possible methods in advance.

> He taught me that you should not bare false witness against your Brother or be quick to sit in Judgment over him because as ye Judge, so shall you be judged because ALLAH has given certain Jobs or Missions to certain Brothers that we know nothing about, and that He alone is the Best Knower of those who have carried out their Mission. And always Remember that a truly Righteous God can act like a Alcoholic, however, the real Alcoholic could not be a True God, that A Real God can act like a drug addict, however, a real Drug Addict could not be a Righteous God, that A Real God could act like a Crazy Man, however, a truly Insane Man could never act like a God and Remember the MASK that an Actor wears is apt to become his FACE if he is not truly RIGHTEOUS, because the Final Proof is in the RIGHTEOUS PUDDING!!! Which is ALLAH'S RECIPE for SUPREME INDIGNATION.[333]

Both Allah and Shaamguadd's statements hint at espionage tactics comparable to those used by the FBI. This also tallies with urban legends that circulate throughout the Black revolutionary genre about guerilla warfare. A prime example of this is found within Black Cinema, in a movie based upon a novel entitled, "The Spook Who Sat Behind the Door." This novel is about a Black Man scouted and recruited by the government to work for the Central Intelligence Agency (CIA). The Black character playing the "spook" had successfully completed rigorous mental and physical training at the CIA Academy. He graduated at the top of his training class. He then went on to work for the CIA and after a short tenure the "spook" decided to resign. The "spook" then went back to the city and recruited young men from street organizations and founded a revolutionary underground movement. The character taught and trained the young soldiers in military tactics by using the knowledge and experience he gained as a CIA agent. Among other tactics, one of his ploys was to have his followers act as drunks and dope addicts in the daytime but function as a high-powered militia at night. The "spook" also found himself in the middle of a riot in which he prevented by calming the potential rioters down. The "spook's" movement grew in influence and effectiveness until the police force placed him #1 on their list of undesirables.

There are interesting comparisons between Allah (the Five Percenters) and the fictitious character called the "spook" and his movement. (1) Like the character that played the "spook" Allah received military training from the government while in the United States Army. He also received additional military training "FBI style" as a Fruit of Islam (FOI). (2) Both Allah & the "spook" were discharged from their respective positions within these organizations and set out to do work amongst the youth. (3) Both recruited inner-city youths for a revolutionary youth movement. (4) Both trained the youth. As cited in a New York Daily News article about Clarence 13X Jowars (Allah) and the 5%, *"According to the police, Jowars has had as many as 500 black followers ranging in age from 15 through their early 20's, in training at one time, teaching them black militant philosophy and tactics of street crime directed against whites."*[334] (5) Both Allah and the "spook" were placed at the top of the list of dangerous militants by the civic authorities. As Barry Gottehrer stated in his book called the Mayor's Man..."The police knew Allah—they put him at the top of their list of dangerous militants in New York City". (6) Both Allah & the spook played major roles in the preventing of riots in their cities.

On Religion

In the interview Allah voiced his disdain concerning the traditional teachings of Jesus and Christianity:

And the Five Percenters, I'm teaching them that they can't go on religion because religion has never did anything for them. Like my mother, she said, "Jesus, Jesus, Jesus," I know he over there in Jerusalem dead in the earth because he hasn't showed me nothing.[335]

The Five Percenter view of the historical Jesus varies from the current Christian tradition. The Five Percent teach that Jesus was an original Black man and that he was a prophet of Allah that taught Islam, not Christianity. The Five Percent teaching on Jesus is based upon a NOI lesson written by the Honorable Elijah Muhammad entitled "Isa's History." In this lesson it teaches that Jesus real name was Isa and he was not born through an Immaculate Conception, but rather his biological father was Joseph. When Jesus was born, Joseph sent Mary and Jesus to live in Egypt to avoid persecution by the Jews. When Jesus turned 14 an old wise prophet found him and informed Jesus of who he was and his mission. The old prophet gave Jesus three lessons on mental telepathy that he would need to complete his mission. Jesus then walked from Cairo, Egypt to Jerusalem, Palestine to teach the Jews Islam. The Jews rejected Jesus and hated Jesus for what he taught. After teaching them for 22 years, Jesus discovered that according to the scriptures the Jews had 2000 more years to deceive the nations of the earth. Jesus then decided to give his life for the truth (Islam). The authorities put up an award for Jesus capture. Two officers apprehended Jesus while he was in front of a store teaching a small crowd of people then slew him. When Joseph heard of Jesus death, he came and got the body from the authorities and secured some Egyptian embalmers who embalmed Jesus body to last for 10,000 years. They buried Jesus in a tomb in Jerusalem. Legend says his body lies in the tomb in such a manner that it reflects in four different directions and no Christian is allowed to see Isa's body unless they pay a price of $36,000 and get a certificate from the Pope of Rome. According to this lesson Muslims guard the tomb of Jesus and all Muslims can go see the body of Isa at anytime without charge.

While on the topic of religion Allah addressed a concept held by some members of the NOI that W. D. Fard is God alone. Some Muslims solely attributed divinity to Fard and were reluctant to apply the same principles to them selves. So Allah reasoned if you depended on Fard alone, how do you account for his absence. Allah:

..Elijah says W. D. Fard is God. Where is he?[336]

Ironically the same question was asked of the Honorable Elijah Muhammad in another interview. When asked about what happened to Fard Muhammad and why he disappeared the Honorable Elijah Muhammad responded:

The Messenger: Well that happened like this; after He had given to me what He wanted to give to me as the teachings and the work of preparedness of our people that it was not necessary for Him to remain here among us, so He taken His leave, as it is said in the Qu'ran that the people is not worthy that God remain among them, but He makes a messenger of that people, that through that messenger He will reach the people- through Him, and the Bible verifies the same. And so He left and He give me a hint about His return, but now there is just as much prophesy that He will return or He will not return as there is of his returning, because the Bible says He will send His angels and they will take care of the gathering of his people. I don't expect Him to return in person, not like that, because there is too much for us to look forward to that He will not, it is not really necessary if He is going to send His Own people as they refer to angels to gather the believers of my people, it's not necessary."
Question: Where did He go and where is He now?
The Messenger: "Well that is something that we actually cannot say. If one would open up such truth, as the truth of God to the people, I do think that He's within His rights to stay out of the sight of the people until He has won everything to Himself as the Bible refers to it like this, that He's something like a king looking for a kingdom. And that He go and He visit the people, then He leave the people, goes away and wait until the time when that He can secure the kingdom. Then He returns to the people that He had made Himself manifest to. So I think that's a pretty good answer." [337]

Traditionally, the Five Percenters do not deny the claim that Allah came in the person of Master Fard Muhammad but the Five Percent do believe that Master Fard came to empower the Black Man to be God. Instead of depending upon Fard alone,

one should utilize his teachings to become independent, as he was independent. The Five Percent necessarily do not anticipate his returning or second coming in the physical form but they (Five Percent) do not deny this either. It is clearly left up to the conjecture of the individual.

Events

On a lighter note, during the interview Allah announced his plans to host a Christmas party for the Five Percenters (which is a surprise because neither Muslims or Five Percenters celebrate Christmas). Following is Allah's quote from the interview:

> "Listen. Barry Gottehrer was trying to get us a building so we could have a Christmas party. Now, Muslims don't believe in Christmas. I would like to have a Christmas party for the Five Percenters. You understand that?"[338]

Though his reasoning wasn't understood at the time Allah stood by his conviction and worked to make this event a reality. As a precursor he attended Mayor Lindsay's Christmas party at City Hall the following month. Mr. Gottehrer recalls a scene from the party where Allah was holding a discussion with Burt Roberts (who was then District Attorney for the Bronx):

> I will always remember walking into a small corner room at the end of the party to find Allah, the city's super militant from Harlem, and Burt Roberts, in a discussion with an audience that included an assistant chief inspector of the Police Department, a deputy fire commissioner, a teachers' union leader, a Wall Street broker, a Hollywood director and several community leaders. "I have no problem with your being Allah," Roberts said, a big grin on his face. "You can be Allah all you want—in Manhattan, in Queens, in Kings County. But you come up to Bronx County and tell people you're Allah and I'll have your black ass in jail."[339]

Despite the jesting, many would be surprised that Allah attended a Christmas party, let alone the thought of hosting one. As stated earlier, he was well aware that Muslims did not believe in Christmas. In fact, he didn't believe in it either. Nevertheless, he still held a Christmas party for the Five Percenters that same year although with an ulterior motive in mind. Shaamguadd explains:

There were X-mas or Kwanza (whichever you preferred) parties every year. Every year all the major stores donated toys for the children, ours and those in the community. Not little toys either, I'm talking about bikes and cars the babies could ride. They had so many toys they couldn't even carry them and everybody had a ball, young and old and there wasn't anything religious about us. Our Father Almighty God Allah said he wanted us to keep having those Xmas parties (and I have documentation to prove he said that) if you think I am pulling your leg. Ask some of the older Gods about those Xmas parties. I look around at some of those parliaments and it makes me think, you, Gods have forgotten or never learned how to have real fun, seeing the smiles on the children faces when the Father was giving out the toys, used to warm my heart. Those smiles was worth more than all the tea in China. Like the Father used to say "If you ain't about that then keep you dead behind home." Don't deprive the children and anything that brings the spirit of the Human Families together once a year for Peace, Love and Happiness. It can't be bad fun.[340]

Outside of special events, the Universal Parliament became a special event in itself. More thought was put into the Universal Parliaments to make them more constructive like the Muslim Bazaars Allah used to attend. Shaamguadd:

We will also do what we can to reorganize our Universal Parliaments so that they will be more informative and entertaining as they were when the Father was hosting them, where the public was invited, we showed films, we had public speakers, telling us where there were educational and employment opportunities.[341]

It was these kinds of actions that began to develop and mold the character of the movement. Education was a priority and as one Five Percenter told the Amsterdam Newspaper, "we are definitely not interested in rioting; the education we are getting is far more important to us." As fate would have it, these words spoken by the Five Percenters would shortly thereafter be put to the test in the face of one of history's most infamous assassinations.

Chapter 18
Five Percenters to the Rescue

Allah and his Five Percenters on the streets of New York City.

On April 5, 1968, the heralded civil rights leader, Dr. Martin Luther King, Jr. was assassinated in Memphis, Tennessee. This tragedy sent shock waves of rage throughout Black America who Malcolm X a few years earlier described as "a powder keg waiting to explode." The initial reaction of the Black masses was to riot, loot and burn down the stores in their vicinity. That night in Harlem, large crowds swelled on the streets, ready to destroy their own communities.

The Five Percenters were out in force under the leadership of Allah. Recognizing the tendency of the people to react violently without any consideration of who, where, what or how to execute their desire for justice, the Five Percenters policed the streets of Harlem to help reinforce peace. Their gallant efforts helped avert a riot that would have left Harlem devastated. As recalled by a Five Percenter:

In April of 1968 Dr. Martin Luther King was assassinated in Memphis. America's black ghettoes blew up into full scale rioting. Black people were enraged and ready to fight. Dr. King was a man of peace and they killed him too. All over this country Black communities exploded. Everywhere there was burning, looting, and destruction of 'WHITEY ESTABLISHMENTS'. In New York City the BOOM was expected to be the loudest and hardest, there was only minor damage done. Largely because of the bond between the Mayor (Lindsay) and Allah. This was the time when people began to call Allah a 'TOM' because he did not condone rioting. Allah felt that destroying our own community (which is what the riots did) was not an intelligent answer to our problems.[342]

This peacekeeping accomplishment brought national acclaim to then New York City Mayor John Lindsay and his administration. In reciprocation, the Mayor's administration had to extend credit to the real heroes of that day – Allah and the Five Percenters.

Following is a memoir of three of Mayor John Lindsay's aides David Garth, Sid Davidoff and Barry Gottehrer recalling the suspense of that night. Their assertions attest to the major role Allah and the Five Percenters played in curtailing the potential erratic situation.

Mayor's Aides On The King Assassination

David Garth, who was a Communication Consultant for Mayor Lindsay, recalls the moment.

The night that Martin Luther King Jr. got shot, half the city was threatened with violence. Harry O'Donnell, the mayor's press secretary, got a hold of me and I got John Lindsay, who was attending some Broadway play with Mary. I picked up John and we picked up Harry and the three of us, and I think one bodyguard, went up to 125th Street and I though my life was over.[343]

Sid Davidoff, an aide to Mayor Lindsay, provides his account of what happened that fateful night.

We went up to a bar we hung around called the Glamour Inn, where there was a group called the Five Percenters. And the

Five Percenters were as bad as anybody could be. Their leader was a guy named Allah. He had been in the Matteawan State Hospital for the Criminally Insane. He had ALLAH stamped on his underwear, and his big thing was "Hey, they let me out, so I must be Allah." He was one of the great street-corner guys. So we got a hold of Allah.

Thousands of people were coming on the street. It was a situation that could have sparked any minute. Both the police and I felt it was just too dangerous to bring [Lindsay] up. But Lindsay didn't care. He was going. All the police could do was advise us that they had no control.

Our job was then to put around him whoever we could to protect him. The Five Percenters were clearly the people who preserved the peace in that neighborhood, by surrounding Lindsay. I mean, people just didn't fool around with Five Percenters. The police just stood on the fringes.

When the people turned on the TV that night—and it was being carried all over the country—people started to see that they had a man who cared, who was out there, who felt as badly as a white Protestant could feel who ran a city of so many blacks and minorities. Who was reaching out for them. I think that's probably what saved the city.[344]

Barry Gottehrer, one of the chief assistants to Mayor Lindsay, and probably the most involved as his liaison to community leaders provided an outlook on the chain of events.

The height of John Lindsay's national stature came in the month following the King assassination. That was when virtually every city had major riots. In New York, we did not have riots, and we began to get tremendous amounts of publicity: "What did Lindsay do differently in New York?" It was the result of all these things that had been done for two or three years, without much fanfare.

We identified very early on—in each of the districts potentially troublesome during this summer—kids or young adults who had leadership ability. They could be pro-police, could be anti-police. They could hate John Lindsay. But these were people whom we could call on if something happened. There might have been a list of 200 of them. Probably, there were 20, 21 communities, ten in each. Through money we raised from the private sector, from the Urban Coalition, we set up a youth leadership program and hired these kids. In effect, we had on this private payroll kids who had leadership ability in every one of these communities.

...During a period of two years, we tried to establish relationships with those people before an incident happened. We tried to find out what their demands were before the riot. We tried to understand where they were coming from.

As a result, when those first real major things happened in '68, like the King assassination, and the press went running up to Harlem to talk to Charles Kenyatta, to talk to Jim Lawson, to talk to Allah, who by then was a hero—son of a bitch—they didn't attack the city and John Lindsay. They'd say, "There are real problems. Everything is terrible. But we have been working with him for a year, trying to solve them."[345]

Allah reciprocated the compliments. He was impressed with the Mayor's attempts to bridge the gap. So much so that on numerous occasions he confessed this openly to the public:

That's why Mayor Lindsay is the greatest Mayor that ever been. He tell the truth. He's a great Mayor. He gets out with the people. [346]

All involved remembered this historic episode for years to come. It was another public victory for Allah and his young organization. City government officials and national media recognized the Five Percenters' role in preventing a riot. The New Yorker Magazine carried an article on the entire event called, "The City On the Eve of Destruction."

The City On the Eve of Destruction

Mayor John Lindsay was attending a musical on Broadway when he first received word that Dr. Martin Luther King Jr. was assassinated. The then mayor scurried out of the theater headed to Gracie Mansion accompanied by his aide David Garth and a Black detective-bodyguard named Ernest Latty.

Understanding the enormity of the situation, Lindsay panicked as he thought: A wild reaction, all over the country...and here. Coincidently or maybe not, Mayor Lindsay was strategically involved with the past writing of the President's Riot Commission Report. His involvement earned him criticism for his notable remarks, *"We've got to admit we're in danger of breaking into two countries, black and white,"* but now, he was facing the real life situation as he remarked, *"They called the Commission Report too strong. But look what's happened."*

The Mayor met and conferred with his other aides Barry Gottehrer, Harry O'Donnell, Sid Davidoff and Pablo Guzman to implement a contingency plan over the next few hours to keep the city calm. Lindsay felt compelled to go up to Harlem in light of strong reservations about how angry Harlemites would react to "white faces."

Police and fire trucks were dispatched to Harlem and to Black areas of Brooklyn in full force. The Urban Task Force satellite officers (that consisted of mainly community leaders and neighborhood contacts) were put on notice by Barry Gottehrer. The contacts reported that things were looking "really uptight: bad," in Harlem. However, what was equally important to the Mayor's administration was that the structure set up by the Task Force was functioning and still in place. This gave the Mayor and his staff the needed confidence to travel uptown to directly face the people of Harlem in their efforts to prevent a volatile situation.

Upon arriving in Harlem, the mayor was advised by central Harlem's 25th police precinct that they lacked the needed manpower to control the possible uprising. In spite of the warning, Mayor Lindsay continued with his plan and began his walking tour at Eighth Avenue and 125th Street. In instances where the people congregating recognized him the Mayor began talking to them in groups, expressing his sympathy about King's death.

As he proceeded on, the mayor made a pit stop at a building across from Frank's on 125th street to meet with Harlem representatives. After the 40 minute meeting, the mayor resumed his walking tour with Latty, another plainclothesman and Barry Gottehrer following close behind. A street corner figure named "Bobby," joined the Mayor's entourage as a self appointed bodyguard. This drew some concern from the entourage because they thought it attracted trouble.

Part of the walking strategy was to help defuse 125th Street; the Mayor was to walk north, drawing some of the crowd to 126th (in the direction of Allah's Street Academy). The decoy to 126th Street was working, but the crowd was getting too big. To top things off, at the CCNY campus uptown, several hundred students were watching a concert when somebody ran into the auditorium and announced that Dr. King was dead.

Leaving the auditorium in the middle of the concert, almost 200 students, began marching down Convent Avenue to 125th Street, until they ran into Lindsay, who asked them to disband.

"We stopped," said one student in the march, "but other people had followed us, you know, and then they started this." The "this" was sporadic looting, rock throwing, and starting some of the 50 fires that were reported that night.

All almost looked lost until from a distance, Lindsay seen Allah and the Five Percenters coming in full force. Not sure of what was about to happen, Lindsay could only pray for the best. To his relief, the Five Percenters came to enforce peace on the scene. As reported in the New Yorker Magazine:

> Lindsay kept going. To one side, he noticed Allah, militant leader of a black youth group called the Five Percenters, signaling his followers north to help the de-fusing plan. This was a result, the Mayor knew, of Allah's contact with the Task Force, but parts of the press still equated any militant with "hate whitey." Later, store looters were identified on television as Five Percenters.
>
> Allah and some Five Percenters were in the crowd close to Lindsay, and rivalry was developing over who was to shepherd the mayor. There was a little jostling and complaining. Gottehrer was pushed aside roughly, but Lindsay seemed in no more than normal danger. Bobby got separated, and gave Allah a brutal shove on his way back. The Five Percenters – who believe their leader is really Allah, the god: many had no permanent person in their lives until he took them off the streets – threatened to beat up Bobby for this insult. He replied by calling Allah something quite not audible, but obviously foul. Others in the crowd had to keep the Five Percenters from tearing Bobby apart.[347]

Although the melee wasn't directed at Lindsay, he decided that this was his cue to leave. However, in the given situation he was too far away from Dave Garth and the prepared get-away car. Percy Sutton, a Black man and Borough President of Manhattan had his limousine near by, and urged Lindsay to use it. Bobby wisely jumped in too, with the bodyguards, and the walking tour was over.

The Mayor and his staff headed back towards Gracie Mansion through Manhattan streets that were emptied by terrified whites.

The next day, Mayor Lindsay and his staff returned to Harlem to carry on their campaign of peace. High on his agenda was to stop to extend his appreciation to Allah and the Five Percenters for their contribution in preserving the peace the previous night.

...At 3:30, Lindsay was back in Harlem for the fourth time in 18 hours, making a stop at the Glamour Inn to thank Allah and his militant Five Percenters for their peace-keeping help. Until last year, the police had considered Allah's group of 800 or so followers to be a violent and anti-white group. Then Barry Gottehrer discovered that what Allah really wanted was some education for his young disciples, and an occasional bus trip to the country. (When Gottehrer, surprised at this small demand, actually arranged for a chartered bus for a day's outing, Allah said it was the first time any white man he knew had kept his word.) Lindsay stood in their favorite hang-out, thanked them warmly, and everyone looked very proud.

Walking cast along a busy but peaceful 125th Street, smiling and shaking the dozens of hands stretched out to him, Lindsay bore little resemblance to the man who, according to the press had been forced out of Harlem last night by hostile, bottle-throwing crowds who wouldn't let him speak. *The New York Times* gave the impression that the animosity between Allah and his followers and Bobby had been directed at the Mayor; possibly because they didn't know who Bobby and Allah were. (Besides getting them a bus, Barry Gottehrer gained the confidence of Five-Percenters last year by getting the *Times* to change a story referring to them as "anti-white"; a misjudgment made by one reporter, and repeated by the journalistic custom of writing from clips.)[348]

Whether or not Mayor Lindsay's second tour of duty in Harlem did anything to pacify or relieve the tensions of Black Harlem is uncertain, but it did little for their white counterparts in downtown Manhattan. "Rumors," noted the Riot Commission Report, "significantly aggravated tension and disorder in more than 65% of the disorders studies...." White New Yorkers was still ostensibly missing from the daily New

York evening scene in fear of Black retaliation. Rumors were rampant on both sides about Black retribution and further White aggression.

Some choice ones circulated that night in white Manhattan: "Negro veterans from Vietnam are planning sniping attacks to panic the city."

In Black Manhattan, the rumors were more fearful. "They've got concentration camps all ready for us in New Jersey."

One thing for sure, the Black militants in Harlem did not waiver on their stance. Militants warned and urged the people to be prepared to go on the offensive or at least be prepared for a white attack. The militants had harsh criticism for anyone that opposed their views and directed some of their animosity toward Allah.

That night black extremists distributed a mimeographed sheet accusing Allah – mainly because of his peace-keeping activities of the night before – of atrocities like "cutting black women" and being in league with the whites. (The sheet also called for the murder of all black policemen.) There was another, older animosity, Allah, considering himself the real Allah, believed Elijah Muhammad should be *his* messenger, which the Black Muslim leader felt was sacrilege.[349]

At 8:30 Friday night Jesse Gray, Harlem tenant leader, stood at the corner of 125th Street and Lenox, urging people to wait for the sound truck to arrive so the rally he had called could begin. Jesse began: "The white man got of the Mayflower shooting and killing Indians...and now it his objective to kill off the Black People."

The next speaker was Charles Kenyatta, aka Charles 37X, who left the NOI to become the commander of a para-military group he founded called The Mau-Maus. Earlier that evening, stirred by the Mayor's personalized tactics in Harlem, he had manned a sound truck to break up a gang of kids threatening trouble. Later, in a television interview, he said: *"Lindsay helps because he'll leave Gracie Mansion on five minutes notice, and he'll talk to the bottom of the barrel."*

Now, Kenyatta addressed the crowd. He used the rhetoric of revolution – *"If this city must be flattened, let's do it downtown. And I'm telling all of these leaders to put up or shut up because a revolution don't have no leaders. This country is up for grabs. We gonna move this thing until King's dream turns into a nightmare."*

Livingston Wingate, a former director of Har-you-Act, was the next speaker. He spoke to an authentic emotion in the crowd, *"King was simply waving the constitution right back at them....And they snatched it, put it in their hip pockets and shot him down...and he wasn't the first either."* His voice trailed off as the crowd took up the chant: *"We want Whitey! We want Whitey!"*

While the crowd was being whipped into a frenzy, Allah was at his Street Academy holding an audience with the Five Percenters.

Allah Speaks At the Street Academy

A reporter taped bits of his speech as Allah passionately addressed the Five Percenters. Allah gave a fiery speech captured in a magazine article:

"Them people out there are stupid. They're just showing my Five Percenters they are blind, deaf, and what?"

"Dumb!" came the chanted answer.

"We are the only ones who are civilized. We are trying to save our people's lives. The revolution must come from within. Clean up your homes first. Our job is to civilize the what?"

"Uncivilized!"

He turned to one member, "If a Five Percenter don't listen, the penalty is what?"

"Death!"

"There is no teaching in a bar. Bakar Kasim and two sisters got busted over in Brooklyn where they were teaching. Some cops come messing with them, and one of the sisters bit him on the hand. He shouldn't have had his hand on her, and the man should have took his head! Now, you know we believe in peace, but I didn't say if we are attacked don't fight! You say you are God, and a sister is in jail for biting a policeman on the hand. Malcolm said he'd rather have the women than the niggers. And another thing I taught you was to respect the American Flag. You respect any what?"

"Government!"

"I'm telling you, my Five Percenters have got to be healthy, strong and good what?"

"Breeders!"

"But you're healthy all right. Some of you brothers outrun a reindeer or a telephone call every time a riot starts. You ain't ready! You can't fight no guerrilla warfare here, because you don't plan nothing. You have to buy from the white man. Why? Because when his superiors give him the orders, the penalty for disobedience is what?"

"Death!"

"You're out there looting. My wife had to go downtown to get some milk. Some brothers are looting. Don't say you're a Five Percenter if you gonna do it!

"You say you the civilized of the world. The white man won't give you this government until you have given your word you will not destroy him."[350]

While delivering his tirades to his young organization, Allah was quickly becoming subject material for the local and national media.

Whatever the black extremists were writing about him, Allah himself seemed monumentally unconcerned. A wiry, squinting man of forty, whose real name is Clarence "Puddin" Smith, he had lived through a break with the Black Muslims. (He once was a member.) Through a murder attempt that left a bullet lodged in his chest. (Allah was "on the list" after Malcolm X.) And through a stay in the Matteawan State Hospital for the Criminally Insane, which probably got him out of a murder rap of his own. (He was allowed to plead insanity. After all, he thought he was Allah.) That bullet, plus an intricate mathematical catechism perfectly memorized by all his followers, proves that he is 'Allah,' the Islamic word for God. To those who doubt him, he says, "If I'm not Allah, who is?"*

In his storefront academy at 127th Street and Seventh Avenue – financed by the Urban League, which is preparing several of his followers for college entrance—he conducted a Friday night teaching session.

"Peace!" about 80 of his followers shouted ritually as he entered. He stood in the middle of the floor and began a tirade, punctuated only by the words he left out, which the Five Percenters efficiently filled in.

Allah is one of many youth leaders, some in contact with Urban Task Force and some not, who helped keep the peace Friday night, along with such groups as Harlem CORE, the NAACP and Haryou's Neighborhood Boards. When the meeting was over, Five Percenters began filing out past a life-sized photograph of the Mayor and Allah. The inscription read, *To Allah, thanks a lot, John V. Lindsay.*'[351]

It was this same autographed picture among other actions of Allah that found disfavor with certain segments of the Black community. This caused other militant factions to attempt to attempt an attack on Allah's efforts. Other militant factions in the community took more extreme action to get their point across to Allah:

....picture if you will a picture blown up almost to the full size of the school window. Any where from the size of thirty six by sixty [36' x 60'] or forty eight by seventy two [48' x 32'], a huge picture with Allah God and John V, Kindsay embraced in brotherhood. The Mayor had autographed the photo thanking Allah for this help in quelling the near riots during the weekend of the assassination of Dr. Martin Luther King Jr. This picture caused many of stirring conversations, however it was only one set of individuals known as Kufere Muslims, a black-seed brother by the name of Azeam whom acted out the agitated conversations.

Remember this is the year five=1968 where the popular status-quo- is hate whitey at all cost. However Allah<God defied the popular status-quo- and embraced an unpopular stance. This provoked and sort of antagonized many of the black leaders and revolutionaries even many in our nation. This brother Azeam had a long lasting feud with the Black Messiah going way back to his name was Karream. When this brother along with a Captain stormed the strong hold on 129th street in an attempt to assassinate the first born, [then Karream and Al-Jabber] meaning the Black Messiah and Prince Allah stopped them in their tracks, however that is another story. This brother Azeam crashed into the school and shot up the picture tore it down and destroyed it, at the time only a few young brothers were in attendance. They went up side the young brothers heads and roughed them up.

Now when the older Gods got wind of it, there was a fierce retaliation, my beloved brother god, first born Uhuru lead the assault, he managed to get this guy Azeam and return the favor in spades. The blessings of Allah was with him for it was the only thing that saved his life.

The picture was never recovered, it stays vivid in my mind, Allah and Lindsay embraced in brotherhood.[352]

Allah Attends Governor's Peace Vigil
Blacks weren't the only ones holding a meeting in the wake of the King assassination, White New Yorkers decided to hold a

memorial for King that Sunday in Central Park. New York State Governor Rockefeller, a member of the white elite, called the mass meeting. Invitations were sent to Black leaders and organizations (including Allah and the Five Percenters) of Harlem with hopes they would attend.

Uptown groups that were invited did attend the event amongst a sea of white liberals and politicians in attendance such as Governor Rockefeller and Mayor Lindsay. Allah shared the podium and spoke some words:

> No longer could we be acted upon, (pawns for the political more astute) Thus his statement; "I am neither Anti-white, nor Pro-Black" at the podium in Central Park, New York, NY. After the march to demonstrate unity after The Assassination of Dr. Martin Luther King Jr. Another verbal exhibition of his ability to transcend boundaries, worlds.[353]

For the most part, the event was a success. Given all the anarchy and tension in the air, everything ended peacefully. As recorded in the New Yorker:

> The ceremonies ended in peace and surrealism. Rockefeller put his arm around the shoulders of Allah, a Baptist minister thanked Kenyatta in a prayer, Percy Sutton referred to Mayor Lindsay as Mayor Wagner, and a Du Bois Club anti-Vietnam banner for Dr. King was held up for an admiring white photographer from the *News*.
> There had been no riot.[354]

This was a shining moment for the New York political machine and Black grassroots organizations. Other cities throughout America weren't so lucky. In more than 40 American cities, there had been outbreaks serious enough to warrant martial law and the use of heavy weaponry by the Federal Guard troops. The article sums up the reasoning for New York City's success:

> In New York, the biggest city, the place where everyone expected it to happen: There had been no riot.
> The real reason was in the ghetto-dwellers themselves. Restraint in the face of despair came from unexpected people,

unexpected groups. Other reasons were smaller, more tenuous, but just as important: sweeping the streets; chartering a bus; arranging a reconciliation between Bobby and Allah (as is now being done); setting up an all-night phone system; having the Task Force ready to go; and electing a mayor who can show himself. "If Lindsay hadn't gone up there," said one black militant, "if he hadn't known who to talk to, we might have felt a lot different."[355]

Thanks to the efforts of Allah and the Five Percenters, what could have been certain disaster, ended in peace. From arguably initiating the long hot summer riot in 1964 and to now stopping a potential riot in 1968.

The Five Percenters had appeared to come full circle. Originally viewed as blood-thirsty headhunters of whites in the city, they now were the ones who saved the city from burning in what easily could have been a riot. No one was to thank for this but Allah and the efforts of The Five Percenters in their community.

Chapter 19
Juvenile

**Allah (Center) and Justice (left) with young
Five Percenters Dubar, Hasheem and Siheem.**

Allah seemed to be a very bitter, angry man, who became
impatient with the questions that members of the staff directed
to him. He later expressed his amazement to Miss Kaminski
and myself at the "narrow mindedness" and "inability of so-
called professional social workers to accept or even try to
understand" the reality of a philosophy that is foreign to
middle-class idealists.
-- T. Evans, NY Parole Agency.

In the wake of the King assassination, Mayor Lindsay and
Governor Rockefeller publicly recognized Allah's role in
maintaining order in Harlem. In the aftermath, Allah received a

commendation for his social work in motivating Black youth to pursue educational opportunities in academic and vocational trades. Most notably, was the Five Percenters participation in youth leadership programs that was unrivaled by any other grassroots organization. The mayor's public declaration gave Allah an heir of legitimacy in the eyes of other civic and social organizations, thus opening up institutional doors for him to walk right through. This he did as he marched on with his mission to reach disenchanted youth.

Professionals in the correctional industry took a strong interest in Allah's curriculum because of the many young inmates converting over to Five Percenter ideology. This created a demand for penal institution personnel to learn more about the movement. Allah was offered invitations from youth correctional facilities throughout New York. He welcomed these offers as part of his personal interest to reach troubled teens, especially those in prison. A Five Percenter addresses the subject:

> Our Father (ALLAH) taught to us that the job of the devil is to get the wrong-doer. So that if a brother or sister violate the law and put in prison to serve time, that brother or sister are called upon to build to reform their deviant behavior. For our Father (ALLAH) have taught us to respect the law of any cipher that we may enter willingly or non-willingly. He also taught us to stand up for the principle of righteousness, and "Don't forget the brother's in prison."[356]

Indeed the Five Percenters were popular in jail, and it became an omnipresent force for teens fresh out on parole. Many parole officers discovered their clients had embraced the teachings after being released from prison. Consequently, on May 22, 1968, Allah was invited to hold a conference with the staff of a parole agency to help clarify his teachings and answer questions. This visit was documented in a memo from the department heads a month later. The memorandum was from a T. Evans and Judi Kaminski with the subject titled "Allah Five Percent" to a Mr. Schwartz dated July 25, 1968. The memo opened up with the purpose of the meeting.

On May 22, 1968 Allah, who is also called the Father or Teacher, along with two of his followers, Omika and Dumar, appeared at a meeting in the library of our agency. Allah is presently the leader of primarily an all black group, known as the Five Percenters.

The meeting was planned when Mr. Evans and Miss Kaminski became deeply concerned over the lack of awareness of some members of the staff regarding the Five Percenters group, it's leader, philosophy and community action. After attending a Parliament at the invitation of one of Miss Kaminski's parolees, who is deeply involved in the group, we took it upon ourselves to request Allah to speak with our staff. Omika and Dumar volunteered to accompany Allah.

The staff discussion at the meeting was to revolve around the philosophy, beginnings, some personal background of Allah himself, and community action of the 5%ers. However, contrary to plans, Allah briefly touched upon each topic before the meeting was open to questions from the staff. Attendance at the meeting by Youth Parole workers and Supervisors, was good, but not nearly in proportion to the number of parolees who have come in contact with the 5%ers group, and are members of the group. Miss Kaminski and I feel that the lack of a better attendance by members of the staff and supervisors is a very pertinent factor indicating a lack of interest by staff in an acknowledgement of the forces and groups influencing and attracting our clients in the communities.[357]

The authorities appeared intrigued by Allah but noted his sense of frustration with their staff. During the interview he vented his disappointment about people who criticized his moves. All wasn't grim however; one remarkable point was his outline of a true Five Percenter.

Allah seemed to be a very bitter, angry man, who became impatient with the questions that members of the staff directed to him. He later expressed his amazement to Miss Kaminski and myself at the "narrow mindedness" and "inability of so-called professional social workers to accept or even try to understand" the reality of a philosophy that is foreign to middle-class idealists.

During the initial part of the meeting, Allah spoke about the attacks on the 5%ers by members of other black, more militant groups such as the Black Nationalist and the Muslims. These other more aggressive groups have called the 5%ers "Toms"

- 273 -

because the 5%ers do not preach or practice the hatred of "whitey", burning of their own buildings, looting etc. Allah went on to say that the "true" 5%er does not steal, rob or use drugs (marijuana, heroin, cocaine, etc.). The "true" 5%er is the Blackman. The "true" 5%er is a poor righteous teacher. Allah then offered his services, in cooperation with our agency, to those parolees who are declaring their allegiance to the 5%ers and yet are violating the basic teachings of the group.[358]

The presentation was followed with a Q&A session for the parole agency's staff. It was at this point that Allah and accompanying Five Percenters were able to help clarify specifics about his teachings.

The question part of the meeting was very informative because it gave the staff an opportunity to express their feelings and to find out more about the 5%ers' philosophy. A question was asked of the status of women. The answer was given by Omika, a parolee. Omika acknowledged her acceptance of Dumar as her master, and her role of inferiority as his wife. According to the 5%ers' philosophy a man and woman are married by virtue of their desire to be so and through ceremony, and do not conform to the traditional American way of marriage of simply paying a $3.00 fee to get a license.

Birth control is not advocated by the 5%ers. A woman is meant to be a breeder of children, in order to increase the population of the 5%ers group. Her other main function is to care for the home and husband.

Certain foods are taboo to the 5%ers. Some of these foods were mentioned, but the one in particular was that of pork. There is a fear that if the 5%er eats pork, trichinosis will invade his spiritual entity.[359]

Another significant aspect of the Q&A was what appeared to be Allah's foreknowledge of his departure from the organization. His forewarning seemed prophetic as if he knew he was destined to "leave" soon.

Allah consistently mentioned that he would leave the 5%ers soon but would or could not state where or when he was going. He further mentioned that it was important for each 5%ers to be knowledgeable in the 5%ers' teachings, because they would have to continue the teachings after he leaves. With a change in leadership, several possibilities exist. One is the possibility of the rise of a younger, more militant leader, a leader who might be less patient and more bitter about the system of the country. Once Allah mentioned to me that most of the 5%ers have been in some type of prison or institution.

There is an educational system in which the "Lessons" are taught at the Academy (7th Ave. between 126 & 127th St.) by Allah. Members of the group who have progressed further in the "lessons", teach those less enlightened then themselves. Bus trips have been arranged on Saturdays, taking 5%ers to Bear Mountain for picnics, as well as to other public facilities around the city.

Miss Kaminski and I feel that the meeting was informative and gave food for thought in order to learn more about the group. Allah extended an invitation to his academy to those interested in learning more about the movement and observing the interaction of the 5%ers as a group."[360]

These informative sessions for the parole agencies served its purpose. Allah's personal appearances at these kinds of institutes became part of his itinerary to spread the word. Allah's stature grew and he was invited to speak to other organizations per popular demand. But his mainstay was teaching at juvenile correctional centers. Such as the impact he made at a Bronx facility named Spofford Youth House in September 1968.

There are other changes, less tangible one, involving relations with staff and inmates, Mr. Nottage says, and he mentions the Five Percenters.

The youths are members of a group of several hundred in the city who have their own rules and rituals and follow the leadership of Clarence 13X, a former Black Muslim whom they call "Allah."

A few years back, the Five Percenters, who kept aloof from the 95 per cent of the black population, were regarded by the police as a militant, antiwhite group and were held responsible for muggings and possible some homicides.

But their style has changed, according to Barry Gottehrer who heads Mayor Lindsay's Urban Task Force and who meets regularly with the group's leaders. He says they are encouraged by Allah to avoid violence and interracial conflict and urged to study.

Mr. Nottage agreed to the Five Percenters' request that they be allowed to hold meetings or parliaments on Sunday when other youths attended religious services. He also permitted Allah to visit the boys. He talked to them on the ballfield one Sunday and he has been invited back.

"If the boys in this group do not want to eat pork, we don't force it on them or make them get along on bread and milk for a meal," says Mr. Nottage.

The reaction to these approaches from Five Percenters varies: A 14-year old youth who uses the Arabic name of Salik spoke freely about himself and the society. He said he had broken his parole and stayed out at night and that he was "accepting the punishment without complaint."

Of the center, he remarked, "This place is all right now that they give us some kind of consideration so we can keep our rules."[361]

Minister Akbar Muhammad (then known as Larry 4X), assistant to Minister Farrakhan at Temple #7 in the late 60s, said he used to see Clarence 13X in the jails when he was teaching. Minister Akbar:

...But he started giving the little children...and I watched him, now, I was a salesman here in Harlem, so I knew all of these streets, I used to see him, and when I would go to jails to teach I would see him in jail.[362]

Additional Achievements

It appeared Allah was at his zenith in life with a list of accomplishments to add to a growing resume. Some sources say Allah began to receive international acclaim as mentioned in a 5% article. Beloved Allah:

In the two previous years from June of 1969, Allah had risen to become a very powerful figure within New York City. He had achieved a kind of international celebrity status; Canadian television did a story on him; a sociologist from Sweden interviewed him; and he had plans to meet with Chinese representatives on June 20, 1969.[363]

Perhaps the greatest commendation came to Allah from up high. Many believe that the highest honor is when a student receives recognition from his teacher. If that is the case, Clarence

13X received the highest honor when he received a form of vindication by his benefactor -- The Honorable Elijah Muhammad. Contrary to the speculation of some, it is reported the Honorable Elijah Muhammad expressed appreciation of the fact that his former student taught the NOI lessons to the youth in the street. Minister Farrakhan reports a conversation he had with the Honorable Elijah Muhammad on the subject:

> Brother, I'm telling you that the Honorable Elijah Muhammad respected those young brothers and sisters who called themselves the Five Percenters. Now, I talked to the Honorable Elijah Muhammad about that group that was developing in New York and now spreading. He said, "That's good. That is good. They are studying that which Allah (referring to Fard) questioned me on and they are studying my answers to those questions."[364]

Whether this information was known to Allah or not, he pressed on with his mission in good faith. It was his faith that would help him face the jaws of death.

Chapter 20
Back To The Essence

Allah was riding a tidal wave of success as he approached the final chapter in his life. There was one more chilling aspect of his existence that he was destined to fulfill. Allah often reminded his Five Percenters that he would not be long amongst them. He hinted at his death on several occasions. He would tell them things like, "If I die I don't want you standing over me crying because if I could I'd reach up and slap you." Or he would say to a friend while gesturing to one of his Five Percenters, "If I die tomorrow and he keeps teaching, how can I be dead?" A Five Percenter recalls a conversation he had with Allah on the subject:

> In 1969 Allah would say, 'When I die", often. I was living in the school at the time. So I would hear him say it often. One night I asked him why he kept saying that. I told him that if someone was going to kill him, let me know who it is, and I would take care of them. He smiled. But he could see from my mannerism, that hearing him say he would die bothered me. After that night he began to say "When I go home" or "After this year" which went right over my head.[365]

In 1969, Allah began to prepare his Five Percenters for life on their own without him. He spoke with all of them in the Street Academy one by one and told them what their qualities were and left each of them responsible for a function for the movement. Allah even revealed to some of the Five Percenters that he was no longer to be considered their "Father" but rather they should view him as their "Big Brother." As Born U-Allah reveals:

> "The Father "would have some of us in the back of the school, and He had already manifested to us that He was no longer our "Father", but He was our "Big Brother."[366]

In any case, Allah felt the powers that be were very near to assassinating him. Allah would attempt to prepare his Five Percenters for his dreadful premonition.

> For the next few weeks Allah would lecture us constantly. Looking back now, I know that he was ARMORING us for the task to come, once he left us. He would drill us constantly. Not only in our lessons but in the lessons of life also. Today I see that Allah KNEW that he would be leaving us soon, so he implanted ALL of himself (GOD) in us. To make us strong for the job ahead of us.[367]

In fleeting moments Allah would say to his young followers that he had to leave them because "the only way to attract the killer is to give blood," and that "if they ever needed him all they had to do was come together."

On the morning of June 12, 1969, it is reported that Allah awoke at the home of his mother. He told her it was the best rest that he ever had. She asked Allah if he could get out of where he had to go. Allah replied, "when they are ready they will kill you." He hugged and kissed his mother goodbye and departed. His mother had a premonition when he left—he would never return.

Allah Has Been Shot

That same evening Allah was at his Street Academy speaking with his Five Percenters. He spoke with them well into the night about male-female relationships. Those who were present still remember the euphoric feeling that he left with them. A feeling so good that they didn't notice that the yellow cab driver whose taxi Allah got into wasn't the cab of his brother A-Allah who he usually left with. A short while later, the man known as Allah, was gunned down by seven bullets in East Harlem. As remembered by a Five Percenter present at the Academy that night:

> June 13, 1969 was a Friday. You know what they say about Friday the 13th. Allah was shot in the elevator of 21 West 112th Street, in a Harlem Housing Project. It was early in the morning (before sunrise) and the building was that of his wife (Dora) and his children. Allah was with us before this happened, in front of the Street Academy. He was talking to us all of Thursday

evening...Soon other Gods were drawn to the cipher. Allah continued to born his soul to us that night...The Father spoke well into the morning hours, it was around 2 or 3 A.M. when he bid us peace. He walked to the curb and got into a Taxi Cab. It was a yellow cab. Prince Allah ran to the Cab before it pulled off and handed something to the Father.

We all stood in front of the Street Academy, after he left, reflecting on what he had said. After a while we began to dispurse. ISLAM UBEKA-LADU-ALRAHIEM and myself went into the Street Academy (where we were staying) we lock the door and went to rest.[368]

What appeared to be any other night at the Street Academy ended with a rude awakening. They received the dreaded news that no one wanted to hear. Allah had been shot to death.

As I dozed off I was looking forward to Allah coming the next day, waking us up. He did this daily. When we heard his key open the door, we all got up and cleaned up the school. Just as I went into my rest a God banged on the door screaming 'ALLAH HAS BEEN SHOT, HE'S DEAD, HE'S DEAD!' We jumped up and ran to the door. It was Raheem a God from that project. We had to find the key to open the Two Way Lock. We finally got the lock open and ran outside. We ran to the corner of 127th Street and one of the Guys that knew the Father took us downtown in his car. When we got to 116th Street and Lenox we jumped out of the car and ran the rest of the way.

When we got to the building it was cordoned off by Police. As we went to enter they stopped us. Then one of them said, "These are his Sons let them in." Some of the Gods had already seen the body and were standing outside the building, many of them were distilling. I entered the elevator with ISLAM UBEKA when we looked at the body UBEKA distilled. I remember one of the things Allah had told me, "When I die I don't want y'all crying for me." He said, "If I could I would jump up and slap somebody crying over me!" I did not cry. Eventually all of us headed back to the school. We were all in a daze, which slowly turned to anger. We headed to the school with the determined idea that ALLAH IS GOD AND HE CANNOT DIE![369]

Many Five Percenters were devastated at the loss of their leader. Although Allah attempted to prepare them for this day, nothing he could say or do would prepare them for the shock of this hour.

June 13th, 1969, The questions were self centered, the reality was there laying before me. How?, Who?, Why?, my protector, my champion, my mentor, my hero, my Father, my GOD! And my best friend who never let me down. When I cannot resolve an issue, I had a tendency to internalize the issue. Feelings of guilt-fear (false expectations appearing real), proceeding anger turning into rage. Sisters wailed-the brothers stood silent, tears running from their eyes, I stood powerless, the powerlessness overwhelming. The positive reinforcements of the brother only last momentarily. "He Lives". "ALLAH CANNOT DIE", I say this because my Earth, who knew him, ask me in private, "how can GOD die?", and I became enraged, I lost it. This was trauma and it was act out in many ways. I think most of the sisters handled it better than we did, because they would cry, and cry together, we suppressed it, now and then we discuss that last evening, never really talking about our own true feelings. (TRAUMA) I have read about a few great men and women, I have only known one, and for me, he is the Greatest! Every son should feel that way about his father, and know the unconditional love we received. This event in our lives helped to shape us, The Nation, And it is time to LIVE.[370]

Not only were the Five Percenters distressed by this tragedy but it also impacted the Mayor's aide Barry Gottehrer who had grown close to Allah. Mr. Gottehrer:

It took me a moment or two to concentrate on what Murphy had just told me. "You get down to the project, and I'll call the police," I said. I misdialed once, then twice. My hands, which usually were steady, now shook. My body was still half asleep but my brain was racing. Allah, that mad man from the Glamour Inn, who believed that he couldn't die who had become one of my closest friends, was dead. First Kenyatta, now Allah—who would be next? What the hell was I doing all in the middle of this. Then, suddenly, the policeman was on the line, speaking matter-of-factly, in a flat tone. Yes, the story was true. Allah had walked toward the elevator on his way up to visit his wife, Dora, and was blown apart by seven of the eight shots that were fired by one or more unknown perpetrators.[371]

Mr. Gottehrer vividly describes the details from the dreadful death scene:

By the time the police got to him, he was lying dead on the floor of the lobby. The shots had smashed into his chest, back, and legs. What was left of the body had been removed by the time I reached the Martin Luther King Towers, but I saw the elevator, splashed with blood, and the irregular chalked outline where his crumpled form had sprawled and I knew this wasn't all a bad dream. The photographers had left, but a number of policeman were still checking over the hallways. The rear wall of the elevator was dented by a bullet; an area bigger than a man's fist was pressed in a full four inches by the force. On the floor, left behind like a bleak souvenir, lay a shard of bone. I walked outside the lobby, alone, very cold, fighting against the acceptance of what had just happened. Suddenly tears were pouring down my face and I vomited into the hedge.[372]

That night, word had spread around Harlem that the man known as Allah was dead. Many who heard the news were in shock and disbelief. This was a sad night in Harlem for those who knew him. As he was controversial in life, Clarence 13X (Allah) would be the same in death. Whispers went throughout the night speculating about who was responsible for the shooting. At that time, there were no leads as to whom killed him-- but this didn't stop the police from fabricating a story.

Chapter 21
The Plot Thickens

With the unholy alliance of the police and media seeking to capitalize off the murder of Clarence 13X (Allah), they quickly went to work to fabricate a conspiracy theory in hopes of igniting a black civil war. Keeping in step with the COINTELPRO system of the FBI, their iniquitous aim and hopes was to create an atmosphere in which the Five Percenters and the Muslims would turn on one another and shed each other's blood. This way they could "kill two birds with one stone." The police enlisted the media to help their cause by printing accusations, fabricating lies and disseminating falsehoods using the newspapers as their medium. This is exactly what they did and would have been successful if not for the foresight of the Five Percenters and the Nation of Islam.

The morning of June 13, 1969, a flood of propaganda circulated throughout the papers. The New York Daily News headline read: *KENYATTA'S PAL KILLED, Cops See Muslim War.*

> In the second such attack in a week, Clarence Smith Jowars, 41, and associate of Harlem Mau Mau leader Charles 37X Kenyatta, was shot and killed yesterday in the elevator of a Harlem apartment house.
>
> Last Saturday Kenyatta was shot and critically wounded as he sat in a car on a Bronx street. He is recovering in Bellevue Hospital.
>
> Police investigating both shootings believe the attacks are opening shots in an all-out war in the Black Community between the militant Black Muslims and dissidents like Kenyatta and Jowars who left the organization to form their own power bases.
>
> "We believe the Black Muslims have had enough of these splinter groups and want to do away with them once and for all," said a police spokesman.
>
> Jowars, described as the organizer and leader of the Five Percenters, a radical group of young blacks reputedly indoctrinated to hate both whites and Black Muslims was shot about 4 A.M. as he walked into a elevator on the first floor of the Martin Luther King Towers, a housing project at 21 W. 112th St.

Jowar's wife, Dora, lives in an apartment on the fifth floor of the building, police said, and Jowars was apparently on his way to see her...

Police said a "person or persons" stepped up behind Jowars and fired seven shots into him at close range, hitting him first in the head and then the back, chest, and legs. He fell dead to the elevator floor as his assailants fled...[373]

The inflammatory article upset the Five Percenters, the Muslims, including Mayor Lindsay and his administration. In fact, all three parties while working independently of one another set out to defuse this negative rumor. Mr. Gottehrer recalls the action the mayor took to dispel the story. Barry Gottehrer:

On the way down to the Mansion I picked up a copy of the Daily News, and read a huge black headline: Muslim Rebel Slain in Harlem: Cops Fear Black Civil War. The story that followed quoted some unidentified police spokesman as saying, "We believe the Black Muslims have had enough of these splinter groups and want to do away with them once and for all." The genesis of the theory, apparently, was that Allah, like Kenyatta, was a former Muslim who no longer deferred to Elijah Muhammad. Throughout the several stories on the murder Allah was referred to as Kenyatta's friend, his associate, or his pal—none of which described their relationship. They were not working together. Kenyatta was not about to worship Allah as god incarnate, and Allah wasn't interested in costuming his followers in mufti and handing them machetes. The two men were acquainted with one another, and respected their differences...

We moved quickly. The mayor called a meeting at Gracie Mansion with Leary and with Fred Lussen, the chief of detectives, and he hit the roof. "I don't give a damn what kind of leads you have," he said, "that kind of story does not get into the papers. You stop those rumors.[374]

The Muslims at Mosque #7 had already prepared a news conference to dismiss any rumors of any involvement in the assassination of Clarence 13X. The outspoken Minister Louis Farrakhan, who was the National Representative of the Honorable Elijah Muhammad and minister-in-charge of New York City, organized the conference to combat the lies that originated with the NYPD. Farrakhan said the NOI was outraged by white insinuations that Muslims were involved in the murder of Clarence 13X. The New York Times recorded the Muslims response:

> In another development, Min. Louis Farrakhan, who was the National Representative of the Honorable Elijah Muhammad, held a news conference at a Mosque at 105-10 Northern Boulevard, Corona, Queens, to protest the newspaper report in which a policeman was quoted as saying that the Muslims wanted to do away with splinter groups, such as Mr. Smith's.
>
> "We the Muslims are extremely outraged by the vicious, wicked, deliberate sowing of divisive, slanderous seeds by The Daily News, which appears to be desiring to cause black people to fight and kill each other," Mr. Farrakhan said....
>
> Mr. Farrakhan stressed that the Muslims had been active in Harlem for many years "with the Five Percenters and many other Black groups who disagree with our views."
>
> "We have not bothered them, nor have they bothered us," he said.
>
> He went on to say that it was not the Muslims who wanted to get rid of splinter groups, but "rather it appears that the police and the white power structure are tired of the Muslims and the black militants and would like to rid themselves of both, instigating, provoking and inciting innocent black people to fight and kill each other through false accusations."[375]

Farrakhan said he was referring to a published report quoting an unnamed police spokesman as saying the two shootings marked the beginning of an "all-out-war" between Muslims and dissidents. Even though the Muslims protested the rumor, the media still wouldn't budge per instructions they received from the police. The Daily News stood by their story and refused to change it per information they claimed they received from the police department (who naturally despised the Five Percenters and Muslims). This is cited within the same article:

> "We got it from the police; we did not make it up," James Patterson, assistant managing editor of the Daily News, said in commenting on the report criticized by Mr. Farrakhan.[376]

This blatant show of police conspiracy left a foul odor with the mayor's administration. Mayor Lindsay set out to find exactly who was the police official that started the rumor in the first place. But to no avail they never found out. Barry Gottehrer:

We never did find out who started the rumors, but we figured that in order to have credibility with the Daily News reporter, he had to be someone fairly high up in the police command. We never found out, either, what fragment of a lead the unknown spokesman based his assumptions on. For all we know, he was a man with a private gripe, or someone who like to pin as many internal plots on blacks as Kenyatta attributed to the white elite. From Kenyatta, you could understand it. From a police department official, it was disgraceful.[377]

Fortunately, as a result of Allah's affiliation with Lindsay, the mayor set out to correct the wrong. The mayor and his administration reached out to the Muslims and extended an apology for the fabrication of the black civil war theory. Mr. Gottehrer:

At the time, Louis Farrakhan, the head of the Harlem mosque of the Nation of Islam, and I did not know each other very well, although in the next year or two we would become close. I grew to respect him very much. Fortunately Inspector Waith knew him extremely well, and was able to talk frankly with him. He told him the News story was a lie, and the police knew it, and Farrakhan took his word for it.[378]

The mayor and Mr. Gottehrer also went to the Five Percenters Street Academy and extended an up close and personal apology to the Five Percenters:

On Saturday the fourteenth, only hours after the News had hit the street, the mayor and I had met with the Five Percenters in their storefront and told them the same thing. I could still not fully accept the death of my close friend, and the mayor felt the loss deeply. On this hot June day, he pushed beyond what mayors usually are expected to do or can do.[379]

Though the Muslims were cleared of any involvement in the assassination of Clarence 13X-- the question was still left open to who did it. With the revealing of more information and hindsight, Five Percenter scholars point out possible conspiracies. One theory plays down the Muslim conspiracy and lays the assassination at the feet of government agencies:

> Did the NYPD routinely stage-manage the news media to cause conflict between the NOI and others? The answer is obvious. Years later, in a 1973 interview, Minister Louis Farrakhan spoke on "anonymous sources" in news reports. He said, "Whenever you are saying what someone else said and don't name the sources, it can easily be assumed that "YOU" are the sources of your own material. If a law enforcement official has something to say, and it is fact, and it can be proved, he should not fear attribution of the statement." In the same interview he mentioned the article in the New York Times where approximately 46 reporters admitted working for the C.I.A. (cf. Seven Speeches by Minister Louis Farrakhan, (Chicago: 1974, reprinted Newport News: 1990).[380]

The police added more confusion around everything when they came back with a different story the second time around. Per pressure from the mayor's administration, the police fabricated another story that put a positive spin on the circumstances leading to Clarence's death:

> The police department response took us by surprise. Before we knew it, Lussen had called a press conference and announced a new lead. He came up with a few more unsolved shootings and tied them all together as part of a ten-man extortion plot; a number of thugs were putting the squeeze on business men and civil rights figures, demanding financial support for a fictitious black militant organization. If the victims failed to pay off, the thugs would resort to scheme, and limited the number of "facts" he revealed because of the sensitive nature of the investigation. Allah and Kenyatta, apparently, had uncovered the racket and been trying to protect the rights of legitimate black protest groups from criminal elements when they were gunned down.
> By the end of the press conference, Allah and Kenyatta looked like patriotic Americans defending the Constitution and the right of free speech. It was as outrageous a story as the one about the black civil war, and as untrue, but the press bought it.

It ran in all the papers, and the black civil war theory vanished as it appeared the previous week.[381]

Even if the press believed the "extortion theory," those close to Allah knew better and had their own suspicions. Old Man Justice, Allah's right-hand man, suspected that Barry Gottehrer and NYC politicians had their hand in the assassination of Clarence 13X. As Barry Gottehrer reports this alleged incident:

> One night I remember riding around town with Murphy and him. Justice...probably half-joking made it plain that he was scared. He had somehow gotten it into his head that Murphy and I had together killed Allah and were now going to kill him. As we swung around the corner, he reached for the door handle. "I'm getting out of this car," he said. He carried on so, Murphy and I began to tease him. "Let's take him over to the river," I said to Murphy. "Let's see if he can swim." Justice shook and stammered, and we took pity on him, but it was plain that he wasn't the man to take charge of 500 tough street kids.[382]

Others say it possibly could have been a Five Percenter that betrayed Allah. It is common knowledge that there were in fact federal and police agents who infiltrated the movement and posed as Five Percenters. This would have given them more than ample an opportunity to get close to Allah in order to plan and carry out his assassination. As pointed out in a 5% publication:

> Who killed Allah? At that time Seventh Avenue was bustling with all types of shady activities from varied sorts. There was gamblers, dope peddlers, con-men, pimps, prostitutes, Muslims, powerful black church ministers, political activists, all coexisting amongst each other. The operators in Allah's assassination could have been any number of the street people found along Seventh Avenue. However, like Jesus, he could even have been betrayed from amongst one of his own; those who are closest to you can hurt you the most. Allah always said that the only one that can ever hurt me is a Five Percenter.[383]

Barry Gottehrer had his own speculation as to who murdered Clarence 13X. He speculated that it perhaps was Allah's gambling habits catching up with him, or maybe a jealous rival:

The police told me that as yet they had no leads. There was no indication that the murder was part of a plot, no immediate link with Kenyatta's shooting. For all they knew it was a simple case of robbery gone wrong. I found out quicker than they where he had been gambling that night. I knew how he hated to lose, how he would set the Five Percenters on the winner to gorilla his money back for him. Or it might have been some rival jealous of his standing with the Five Percenters. Allah used to tell me that the young people were often approached by people who tried to buy them off, telling them, "You can't deal with Whitey. Don't go to his schools, don't work for him. Stay on the street."[384]

Many Five Percenters firmly believe that the assassination of Clarence 13X was carried about by government agencies. After all, it was the government who would benefit the most. Prince Allah Cuba:

Was it the product of a conspiracy activated by counter-intelligence agents? I can say, based on my own knowledge of the methods of these agencies, based on the analysis of their past activities, that the assassination of the man Allah was definitely carried out by individuals acting in the interest of the police agencies.[385]

Shahid M. Allah also suggests the same in a pamphlet he wrote that points towards FBI involvement in the murder of Clarence 13X:

There were those within the power structure of this country that did not appreciate the wonderful job that Allah had done with the youth of New York City back in the sixties. Accordingly, on the night of June 12, 1969 some unknown assailant pumped seven bullets at point blank range into the physical person of Allah, as He stood in the elevator of the Martin Luther King Towers on 112th Street in East Harlem, NY. Above all the speculation into who killed Clarence 13X Smith (Allah), there is much evidence pointing at the Federal Bureau of Investigation (F.B.I.)! Even today the United States government only releases discretionary files via the Freedom Of Information Act to all those who desire to examine the role that the devil played in Allah's assassination. This is due to the fact that many of the agents are still among the living! Thus, the saga continues. The goal of White establishment is still the same: STOP THE RISE OF THE BLACK MESSIAH! They seek to nullify and do away with that Minister Louis Farrakhan refers to as "THE VANGUARD OF THE NATION (Of Islam)." (Friendship Baptist Church, 06/02/88).[386]

The Mayor Offers His Condolences

On Saturday, June 14th, Mayor Lindsay and Barry Gottehrer met with the Five Percenters at their Street Academy to offer their support and condolences. As recorded in a New York Times Article entitled, "HARLEM MILITANTS OFFER PEACE VOW: 5 Percenters Tell Lindsay They Will Stay in School Despite Smith Slaying." The article opens with the mayor's intent for the visit.

> Mayor Lindsay went to Harlem yesterday and received the pledges of a group of young blacks—mourning the murder of their leader on Friday—that they would avoid violence and continue their efforts to get an education.
>
> The youths were members of the Five Percenters, who are enrolled in a storefront street academy that was operated by Clarence 13X Smith.
>
> Mr. Smith—who was known to his followers as Allah—was killed early Friday when a fusillade of bullets was fired into the lobby of a Harlem apartment building. Seven bullets struck him.
>
> As the Mayor sat in short sleeves in a sweltering storefront, his eyes sometimes downcast, one youth after another assured him that the group would continue to seek an education.[387]

Mayor Lindsay, who respected Allah a great deal, felt it necessary to get up close and personal with the youth group at the Street Academy. The admiration was reciprocated as the youth opened up to the Mayor.

> "We're not going to change—education is the greatest thing in the world and we realize it," one said.
>
> "He's not gone," he said of Mr. Smith. "He's still here."
>
> Wandering listlessly around the long narrow store at 126th Street and Seventh Avenue, the youths ambled toward the crowded entrance saying, "We are the best, the Five Percenters, and there ain't going to be no change. We'll keep civilization going."

Mr. Lindsay left Grace Mansion to attend the 2:30PM meeting where about 49 young men and a sprinkling of women and children awaited him.

As he entered the room there were greetings of "Peace" and the Mayor replied, "Peace, peace."

Standing in the middle of the room, next to a crowded bookshelf, Mr. Lindsay said:

"Brothers, first I hope you know the sadness in my heart at Allah's death. His contribution was an important one these last few years—most especially in the world of education."

Mr. Lindsay pointed out that six youths present in the room were scheduled to go to college next term as a result of their involvement in the "street academy" which is one of a series set up by the Urban League with the help of the Mayor's urban task force.[388]

This wasn't the Mayor's first visit to the Street Academy. He had visited before, only this time it was under solemn circumstances. Mayor Lindsay had nothing but good words to say about Allah and encouraged the Five Percenters to live up to Allah's vision. The youth made pledges to carry on with the mission.

Praising Mr. Smith, a black militant who was ousted from the Black Muslims some years ago by the late Malcolm X, Mr. Lindsay said he had a "natural ability to communicate."

The Five Percenters were formerly a Harlem teen-aged group dedicated to performing acts of terrorism. The name derives from an assertion that 85 percent of the black people act like cattle, that 10 percent are Uncle Toms and the remaining 5 percent are those who would free the remaining 95 percent.

"I hope," the Mayor told the saddened gathering, "that the tragic and senseless and brutal demise of Allah—that the act that will come is a recommitment on your part, a pressing on to the business of living and education."

One after the other the youths---some wearing dashikis---praised Mr. Smith and pledged to continue their studies.

One youth said: "The 5-percenters are not at war with anybody and not looking' for war with anybody.

...another said: "The only way we can show that we loved him is to build—to get our own carpenters, doctors, lawyers, painters, electricians—that's how we can show that we loved him."[389]

The death of Clarence 13X united facets of the community to say their last farewells to the man called Allah. It was a most difficult time; especially for the children who called him "Father."

Chapter 22
Peace Allah

Allah "The Father"

The funeral for Allah was held on Monday afternoon at Unity
Funeral Chapel on 8th Avenue and 126th Street. It was a massive
event as Harlem bid farewell to the man they affectionately
called "Puddin." Four hundred people packed the chapel. Gods
and Earths repeated the sentences "Allah cannot die! Allah is
God, and God lives forever!"—as they passed the walnut casket
bearing the earthly remains of the man who had reached out and
taught them. The New York Amsterdam Newspaper wrote their
last article on Allah as if an obituary for the slain leader. The
headline ironically read, "Allah Still Lives," by Les Matthews.
The article opened capturing moments of the funeral and cause
of death.

> "Allah cannot die!" "Allah is God, and God lives forever!" These
> sentences were repeated hundreds of time by solemn and
> sometimes weeping Five Percenters as they passed the walnut
> casket bearing the earthly remains of Clarence 13X Smith who

was affectionately called "Puddin" by a number of his intimates. He was in repose at Unity Funeral Chapel on Eighth Ave. at 126th St. Saturday, Sunday and Monday before the afternoon rites.

Allah still lives in the mind and hearts of thousands of youngsters including some young men and women in Manhattan, Bronx, Brooklyn and Queens. Allah could communicate with youngsters. His every wish was their command.

Clarence 13X Smith was shot to death on the morning of June 13 on the first floor of the Martin Luther King Towers, 21 W. 112 St., by one or more gunmen who apparently trapped him in the quiet hallway. They pumped seven bullets into his body. They did not give him a chance, and, he carried no weapons.[390]

Mr. Matthews mentioned the humble beginnings of the dearly departed and outlined the start of his rise.

Attempts were made on his life in 1965, two years after he was expelled from the Muslims by the late Malcolm X who said Clarence Smith was a rebel. "He refuses to abide by the rules and we gave him many chances. I think he would fare better out of the Mosque," Malcolm said.

Clarence decided to start his own program and started to round up the youths. He rounded up the wayward, the dropouts and youngsters who apparently could not stay out of trouble. He named them the Five Percenters. He used his Muslim training as a guide and gave the youngsters lessons in his new religion. His party grew but he ran into trouble with the authorities and was arrested by Det. Troy Windham and sentenced to Matteawan State Hospital. It was while he was in the hospital that he changed the thinking of his group. He taught them not to hate, impressed upon them to go to school, work, learn a trade or profession. He sent them lessons from the hospital and sent me word that he had a new look at life.[391]

Les Matthews, a long time Harlem resident and news reporter dubbed "Mr. 125th Street," had developed close ties with Allah throughout the years. Within his article he revealed more intimate moments and details of Allah's life.

During the riot that followed the assassination of Dr. Martin Luther King Jr., he walked through 125th Street calling his "children", admonishing them when he found them doing wrong and asking them if they had forgotten Allah's teachings. The little "Gods" as he later referred to them, accompanied him to their headquarters on Seventh Ave. and 126th St.

All did not run smooth because an officer, not acquainted with him roughed him up and hauled him to the W. 123rd St. station house. He looked at me and said loud and clear: "I want you to write what this black cop did to me. Allah. Just write the truth. I am getting my children off the streets and he hauled me in here. Do you call that justice?" He was later released.

Allah had several run-ins with the authorities but they were minor. One of his greatest weaknesses was shooting dice. He once told an officer: "I am going to shoot dice until I die."

Allah also had attracted the attention of Mayor Lindsay who visited him several times in the Urban League Academy on Seventh Ave. at 126th St. A huge picture of Allah with the Mayor was in the window for months. The Mayor also arranged for several of Allah's followers to go up in an airplane and assigned Barry Gottehrer, head of the Mayor's Urban Action Task Force, and Ted Gross, to work with Allah.

Gottehrer who was introduced to Allah by James Lawson, attended several of the Five Percenters' Parliaments in Mt. Morris Park and in the Bronx. Hundreds attended the sessions and listened intently as Allah spoke.[392]

In his conclusion, he mentioned another occurrence, provided some background information and highlighted certain aspects of Allah's character.

Allah was a rare man who did not mind what was written about him or said about him as long as it was the truth. He often remarked about the article that appeared in this paper about him following a Sunday afternoon upheaval at 125th St. and Seventh Ave., and said: "Was it that bad. I don't remember but something drove me to it because I wouldn't do a thing to hurt my children."

He was born in Danville, Va., 41 years ago and moved to the city in his early teens with his brothers John, Louis, Weldon, Ernest and Charles. He had a sister, Mrs. Bernice Inge. He was married 19 years ago and the union between him and his wife, Dora, produced four children, Perry, Clark, Debbie and Christina. Although he lived at 249 W. 139th St. he visited his family often.

Allah was a man who loved peace. He warned his followers against using dope. He was not a soapbox speaker but he got his message across.

His funeral attracted more than 400 and the crowd was swelled with more than two dozen police officers who are seeking the killer or killers of the youth leader whose funeral procession included seven bus loads of youngsters from the Bronx, Brooklyn and Manhattan.

They accompanied his body to Ferncliff Cemetery in Hartsdale, N.Y. where it was cremated. He was dressed in a double-breasted suit and wore a crown for he's a king, one that will never die.[393]

One Five Percenter reminisces on his thoughts during this period of mourning for young Gods and Earths:

"The Father's funeral" was held on 8th ave, between 126th and 127th street. Gods from all over was there. Some Gods never got over it, that night as I laid in my bed, I thought about the "Father" and the influence he had on my life. I thought of how one time Allah punched me in my chest, because I wouldn't take money that he was offering to me. I thought of how He had sent me, Zumar, Shariek, and El-Bar-Sun on a mission to Fire Island to rap with a new crop of graduating Police Officers.

I thought of how He was looking for me, for something that I had did. I thought of the first time that I met Him, I laid in my bed thinking about the Man, who we called "Father" and cried.[394]

Many felt the tragic loss of Allah. In Harlem, like Malcolm X, he was one of their shining Black princes being laid to rest. Barry Gotthehrer who grew close to Allah recalled the scenes from the funeral and wake:

On Monday afternoon I went to Allah's funeral. Over the weekend his body, patched together by the undertaker's art, had lain in an open coffin at the Unity Funeral Chapel, the biggest funeral parlor in Harlem, a block west of the Glamour Inn. By chance, none of the fusillade of bullets had hit Allah's face. They had put a double-breasted suit on him, and arranged a gold crown on his head.

Four Hundred people came to the funeral, including several dozen policemen on the job, and seven busloads of youngsters.

They came from the Bronx and Brooklyn as well as from all over Manhattan.

People sobbed, screamed, fell down in the aisle. Some women became hysterical and had to be carried out. Several people fainted. It was an overwhelming atmosphere. One had the feeling that anything might happen, that someone might flip out and start firing a gun into the crowd.

A minister said a prayer and gave a sermon. A girl Five Percenter led in the singing of a song she had written, called "Allah."

I couldn't bring myself to go out to Ferncliff Cemetery, in Hartsdale, New York, where Allah was to be cremated. The hearse set out, trailed by the slow parade of limousines, buses, and souped-up, ancient cars.

Four hours later I was at Allah's brother's house for the wake, where everyone concentrated on hard drinking. In the midst of our sadness, we ended up having a party. [395]

The remains of Clarence 13X was cremated and his followers sprinkled some of his ashes over Mount Morris Park. With the loss of their fierce leader, the Five Percenters faced their biggest trial yet. Some were in denial that this dreaded day had come. Others attempted to prepare themselves in advance for this day. Many still were in shock and disbelief. But all would have to face the task at hand.

Chapter 23
The After Math

JUSTICE WITH YOUNG GODS

Old Man Justice pictured with a group of young Five Percenters.

After the death of Clarence 13X (Allah) the Five Percenters
were faced with a leadership crisis. This was their first time
without a commander-in-chief. People pondered about who
would be next to lead the courageous group. The answer wasn't
so obvious as to whom if anyone could fill the shoes of Allah
who Barry Gottehrer aptly described as "a hard act to follow."

Many people outside the movement thought that Allah's
right-hand man, Old Man Justice, would be the logical choice.
But Justice shied away from being a leader for the movement. In
fact it was a custom for Five Percenters to greet each other with
the greeting "Peace Allah." However, when anyone said this to

Old Man Justice, he defied the custom by replying, "I'm not Allah-- Allah is my man."

> This person, who I am about to manifest his truth about his name, is none other than "Justice C. Allah". I am using Allah being his name because it is our family name, never the less "Justice C", or the "old man" as we called him never liked anyone to call him "Allah" because he did not like it. He used to say that he was not cause "Allah" was his man. He went on to say that his name was "Justice".[396]

Justice in his twilight years never desired to be the leader over the movement. He rather favored his role as a guide instead. A Five Percenter biography recalls memories of Old Man Justice during this time period:

> We called him Free Cipher Akbar in the beginning. He was about the only brother who was older than Allah when the 5% Nation started. His name was changed to JC or Justice Understanding in 1967. His role was to guide us. He never wanted to lead us. He was "crazy like a fox" and he knew all of the street hustles and cons. Two times he had to guide us in the place of Allah (1965-1967) when Allah was in Mattawan. And (1969-1978) when Allah returned to the essence. Justice was our Big Brother. His favorite quotes was Filthy Mac NASTY...AND DIRTY LOWDOWN." He was like that older family member who you could hangout with or get high with when you were young. The one who hipped you to "Streetlife." If you asked him about lessons, Justice would say, "I don't know how to quote them, but if you say them, and I'll tell you if it is right. He was "an example of the power" for many of the Gods & Earths who came around after Allah went home... After the Father went home Justice kept us together.[397]

The other alternative was to look toward other elders such as Shahid. However, Abu was embroiled in his own personal affliction that prevented him from taking on a leadership position. As he admits in an article.

> Clean for the past 12 years, Abu is forthright about his drug wrestling but says it doesn't eclipse his designation as God. In fact, he credits NGE with helping him win his battles over addiction.

"I thought I could do wrong the right way," he says recalling how many times he's been jailed, "but my criminal history shows and proves otherwise. We live in an addictive society and products of the environment develop addictive personalities. The addictive personality thinks that negativity is positive."

Abu's addiction might have cost more than just personal grief, though. In 1969, when Clarence 13X was mysteriously murdered, Abu claims says he was asked who would now lead NGE. "Strung out like a research monkey," as he tells it, the best response Abu say he could come up with was, "not me." Since then NGE has had no central leadership. The rationale among them is that with no leader, no one would have a target to assassinate. [398]

Another elder that was a good candidate was Hebekha who was very strong in the knowledge plus he had the experiences of being in the Temple. However, Hebekha decided to return back to his roots by going back to the Temple #7.

Ubeka (the brown seed) was a great teacher of this knowledge, before he became a Muslim after the Father went home.[399]

If the elder cadres weren't ready to man the helm, perhaps it was choice to select amongst the younger candidates. Some within the organization felt that Clarence's first begotten Black Messiah or Knowledge Allah was able to rise to the challenge:

Many people from outside the Nation thought that Allah's longtime friend, Justice, would fill the role that Allah had left. Those within the Nation felt that Knowledge Allah had been groomed by Allah well enough to do the job.[400]

Some Five Percenters even questioned the necessity for leadership at all. It is alleged by some that Allah told his Five Percenters that they did not need leadership as individuals because they should be leaders of themselves and their families. Other sources profess that Allah taught that they needed collective leadership as a people because the Black nation needed their own government if they were going to be self-sufficient. Consequently, without anyone assuming the mantle of leadership in the movement, the Five Percenters were "dead" for a year.

> After the death of Allah the Gods were, as Allah had predicted, dead for a year. They were devastated by his loss. For a year there was increased drinking and drug use.[401]

The loss of Allah took its toll on the young organization and for a year different vices began to plague some members. Universal Shaamguadd expounds:

> The OSTRICH SYNDROME is the most popular way that FIVE PERCENTERS tend to fall victim without realizing their even taking a Fall. The OSTRICH being a large bird that when it finds itself in danger tends to bury its head in the Earth, foolishly feeling that it cannot see the Danger that it is safe while all the time his Behind or Body remains exposed.
>
> It's the same thing with Human Nature when some people don't get things their way or feel life isn't treating them right they bury their Minds or Heads in the Earth. By earth, I mean 6. Equality (Drugs, Alcohol, Money, Food, Women, Cars, Crime, etc.). All seems well while the Head is in Equality. However, if the Equality doesn't do permanent damage to the Head or Mind, when one finally pulls his Head out of 6 (the EARTH) he finds that not only is the problem or danger still there, it usually has increased in size or in it's threat, this is what happened to most of us after the Father left us.[402]

Gykee Mathematics bares witness to Shaamgaudd's observation and tells his story:

> After the Father's return home, we hadn't been drawn up to his maximum equality the bottom fell out for many of us, we all took it very hard.
>
> I should say for me my woes and trouble progressed and intensified, never just once having the reasoning to say maybe my drinking and drugging had something to do with it. The start of the year seven=1970 found many of us in oblivion for it came and let many of stay sedated or in a drunkard stupor, me myself was in both. Despite the authorities offer to us to go to plays at the theaters, trips and all sort of things to appease and console us, not knowing how we were going to react, nothing seemed to matter to many of us at that point.[403]

Allah had predicted the low numbers that would possibly result from his physical death. He used to hold conversations with his right hand man Justice about it.

> I can recall Allah saying: "If he just got one of us, he would have done his job." A conversation with Old Man Justice, pertaining to the number of Five Percenters there would be. He stated: "Maybe nine or seven, five even and not to be surprised if there were three or just one."[404]

No longer were there overflowing Parliaments of hundreds of teens propagating the "knowledge of self." The audiences had dwindled down to ones.

> I remember one "Parliament" in the year=1970, where there was nine of us in the same "Harriet Tubman School" where the rallies are held now. I could only think that the brothers and sisters at the time had become very, very dismayed. Something the Father had told us to not ever become and if we did to call on him and he would be there, meaning when we all come together in his name, he would be there for us.[405]

With things looking grim, some Five Percenters seen a silver lining to this dark cloud of their recent loss and subsequent stupor. Some determined the chain of events was not coincidence but perhaps due to divine foresight. In synch with Allah's prediction theory, some Five Percenters attempt to bring meaning to the loss of Allah's physical existence.

> Though His physical person is gone, His Divine Mind remains! Messenger Elijah Muhammad attests to this: "The Black Man is always here, but no single man lives forever. Do you know why? After the scientist (angel) lives here and learns all about the Earth and knows what is to come to his Earth tomorrow (tomorrow could be 1,000 years or 20,000 years) he is not particular about staying around to see it come in, because he already knows. So he gets tired and starts to live a life which come in, because he already knows. So he gets tired and starts to live a life which he knows will have an end to it..." (Theology of Time) So Allah is indeed the God![406]

Other Five Percenters who remained in the fold had witnessed the small numbers and made a concerted effort to rebuild.

> After Allah returned, the Nation of Gods and Earths [which He said we would be known as] went thru low tide. The Parliaments in Mt. Morris Park, Fort Greene Park, and Harriet Tubman School use to be full and over flowing before this happened, but after Allah's return the Parliaments began to thin out more and more. The "Piece (Peace) without the magnetic" began to jump ship and abandoned the Nation, the ranks thinned all the way out, until only the true and living would not let the Nation die out. They were the Piece (Peace) with the magnetic:. They held onto the Nation when others let go. They were the "few" that held our Nation together after Allah returned, and they will always have my Peace. Even though some of them drank and got "stimulated", they stayed, and I love and respect them more then those who didn't get "stimulated", but abandoned the Nation.[407]

Show and Prove

Be that as it may, within a year and a few months time, at the end of 1970, there were two events that signaled to the Five Percenters that they were en route to a healthy recovery. The first to trigger the resurgence was a party given together by Prince Allah (of Queens) and Born Allah (of the Bronx). The two attended Harlem Prep School together and gave a party in Hollis, Queens on December 4, 1970. This social attracted Gods and Earths from all over. Born Allah elaborates:

> When Prince and Born gave a dance that brought everybody to the Desert (Queens), a viable rose sprung to life within the Nation. Gods and Earths came from all five boroughs and as far north as Massachusetts and as far as Philadelphia to the south. We were entertained by Sabu and his Ensemble, a group which formed the nucleus of G.Q., who with their monster hit single "disco nights" later become the no. 1 disco group of 1979. Sabu Allah and Raheem Le Blanc from Pelan, the first musicians to arrange music for the Enlightener (our National Anthem), played the night away. The dance was a great success and the Gods and Earths demanded that Prince and Born do something like it again.[408]

The second event occurred that same month on New Year's Eve; when the Gods and Earths from all four boroughs came to the street academy to bring in the New Year. This renewed the memory of Allah's words when he told them, "If they ever needed him all they had to do was come together."

The following year, 1971, the Gods and Earths got it together and came back alive as a nation under the name of, "The Five Percent Nation of Islam" aka "The Five Percent Nation." The titles were derived from the claim that they were the Five Percent or the *"poor righteous teachers"* within the grander scale Nation of Islam that theologically comprised of all original people of the Earth. Numerous teams of Five Percenters became active in the city and sponsored events in their local areas. The most popular were the math, science, sewing and first aid classes sponsored by the group. Other members ventured outside of New York City to spread the teachings to other states such as New Jersey, Connecticut, Pennsylvania and Massachusetts. As a result, these states became part of the Five Percent terrain.

Given the large number of the Five Percenter student population at Harlem Prep, the institution morphed into a stronghold for the movement. Gods and Earths began teaching at Harlem Prep and represented the school at science seminars. Two prep students Born and Prince were also making plans to host a scientific and educational affair on behalf of the Five Percenters called *"The Educational Show and Prove."*

> The real plans for the Educational Show and Prove came about as a result of Prince Allah from the Oasis (Queens), and Born-Allah from Pelan (Bronx) having a desire to "Show and Prove" that the Nation of Gods and Earths did not die when the Father returned to the essences in 1969...
>
> At the April and May Parliaments, Born and Prince announced the upcoming "Educational Show and Prove" to be held at Harlem Prep. located on 135th street and 8th avenue, Harlem, New York City, USA. It was also made known that there would be a scientific projects, arts, songs and dance, a Karate exhibition and every other kind of talent representation that the Gods and Earths want to show and prove.[409]

The two decided to host the event on June 13th, which was the anniversary of Clarence's assassination. Allah's immediate family was invited as the guests of honor. Gods and Earths from all over dedicated themselves to making the event a reality and the Five Percenters had a goal in front of them which to galvanize around.

A few days after the show and prove announcement, the City of New York declared their plans to have a *"Children's Day."* It was to be held at another location simultaneously on the same day as the Show and Prove, setting up the two events to undoubtedly rival each other. Not to be outdone by the opposition, the Five Percenters prepared themselves for an outstanding event in hopes of attracting many children. A team of Gods and Earths pulled together and worked diligently to provide the necessities for the affair to happen.

> The final day for preparations came that Saturday on June 12, 1971, with buying food, costumes, dress rehearsal and making the final arrangements for all the equipment to be on hand the next day. Prince and Born along with God Supreme, Gykee, God Dumar, Al Shakeim, Takesha, LuAsia, El Latisha, Lateef, Dihu, Janel, Knowledge Allah, Tall Yusif, Gevasia, Makebea Washika, God Aliem, both Prince's and Born's Old Earths and a host of Gods and Earths worked diligently to set the stage for the next day of food, folks and big fun![410]

After completing the final preparations, the Show and Prove event was ready to proceed with great anticipation, in spite of the rival event sponsored by the city. However, in a stroke of luck or divine intervention for the Five Percenters, rainy weather had foiled the city's plans.

> The first "Show and Prove" was held at Harlem Prep. on June 13, 1971. It was this particular Sunday on Father's Day that the city declared (about a month and a half after we announced our Show and Prove), "Children's Day" in Harlem to be held in Mount Morris Park. We recognized and understood that the babies were the greatest as Allah, the Father taught us "Allah U Arkbar". Therefore, our Father's Day has actually always been our Children's Day as well.
> However, many people felt the city had tried to divert the children from attending the Show and Prove given by the Gods and Earths. It really didn't matter much because that day it rained about 4 o'clock and the rain drove everybody indoors.

Allah being the best of planners; We therefore planned well in advance to have an indoor affair from 2 p.m. to 10 p.m.[411]

As fate would have it, as the city's event was rained out, the attendees opted to go to the educational show and prove at Harlem Prep instead. The children were admitted for free and received free dictionaries at the door while adults received raffle tickets for a door prize. With the crowd at full capacity, the Five Percenters started the program and show.

God Dumar M.C.ed and opened up with an introduction of the days events. The first to go on was LaTisha from Mecca (Manhattan). She sang a song written by I-God entitled "Allah's Blessings"....Next 5 young Gods from Pelan beat the congas like they had never left the motherland... An announcement was made that Amar, a Visual Arts student at Harlem Prep. had made the first documentary produced by a God of the Nation and that Prince Allah would be the commentator for its public viewing that would be shown in the screening room, also that food would be served downstairs. Most of the crowd of 2,000 tried to go downstairs at the same time! Surprisingly enough there was no problem in controlling this capacity crowd who had came to commemorate the Father and everyone acted righteously. For the next hour or so the video tape was viewed, the people ate and generally socialized while music was played over the P.A. system. During this time the childrens exhibits were presented. A young God won the "The Allah Science Award" with his exhibit, "What makes rain, hail and snow". He used an ac/dc battery, a 100 watt light bulb and a pan filled with water to create vapor, which formed water drops that we were able to detect with the naked eye, and when the drops became too heavy, gravitation caused the water to distill back into the pan. Many other awards were given out. At 7 to 8 P.M. a Karate exhibition by "Green Eyes" Zumar Allah from Mecca and Jabar Abdul Jabar, a certified Black Belt, performed incredible feats. From about 8 P.M. to about 8:45 the Earths presented a fashion show, afterwards the Earths from Pelan treated the audience to songs and dance from the Motherland. At 9:30, Sabu and his Ensemble led a 16-piece band that played a variety of music. Although the Show and Prove was to end at 10 P.M. the people danced to 2 o'clock in the morning![412]

Needless to say the event was a huge success and another milestone of achievement for the young organization, especially in the absence of its deceased leader. This solidified the confidence needed for the group to push forward and the endeared *"Show and Prove"* has become a staple for the organization ever since. Born Allah sums it up:

The Father's Educational Show and Prove that Sunday in June of 1971 was a great day and night to commemorate and remember our Allah by having the children show forth their greatness. It was that day that the Gods and Earths instituted an institution that will last forever, just as our Universal Parliaments.[413]

Chapter 24
Life After Death

Young Five Percenters at Annual Educational Show and Prove Event.

The Seventies

The Show and Prove event was the catalyst for the rebirth of the Five Percenters and the event's co-founder Born Allah appeared to be headed for a bright future. He had just graduated from Harlem Prep class of '71 and was offered an athletic scholarship to Florida A&M University. But before he could take advantage of this opportunity his plans were sidelined because of an unfortunate dispute involving a neighborhood man and a young Five Percenter. Always known for helping others, it was his coming to the aid of others that led to his own imprisonment. Born tells his story:

> "...A man was holding a gun on one of the young brothers, age thirteen. I approached...and asked him what was he doing with 'that gun on my young brother?' He said that the young brother had a mini-bike which belonged to his son. At that point, the

young brother ran and the man turned the gun on me and ordered me to put the mini-bike in the back of his car, which I did.

"There was a group of other Five Percenters on the street at the time and they began to approach the man when they saw him with the gun on me. As my back was turned, just after placing the mini-bike in his trunk, I heard a shot ring out. I tensed my body to absorb the bullet but I felt none. I looked back and saw this individual firing wildly towards the ground where the brothers were approaching from. I was able to divert his attention...the brothers gained on him...the man turned and fled. The brothers pursued. He was later found dead and I was charged with the murder."[414]

Prior to this tragedy, Born was "put in charge" of the Bronx by Allah himself. Some always thought that this made him a target of the local police and the Bronx District Attorney who equally shared a disdain for the movement. Some Five Percenters feel that Born was a victim of racism and politics as he was sentenced to 25 years to life in prison.

During the 70's, Five Percenters maintained their definitive influence amongst the inner city youth of New York. Many youth organizations, social clubs and gangs began to die out during this period. Some abandoned the gang lifestyle to join the ranks of the Five Percenters. Others opted to start similar conscious movements. One example was a Bronx gang called the Black Spades, who gave up their gang ties to embrace black consciousness and became known as "The Zulu Nation," complete with lesson sets similar to the Five Percenters.

The early seventies also was the heyday of the Nation of Islam. The Five Percenters drew inspiration from their parent organization as it was flourishing on all levels during this era. One example of the Muslim's success was a huge event sponsored by the Muslims in 1972 called *"Black Family Day"* given on Randall's Island in which Minister Farrakhan spoke to over 70,000 people. The Muslims had partnered with some Five Percenters and allowed Prince Allah to oversee vending at the event. The NOI had reached all-time highs in their progression as detailed in a Five Percenter article written in February of 1974 that compared the two movements.

Why are the Muslims in the foreground and the Five Percenters in the background today? The Honorable Elijah Muhammad has been teaching for the past 44 years and within this amount of time the Nation of Islam has grown tremendously. He has 71 Temples throughout the cities of the United States. The wealth of the Nation of Islam has increased along with the growth of the population. Therefore over the period of 44 years under the leadership and Guidance of the Messenger of Allah the Muslims have been successful in establishing businesses thereby changing their living conditions. These businesses provide the Muslims with employment. The Muslims do not waste money on sport and play, smoke and drink, instead they pool their resources for one common cause. One only has to read the Muslim Newspaper "Muhammad Speaks" to bear witness to the progress of the Nation of Islam under the Leadership of the Honorable Elijah Muhammad. The total population can easily see how the Nation of Islam has made a positive change in the Black Community. The culture and refinements of the Muslims also attracts the Black Community, for they give and receive the utmost respect at all times. The Nation of Islam has reached worldwide recognition by both enemies and friends (brothers) in other countries. International business [sic].

[sic] Grassroots but now they have attracted the interests of the Black Middle Class and are drawing professionals and expertise there from. Young Muslim Scholars are encouraged to learn professions, technology and engineering. There are no idle Muslims to be found only building and productivity. A large percentage of Muslims embrace Islam in the devil's penal institutions. When these Muslims are released from prison they are received with opened arms by the Nation of Islam, given work to do and they live respectable lives without returning to prison. The Muslim Brotherhood is unsurpassed.[415]

Although the Muslim dynasty appeared to be invincible at the time, it would face a grave crisis in which they received moral support from their younger brethren the Five Percenters.

Physical Departure of the Hon. Elijah Muhammad

On Feb. 25th, 1975, it was reported that the Hon. Elijah Muhammad had passed away at Mercy Hospital in Chicago of congestive heart failure. This was a time of mourning within the Nation of Islam as well as the Five Percenters who held a great respect for the Messenger of Allah. Many of the Muslims were already in Chicago as scheduled for their Savior's Day convention that was to be held on Feb. 26th. At the Savior's Day convention it was announced that the Messenger's son, Wallace D. Muhammad, was voted as the new leader of the NOI.

Over the next couple of years Wallace made drastic changes. He moved the NOI to orthodox Islam and subsequently questioned the teachings (lessons) of his Father and Fard. He changed the Nation's name from the "Nation of Islam" to the "World Community of Al-Islam in the West," ultimately naming it the "American Muslim Mission." In addition, Wallace dismantled the paramilitary wing of the NOI--the Fruit of Islam (FOI) and relaxed the disciplined instituted by his father. This had a rippling effect as some Muslims went back to their old lifestyles of the "dead" world and abandoned Elijah's ideology. Shahid M. Allah cites this impact:

> In his 1974 Saviour's Day Address: The Last Sermon Messenger Elijah Muhammad said, "The Bible says of the DAY OF JUDGEMENT" you will see God as He is. This is the day that I can gladly say that He is 'He.'... FOR 43 years, I have been teaching that God is man. For 43 years I have been teaching you that one day you'll wake up and agree with me..." And as ELIJAH taught that from the rostrum at the South Shore country club in Chicago, Illinois, Allah's Gods and Earths diligently taught the same TRUTH in the streets. ELIJAH MUHAMMAD is the Moses of the Bible and Holy Qur'an. This cannot be refuted. Moses (Musa) means Civilizer. The Book of Malachi reads: "BEHOLD, I SEND YOU ELIJAH (MUHAMMAD) BEFORE THE GREAT AND DREADFUL DAY OF THE LORD.." And in 1975, when the physical person of the Most Honorable Elijah Muhammad was withdrawn from the world scene ALLAH (THE GODS) remained! And the trial would come down on the Nation of Islam.[416]

Within the teachings of his new American Muslim Mission, Wallace changed his name to Warithudeen Mohammed and declared that the Honorable Elijah Muhammad was no longer considered to be the Messenger of Allah. He criticized many of his Father's teachings as contradictory to Islam as taught in the East. It was during this time that the American Muslim Mission made it increasingly unpopular to invoke the name of Elijah Muhammad or let alone teach his lessons. This was the case with most of Elijah's ministers who followed the path of Wallace and no longer advocated the teachings of Elijah Muhammad. This point is mentioned in the Five Percenter Newspaper:

> The next example is the Muslim followers of the HONORABLE ELIJAH MUHAMMAD. When the MESSENGER OF ALLAH returned to his essence, some of his followers began to stray from his teachings. This resulted in their losing knowledge of WHO IS THAT MYSTERY GOD? And reverting back to worshipping a SPOOK. The Messenger's greatest teaching is that GOD IS NOT A SPOOK. But since those followers who strayed were convinced to disregard their LESSONS, they forgot that (WE) THE SON OF MAN HAVE SEARCHED FOR THAT MYSTERY GOD FOR TRILLIONS OF YEARS AND WERE UNABLE TO FIND THIS SO-CALLED MYSTERY GOD SO WE HAVE AGREED THAT THE ONLY GOD IS THE SON OF MAN (US). I am not a follower of MINISTER LOUIS FARRAKHAN but I respect him for sticking to the teachings of the Messenger when others strayed from them.[417]

On the contrary these trying times for the NOI became a defining moment for the Five Percenters because it was the Gods and Earths who continued to teach and uphold the lessons of the Hon. Elijah Muhammad in his absence. Simultaneously, Minister Farrakhan had regrouped and reestablished the Nation of Islam under its former teachings. For the Five Percenters defense of the lessons in the face of the American Muslim Mission and differing views of orthodox Muslims, the Five Percenters earned the respect of the Muslim followers of the Honorable Elijah Muhammad. Minister Farrakhan cites this point in a lecture he gave in 1977. The Minister expounds:

> And one thing that that brother (referring to Clarence 13X) did, he taught the lessons of the Honorable Elijah Muhammad to young brothers and sisters. And many of those who brother represent, that are a part of the 5% Nation, they didn't take this fall that we took because they were rooted in the lessons of the Honorable Elijah Muhammad. And that's why the Honorable Elijah Muhammad before he left us he kept telling us to study the lessons, study the lessons, study the lessons. Because the lessons weren't just for yesterday, they are for yesterday, today and tomorrow. And because we forgot the lessons we fell victim to deceit.[418]

As these chains of events unfolded, it was Minister Farrakhan, who after two years of following Warithudeen trail-blazed the path back to the teachings of the Honorable Elijah Muhammad for the NOI. As Minister Farrakhan successfully resurrected the NOI many followed in his path and reclaimed the teachings of Elijah Muhammad. Farrakhan reassumed his title and post as "The National Representative of the Honorable Elijah Muhammad" and reestablished the militant Fruit of Islam (FOI). Farrakhan went on to repurchase the properties of the NOI that were lost under the leadership of Warithudeen and successfully rebuilt the Nation of Islam attracting many followers—old and new.

The Honorable Elijah Muhammad wasn't the only loss felt by the Five Percenters. This decade also claimed the life of Allah's right hand man-- Old Man Justice.

> Justice began to have seizures. During one seizure he fell into a tub of hot water. He was hospitalized his entire body was scalded. His strength began to fade after that. We hoped that he would rest. But he had to "hangout." A few months later Justice had another seizure and returned home it was July 19, 1978. We put our monies together for his Funeral Service and Cremation. The one thing you will remember about Old Man Justice is his laugh and his smile.[419]

Despite the loss of Justice, the Five Percent Nation of Islam still was gaining momentum and its presence was being felt in the streets of the Greater New York Area. Part of this was due to their militant discipline and uncompromising stance on the NOI lessons. Many youth were attracted to the no-nonsense image portrayed by the Five Percenters and their mastering of the spoken word. Their impact and influence was felt in the public school systems amongst their peers and their teachers.

> From the mid-seventies on into the late eighties the influence of the 5% (Gods and Earths) swelled to enormous proportions up and down the East coast, Mid-West and even as far as the West coast (i.e. California). Righteousness was running rampant in high schools like Springfield Gardens, located in Springfield Gardens, Queens, NY. Young Gods with attributes like: Prince Saluhdin, Master Saviour, Supreme Lamiek and Allah Supreme consistently check-mated their White school teachers daily! No

lie about Allah (Clarence 13X Smith), Master W.D. Fard Muhammad, the Most Honorable Elijah Muhammad or the Hon. Louis Farrakhan could be told without it being refuted by one of the Gods or Earths.[420]

It was common for Five Percenters to often hold impromptu ciphers in the streets or in public schools as other interested curious youth looked on. These ciphers were often initiated by a member of the Five Percent Nation of Islam asking another Five Percenter, "How do you see today's mathematics?" That question would initiate a "build session" in which a Five Percenter would poetically begin to recite his lessons in a rapid-like fashion in correlation to that particular date. These ciphers (conversations) became public exhibitions and mesmerized onlookers. Yusef Nurrideen speaks on this phenomenon:

> When dozens of these novel concepts come at you in the rapid-fire, mile-a-minute talking pace of a Five Percenter it is a mind-expanding experience...a visit to another world where normal rules of logic are suspended and an entirely new set of rules apply. The terrain of this world is landscaped by the mythology provided in the lessons of the NOI, and the "divine sciences" created by Clarence 13X, the Supreme Mathematics and Alphabet.[421]

It was build sessions like these that propelled the Five Percent Nation of Islam into the limelight and made the movement so attractive as it allured more youth to its fold. During the mid 80's, Black youth began to identify with Black Nationalism on a large scale. This era put the Five Percenters at the helm of consciousness amongst the youth because of their awesome ability to articulate on a political as well as a social level. This kind of activity peaked the interest of the media.

> The hypnotic, mathematical, rhythmic Black theology of the 5% proved to be so successful that White daily newspapers like NEWSDAY commenced to print bad press about us, to discredit an indestructible foundation – the Nation of Gods and Earths! In an article entitled "A 'Nation' Unto Themselves" by NEWSDAY journalist, Sid Cassese, it was written, "They call themselves Gods...They speak to each other in a mathematical code and offer their dogmatic teachings in a terse, staccato, seemingly

rote-learned rap. 'Peace' is their greeting and their amen..."
(Newsday, December 5, 1982) Irregardless of the bad press the
Gods and Earths continued to teach all those who had not heard
the Life-Giving teaching of Messenger Elijah Muhammad. One
could often find the 5% educating the youth on basketball courts,
house parties, barber shops, concerts, discos, college campuses,
places of employment, and even houses of worship. Day by day,
week by week, month by month and year by year the influence
of the Gods and Earths has grown to enormous proportions. We
thank Allah for this; because He had the courage to come forth
from Temple No. 7, back in the early sixties, when Malcolm X
was the Minister, to share the Knowledge with the youth out in
the streets! "...Your sons and daughters shall prophesy..your
young men shall see visions." (Joel 2:28) This is what Allah
blessed the youth with.[422]

Hip Hop

These communications of free expression ultimately helped
spawn an art form amongst Black youth. Yusef Nurrideen:

> One area in which all Five Percenters or Gods have exhibited
> remarkable master or self-actualization is the ability to
> communicate effectively. As conversationalists they are
> unequalled. The fascinating, even mesmerizing, appeal of the
> movement to the youth comes from the Five Percenter's
> eloquent and spell-binding usage of African-American inner-city
> slang. Using the potency and the vitality of the black dialect
> they open up new avenues of logic and thinking, or original
> ways of perceiving the world.[423]

It was this same mastery of the spoken word and self-
expression that allowed the Five Percenters to play an intricate
role in the beginnings of an urban subculture that was
established by urban youth. This genre later became known as
"Hip-Hop" or *Rap Music* that began in the late 70's. Kool Herc,
who is recognized as one of the pioneers of Hip Hop admits the
effect the Five Percenters had on him and his craft. This form of
music would eventually sweep the United States and the World.

The Five Percenters became a primary force in the beginnings
of Hip-Hop with the advent of rap groups such as "The World
Famous Supreme Team," with their smash records "Hobo
Scratch" "Buffalo Girls" and "Hey DJ." The Supreme Team
hosted it's own radio show on WHBI and systematically played

the Five Percenter National Anthem called "The Enlightener" (a hymn that sung praises to Five Percenter founders Allah and Justice) before and after their show. The Supreme Team later recorded some of Hip-Hop's earliest hits that became the background music to the dance craze known as "Break Dancing."

Many other 5% rap groups later emerged on the scene during the '80s. The most notable were artists such as Eric B. & Rakim, Just-Ice, Big Daddy Kane, Lakim Shabazz and King Sun. All the said above groups often invoked Five Percenter teachings and imagery throughout their records and music videos. In fact, the Five Percenters have been acknowledged as being the source for common Hip Hop popular phrases that include ("Peace", "Word is Bond", Peace "G", "Cipher", "Building", "Break it Down", "Dropping Science or Knowledge", "Represent", and "Show and Prove") amongst many other phrases. These phrases show the impact that the Five Percenters had on the Hip Hop culture yesterday and today.

Organizational Efforts

During the early 80's, Universal Shaamguadd gained popularity within the movement when he founded a Five Percenter newsletter entitled the *"Sun of Man."* This newsletter was one of the first of its kind and was used to spread and centralize Five Percenter teachings utilizing their own medium. The newsletter addressed current events, health issues, history and other issues affecting the Black community and the Five Percenters. These kind of steps increased visibility of the organization to the general population.

Five Percenters efforts earned them respect from civil and religious leaders. One prime example of this is when Minister Farrakhan delivered his historic address at Madison Square Garden on October 7, 1985. The Garden was sold out as well as the overflow room at the Felt Forum next door as there was over 25,000-35,000 people in attendance. The Five Percenters were out in force in great numbers. At one point in his speech Farrakhan took the time out to recognize the unity between the Five Percent Nation and the Nation of Islam. Yusef Nurrideen points this out in his article:

As the Five Percenters political ideology becomes more developed, they increasingly identify with the aims and aspirations of the Nation of Islam. Although members of the old Nation would dismiss them as "Scientists," Minister Louis Farrakhan in his October 1985 Madison Square Garden address to a overflow crowd of 25,000 New Yorkers at one point specifically addressed his "beautiful brothers and sisters of the Five Percent Nation" in a message of unity. Several hundred Five Percenters in the crowd cheered in response. Some Five Percenters now say that the only difference between themselves and Farrakhan's NOI is the latter's strict dress code (e.g., suits and bow ties).[424]

Rap Artist Rakim Allah seen in his video "Move The Crowd" displaying the Five Percent insignia "The Universal Flag of Islam."

In a 1986 issue of the Sun of Man newsletter, in an effort to organize the Five Percent Nation of Islam, Universal Shaamguadd addressed the issue for organization in his publication. He announced and suggested the name under which they could organize. The title he along with other Five Percent pioneers proposed for the Five Percent Nation was "Allah's Nation of Islam" which was to be the name under which they would reorganize:

Our Father Almighty God Allah told us that all of these things would come to pass and that the solution to these problems would be right under the peoples' noses, and that they would not be able to see it because they didn't have the understanding.

I see these things as a warning from Allah, because he taught us that we were the solution to world problems and that it was our duty to do all with in our power to make them see and understand this, and it is with this and other things in mind that we have come together to try to restruct our Nation under the title of Allah's Nation of Islam. We will still be the Five Percent Nation, and the Gods and Earths and the Nation Builders, however, our Formal Title will be ALLAHS NATION OF ISLAM.

There will be a National Council of Allah to oversee National activities as well as State Council and Community Councils with area wide representation. It is our hope that a National Council will be able to show the world that we are of the solution not the problem a lot of the people accuse us of being. We also plan to deal directly with the media, in a more direct as well as local and national politics on a more realistic and personal level. To show and prove that we are an asset to society rather than the liability they have labeled us. We also plan to publish a National Paper, one that will combine and reflect the teachings of our nation as a whole and bring some of our issues to the forefront of social awareness. [425]

Soon afterwards there were two National Newspapers published by the Five Percenters called "The Word" and "The Five Percenter." A Five Percenter journalist Shabazz Adew Allah recalls the history:

Historically speaking, "The Five Percenter", as a monthly publication was co-founded by EL-AM JAB BORN ALLAH, KOFI ALLAH, MESSIAH B. ALLAH, QUEEN ARABIA EARTH AND SALAAM ALLAH in 1987. This is the same year that BELOVED ALLAH, GOD ALLAH MIND, SHAHID M. ALLAH, ASIA EARTH, DAMEENA EARTH AND GOD ALLAH SUPREME KAZI presented the first edition of the first nationally recognized news publication, "THE WORD". It's theme was/ is "ONE WORD CAN CHANGE THE COURSE OF A NATION". 1987 was a year of intellectual challenge, and the Gods and Earths wasted no time in pulling together their collective skills to meet the challenge.[426]

Both papers were embraced by the movement and enjoyed national circulation. Many Five Percenters took pride in establishing their own media as they had a platform to tell their own story and report their own news.

As the Five Percent Nation of Islam made moves on an organizational level it was faced with some setbacks. Moves were being made to seize the Street Academy from the Five Percenters of which they had a 20-year lease from the city that was good from 1967 through 1987. The first attempt was made ten years prior in 1977, when the Harlem Commonwealth Council prematurely attempted to oust the group from the land in order to build a Senior Citizens complex. The Five Percenters put up a strong resistance and the city opted to honor the lease until it's fulfillment in 1987. After winning the battle with the Harlem Commonwealth Council, ironically the Street Academy became stagnant over a ten-year period and had little impact on the movement. As relayed in an article that appeared in the Five Percenter Newspaper in 1989:

> The so perceived Hub of the Nation, the Allah School in Mecca building, has seemingly been frozen in time eleven years since staving off the Harlem Commonwealth Council's sinister attempt to seize the structural monument at 2122 Seventh Avenue. The role it has played on our Nation's guidance and growth though seemingly important has for nearly two decades stood ominously a curious ambiguity. Mainly as a shelter to national membership seeking refuge from the elements, No other clear programmatic function of Allah School was universally defined and accepted...
>
> The overbearing image of sacredness accompanying the Allah School in Mecca building is derived only from its association to our great Father's legacy. For many and possibly most of the Nation, it has been idolized as a source of Unity, Security, and Pride. Realistically though such fundamentalist folly has earmarked a misguided mind set of whimsical well wishing and more dangerously, false unity, false security and false pride.[427]

While fighting to keep the street academy after the expired lease in 1987, another untimely misfortune arose. To compound the already existing issue, a fire occurred at the Allah Street Academy in 1988 that left the building severely damaged. Due to organizational challenges and lack of funds the future of the school's needed repairs looked bleak. Many within the movement suspected arsonists perhaps hired by the powers that be and/ or economic opportunists. But because of the academy's prior managerial problems, the news of the school's potential demise met with mixed emotions by the Gods and Earths. As reported in The Five Percenter Newspaper in 1989:

On Tuesday, December 6, 1988, a historic shrine in Mecca was gutted in a fiery inferno that suspiciously raged uncontrollably at 2122 7th Avenue. In the smoldering aftermath virtually nothing but the walls, a Universal flag, and a black and silver sign reading "Allah School In Mecca" remained. Accounts, given to the Five Percenter, of the SEEMINGLY ALARMING event allege that the fire ignited and spread throughout the one story structure instantaneously engulfing it in roaring flames...

In various statements to the Five Percenter, nation members reveal feelings about the event ranging from distressed grief all the way to rejoiced jubilation. The reason for such diverse, reactions is said to be because the 'Allah School Issue' had greatly polarized the nation as to what the appropriate course of action was regarding the all but condemned structure.

Overwhelmingly, however, the consistent suspicion held by almost all spoken to was that the building was indeed a target of arson. It should be noted that at the time of the fire a vigorous battle was being fought by some nation members to stave off the imminent loss of the property. An order to vacate the property September 1988 was issued by the city of New York and litigation to halt this process was in motion...

As one young nation member puts it, "I feel bad because of all the history of the father contained in the structure." This statement was met with the reply by an older nation member that the "history was carried in the minds of the people and not in the building," he said. He also added, "the Father was barely in the building two years." Since it was established in 1967 and he left in 1969.

In any event, the building now stands there a boarded up burnt out shell seemingly waiting for the circling vultures to soar in and pick apart its remains. The questions on the minds of many and perhaps the most relevant ones are: was this really a catastrophe or was it a blessing in disguise and also WHERE TO NOW ALLAH SCHOOL?[428]

As it was in other cases, Allah's Five Percenters were no strangers to adversity. As news of the academy's bleak future reverberated in Five Percent circles, many heeded the call for help. There was a new cause to join forces around. The Gods and Earths designated to fix and keep the academy open promoted the rallying cry "Save Our School" or "SOS". Petitions were being signed and money was being collected for repairs. Five Percenters pooled their resources and came together to remedy the situation. To help the matter, a soon-to-be popular rap video was shot on location at the newly renovated Allah School that helped rejuvenate the institution.

As the tide of black consciousness was still rolling strong amongst urban youth, Hip Hop was again used as a medium for Five Percenter messages. In 1990, two popular 5% rap groups *Brand Nubians* and *Poor Righteous Teachers* burst on the rap scene. Brand Nubians did their first music video *"Wake Up"* on location in front of the newly renovated *Allah School In Mecca* in 1991. The image of the Allah School and lyrics loaded with 5% references was being seen and heard on TV screens throughout the world. Poor Righteous Teachers also came out with rap videos that were full of Five Percenter imagery and teachings. Other Five Percenter popular rap artists emerged on the scene in the mid nineties such as the members of the *Wu Tang Clan, Digable Planets, Black Moon, Busta Rhymes, AZ* and *Erykah Badu* just to name a few. These groups as well as others made guest appearances at the annual Show and Prove events.

With it's recent renovations and appointment of a managerial staff to run the operations of the school, the institution began to come into it's own. It became a meeting place for Five Percenters to congregate, hash out new ideas and implement plans. One among them was another attempt to rename the movement. A few years earlier a short biography of Allah was written in 1987 that made the posthumous claimed that Allah said, *"His death would born the Nation of Gods and Earths."* Some of the staff began to use this name in conjunction with other existing names although the name wouldn't catch on until a few years later.

Another welcoming force in the Five Percent was its influence on college campuses, particularly historically Black colleges. A prime example is the popularity it gained at Martin Luther King's alma mater, the prestigious Morehouse College campus in Atlanta, GA. In the early nineties an influx of Five Percenter students enrolled at the college were very active and influential on the Atlanta scene. The team of students held lectures, educational forums, conducted student debates and participated in tutorial programs for neighborhood youth. Universal Parliaments were conducted weekly on the Atlanta University Campus with hundreds of students and non-students in attendance.

These Five Percenter students became ideal role models for the organization, as they were refined, articulate, well educated and polished in their presentation. The students shunned drinking and smoking (which is a remarkable feat at any college) and were highly respected by their peers. Their diplomatic efforts gained them friendships with other religious and civic organizations such as the Nation of Islam, the orthodox Muslim community, fraternities, sororities, Christian organizations, political groups and nationalists. Even England's British Broadcasting Company (BBC) contacted the Five Percenters and Muslims to air a documentary. Among them a young Five Percenter and NOI student minister, True Islam, was featured in the BBC's documentary of Morehouse College. Similar Five Percenter activity also took place on other college campuses throughout the country.

Million Man March Participation

The presence of the Five Percenters and its impact could best be measured by another seemingly impossible milestone event that occurred in 1995. Minister Farrakhan, who was on a "Men's Only" speaking tour in which he addressed Black male audiences around the country had announced his plans to have a "A Million Man March" at D.C., the nation's capital. The event was scheduled to take place on Monday, October 16, 1995 and was billed as "The Day Of Atonement."

News of the proposed event appealed to the Five Percenters who were a predominantly male group. Another reason was the group's relation to the convener Farrakhan, who some Five Percenters now claim kinship given his status in the NOI puts him on par with the Most Honorable Elijah Muhammad. For 2nd generation Five Percenters Farrakhan is to the organization what the Honorable Elijah Muhammad was to the 1st generation of Five Percenters. Or even in the least of cases, it merely could have been a show of Black unity on behalf of the Five Percenters. Whatever the reason, it was important enough to carry an article of support in the September 1995 issue of the Five Percenter Newspaper.

> We are in full support of the ONE MILLION MAN MARCH, to be on October 16, 1995. It is high time for Us Men of the Black Family to get together for one common cause. Justice for our people lay only in our ability to overcome the DIVIDE and CONQUER syndrome which has permeated our kind since the days of slavery. All other races have the power to UNITE for an upliftment and improvement of their people... We are thrilled and optimistic of a new DAY and TIME, when we American Men (Black men) put the welfare of our Black people first and foremost.. Good luck to all of you overtaking this historical and glorious event. Only the minions will try to discredit this day of great deed in its inception... They will say: "IT WON'T WORK". Because they do not want it to work. But the power of Black Unity and Black love will make it work!!!!!!!![429]

Caravans of Five Percenters from all over the country made the trek to DC and showed up by the thousands. One could see the presence of the group as the greetings "Peace God!" was exchanged by hundreds of men and impromptu ciphers commenced everywhere in DC. The DC chapter of the Five Percent Nation had hosted a rally the day before and enjoyed a sizable turn out.

That Monday on the mall, the Five Percenters involvement was evident as there was a huge banner that read "The 5% Nation of Islam" with two big painted head busts of Allah and Justice. Young men were bejeweled with the Universal Flag of Islam pins and shirts as some vended on the mall. Many compared the event to the eastern "hajj" in Mecca which Muslim pilgrims travel to worship at the Kaaba in Arabia. Except that this hajj took place in the West and was the day of the Black Man and on a smaller scale a reunion for the Five Percenters. The experience was overwhelming and prompted a special edition of the Five Percenter Newspaper that reported the experience.

> On October 16, 1995 OVER ONE MILLION Blackmen assembled in Washington D.C. in response to a call for a MILLION MAN MARCH there by Minister Louis Farrakhan and Dr. Benjamin Chavis.

GODS IN THE HOUSE. Many GODS from all across America were in attendance at the history making event which surpassed all previous attendance numbers to date (1.2 to 1.5 MILLION) even though the Devil's Media LIED placing the count at 400,000. All Who were there know that we passed 1 Million before noon. The meeting of Oh So many GODS from across America and seeing SHAHID (JOHN 37X) WHO LEFT THE MOSQUE WITH ALLAH and CO-FOUNDED THIS NATION WITH HIM AND JUSTICE. Made it especially rewarding for us.[430]

The Million Man March attracted well over it's desired figure of one million. It was the largest gathering ever in the United States, Black or white. In the microcosm of that macrocosm, it was the largest gathering of Five Percenters ever too. At the very least it showed their strength in numbers and the explosive potential to make a positive change in modern society.

Speaking of modern, another contemporary tool of communication was experiencing its modest beginnings. It was the advent of the "world wide web" or the "internet." The Five Percenters introduction to the Internet started out humbly enough circa 1997 as "wannabe" Five Percenters from suburbia posted websites with familiar symbols and references from 5% rap groups they idolized. Although maybe sincere, these first Internet surfers were typically from remote areas that were never exposed to actual Five Percenters and the contents on their websites depicted such. As more authentic Five Percenters gained access to the web the makeshift websites and their owners were discovered and admonished. Although all wasn't lost because this prompted the makers of these sites to travel to Allah School In Mecca where they could meet Five Percenters and receive the teachings thus now giving them an heir of legitimacy.

On the flip side of the coin, this proved to be of equal benefit for the Allah School In Mecca because it now could develop a strong hold on a new generation. Seemingly so because prior it onlt had a waning influence on tenured 5% in the greater New York area as the 5% were already accustomed and familiar with the teachings so they didn't need to depend on the edifice – they seen themselves as the edifice. But this wasn't so for the new generation and the word from Allah School In Mecca was taken as "the gospel."

One point of concern is that the younger converts who receive the teachings the unconventional ways didn't have the benefit of learning "the culture" as their predecessors who grew up in communities rampant with other Five Percenters. Abu Shahid addressed this concern with a reporter:

> But the result today shows fragmentation and a nation so spread out that it's difficult to maintain communication between Gods and Earths from other states and countries – even as they believe their numbers continue to grow.
>
> "With more quantity you get less quality," says Abu. "Newer elements pop up watering down the solution saying foolish things like [NGE teachings] aren't needed." Given how many movements wane from their founding fathers' intentions as they grow older, Abu hopes that this doesn't happen to NGE and the principles he helped foster.[431]

When I conducted my interview with Shahid and asked what his statement meant, he advised:

> "I mean the Lessons, do not get away from the Lessons. The Lessons are the cornerstone of the Nation. The same Lessons that the Father and I received in the Mosque. It means the same thing today. What you teaching must be consistent with the Lessons."[432]

Shahid's point is valid amongst the contemporary Five Percenters. With the addition of a newer generation some have brought their own ideas to the theology. Different persons have attempted to invalidate the lessons and the more extreme ones attempt to vilify its authors who are the NOI founders. Evidence of this can be seen on the Internet. Anyone who participates in the undermining of the lessons and its founders are often dismissed as "Five Pretenders" or "Jive Percenters" by those firmly rooted in the lessons. The current Five Percenters are streamlining their efforts to reinforce "the lessons" as the unabated criterion for their teachings as it is securing its place at the forefront of the movement.

Chapter 25
Contemporary Five Percenters

Allah School In Mecca

The contemporary Five Percenters have come a long way since their inception in 1964. The early Five Percenters of the 60's, 70's and 80's are much older today. What once started exclusively as a youth movement has just as many older adults in its ranks. This has caused some to take a more organized approach to the doctrine. Steps have been made to bring more structure to the movement similar to the "religious" organizations that they once criticized. Much cannot be done to avoid the comparison, as any group who wishes to flourish and thrive must develop some kind of structure.

Demographics

The contemporary Five Percent may not have the potency and rigor it once had in the 1960's, it does have greater numbers to date, thus showing mass potential. The actual size of the movement is difficult to gauge, as there is no roster of membership. Due to it's loose knit nature and denial as a real organization or religious group it doesn't deem it necessary to count its numbers in a conventional sense. It is clear that at least tens of thousands of young Blacks have come through its doors and many still remain and identify themselves as part of the collective. With that in mind, the majority of Five Percenters are not involved with the latest organizational efforts to develop a solid structure similar to other groups such as the Nation of Islam, but as to those who are involved, they have large numbers to work with. That gives you some idea of the far-reaching effects and size of the movement.

The logistical membership of the Five Percenters has somewhat changed over the last four decades. As it once started out as an exclusive all youth movement that catered and consisted of troubled teens, the median age is older today and it is safe to say that it could now be considered a responsible adult group whose mission statement is to "teach the children." Many of the children in the movement are the actual biological children of its members. Moves are being made to bring more young children into the fold reminiscent of the 60's, 70's and 80's. A positive aspect is that many of the adult members were true to the edict spoken by a young Five Percenter to Mayor Lindsay after Clarence 13X's death when he said, *The only way we can show that we loved him is to build—to get our own carpenters, doctors, lawyers, painters, electricians—that's how we can show that we loved him.* Today, Five Percenters come from all walks of life and have attained the occupations mentioned in the young man's statement. They are a microcosm of the rest of working America. Many of their members are productive citizens in society as they are professionals, entrepreneurs, teachers, laborers, artists, lawyers, students and the list goes on.

Quite surprisingly, there are numerous Five Percenters that are in the United States Military. Although amongst Five Percenters it is not popular to be in the Service, there has been quite a few that have joined or either were converted while in active duty. Nevertheless, the Five Percenters have successfully integrated into the Service. It should be noted that Five Percenters do not encourage any of their members to join the service but it is encouraged for Black People who are in the service to become Five Percenters.

The Five Percenters are no longer geographically limited to the eastern region of the United States (although that area still has the highest concentration of Five Percenters). Its members are now located in every peak and valley of America. The presence is strong in states such as: New York, New Jersey, Pennsylvania, Massachusetts, Connecticut, DC, Maryland, Virginia, The Carolinas, Georgia, Florida, Louisiana, Texas, Illinois, Ohio, Michigan, Wisconsin, Colorado, Washington, California and other states. Its presence is greater in the major cities but many are found in suburban areas and even rural parts of the country. The Five Percenters have established a solid presence in Canada as well as overseas in London, England. A few other areas overseas have a Five Percenter presence mainly through the adherents that are in the United States Armed Services stationed in Asia, Africa and Europe.

The Five Percenters still have large numbers within the penal institutions of America. Many inmates convert while in prison. Its influence within the correctional system along with some purported acts of aggression has prompted some institutions to label the Five Percenters as a gang. Leading the charge was the South Carolina Department of Corrections, which in 1995 designated the Five Percenters as "a Security Threat Group." Inmates that claimed to believe in the Islamic sect are denied their rights in prison and in many cases placed in solitary confinement unless they complete a form denouncing the Islamic sect. Subsequently, a group of inmates (Plaintiffs) with the assistance of the ACLU and Southern Center For Human Rights filed a lawsuit in the United States District Court against the Department of Corrections (Defendants). In December 1997 the Court ruled in favor of the Defendants. The action was appealed to the U.S. Fourth Circuit Court of Appeals by attorneys representing the inmate plaintiffs and in March 1999 the Court of Appeals upheld the lower court decision in favor of the Defendants. This decision although not legally binding outside of (SCDOC) has been upheld in practice within other correctional institutions across America denying Five Percenters their religious rights.

In the state of New York the persecution was just as severe until a recent turn of events. A Five Percenter inmate named Intelligent Tarref Allah was able to obtain a lawyer from

Sullivan & Cromwell, a prestigious Manhattan law firm, and the Five Percenters' case was taken to the Supreme Court and met with success. On July 31, 2003, a Federal Court District Judge in Manhattan ruled that the Five Percenters could practice their "religious" beliefs within the New York Department of Corrections. The New York Times reported the decision:

> But on July 31 Judge Naomi Reice Buchwald of Federal District Court in Manhattan ruled that Mr. Allah is entitled to the same religious freedoms as the thousands of practicing Jews, Muslims, Christians, Hare Krishnas and Wiccans incarcerated in New York State's prisons.
>
> In the universe of prisoners' rights, the ruling was groundbreaking because it would force state prison officials to allow Five Percenters, whom observers see as an extremist group, to have access to the literature and carry out the rituals of what they say is their religion, the Nation of Gods and Earths.
>
> Judge Buchwald also ordered state prison officials to report back to her within 60 days on their progress in accommodating Five Percenter requests for monthly "Parliament" meetings; special prison dinner menus and post-sundown cafeteria schedules during periods of fasting; and special celebrations during Five Percenter holy days, including the birthdays of Elijah Muhammad, the Nation of Islam founder, and Clarence 13X Smith, the founder of the Nation of Gods and Earths.[433]

This landmark decision allows the Five Percenters the freedom to practice their faith within the walls of the New York State prisons. This unprecedented victory both instills inspiration in Five Percenters in other correctional institutions throughout the country while at the same time escalating reluctance on behalf of other prison officials who fear they may have to take the same course.

In other institutions specific to higher learning, the Five Percenters still have their niche on the college campuses. Their influence is more predominant on historically Black college campuses such as Morehouse College, Clark Atlanta University, Howard University, North Carolina A&T, North Carolina Central University, Hampton Institute, Florida A&M and Grambling University. Many Five Percent adherents go on to attend Graduate Schools to further their studies in academic disciplines. It is expected that once they receive their credentials they will utilize it to help build their communities and proselytize their teachings.

One example is Five Percenter True Islam, who after graduating from Morehouse College enrolled in the Islamic Studies PHD program at the University of Michigan. He since then has obtain his Masters Degree and has written five books to his credit: "The Book Of God" "Allah The Original Man" "King of Kings, Lord of Lords" "How Came The Black God Mr. Muhammad" and "The Truth Of God." His books are all dedicated to showing and proving to the world of religion and academics that the teachings of the Honorable Elijah Muhammad are academically correct and without flaw. He has traveled to and participated in seminars to prove his theories throughout America and even overseas to Germany. His work has earned him awards and honors by the hosting councils. He is scheduled to earn his PHD in 2007.

5% Institutions

Five Percenters have developed their own provisional institutions throughout America. Different "Allah Schools" have opened and closed its doors in the Eastern, Southern, Midwestern and Western parts of the United States. The movement's physical and standing Headquarters is still located at "The Allah School In Mecca" in Harlem, New York. There is no one specific person "in charge" but there are people assigned to specific functions of its daily operation. There is still the threat of outsiders (commonwealth groups with financial interests) to seize the school from the movement. The Allah School administration is aware of their tactics and continues to take precautionary measures to thwart off these organizations. The Allah School hosts "General Civilization Classes" for Five Percenters who wish to learn more about their studies. On the other side it moonlights as the "Allah Youth Center" which hosts outreach programs for neighborhood youth. The school's doors remain open to all members, sympathizers and even tourists. Most of the tourists are members who live outside of New York City and travel to Harlem to see "the root of civilization." In fact tours are actually provided showing out of town Five Percenters different historical landmarks pertaining to the history of Allah. This usually takes place during National Events held in New York City and hosted by the School.

The "Show and Prove Educational" is still the most popular annual event of the organization. It has consistently taken place over the past 33 years since it's inception. Science awards are still given out to the bright young students with the best science projects. It is always a surprise to see what music groups will perform. With so many Five Percenter music celebrities makes for many options and guest appearances. Acts such as Wu-Tang, Brand Nubians, Poor Righteous Teachers, Erykah Badu, Common Sense, Gangstarr and others have performed at the event in the past. Another annual gathering has become known as "Father's Day," that takes place on or about February 22nd, which is the birthday of the Nation's founder Allah. This event is similar to a special Universal Parliament that places emphasis on the achievements of Allah and his history. These two annual events are considered homecomings, as it resembles reunions between members of different parts of the country. It is not uncommon for members to hold dancing room balls the weekend of the events. Another gaining popular annual event is "Family Day" which is hosted outside in Philadelphia's Fairmount Park during a summer month. Other "Family Days" are hosted in other regions of the country as well.

In recent times, the Allah School administration has charted the country into 9 regions to help its organizational efforts. Each region holds a regional conference meeting in which a member of the school's administration usually heads. The regular monthly Universal Parliaments are still held the last Sunday of every month. In New York City, the Parliaments take place in the auditorium of Harriet Tubman Elementary School located around the corner from Allah School In Mecca. During the summer months the Parliaments are moved outside to a park located in the Fort Greene section of Brooklyn. This custom is practiced throughout all American cities that have Five Percenters. Meeting places are conveniently posted on Five Percenter websites showing the locales for the viewers perspective city.

One field the Five Percenters have taken a liking to is communications. Gods and Earths utilize print media such as newspapers, newsletters and the World Wide Web to get the word out to the masses. There are many other 5% organizations that function in conjunction and independently of the current administration. Amongst them are: The Sun of Man Publications, The Word Newspaper, The Five Percenter Newspaper, The Allah Team (All in All Productions), Allah's Universal Development Inc., The Black Family Newsletter, The Universal Truth, Thy Kingdom Come Productions, The National Statement, The Great Enlightener, NGE Power Paper, Black 7 On-line magazine and The 14th Degree and Beyond Earth Committees.

So many different 5% forums and perspectives promote a true sense of democracy among its adherents. Its democratic system allows its citizens the freedom of thought that promotes progression and tolerance of inalienable rights that rival even America's current democratic system. But the aim is to establish a righteous government based upon divine principles. Much like the spirit of the Universal Parliaments established by its founding Father Allah. Its constitution is the NOI lessons, Supreme Mathematics and Islamic principles. The Five Percenters developed a slogan that sums up their mission statement, *"Unification is the Directive, Truth is the Criterion."* It is within that pursuit and criterion that the Five Percenters will find their way.

The End.

Appendices

I. 5% Schools Of Thought
–An Exploratory View of Theological Diversities within the Five Percenters.

II. The FBI Files On Clarence 13X And The Five Percenters
–The files of the FBI's COINTELPRO directive against Clarence 13X and The Percenters.

III. The Wisdom Of Allah: Clarence 13X Speaks!
–Interview Conducted With Allah (Clarence 13X) At Otisville Training Institute For Boys On November 15, 1967.

IV. The Allah School In Mecca
-Insights Into The Curriculum of The Allah School In Mecca.

Appendix I
5% Schools Of Thought

An Exploratory View of Theological Diversities within the Five Percenters

5% Contrasting Ideologies

[Author's note: The following appendix captures various different ideologies that have existed within the Five Percenters. Certain past and present philosophies are highlighted within the movement.]

Prior to his untimely death, Universal Shaamguadd recalled a prophetic statement made by Allah in regards to the future of the Five Percenters. Shaamguadd:

> Now in all fairness The Father also said that from one shall come many...Just as many nations have came from the teachings of Muhammad of 1400 and many nations have come from the teachings of the Honorable Elijah Muhammad (May the Peace and Blessings of Allah be upon Them.) I AM sure that many nations will be born from the teachings of Almighty God ALLAH whatever path you'll may decide to take I hope that we will remain one in PEACE and one in ISLAM, and may the Supreme Guidance of ALLAH be with you. PEACE.[434]

As it is with any group of human beings, the Five Percenters are not a monolithic society. With the advent of the new millennium the contemporary Five Percent have engaged in discussion and debates on the theology of the movement. As a result, different schools of thought were brought to the surface within the movement. Since the Five Percenters pride themselves on being free and independent thinkers, the different schools of thought within the movement sometimes can be as numerous as its members. One important aspect is the different schools of thought and members all co-exist with one another. There has yet to be a "split" because of any ideological differences. This is largely due to the Five Percenters creed of free thought and democracy amongst it's own. The only exception to that would be any moral or ethical violations that could earn banishment or exile from the group.

As the Five Percenters are free spirited it is extremely difficult to access the diversity of all views within the organization. However, one could possibly conclude that of all the different perspectives it appears to be at least two major stances established within the movement. Both stances appear to be centered on the way Five Percenters view themselves in relation to their organizational ancestry or "the Root," (i.e. Nation of Islam, Master Fard Muhammad, the Honorable Elijah Muhammad) which they profess borne "the Fruit," (Allah-Clarence 13X and the Five Percenters).

In an attempt to define its relation to the NOI and its teachings meaningful dialogue has been exchanged between the Five Percenters. The best way this author sees to describe it is whether or not the Five Percenters by definition could be considered an "Extension" or a "Division" of the Nation of Islam. These two stances are related to how they define themselves in relation to the Nation of Islam and its teachings (lessons).

There are some Five Percenters who agree with the points of the Nation of Islam and its core teachings. These Five Percenters fit the definition of an "Extension" within the Nation of Islam and its teachings as defined in the word and its root word:

Extend- (1) to stretch out or draw out to a certain point (2) to enlarge in area, scope, influence, meaning, effect, etc.; widen; broaden; expand; spread (3) to present for acceptance; offer; accord; grant (4) to give added bulk or body to (a substance).

Extension- (1) the amount or degree to which something is or can be extended; range; extent. (2) a part that forms a continuation or addition. (3) a branch of a university for students who cannot attend the university proper.

Hence, those who see themselves as an extension of the NOI tend to embrace the fundamental concepts of NOI theology. These Five Percenters believe that Allah's original intent and purpose of founding the Five Percenters were to spread the teachings of Islam (as taught in the NOI lessons) to the "babies" in the street who didn't attend the Mosque. These Five

Percenters identify themselves in the lessons as being part of a larger Nation of Islam that encompasses all the human family who "are striving for righteousness" and Black People in particular. As a rule of thumb, these Five Percenters comply and teach in accordance with the teachings of Allah (Supreme Mathematics and Alphabets) and W. F. Muhammad and Elijah Muhammad teachings (120 lessons as well as the body of knowledge found within NOI literature). Although the Five Percenters of this frame of thought recognize a divine connection between themselves and the NOI, they still cite the need for the Five Percenters and it's unique identity and purpose within the grand scheme of things.

Be that it may, in another spectrum; there are some Five Percenters who disagree with some major points of the Nation of Islam and its core teachings. Some of these Five Percenters fit the definition of a "Division" of the Nation of Islam and its teachings as defined in the word and its root word:

> Divide- (1) to separate into parts; split up; sever (2) to separate into groups; classify (3) to make or keep separate by or as by a boundary or partition (4) to cause disagreement between or among; alienate.

> Division- (1) a divide or being divided; separation (2) a difference of opinion; disagreement (3) anything that divides; partition or boundary.

Some of these Five Percenters who are partial to the NOI teachings believe that Allah left the Mosque because of a disagreement with the NOI teachings and established a counter-teaching or a whole new "nation" that contrasted with their ancestral organization (NOI) and their teachings (lessons). These Five Percenters tend more to innovate on the NOI teachings rather than adhere or acknowledge the fundamental concepts. Some of these Five Percenters even reject the term "Five Percenter" as well as other core tenants of the NOI lessons in an attempt to redefine themselves under different names to further alienate themselves from that past. Although perhaps not the original intention, some have selected to refer to the movement under the modern term "Nation of Gods and Earths" or the "NGE."

A prime example of this is the NOI lesson from which Allah gave the Five Percenters their namesake and mission. The term "Five Percenter" itself was once considered an endeared term coined by the movement's founder Allah himself. However, in present-day times the term is now considered offensive and irrelevant to some NGE members who dismiss the term in reference to the movement as incorrect. In question is the Lesson that serves as the foundation of the movement (formally known as the 5%) because of its inclusion of the words "Muslim and Muslim Sons" (the latter is a NOI term that means Mason) in the definition of Five Percent.

Some NGE members have redefined the term Five Percenter and gave it a new meaning as they no longer subscribe to the NOI definition as mentioned in the Lessons. Some NGE members have embraced an alternative teaching that they claim originated with Allah. The beginnings of these posthumous claims were introduced or mentioned almost two decades after his death. An article appearing in the Five Percenter Newspaper makes the claim:

> For the next few weeks Allah would lecture us constantly. Looking back now, I know that he was ARMORING us for the task to come, once he left us. He would drill us constantly. Not only in our lessons but in the lessons of life also. Today I see that Allah KNEW that he would be leaving us soon, so he implanted ALL of himself (GOD) in us. To make us strong for the job ahead of us. He told us in 1969, "After this year y'all will no longer be the 5%, you'll be the NATION OF GODS & EARTHS...THE 5% WILL BE THE WOMEN & CHILDREN".[435]

Name Game

This same dialogue has also prodded questions surrounding the naming of the movement. Shortly after Shaamguadd announcement attempting to solidify the name Allah's Nation of Islam, there was a claim that emerged that taught an alternative story about Allah that conflicted with Shaamguadd's testimony. According to this plus lesson, Allah never maintained that his movement was in any part to be called the Nation of Islam as the Five Percenters previously taught according to NOI Lessons (that all original people naturally were in the Nation of Islam). In contrast this claim advocated that Allah said they weren't even to be called Five Percenters. A group of individuals had issued a "history" or "plus lesson" to substantiate the doctrine. These plus lessons included revelations about Allah that were previously either unknown or unpopular to the movement for the previous two decades. The most noticeable was the new name change attempt of the movement that came from a posthumous claim made in 1987. The plus lesson aptly titled "The Greatest Story Never Told" made the unprecedented claim:

> In 1968, Allah started giving indications to his Five Percenters that he would be departing. He would tell them things like, "After this year there won't be any Five Percenters anymore. You will be the Nation of Gods and Earths, not the Nation of Islam...[436]

Some Five Percenters have used this name change claim as a justification to develop an alternative doctrine based upon a reinterpreted version of the NOI lessons that they profess originated with Allah. However, not all Five Percenters share this point of view. There are Five Percenters who question if Allah ever changed the name of the movement and cite the known previous history of the Five Percenters as their evidence. Some Five Percenters point out the fact that while the Five Percenters are known as the Gods and Earths there are no mentions of a "Nation of Gods and Earths" contemporary with the history of Allah while he was alive or even 12-15 years after his death. They point to numerous documents that were contemporary with the time Allah walked amongst them as their evidence. The weightiest testimony is an audio of Allah himself recorded in the year 1967 referring to his organization on numerous occasions as the Five Percenters. However, those who favor the name Nation of Gods and Earths emphasize that the new name was not to go into effect until after the death of Clarence 13X anyway because according to NGE legend Father Allah stated that "his death would born the Nation of Gods and Earths." Still some traditional Five Percenters don't support this claim because of the lack of evidence and it's similarities to posthumous claims made by other religions of question (in particular Christianity). To other Five Percenters, the name of the organization isn't that great of a deal in which they feel should not even be argued. So to these Five Percenters a debate over the name is a non-issue.

Master Fard Muhammad: Prophet or God?

Another point of dialogue between Five Percenters surrounds NOI founder and co-author of 120 lessons Master Fard Muhammad. Historically, Five Percenters taught the traditional history of W. F. Muhammad as relayed by the Honorable Elijah Muhammad, that "Allah Came In The Person of Master Fard Muhammad." However, in contrast to earlier Five Percenter accounts, some members who identify under the banner of the NGE issued plus lessons and statements in the late 80's and mid 90's telling a rather different perspective on Fard Muhammad. In an attempt to disassociate themselves from the NOI and Fard, a decree was issued questioning Fard's credibility. In a strange twist one perspective claimed or suggested that Fard was/ is considered a "devil" because of his mixed parentage. This doctrine is supported by the claim of an alleged confrontation that took place between Allah and the Muslims during a Universal Parliament. Purportedly during this alleged incident Allah challenged Fard's divinity and even suggested that Fard was a "devil." The "Greatest Story Never Told" dramatically relays the alleged incident:

> At one point in the parliament there was a disturbance caused by some Muslim followers of the Honorable Elijah Muhammad who were members of Temple No. 7 when Allah was there. They had come to question him as to why he was teaching the youth of the nation that he was Allah. Allah responded that "the muslims of the Nation of Islam have never seen W. D. Fard and they worship him as Allah. But they say that they don't worship a mystery god. So you are worshipping in blind faith. Elijah said we had to stand on our own two feet. You can bring Elijah, and any of his ministers to Rockland Palace and he will tell you that I am Allah. You or any muslims can't judge me or my sons and your lessons say that anything made weak and wicked from the Original man is devil, and you are running around worshipping a Half-Original Man and not the blackman." The muslims departed as the Five Percenters celebrated a moral victory with thunderous cries of "All praise are due to Allah!"[437]

Though this passage would become popular amongst NGE newcomers, some of the traditional Five Percenters question the authenticity of this report. Others go deeper still to advocate that this is an attempt to change the teachings of the Five Percenters. Some believe that the overall attempt to change the name and teachings of the 5% is a government conspiracy reminiscent of the time when Allah was in Matteawan. Concerned Five Percenters cite that the intention and the conspiracy is the same as it was then—take the focus off the original teachings (120 lessons) as taught by the NOI to derail the original purpose of the movement. Some Five Percenters believe that alleged false claims have become part of a false propaganda campaign promoted by government sources.

> The long term project to prevent the growth within the movement toward the viable goal of freedom, justice, and equality has been code named Operation Cobra.
> As in the earlier movements of Martin Luther King, Malcolm X, the Nation of Islam, and the Black Panthers, the methods are the same: misinformation, disinformation, rumors, slander, and lies. The misinformation is accomplished by anonymous (so-called) "PLUS DEGREES" predicated upon a religious basis, and calculated to evoke worship of the physically dead leaders (referring to Clarence 13X). Knowing that the dead can not lead the living, the disinformation is accomplished by putting words in the absent person's mouth he never said.[438]

On another note, in an effort to champion or establish an official NGE stance, a decree was issued in 1996 by Dumar Wa'de Allah who is proclaimed to be *The National Representative of the Nation of Gods and Earths*. In his missive he states his claim and reasoning about some disagreements with NOI teachings as it relates to NOI lessons. The main point surrounds the identity of Master Fard Muhammad. He states why he believes Fard is not considered to be Allah (God) and says he witnessed Clarence 13X advise the same. Dumar Wad'e:

> The Father taught us (Gods) that the more he studied the lessons and gained a Supreme Understanding of these lessons, he realized that Master Fard Muhammad could not be Allah. The Father revealed to us, how the 30th degree in the 1-40 proved that the Blackman is God. The Father also applied understanding to the first degree in the 1-10 and 1-40, proving to him that the Original Man is Master Fard Muhammad's Father.

REVIEW: My name is W.F. Muhammad I came to North America by myself. My uncle was brought here by the trader 379 years ago.

FACT: An uncle is the brother of the Father. Brothers are of the same seed, making them of one root and origin.

REMINDER: As time changes, you must change.[439]

Regardless of the above view concerning W. F. Muhammad, there are still Five Percenters and members of the Nation of Gods and Earths who still persist and continue to teach the traditional history of Master Fard Muhammad as given by the Honorable Elijah Muhammad. Even another NGE representative in an effort to correct the misperception of W. F. Muhammad that existed within NGE philosophy wrote an article vindicating Fard. The following information vindicating Fard, Elijah and the lessons appeared in the Nation of Gods and Earths Newspaper:

> Those of you who deny W. F. Muhammad need to Open your third Eye and see the relation between The Root and The Fruit. If the Root is fake then the Fruit is fake. Don't let people use Wisdom to play on your Knowledge. Our ROOT was truth and we are a higher form (FRUIT) of that truth.
>
> When people try to invalidate Master Fard Muhammad/ the Honorable Elijah Muhammad/ and the Lessons/ and you accept those teachings; you are metaphorically denying yourself. Quit making issue out of toilet tissue. Quit pouring fragrances on feces. Our Nation was founded in THE TRUTH and it is that truth that the Mason among us is trying to RE-CONCEAL. To Rock the once AWAKENED BLACKMAN BACK TO SLEEP![440]

Instead of Fard achieving the status of God, amongst some members of the NGE, Clarence 13X is now considered to be the Supreme Allah ranking over all other Prophets, Messengers and Gods who came before him. As a result of this adulation of Allah (Clarence 13X), those who are considered his "First Borns" a.k.a. "Elders" are naturally admired and revered to some as the elite in the movement because they personally met "God" or "walked with the Father" in person. Ironically, this has enabled certain elders who make this claim to have power over their constituents similar to a priest hood reminiscent of the very religious system they condemn. This influence has often been heightened by plus lessons or stories written about the supposedly mystic powers of Allah according to certain elder accounts. A Five Percenter researcher within the movement makes his observation and comparison:

> But, in point of fact, there is an interesting parallel between Jesus and Allah. Jesus' "Apostles," like Allah's "First Born" went on to produce a mythology surrounding his person, while essentially developing their own privileged priesthood, with their own status highlighted by the sanctity attached to the absent deity, and their association with him. The doctrine of "apostolic succession" enabled Peter to build the Catholic Church in Rome. For many, with character defects galore, their only saving grace was their association with Allah in the 1960s, when they, themselves, were children. As to their adding on...We have seen the level of their progress in over 20 years. That level of progress can be measured in comparison with the body of mythological literature created during the same period.
> As Jesus own "first-born to knowledge" had him walking on water and changing water to wine, we have had our own "apostles" claiming miracles on 125th Street. Without a doubt, the passage of time is the most effective agent in the myth making process. No one would have believed that if it was said in 1968.[441]

As in anything, this general assertion didn't pertain to all Elders. Many Elders are sincere in their ways and actions. As it is with any community, the Elders have a wealth of experience and wisdom that could help guide the young. The same can be said of the Elders amongst the Five Percenters although it must be an earned respect.

The deification of Clarence 13X (Allah) has not gone unnoticed by some NGE adherents. When the alleged fabricated and concocted histories about Allah reached a threshold among some NGE adherents, a NGE representative wrote an article addressing the supernatural overtones that entrenched its way into some of the Nation of Gods and Earths doctrine. In an article that appeared in the Five Percenter Newspaper Shabazz Adew Allah addresses the subject:

"All praise is due to Allah. Allah is all of us. But we have a Supreme One that we can throw this name 'Holy' upon. He is Allah, The One over all us; The Most Supreme One, the Wisest One, the Mightiest One; The One that Sees and Hears that which we can't see and hear. That is He. He is rooted in all of us. Every righteous person is a god. We are all God. When we say "Allah" we mean every righteous person..."

The above quote is taken from the book "Our Saviour has Arrived", written by the Honorable Elijah Muhammad. The subject can be founded on page 26, Chapter 10, Titled "I Want To Teach You". In this lesson Elijah Muhammad teaches on the topic of the Reality of God, Who and What Is Allah. And from the above, he explained His concept of Allah quite clearly, with the exception of One important aspect. Elijah Muhammad did not make plain in this lesson that "The One over all of us..." which he was referring to was Mr. Fard Muhammad, i.e. the mentor and saviour of Elijah Muhammad. This "Concept of Allah" is held by many brother's and sister's within the ranks of our Nation of Gods and Earths. The difference is that you have replaced the name of Master Fard Muhammad, as given by the Honorable Elijah Muhammad and you gave the title to the Father of the Nation of Gods and Earths (formally known as the Five Percent). You say you give this title to the Father because you love, respect and find this Title most fitting for the Father, because he Fathered this Nation of Gods and Earths and the knowledge of His wisdom resurrected you from ignorance. So you glorify the Father and you put Him above yourself and you desire to throw the name 'Holy' upon Him (the Father). So the names have changed from Fard to the Father, but the Concept remained. But is this really the concept of Allah, as given to us by the Father? I think not! The Father have never advocated for us to glorify Him or give praise to His name like many have taken the Truth of God and mixed it with religious undertones that is mystifying the Life and Teachings of the Father. I know that you are one who love and respect the Father, but you are glorifying the Father in a most unglorifying way. There are stories being circulated that supposed to represent historical events where the Father did things like move a star across the sky with his finger, melted clouds with his wisdom, etc., these fairy tales were made-up and given to take us further away from the Truth of God, by making the Father appear to be some Big headed scientist with unnatural mystical and magical power's. You are doing this Nation a great wrong with your religious undertones with reference to the deeds, aims and teachings of the Father with regard to the Nation of God and Earth.[442]

Whether or not NGE members intended for it's following to idolize Allah (Clarence 13X), it must contend with the fact that for some members of the NGE (specifically the Internet generation) the stories about Allah has taken precedence over the Lessons of the former 5% Nation of Islam. Whereas the Lessons were once the unabated criterion for all, for some it has now been replaced with tales or histories of "the Father." Youth often scramble now to cling to ranking elders who claim to have walked with the Father. In extreme cases, the youth no longer cram to recite the lessons to one another, that custom has been substituted for the exchanging of stories or hadith about the founding Father Allah. Prince Allah Cuba harshly sums it up in his conclusion:

> Since the passing of Allah in 1969 the Five Percent has gone through many changes. Some of these changes have been toward a reactionary and socially backward direction; true, poor, righteous teachers had nothing to do with that. It was to the interest of the state and the devil to turn the Five Percent into a harmless religious cult built around the person of the absent Allah; this was done.[443]

Overall, it is safe to say that the ideal goal is for Five Percenters to continue the healthy balance of respect and admiration for its founder without sacrificing the identity of its individual members by becoming dogmatic in the process. Traditional Five Percenters have been high achievers in their ability to balance the two.

Islam and I-God

Another point of discussion between the Five Percenters and/or the NGE is ISLAM itself. Historically, Elijah Muhammad taught that *"Islam is Mathematics and Mathematics is Islam."* Elijah Muhammad emphasized that Islam was not a religion but it is the very nature of the Original people. The Honorable Elijah Muhammad elaborates:

> Islam is not a religion. We call it a religion, but it's not a religion, because it is the nature of us; therefore, the nature of us can't be

called a religion. That's why the 30th chapter and the 30th verse of the Holy Qur'an teaches you that Islam is not a religion, but it's the nature in which we were born. [444]

Allah and traditional Five Percenters appeared to teach the same of Islam in agreement with Elijah Muhammad. However, in recent days and times, some members in the NGE reject the term Islam as they define it as "a religion" which has been deemed unsuitable for members of the NGE. At best, the more reluctant NGE die hards accept the term ISLAM only when used as an acronym meaning "I-Self-Lord-Am-Master," which ironically was coined by Noble Drew Ali and/ or the Hon. Elijah Muhammad.

In the place of Islam, some members in the NGE have totally replaced this term with a new culture referred to as *"I-God."* In as where Islam according to the NOI lessons carried with it an inherent moral system called the *"prescribed laws of Islam to the said person of that ability,"* the culture "I-God" according to some, allows its adherents to make up their own rules and regulations. The rules are normally established on an individual basis and are tailored to fit the individual's own personal lifestyle-- be it positive or negative. Lord Jammar of Brand Nubians touches on this concept during an interview with SPIN magazine:

> Gods are free to make up their own rules. When asked about references to "smoking spliffs" in their lyrics (marijuana is totally forbidden by the Nation of Islam), Lord Jammar of Brand Nubian bristled: "See, in the Five Percent Nation, each man is the sole controller of his own universe. If you're the god of your universe, you set up your own laws."[445]

Since the culture of "I-God" is more of an individualistic way of life it is sometimes in contradiction with "Islam" which constitutes a communal way of life of ethics observed by a community or group. In that case, what the average Islamic Community (Five Percenters included) consider to be vices are in some instances acceptable in the culture referred to as "I-God" because of the philosophy that if you are God "you don't have to submit to any laws but your own laws you make for yourself." However, in a different regard, this version of "I-God" on one level appears to conflict with the traditional teachings of Allah and the Five Percenters who believed in free will but only if it led to righteousness. Historically speaking, Clarence 13X as well as many members of the Five Percent Nation of Islam taught that you must obey the laws of the land in which you live as well as those in authority over you as long as it does not conflict with Islam.

It must be noted that all Five Percenters do not view the culture of I-God the same. Some Five Percenters interpret the letter "I" in I-God to mean Islam as well. So to them I-God is the same as "Islam-God." These Five Percenters of this frame of mind see no contradiction in the two terms Islam and I-God. In fact, some Five Percenters agree that Gods should have the freedom that's represented in the culture "I-God" but only if it is considered "the freedom to do righteousness" as Islam denotes. So these Five Percenters by definition see the culture I-God to be just as strict or ethical as noted in Islam. It would even be safe to say that on a whole Five Percenters still view Islam to be synonymous with Elijah Muhammad's interpretation as "Mathematics" and it is the accepted culture that is in accordance with the NOI lessons.

To Be or Not to Be Muslim

Another controversial debate within the movement has been the question whether or not Five Percenters are "Muslims." According to Elijah Muhammad the Black Man by nature is born a Muslim. The Messenger defined the term Muslim as a *"Righteous Person,"* *"One that submits to do the will of Allah,"* as well as *"One of Peace."* It is also evident in the NOI lessons that the Black Man is God and he is by nature a Righteous Muslim. Elijah Muhammad taught that the two terms Allah and Muslim when used in reference to the Black Man were synonymous with one another. Elijah Muhammad elaborates on this sentiment in his book *"Our Saviour Has Arrived"*:

> When we say 'Allah,' that Name means God and covers ALL MUSLIMS. ALL MUSLIMS ARE ALLAH'S, but we call the Supreme Allah the Supreme Being.[446]

Although Five Percenters have supported this statement in the past and while many still do, during these recent times it has found disfavor with many members of the NGE philosophy. As a result, less emphasis is placed on the NOI lessons as the NGE invest little in the literal interpretation by its authors. Instead the NGE administration decided to "renew its history" by teaching a reinterpreted version of the NOI lessons. Within this "renewal" or "greater understanding" the interpretations of the NGE administration were upheld while the meanings from its original authors (Elijah Muhammad and Fard Muhammad) were disregarded. As a result, while some die-hard Five Percenters hold fast to the oral tradition of reciting the lessons, some NGE members no longer feel pressure to recite or quote verbatim the Lost-Found Muslim Lessons of the NOI which are the literal words of Fard and Elijah. Hence, even the title of the "Lost-Found Muslim Lessons" serves as a deterrent to some NGE members from reciting or studying them because of some of the NGE who claim they are not Muslims. So the logic is if you are not Muslim than what sense does it make to study "Muslim" lessons. In an effort to establish and solidify recent NGE theology, the National Representative of the NGE issued a statement denying the Muslim tenant found within the NOI lessons.

Exhibit A

[Author's Note: Following is part of an essay written by the National Representative of the Nation of Gods and Earths, Dumar Wa'de Allah]

A National Statement

The Science of THE LESSONS:

The National Statement that is being presented in Now CIPHER VICTORY month will explore a very important issue that confronts the youth and Five Percenters within the Nation of Gods. This issue is pertaining to the science of the lessons. Specifically 120 degrees. The Gods have agreed that the time to renew and provide a understanding about the science of the lessons is needed within our Nation. Gods and Earths, in 1996 the Nation is making it very clear, we are not muslims or muslim sons. Our Nation is not an organization, gang, religious group or splinter sect. The Nation of Gods and Earths are real people walking, talking and building with the human families on the planet earth.

QUESTION: If the Gods are not muslims, why do they quote muslim lessons?

This is a question that many brothers and sisters are asking openly and in secrecy. If you read this edition of the National Statement very carefully, that question will no longer exist within your head.

A JEWEL TO REMEMBER: As time changes, you must change.

Once upon a time in America, the original people had lost all knowledge of self. After a period of time, many of our people began to reveal different aspects of the original man history. These individual revelations were only a part of the total history.

RESEARCH: Use your mind to research and study the time line to identify the original people that presented part of your birth record.

In keeping this edition of the National Statement plain and simple, we will now focus on W.F. Muhammad. According to the teachings of the Honorable Elijah Muhammad, W.F. Muhammad, also known as Master Fard Muhammad revealed himself to the so-called Negro in the 1930's and taught that the Blackman (Original people) in America was of the lost tribe of Shabazz and their ancestors were muslims. During this time, one of Master Fard Muhammad students named Elijah was under his constant study and teaching. The science of knowledge that W.F. Muhammad taught Elijah, came to be known as muslim lessons. As time passed and Master Fard Muhammad disappeared like a thief in the night, Elijah made it mandatory that all his followers learn to recite the lessons. Elijah also began to teach his followers, that he was taught by Allah, who appeared in the person of Master Fard Muhammad. From 1934 to 1964 these teachings were never questioned by his followers. What happened in 1964? A change came about. The knowledge was born, bringing forth true equality of the original peoples culture. During this time of the Blackman (original people) resurrection, Our Father was under the teachings of Elijah Muhammad and studied the lessons.

QUESTION: Are there any muslims other than righteous?

Many brothers lack the understanding of the law of reverse polarity, and answer the question as a muslim. Their answer is not negative, it only shows that they lack the understanding of how to draw this question up in living mathematics. This National Statement is telling the world that the Nation of Gods and Earths are not muslims, that the original man, in his original state of mind, is the maker, the owner, the cream of the planet earth, the Father of civilization and God of the universe.

FACT: A muslim is a religious man. The question that I present to the readers is...... Do you understand the science of how the Gods are taking the devil off their planet?

REVIEW: Planets are something that are made or grown from the beginning.

FACT: The Earth and Moon are made planets (the mental and physical part of the original black woman). The Sun is a grown planet. (the mental - sun 1 and physical - son) of the original man. As Gods, we teach that the original woman is the Earth and is the Home of Islam. (Nature of the Original People). Yet, many brothers want their women to be bonded to The 14th degree in the 1-14. What is the meaning of M.G.T and G.C.C.? Gods, how can you ask your woman to apply herself under the Muslim Girls Training and General Civilization Class, when, in fact, she is not a muslim; and you are the Father of her Civilization.[447]

As it is in most cases, different Five Percenters see this subject differently. Another group of Five Percenters who support the original teaching that Allah (God) is a Muslim wrote a rebuttal supporting the claim of the 120 Lessons. In an effort to vindicate 120 lessons as well as W. F. Muhammad, Elijah Muhammad and Father Allah, they wrote an essay as a rebuttal proving the NOI lessons claim that Black People are righteous Muslims as well as Gods.

[Author's Note: Following is part of an essay written by Five Percenter scholar True Islam]

"Is Allah a Righteous Muslim?"
by True Islam

Over the past few years, a debate has quietly raged within the Five Percent Nation over whether or not Gods were Muslims. Many believe that a Muslim is "one who submits" and therefore Gods, who allegedly submit to no one and nothing, cannot then be Muslim. There are also those who allege that the Father Allah taught that we are not Muslim, yet such persons fail every time to produce proof of such claims... THE LESSONS HAVE ALWAYS BEEN OF PARAMOUNT IMPORTANCE IN THIS NATION. Those brothers who are now trying to deny the The Lessons their rightful place and propagate a doctrine which is contrary to the message of The Lessons, are disrespecting the Father and the Mission that he left the mosque to accomplish... So, what did the Honorable Elijah Muhammad, as the bridge between Master Fard Muhammad and the Father Allah, teach? First and foremost, he taught that the Black Man is God.

"The Black Man is the God of the Earth. He is the Creator. I don't care how you have been mistreated, still your Father was a Black Man and He is the One who created this Earth and is now taking it over. This is our Earth."[1]

Muhammad says Master Fard Muhammad said to him one day
"They just waited. They're so glad that the day has come now that they can show you now that the Black Man is God!"[3]

The Black Man, Muhammad teaches, is God, and our rightful name is Allah.

"As far as the Name goes, I am Allah and you are Allah. I am not anything more than you in that way. We are all Allah."[4]

And Allah, Muhammad teaches, IS A RIGHTEOUS MUSLIM. The Original God, the first Creator, was a Muslim.

"We were created Muslim from the very beginning. Our Father, who created the Heavens and the Earth was a Muslim...Muslim means a righteous person...You were created Muslim."[5]

He says again:
"You are born a Muslim. You were not made a Muslim, you were created a Muslim from the start. God, Himself, was a Muslim and all of His people are Muslims."[6]

Allah the Original Man himself was a Muslim, and all natural Muslims are Allah's, collectively and individually:

"When we say 'Allah,' that Name means God and covers ALL MUSLIMS. ALL MUSLIMS ARE ALLAH'S, but we call the Supreme Allah the Supreme Being. And He has a Name of His Own. This Name is 'Fard Muhammad.'"[7]

And He came, by Himself, not to just make us followers, but to grow us into true God-hood.

"The Father is our own Kind. He wants to make you and me: not just believers, but Gods......There is no doubt that we are really Gods, but we lost our power and knowledge as shown by the parable of Jesus. 'Salt is good as long as it has saving power. When it no longer has saving power it is not good for anything, but to be thrown out and trampled under people's feet.' This is referring to us. We had knowledge and we will be powerful when we are restored to what we originally were. But, we have been robed of power through depriving us of the Knowledge of Self...Allah taught me that He would like to restore you...You have lost everything of Self. Now He wants to restore you back to Self. Then you can do what we are preaching that He is doing if you will believe and follow Him. He didn't come here just to show us who He was. He came here to show us who He was, who we are, and to make us rulers."[8]

The Lessons are just as explicit on the Black Man being God and God being a Righteous Muslim. In Student Enrollment # 1, Master Fard Muhammad asked, *"Who is the Original Man?"*. The Honorable Elijah Muhammad answered:

The Original Man is the Asiatic Black Man, The Maker, The Owner, The Cream of the planet Earth, the Father of Civilization, the God of the Universe.

In the knowledge degree of the ***Lost-Found Muslim Lesson # 2*** (1-40), Muhammad stated: *"The Holy Koran or Bible is made by the original people, who is Allah, the supreme being, or (black man) of Asia."*

The original Man/People is/are God whose proper Name is Allah. In the understanding degree of the Student Enrollment (1-10), Master Fard Muhammad asks, *"What is the population of the Original Nation in the wilderness of North America and all over the Planet Earth?* Muhammad responded:

"The population of the Original Nation in the wilderness of North America is 17,000,000. With the 2,000,000 Indians makes it-19,000,000.

All over the Planet Earth is 4,400,000,000.

These 17,000,000 members of the Original Nation are Original People and are therefore Allah. But they are also Righteous Muslims. In English Lesson C1 (1-36) a dialog is recorded between Master Fard Muhammad and the Honorable Elijah Muhammad. It starts off:

*My name is **W.F. MUHAMMAD**.*

I came to North America by myself.

My uncle was brought over here by the Trader three hundred seventy-nine years ago.

His Uncle is the Original Man in the wilderness of North America who was brought here by the Trader, Sir John Hardy Hawkins in the year 1555. The Original Man here is the brother of the Original Man in the East, one of whom was Alphonso Allah, the father of Master Fard Muhammad. And because we are the brother of His father, we are called "uncle". The Lesson goes on to say that the Devil, after planting fear in the uncle, fed him the wrong foods which made him other than himself. *"What is his own self?"* the Honorable Elijah Muhammad asks. Master Fard Muhammad answers:

14. His own self is a righteous Muslim.

15. Are there any Muslims other than righteous?

16. I beg your pardon! I have never heard of one...[9]

19. How many original Muslims are there in North America?

20. A little over seventeen million.

21. Did I hear you say that some of the seventeen million do not know that they are Muslims?

22. YES, SIR!

23. I hardly believe that unless they are <u>blind, deaf, and dumb.</u>

24. Well, they were made blind, deaf, and dumb by the devil when they were babies.

In the above exchange, Master Fard Muhammad identifies the 17 million members of the Original Nation in the wilderness of North America as RIGHTEOUS MUSLIMS. These are the same who are the Original People who is Allah. ALLAH IS A RIGHTEOUS MUSLIM. I once heard a God try to argue that the "uncle" that is here referred to as Muslim was the 85%. The Five Percent, he said, were not Muslim. The Lessons, however, destroys that argument. Above degrees #19-24 explicitly states that the whole 17 million are Righteous Muslims. The 85%, THE BLIND, DEAF, AND DUMB AMONG US, are those who argue that they are not Muslim for lack of knowledge. Also, in the knowledge equality degree of the 1-40, it makes it plain that the FIVE PERCENT IS MUSLIM.

Who is the 5% in the Poor Part of the Earth? They are the poor, righteous Teachers, who do not believe in the teaching of the 10%; and who are all-wise; and know who the Living God is; and Teach that the Living God is the Son of man, the Supreme Being, the (black man) of Asia; and Teach Freedom, Justice and Equality to all the human family of the planet Earth. Otherwise known as Civilized People.

ALSO IS MUSLIM AND MUSLIM SONS.

Some brothers have grafted the Lesson to make it read

Also called Muslim and Muslim sons.

This is not what the degrees says. It is devilishment to graft the Lessons to support ones made up doctrine.

31. To make devil, what must you first do?

To make devil, one must begin grafting from original.

Many Gods are running around with "devil lessons" which were grafted from the originals. But this degree explicitly states that THE FIVE PERCENT IS MUSLIM.

The Original Nation is called the Nation of Islam. Many Gods, who lack proper knowledge, disassociate themselves from the Nation of Islam because they identify it with the Mosque. This is an emphatic now cipher. The whole Original Nation of 4,400,000,000 Original People constitute the Nation of Islam. Those of us who were brought to the wilderness of North America by the Trader are called the Lost-Found Members of the Nation of Islam. We are the Five Percent within the Lost-found Nation of Islam. But the only eternal nation is the Nation of Islam.

9. *What is the birth record of the said, Nation of Islam?*

   The said, Nation of Islam, has no birth record. It has no beginning nor ending.

10. *What is the birth record of said, others than Islam?*

   Buddhism is 35,000 years old.
   Christianity is 551 years old.[10]

HOW OLD IS YOUR NATION?

There are many gods among us who say they are not Muslim because they don't "submit". In fact, they may be telling the truth. Though by nature we were created Muslim, willful rebellion against the Universal Law of Mathematics will indeed earn us a different name. In the *Holy Qur'an*, which was written by the Original People who is Allah, it reads:

And We indeed created you, then We fashioned you, then We said to the angles: Make submission to Adam. So they submitted, except Iblis; He was not of those who submitted.

He said: What hindered thee that thou didst not submit when I commanded thee? He said: I am better than he (Adam); Thou has created me of fire, while him Thou didst create of dust.

He (Allah) said:Then get forth from this (state), for it is not for thee to behave proudly therein. Go forth, therefore, surly thou art of the abject ones." (7:11-13)

The above is a symbolic picture of the Self Creation of Allah The Original Man (A.T.O.M. or Adam). It is clear that from the very beginning of this Nation, there were those among us who developed a particular temperament which caused them to willfully violate the Holy Sharia or Law of Islam which was always paramount in this Nation. Maulana Muhammad Ali says the creation from fire and from dust represents two different temperaments within the Original Nation. Those who are made from dust represents the perfect man who is humble and meek while those among us who are made of fire are the proud and arrogant.[11] Those individuals who say "I don't submit to nobody or nothing, I'm God!" Not only are these individuals blatant liars, they are called in scripture *Iblis.* Said persons of this temperament are punished by the Nation of Islam by exile or banishment. In Islam, for the last 66 trillion years, the Holy Sharia has been the Rule, for rule or ruler is that which the King (Allah) uses to keep everything right and exact. No one is ever above the Law of Islam. Even the Great Gods who sat in the Circle of Twelve were subject to the Law. One of the Great Gods 50,000 years had an idea that didn't find favor among the other 11 Imams or Scientist of Islam. He persisted in his idea and was thus banished from the Holy City Mecca. Shabazz and his family were exiled into Africa which, at that time, was used by the Great Gods as a place of exile for all rebels. The ancient Sumerians referred to Africa as the *ABZU* which came to mean "Underworld" and "world of the Dead".[12] The Anunnaki, which are the 24 Scientists in Sumerian theology, sentenced rebel Gods, including members of their own Circle, to exile in Africa or the Abzu. The penalty (Just-Ice) for rebellion against the Law of Islam is banishment and a "cutting off from heaven." This means the guilty party is denied the Supreme Wisdom and Guidance that emanated from the Holy City Mecca, the Root of Civilization. The natural consequence of this is that the society or family who were "cut off" falls into debasement and savagery. When Shabazz rebelled, his family fell into savagery in Africa, our land of exile. There is no denying this. This is fact. The banishment of Shabazz and his Family is recorded in the Sumerian cuneiform tablets. They refer to Shabazz as "En.Ki." which means "The Lord who was cut off."[13] He was one of the Lords, the Twelve Major Scientists, but he was cut off when he refused to submit to the Decree of the Council. To the Abzu Enki was banished. Why are the Indians in North America? Because they violated the Law of Islam 16,000 years ago and were exiled here. All members of the Universal Nation of Islam are required to submit to the Law of Mathematics. We all have the option, however, of not submitting. There is a penalty (Just-Ice) for such rebellion. Just because you are God, doesn't mean you don't have to submit to Allah's Mathematics.

Some brothers see the fact that Allah is a Muslim as a contradiction. It's not just a contradiction, it's a paradox, for such is the nature of Truth. The Truth is the Light. And Light, by it very nature, is a contradiction; a contradiction which physicists called the Great Paradox of Light. Fritjof Capra, in his *The Tao of Physics*, explains:

"In atomic physics, many of the paradoxical situations are connected with the dual nature of light or-more generally-of electromagnetic radiation. On the one hand, it is clear that the radiation must consist of waves because it produces the well-known interference phenomena associated with waves...On the other hand, electromagnetic radiation also produces the so-called photoelectric effect: when ultraviolet light is shone on the surface of some metals, it can 'kick out' electrons from the surface of the metal, and therefore it must consist of particles....The question which puzzled physicists so much in the early stages of atomic theory was how electromagnetic radiation could simultaneously consist of particles (i.e. entities confined to a very small volume) and of waves, which are spread out over a large area of space. Neither language nor imagination could deal with this kind of reality very well."[14]

We now know that this seeming contradiction is a fundamental aspect of the nature of light itself.

"Every time the physicist asked nature a question in an atomic experiment, nature answered with a paradox, and the more they tried to clarify the situation, the sharper the paradoxes became. It took them a long time to accept the fact that these paradoxes belong to the intrinsic structure of atomic physics."[15]

Reality is a Paradox. The Truth, like light, is a Great Paradox. The Original Man is Allah, and Allah is a Righteous Muslim.

Who among us is willing to deny Allah's Mathematics? Who among us is willing to deny The Lessons? And who among us is willing to deny the Honorable Elijah Muhammad, the bridge between the Knowledge and the Understanding? To say that Allah is not a Muslim, is to deny all of the said above. And to deny the said above is to deny the Father himself. WHO AMONG YOU ARE PREPARED TO DO SUCH? Just because a few *individuals* who think they are leaders over a Nation WHICH HAS NO LEADERS, issue a statement denying Truth, it doesn't make Truth any less true. You are again, *"teaching for doctrines the commandments of men."* BUT A DEVIL DOESN'T FOOL A MUSLIM. NO, NOT NOWADAYS.

PEACE TO THE NATION OF ISLAM![448]

Conclusion

In light of existing theological differences, as in the two examples provided, the Five Percenters respect each other's opinions for the common cause of "civilizing the uncivilized." Allah's revelation of Supreme Mathematics promotes a mutual respect for differences without hindering the pursuit and discovery of truth for the individual. So in many instances while Five Percenters continue to "sharpen their sword" (debate) with one another there is always a peaceful parting out of the ways out of respect for an individuals understanding. Hence, there is a popular saying amongst Five Percenters that reads, "We may be 'A-alike' and we may even 'B-alike'-- but that doesn't mean we may (see) 'C-Alike'."

Appendix II

The FBI Files On
Clarence 13X (Allah)
And The Five Percenters

SELECTED DECLASSIFIED GOVERNMENT DOCUMENTS ON CLARENCE 13X SMITH (ALLAH) AND THE FIVE PERCENTERS

[Author's Note: Following are transcripts of Official FBI Documents obtained under the FREEDOM OF INFORMATION ACT. The FBI kept close tabs on Clarence 13X(Allah) and The Five Percenters. The FBI partnered with the Bureau of Special Services (BSS), which was a special division of the New York City Police Department (NYCPD) and other special agencies.]

[Author's Note: The first file presented is the actual COUNTERINTELLIGENCE (COINTELPRO) memo that defined the diabolical purpose of these investigations.]

[U. S. GOVERNMENT MEMORANDUM LETTERHEAD]

Date:	**8/25/67**
To:	**SAC, Albany**
From:	**DIRECTOR, FBI**

COUNTER INTELLIGENCE PROGRAM
BLACK NATIONALIST – HATE GROUPS
INTERNAL SECURITY

[...] The purpose of this new counterintelligence endeavor is to expose, disrupt, misdirect, discredit, or OTHERWISE NEUTRALIZE [emphasis added] the activities of black nationalist hate-type organizations and groupings, their leadership, spokesmen, membership, and supporters, and to counter their propensity for violence and civil disorder. The activities of all such groups of intelligence interest to the Bureau must be followed on a continuous basis so we will be in a position to promptly take advantage of all opportunities for counterintelligence and inspire action in instances where circumstances warrant. The pernicious background of such groups, their duplicity, and devious maneuvers must be exposed to public scrutiny where such publicity will have a neutralizing effect. Efforts of the various groups to consolidate their forces or to recruit new or youthful adherents must be frustrated. No opportunity should be missed to exploit through counterintelligence techniques the organizational and personal conflicts of the leaderships of the groups and where possible an effort should be made to capitalize upon existing conflict between competing black nationalist organizations. When an opportunity is apparent to disrupt or neutralize black nationalist, hate-type organizations through the cooperation of established local news media contacts or through such contact with sources available to the Seat of Government, in every instance careful attention must be given to the proposal to insure the targeted group is disrupted, ridiculed, or discredited through the publicity and not merely publicized...

You are also cautioned that the nature of this new endeavor is such that under no circumstances should the existence of the program be made known outside the bureau and appropriate within-office security should be afforded to sensitive operations and techniques considered under the program.

No counterintelligence action under this program may be initiated by the field without specific prior Bureau authorization.

[Author's note: Seat of Government is an official designation created by J. Edgar Hoover to refer to his own office.]

COUNTERINTELLIGENCE PROGRAM
BLACK NATIONALIST – HATE GROUPS
RACIAL INTELLIGENCE

3/4/68

GOALS

For maximum effectiveness of the Counterintelligence Program, and to prevent wasted effort, long-range goals are being set.

1. Prevent the COALITION of militant black nationalist groups. In unity there is strength; a truism that is no less valid for all its triteness. An effective coalition of black nationalist groups might be the first step toward a real "Mau Mau" [Black revolutionary army] in America, the beginning of a true black revolution.

2. Prevent the RISE OF A "MESSIAH" who could unify, and electrify, the militant black nationalist movement. Malcolm X might have been such a "messiah;" he is the martyr of the movement today. Martin Luther King, Stokely Carmichael and Elijah Muhammad all aspire to this position. Elijah Muhammad is less of a threat because of his age. King could be a very real contender for this position should he abandon his supposed "obedience" to "white, liberal doctrines" (nonviolence) and embrace black nationalism. Carmichael has the necessary charisma to be a real threat in this way.

3. Prevent VIOLENCE on the part of black nationalist groups. This is of primary importance, and is, of course, a goal of our investigative activity; it should also be a goal of the Counterintelligence Program to pinpoint potential troublemakers and neutralize them before they exercise their potential for violence.

4. Prevent militant black nationalist groups and leaders from gaining RESPECTABILITY, by discrediting them to three separate segments of the community. The goal of discrediting black nationalists must be handled to, first, the responsible Negro community. Second, they must be discredited to the white community, both the responsible community and to "liberals" who have vestiges of sympathy for militant black nationalists [sic] simply because they are Negroes. Third, these groups must be discredited in the eyes of Negro radicals, the followers of the movement. This last area requires entirely different tactics from the first two. Publicity about violent tendencies and radical statements merely enhances black nationalists to the last group; it adds "respectability" in a different way.

5. A FINAL GOAL SHOULD BE TO PREVENT THE LONG-RANGE GROWTH OF MILITANT BLACK ORGANIZATIONS, ESPECIALLY AMONGST THE YOUTH. SPECIFIC TACTICS TO PREVENT THESE GROUPS FROM CONVERTING YOUNG PEOPLE MUST BE DEVELOPED. [emphasis added]

TARGETS

Primary targets of the Counterintelligence Program, Black Nationalist-Hate Groups, should be the most violent and radical groups and their leaders. We should emphasize those leaders and organization that are nationwide in scope and are most capable of disrupting this country. These targets, members, and followers of the:

Student Nonviolent Coordinating Committee (SNCC)
Southern Christian Leadership Conference (SCLC)

Revolutionary Action Movement (RAM)
NATION OF ISLAM (NOI) [emphasis added]

Office handling these cases and those of Stokely Carmichael of SNCC, H. Rap Brown of SNCC, Martin Luther King of SCLC, Maxwell Stanford of RAM, and Elijah Muhammad of NOI, should be alert for counterintelligence suggestions. [...]

[Author's Note: Following are the exclusive FBI files relating to Clarence 13X Smith and The Five Percenters.]

SUBJECT: **Clarence 13x Smith**
FILE NUMBER: **100-444636**
SECTION NUMBER: **[blank]**
SERIAL (S):   **[blank]**

[U. S. DEPARTMENT OF JUSTICE; FBI LETTERHEAD]

To: Director United States Secret Service, Department of the Treasury, Washington, D.C. 20220

Re: Clarence Edward Smith

Dear Sir:

The information furnished herewith concerns an individual who is believed to be covered by the agreement between the FBI and Secret Service concerning Presidential protection, and to gall within the category or categories checked.

(X) Because of background is potentially dangerous; or has been identified as member or participant in communist movement; or has been under active investigation as member of other group or organization inimical to U. S.

(X) Subversives, ultrarightists, racists and fascists who meet one or more of the following criteria:

Evidence of emotional instability (including unstable residence and employment record) or irrational or suicidal behavior.

Prior acts (including arrests or convictions) or conduct or statements indicating a propensity for violence and antipathy toward good order and government.

Very truly yours,
(signed) John Edgar Hoover

[U. S. GOVERNMENT MEMORANDUM LETTERHEAD]

Date: **10-22-65**
To: **DIRECTOR, FBI**
From: **SAC, ST. LOUIS (100-20019)**

Subject: **CHANGED**
CLARENCE SMITH JOWARS, aka Clarence **Edward-Smith SM – NOI**
(00:NY)

The title of this case is being marked changed to reflect the name CLARENCE EDWARD SMITH as it appears in the U.S. Army service records.
Re NY let to Bureau, 9-17-65.

A review on 10-14-65, by IC [Name redacted] of the U. S. Army service records on file at MPRC, SLMO, indicated CLARENCE EDWARD SMITH, SN 51 207 085, was inducted into the U. S. Army on 10-30-52, and entered on active duty on the same date at New York, N. Y. He was honorably released from active duty on 8-21-54, as a PFC at Camp Kilmer, N. J., and transferred to the U. S. Army Reserve to complete his military obligation.

He served in the U. S. Army Reserve, inactive status, from 8-22-54 to 9-30-60, at which time he was honorably discharged.

He had foreign service in Japan and Korea and was awarded Korean Service Medal with one Bronze Service Star, Combat Infantryman's Badge, Presidential Unit Citation (Republic of Korea), United Nations Service Medal, and the National Defense Service Medal.

His character and efficiency ratings ranged from unknown to excellent and there is no record of courts-martial or AWOL

The following descriptive and background information is contained in the Army service records:

SL 100-20019

Date and place of birth	2-22-28, Danville, VA
Height	5'11"
Weight	162
Race	Negroid
Hair	Black
Eyes	Brown
Blood Type	"B"
Education	Two Years High School
Civilian Occupation	Shines shoes and shipping clerk
Military Occupation	Light weapons infantryman

[Author's note: Other information is provided pertaining to former addresses, names of relatives (omitted) and medical records. Author has not printed per irrelevance]

[U. S. GOVERNMENT MEMORANDUM LETTERHEAD]

Date: **9/17/65**
To: **DIRECTOR, FBI**
From: **SAC, NEW YORK (100-150520)**

Subject: CLARENCE SMITH JOWARS aka Clarence Smith Jowers, Clarence 13X Smith, Clarence 13X, "Allah", Puddin, SM – NOI (00:NY)

ReNYairtels and letterhead memorandums to the Bureau dated 6/ 2/ 65, 6/ 9/ 65, 6/ 22/ 65, and 7/ 9/ 65, all captioned; "DISTURBANCE BY GROU CALLED 'FIVE PERCENTERS', HARLEM, NEW YORK CITY, 5/ 31/ 65; RACIAL MATTERS", which contained information concerning captioned subject under the name CLARENCE 13X SMITH aka "Allah", and which further reflected that subject was the recognized leader of the "Five Percenters".

It is noted that records of the Bureau of Special Services, (BSS), New York City Police Department, (NYCPD), reflects subject's true name as CLARENCE SMITH JOWARS and as CLARENCE SMITH JOWERS, however, for uniformity, subject's true last name will be carried as

JOWARS until such time as investigation determines the true spelling of subject's last name.

[Name redacted] BSS, NYCPD, advised SA [Name redacted] on 9/ 9/ 65, that the NYCPD has developed the following information concerning the subject:

CLARENCE SMITH JOWARS aka Clarence 13X, a Negro male, born 2/ 21/ 28, in Virginia, city not known, NYCPD # B 612230, resided in Apartment SE, 21 West 112th St., NYC, from August, 1954, through January, 1964. Subject has Social Security Number 228-28-0034. Subject served in the US Army under the name CLARENCE SMITH JOWARS or CLARENCE SMITH from 10/ 29/ 52, through 10/ 29/ 54, and had Army Serial Number 51207085. Subject had the rank of Private First Class, served in Korea, and was last assigned to Company "F", 39th Infantry, Ft. Dix, New Jersey.
Page 1

[The Next two paragraphs are redacted]

From February, 1950, through August, 1954, subject resided at various addresses in the Harlem area of NYC, and has been employed by various businesses in the NYC area. On 3/ 29/ 60, subject reportedly obtained aid from the Veterans Administration in the amount of $129.60.

[Name redacted] advised that the arrest record for subject had temporarily been removed from subject's file, however, he would furnish this information as soon as it is available.

Subject, who was arrested on 6/ 1/ 65, by the NYCPD, details of which are set out in referenced airtels and letterhead memorandums, is still confined, NYC, on $9,500 bond.

[Name redacted] further advised that subject appeared in New York Supreme Court, Part 30, (Felony), on 9/ 9/ 65, and his case was postponed until 9/ 23/ 65. Subject continued to be confined to Bellevue Hospital, NYC, where he is undergoing psychiatric treatment.

LEAD:
ST. LOUIS

AT ST. LOUIS, MISSOURI.
1.   Will, at Military Personnel Records Center, review subject's military personnel file under U.S. Army SN 51207085.

2.   From review will determine if subject's true name is CLARENCE SMITH JOWARS, CLARENCE SMITH JOWERS, or CLARENCE SMITH.

3.   Will furnish the NYO all available background data including date and place of birth, and names of relatives.

[U. S. GOVERNMENT MEMORANDUM LETTERHEAD]

Date: 6/1/65
To: **DIRECTOR, FBI --21--/157-6-34**
From: **NEW YORK /157-892/**

DISTURBANCE BY GROUP CALLED "FIVE PERCENTERS", HARLEM, NYC, MAY THIRTYONE LAST. RACIAL MATTERS (U)

On June one instant, BSS, NYCPD, advised that at approximately six thirty pm, Negro NYCPD Patrolman observed a group of Negroes creating a disturbance at One Hundred Sixteenth St., and Lenox Ave, NYC, and told them to cease their activity. Group berated and cursed patrolman and continued on Seventh Ave. Patrolman did not attempt to arrest them.

At approximately six fifty pm, cab driver informed same Patrolman that mob of Negroes had two policemen pinned up in Hotel Theresa, One Hundred Twenty Fifth St. and Seventh Avenue, NYC, and were threatening them.

Police reinforcements arrived at Hotel Theresa, NYC, and arrested following individuals on charges of felonious assault, resisting arrest, and conspiracy to commit a felony.

A male Negro, thirty five years old, who stated his name was Allah and that he was born in Mecca and that he resided at Harlem Hospital, NYC. No previous record for him located. His NYCPD B NUMBER is six one two three zero. (U).

James Howell, aka Akbar, male Negro, thirty seven years old, resides [address redacted], NYC, [line redacted].

Gumeal, male Negro, twenty one years old, resides [address redacted], NYC, [line redacted].

[Author's note: The following 4 paragraphs including the names and addresses of the other 4 defendants were all redacted].

All six above Negroes are employed and state they are members of organization called "Five Percenters" which means, according to them, the Five Percent of the Muslims who smoke and drink. [name redacted] stated they have no headquarters and "hang out" on the street corners of Harlem. (U)

According to a Negro named Wilbert Lee, filed a complaint of felonious assault against the Negro named Allah, who is self-proclaimed leader of "Five Percenters." Lee charged he was struck on head by stick wielded by Allah. Allah in turn states he was acting in self-defense because he saw gun in Lee's possession.

Above six Negroes arraigned before Judge Francis X. O-Brien, Felony Court, NYC, On June one instant, and all held in three thousand to five thousand dollars bail on charges of felonious assault, resisting arrest, and conspiracy to commit felony. Allah received additional charge of narcotics possession since he had marijuana cigarette on person when arrested.

Case adjourned by Judge O-Brien until June eighteen next.

Approximately sixty Negro followers of "Five Percenters" in court on June one instant, when six Negroes above were arraigned. When six defendants appeared, the sixty followers rose to their feet and shouted "Peace" holding their palms upraised. Judge O-Brien and informed the Judge that He, Allah, is God and threatened to kill Wilbert Lee and NYCPD Patrolman who arrested him.

All six Negroes who were arrested currently in city jail in lieu of bail.

NYO indices reflect no identifiable info Re "Five Percenters" or any of above-named Negroes. LHM follows.

NYO contacting logical sources for any additional information.

END
WA..FOR..8
WA.....SXC R 8

FBI WASH DC

[U. S. GOVERNMENT MEMORANDUM LETTERHEAD]

DATE: 10/19/65
TO: DIRECTOR, FBI
FROM: SAC, NEW YORK (100-150520) (F)

SUBJECT: CLARENCE SMITH JOWARS aka SM – NOI (00:NY)

ReNYlet to Bureau, 9/17/65.

On 10/15/65, [Name redacted] BSS, NYCPD, advised [Name redacted] that subject last appeared in New York State Supreme Court, Part 30, (Felony), NYC, on 10/13/65, where Bellevue Hospital officials advised the presiding judge that they needed 10 additional days to complete their psychiatric treatment of subject. Subjects' case was adjourned until 10/27/65, and he continues to be confined NYC on $9,500 bond.

[U. S. GOVERNMENT MEMORANDUM LETTERHEAD]

DATE: 10/11/65
FROM: SAC, NEW YORK (100-156139) (F)
SUBJECT: PUDDIN
                6 Feet, 140 Pounds, Slim Build, Goatee
                SM-NOI
                (00: NY)

Rebulet to NY, 8/24/65, captioned, "NATION OF ISLAM; IS-NOI", and Savannah Dual Captioned letter to the Bureau, [Sentence is redacted] dated 8/18/65.

ReSavannahlet furnishes information concerning an interview of [Name redacted] who identified the subject and the other named JOHN as fanatical members of the Black Muslims in NYC, who are leaders in the movement and instigators of violence.

A review of the files of the NYO reflect that PUDDIN might possibly be identical with CLARENCE SMITH JOWARS aka CLARENCE

- 367 -

SMITH JOWERS, CLARENCE 13X SMITH, CLARENCE 13X, "ALLAH", "PUDDIN". (NY 100-150520).

CLARENCE SMITH JOWARS is a Negro, male, and was born on 2/21/28, in Virginia. According to the Bureau of Special Services (BSS), NYCPD, JOWARS is a self-proclaimed leaders of the "Five Percenters", who are the 5% of the Muslims who smoke and drink. The 5% according to the BSS, have no headquarters and appear to be a loosely knit group that "hangs out" on Harlem street corners.

On 6/1/65, JOWARS was among six male Negroes who were blocking the sidewalks and were interfering with street traffic in front of the Hotel Theresa, 2090 7th Avenue, NYC. When told to move on by two police officers, they turned on the officers, called on bystanders to attack the officers, and shouted anti-white and anti-police invectives. Additional police assistance was necessary to arrest the six individuals.

(1)

It is noted that an article in the New York World Telegram dated July 30, 1965 refers to JOWARS and his arrest by the NYCPD and states that Harlem knows him by the name "PUDDIN".

JOWARS is presently being confined at Bellevue Hospital, NYC, where he is undergoing psychiatric observation, and is awaiting trial.

It is requested that Savannah reinterview [Name redacted] and display the enclosed photograph of JOWARS to them to determine if JOWARS might be identical with the subject.

(2)

[U. S. GOVERNMENT MEMORANDUM LETTERHEAD]

Date: **11-16-65**
To: **DIRECTOR, FBI (100-444636)**
From: **SAC, NEW YORK (100-150520)**

Subject: **CHANGED**
                  CLARENCE EDWARD SMITH, aka
                  SM – NOI
                  (00:NY)

Title marked "Changed" to show subject's true name as CLARENCE EDWARD SMITH as reflected by military records. Title previously carried as "CLARENCE SMITH JOWARS aka Clarence 13X Smith; ET AL".

ReNYlets to the Bureau dated 9/ 17/ 65, and 10/ 19/ 65, and St. Louis letter to the Bureau, 10/22/65.

On 11/ 2/ 65 [Name redacted] BSS, NYCPD, advised SA [Name redacted] that subject last appeared in New York State Supreme Court, Part 30(Felony), NYC, on 10/ 27/ 65. Subject continues to be confined Bellevue Hospital, NYC, on $9,500.00 bond.

[Name redacted] advised that he made inquiry at the above court and it is expected that when subject appears in above court on 11/ 16/ 65, subject will be adjudged criminally insane and will be committed to a mental institution. He stated he would advise of the outcome of this matter.

For the information of Richmond, subject is a former member of the Nation of Islam (NOI) in NYC. He was arrested on 5/ 31/ 65, by the NYCPD as being the ringleader of a group called the "Five Percenters", a Negro Youth gang in the Harlem section of NYC.

Subject is a Negro male, born 2/ 21/ 28 or 2/ 22/ 28, at Danville, Virginia. [A complete line is blacked out by the FBI]

LEAD:
      RICHMOND
          AT DANVILLE, VIRGINIA. Will check birth records and verify birth, furnishing correct date of birth, name given at birth and full name of parents.

[U. S. GOVERNMENT MEMORANDUM LETTERHEAD]

Date: 11/26/65
To: **DIRECTOR, FBI**
From: **SAC, NEW YORK (100-156139)**

Subject: **PUDDIN, 6 FEET, 140 POUNDS, SLIM BUILD, GOATEE, SM – NOI (00:NY)**

ReNYlet to Bureau, 10/11/65

For the information of the Bureau and Savannah, CLARENCE 13X SMITH who is most probably identical with the subject, appeared in New York State Supreme Court on 11/ 16/ 65, and was found to be unable to understand the charges against him. He was remanded to the custody of the New York State Department of Mental Hygiene for indefinite confinement.

LEAD:
SAVANNAH

AT SAVANNAH, GEORGIA SY is requested to advise whether [XXXXXXXX] identified photograph of CLARENCE 13X SMITH as being identical with "PUDDIN."

[U. S. GOVERNMENT MEMORANDUM LETTERHEAD]

Date: **12/1/65**
To: **DIRECTOR, FBI (100-444636)**
From: **SAC, NEW YORK (100-150520)**

Subject: **CLARENCE EDWARD SMITH aka SM-NOI (00 : NY)**

ReNYlet to Bureau, 11/16/65

On 11/ 16/ 65, [Name redacted] BSS, NYCPD, advised SA [Name redacted] that on 11/ 16/ 65, subject, who is the leader of the "Five Percenters", appeared in New York State Supreme Court, NYC, and was found "unable to understand the charges against him". Subject was remanded to the custody of the New York State Department of Mental Hygiene for an indefinite confinement.

The NYO will, upon completion of outstanding investigation, prepare a report in this matter.

PART TWO

[FEDERAL BUREAU OF INVESTIGATION LETTERHEAD]

Office of Origin: NEW YORK
Date submitted: 1/17/66
Investigative Period: 6/15 – 12/23/65

Subject: CHANGED, CLARENCE EDWARD SMITH aka Clarence Smith Jowars, Clarence Smith, Clarence 13X Smith, Clarence 13X, "Allah", "Puddin"

Report made by: [Name redacted]

SUMMARY REPORT
  Title "changed" to reflect alias of CLARENCE SMITH

REFERENCES

Nyairtel to Bureau dated 6/ 2/ 65 captioned "DISTURBANCE BY GROUP CALLED 'FIVE PERCENTERS', HARLEM, NYC, 5/ 31/ 65, RACIAL MATTERS".

Nyairtel to Bureau dated 6/ 9/ 65 captioned "DISTURBANCE BY GROUP CALLED 'FIVE PERCENTERS', HARLEM, NYC, 5/ 31/ 65, RACIAL MATTERS".

Nyairtel to Bureau dated 6/ 22/ 65 captioned "DISTURBANCE BY GROUP CALLED 'FIVE PERCENTERS', HARLEM, NYC, 5/ 31/ 65, RACIAL MATTERS".

Nyairtel to Bureau dated 7/ 9/ 65 captioned "DISTURBANCE BY GROUP CALLED 'FIVE PERCENTERS', HARLEM, NYC, 5/ 31/ 65, RACIAL MATTERS".
Nylet to Bureau dated 9/17/65.
St. Louis letter to Bureau dated 10/22/65.

Nylet to Bureau dated 10/ 18/ 65 captioned "DISTURBANCE BY GROUP CALLED 'FIVE PERCENTERS', HARLEM, NYC, 5/ 31/ 65, RACIAL MATTERS".
Nylet to Bureau dated 11/16/65.
Nylet to Bureau dated 12/1/65.
Richmond letter to NY dated 12/21/65.

-A-

ADMINISTRATIVE

This report is classified "Confidential" because of the information contained therein from NY T-1 through NY T-5 who are informants furnishing information of continuing value and whose effectiveness could be impaired if this information is revealed and would thereby have an adverse effect on the national security.

It is noted that information concerning all of the NOI affairs attended by the subject are not set out in detail in this report inasmuch as many of these affairs could not be determined to of a seditious, anarchistic or revolutionary nature.

It is noted that prior investigation by the NYO into the "Five Percenters" revealed that it was a Negro youth street gang in Harlem that had been influenced by CLARENCE EDWARD SMITH aka, a former NOI member who called himself "Allah". Under his influence these youths became indoctrinated in the perverted NOI form of Muslim ideology with anti-white racial overtones. Many of these youths have adopted Muslim names although investigation revealed that they were not members of or affiliated with the NOI, MMI or the OAAU. Inasmuch as the gang was composed of teenagers without any real overall setup or headquarters, the NYO conducted no extensive investigation or the group since they represented a local police problem.

On 10/ 15/ 65, SA [Name redacted] conferred with [Name redacted] BSS, NYCPD and [Sentence redacted] BSS. The results of this conference are not being set out in the details of this report on the specific request of [Name redacted] that none of the information be disseminated outside of the FBI in view of the continuing extensive investigation by the NYCPD into the "Five Percenters". Because of the nature of the information, BSS could not be concealed by a "T" symbol without it being apparent that the concealed source was some branch of the NYCPD. The information obtained by SA [Name redacted] during the above conference is as follows:

-   B –

The NYCPD is continuing to conduct a full-time, extensive investigation of the "Five Percenters" which includes daily interrogation of gang members and nightly surveillances of them. The NYCPD feels that this extensive coverage has succeeded in deterring the activity of the gang and has opened the way for numerous arrests for assaults, muggings and marijuana smoking charges by gang members.

The NYCPD investigation has determined that there are approximately 200 "Five Percenters" in NYC, ranging in age from 12 to 21. Approximately 125 of then are centered in Harlem, and the remaining 75 are scattered over Bronx, Brooklyn and Queens. The gang is responsible for numerous assaults and muggings, chiefly aimed at whites on the fringe area of Harlem. However, if the gang is unable to find a white victim they have no reservations about choosing a Negro victim. The gang has also caused a great deal of trouble in schools where they have disrupted classes, demanded to be called by their Muslim name and have assaulted some teachers.

The leader of the "Five Percenters" was CLARENCE EDWARD SMITH who is incarcerated and undergoing psychiatric examination. He is known to gang members as "Allah", Clarence 13X or "Puddin".

The gang has no meeting place other than the street, school yard and public parks.

The current meaning of "Five Percent" is that 85 percent of Negroes are cattle, 10 percent are Uncle Toms and the remaining 5 percent, which they are, are the real leaders of the Negro people. The Muslim indoctrination they receive in addition to the adoption of a Muslim name is the memorization of the questions and answers put out by the NOI which NOI members must learn before receiving their "X" name. This list of questions and answers appears to have originated with SMITH who was an NOI member under the name of CLARENCE 13X SMITH, and he undoubtedly obtained it when he joined the NOI.

The NYCPD investigation has developed no tie or relationship by the "Five Percenters" with the NOI, MMI or the OAAU.

The investigation has developed nothing to indicate that the gang is armed or has a cache of arms and weapons stored in Harlem. Undoubtedly some of the members have weapons or homemade-type zip guns, but there is no evidence of wholesale arming of the gang. There is also nothing to indicate the gang has training in garroting or hand to hand killing methods.

[Name redacted] mentioned above, described the "Five Percenters" as a particularly vicious type of street gang that has found in this Muslim overtone a mysterious type of ideology that seems to unite and inspire them. Consequently, the NYCPD is following their activities very closely to control and identify them.

As pointed out in referenced NY airtel dated 10/ 18/ 65, the "Five Percenters" is a teenage Negro street gang. Its leader is currently incarcerated and the NYCPD is conducting an extensive investigation of the gang. Therefore, the NYO feels that the "Five Percenters" represent a local police problem and no investigation of the "Five Percenters" itself is being conducted.

One extra copy of this report is being furnished the Bureau and being prepared for the NYO for dissemination to US Secret Service upon Bureau authorization.

FD 122 is being submitted recommending subject be included on the Security Index (SI).

INFORMANTS: [5 informant names are redacted]

The identities of other confidential sources contacted during the investigation of the subject and who were unable to furnish any information concerning the subject are:

[7 names are redacted]

LEADS

NEW YORK

AT NEW YORK, NEW YORK. Will await Bureau approval of subject's inclusion on the SI.

2. Upon approval of subject's inclusion on the SI, will furnish one copy of instant report and photograph of subject to US Secret Service, NYC.

3. Will determine from Department of Mental Hygiene, State of NY, location of subject's incarceration and attempt to place stop would subject be released

[U. S. DEPARTMENT OF JUSTICE; FBI LETTERHEAD]

Report of:	**[Name redacted]**
Office:	**New York, New York**
Date:	**1/17/66**
Field Office File at:	**100-150520**
Title:	**Clarence Edward Smith**

Character: SECURITY MATTER – NATION OF ISLAM

Synopsis:

CLARENCE EDWARD SMITH, Negro male, born 2/28/28 at Danville, Va. last resided 21 West 112th Street, NYC and currently in custody NY State Department of Mental Hygiene for indefinite confinement. SMITH currently unemployed and last known employment was Earth Painters Improvement Co., 1087 Union Street,

Brooklyn, NY. SMITH served in US Army from 10/ 30/ 52 to 8/ 21/ 54. Military record set out. [Name redacted] SMITH, FBI # 426 220F, arrested by NYCPD 5/ 31/ 65 under name "Allah" for felonious assault, conspiracy to commit same, resisting arrest, assault with deadly weapon, disorderly conduct, as leader of Negro youth gang called "Five Percenters". SMITH remanded custody of NY State Department of Mental Hygiene for indefinite confinement. Arrest record set out. SMITH reportedly member of NOI Mosque #7, NYC and attended NOI affairs from 9/1/61 through 3/23/65. NOI activity set out. Description set out.

A. Birth

CLARENCE SMITH, a Negro male, was born on February 22, 1928, at Danville, Virginia. [Sentence redacted].

On November 22, 1965, Mrs. ELVA LYONS, Receptionist, State Bureau of Vital Statistics, Richmond, Virginia, advised that her files, located in Volume Number 1985A, is Certificate Number 57978, which reflects that CLARENCE EDWARD SMITH, Negro male, was born February 22, 1928, in Danville, Pittsylvania County, Virginia.

B. Residence

In January, 1952, CLARENCE SMITH, a Negro male, born February 22, 1928, resided at 215 West 134th Street, New York, New York.

A review on October 14, 1965 of the United States Army service records on file at the Military Personnel Records reflected that CLARENCE EDWARD SMITH, Negro male, born February 22, 1928, United States Army Serial Number (SN) 51 207 085 as of September, 1960, resided at 21 West 112th Street, New York, New York.

On June 7, 1965, [Name redacted] Bureau of Special Services (BSS), New York City Police Department (NYCPD) advised SA [Name redacted] that CLARENCE 13X SMITH, also known as "Allah", who resides at 21 West 112th Street, New York, New York, was arrested by the NYCPD on may 31, 1965, as being the ringleader of a Harlem street gang known as the "Five Percenters" and for unlawful assembly.

On November 16, 1965. [Name redacted] BSS, NYCPD, advised SA [Name redacted] that on November 16, 1965, CLARENCE 13X SMITH, who had been in the custody of the NYCPD since May 31, 1965, appeared in the New York State Supreme Court, New York, New York, and was remanded to the custody of the New York State Department of Mental Hygiene for an indefinite confinement.

C. Employment

CLARENCE SMITH, Negro male, born February 22, 1928, was, as of September, 1962, employed by the Earth Painters Improvement Company, 1087 Union Street, Brooklyn, New York.

On November 9, 1964, [Name redacted] BSS, NYCPD, advised SA [Name redacted] that CLARENCE 13X SMITH of 21 East 112th Street, New York City was employed by the Earth Painters Improvement Company, 1087 Union Street, Brooklyn New York.

On June 7, 1965, [Name redacted] BSS, NYCPD, advised SA [Name redacted] that CLARENCE 13X SMITH who resided at 21 West 112th Street, New York City, was unemployed.

[Name redacted] BSS, NYCPD, advised SA [Name redacted] on November 10, 1965, that CLARENCE 13X SMITH, who has been in the custody of the NYCPD since May 31, 1965, on charges of unlawful assembly and as being the ringleader of a Harlem street gang known as the "Five Percenters", appeared in New York State Supreme Court, New York City on November 16, 1965, and was remanded to the custody of the New York State Department of Mental Hygiene for an indefinite confinement.

D. Military Service

A review on October 14, 1965, by IC [Name redacted] of the United States Army service records on file at APRC, St. Louis, Missouri, indicated that CLARENCE EDWARD SMITH, Negro male, born February 22, 1928, United States Army SN 51 207 085 was inducted into the United States Army on October 30, 1952 and entered on active duty on the same date at New York, New York. SMITH was honorably released from active duty on August 21, 1954 as a Private First Class at camp Kilmer, New jersey and transferred to the United States Army Reserve to complete his military obligation.

SMITH served in the United States Army Reserve, inactive status, from August 22, 1954 to September 30, 1960, at which time he was honorably discharged.

SMITH had foreign service in Japan and Korea and was awarded Korean Service Medal with one Bronze Service Star, Combat

Infantryman's Badge, Presidential Unit Citation (Republic of Korea), United Nations Service Medal and the National Defense Service Medal.

His character and efficiency ratings ranged from unknown to excellent and there is not record of court-martials or absence without official leave (AWOL).

MPRC records contained Report of medical Examination dated August.

[Author's Notes: Rest of information pertains to medical history and isn't relevant]

E. Marital Status

Records of MPRC, St. Louis, Missouri, as reviewed by IC [Name redacted] on October 14, 1965, reflected that CLARENCE EDWARD SMITH was married, [Name redacted].

On September 9, 1965 [Name redacted] BSS, NYCPD, advised SA [Name redacted] that investigation of CLARENCE 13X SMITH by the NYCPD has reflected that SMITH was married [Name redacted].

F. Arrest Record

Information was received from the Identification Division of the Federal Bureau of Investigation (FBI), Washington, D. C. on November 12, 1965, which reflected that CLARENCE EDWARD SMITH, FBI Number 426 220 F, has the following records in the files of the FBI Identification Division:

[Author's Notes: document then relays that they have Clarence's fingerprints from his Army days (10/ 30/ 52) and his arrest record (5/31/65) with 6 counts (1) fel A on officer (2) fel aslt on complainant (3) 580 PL consp (4) 1851 PL resist arr (5) 1897 PL 6 foot board (6) dis-con]

On June 1, 1965 [Name redacted], BBS, NYCPD, advised SA [Name redacted] that at 9:15 PM, May 31, 1965, six Negro males were blocking the sidewalk and interfering with street traffic in front of the Hotel Theresa, 2090 Seventh Avenue, new York City. When told to move on by two police officers, these six Negro males turned on the officers, called on bystanders to attack the officers, and shouted anti-white and anti-police invectives.

[Name redacted] advised that all six of these Negro males were arrested by the NYCPD. He informed that all of these individuals had Muslim type names or aliases, but all denied being members of the Nation of Islam (NOI) or the Muslim Mosque, Incorporated (MMI). However, some of these individuals appeared to have some knowledge of the NOI. These six Negro males claimed to be members of the "Five Percenters", which they claimed meant the five per cent of Muslims who smoke and drink.

[Name redacted] advised that one of the above six Negro males who was arrested identified himself as "Allah", a Negro male, believed to be identical to CLARENCE 13X SMITH. "Allah" was the ringleader of the above six Negro males who were arrested and was the self-proclaimed leader of the "Five Percenters". "Allah" was assigned NYCPD Number B 612230.

[Name redacted] advised that "Allah" was charged with felonious assault, conspiracy to commit same, resisting arrest, assault with a deadly weapon, disorderly conduct, possession of a marijuana cigarette and malicious mischief.

[Name redacted] informed that "Allah" was arraigned on June 1, 1965, in Manhattan Felony Court, New York, New York, and was incarcerated in new York, New York, in lieu of $9,500.00 bond.

On June 7, 1965 [Name redacted] BSS, NYCPD, advised SA [Name redacted] that "Allah", NYCPD Number B 612230 had been identified as being identical to CLARENCE 13X SMITH.

On June 24, 1965, [Name redacted] BSS, NYCPD, advised SA [Name redacted] that on June 24, 1965, CLARENCE 13X SMITH appeared on felony charges in New York Supreme Court, Part 30 (Felony), New York, New York, and was committed to Bellevue Hospital, New York City, for psychiatric examination.

[Name redacted] BSS, NYCPD, advised SA [Name redacted] in November 2, 1965, that CLARENCE 13X SMITH HAD appeared on felony charges in New York Supreme Court, Part 30 (Felony), New York City, on various dates from June 24, 1965 through October 27, 1965. At each appearance SMITH was remanded to the custody of Bellevue Hospital, New York City, for additional psychiatric examinations. [Name redacted] further advised that SMITH was next scheduled to appear in the above court on November 16, 1965, and that the judge of the above court had stated that in all probability, SMITH would be adjudged criminally insane and would be committed to a mental institution.

On November 16, 1965 [Name redacted] BSS, NYCPD, advised SA [Name redacted] that on November 16, 1965, CLARENCE 13X SMITH appeared in New York Supreme Court, Part 30 (Felony), New York, New York, and was found "unable to understand the charges against him". On the same date, SMITH was remanded to the custody of the New York State Department of Mental Hygiene for an indefinite confinement.

On December 3, 1965 SA [Name redacted] caused a search to be made of the records of the New York Supreme Court, New York County, New York, New York. This search reflected that on November 16, 1965, CLARENCE 13X SMITH, also known as "Allah", appeared in Part 30 (Felony) of above court, was found "unable to understand the charges against him", and was remanded to the custody of the Commissioner of Mental Hygiene of the Department of Mental Hygiene for the State of New York for an indefinite confinement.

AFFILIATION WITH THE NATION OF ISLAM (NOI)

Characterizations of the NOI, NOI Mosque Number (#) 7, Fruit of Islam (FOI), Muslim Girls Training (MGT), Muslim Mosque, Incorporated (MMI) and the Organization of Afro-American Unity, Incorporated (OAAU) are contained in the Appendix section of this report.

The New York, New York Branch of the NOI is known as Mosque #7 located at 102 West 116th Street, New York, New York. However, this Mosque was destroyed by fire on February 23, 1965. There are three meeting places for Mosque #7 which are located and identified as: 105-03 Northern Boulevard, Queens, New York, known as Mosque #7B; 120 Madison Street, Brooklyn, New York, known as Mosque #7C; and 878 Prospect Avenue, Bronx, New York, known as Mosque #7D.

A. Attendance at NOI Meetings

CLARENCE 13X was observed in attendance at [Name redacted] NOI meetings held on various dates from [Word redacted] at NOI Mosque #7, 102 West 116th Street, New York, New York.

CLARENCE 13X was observed in attendance at [Word redacted] NOI meetings held on various dates from [Word redacted] at NOI Mosque #7, 102 West 116th Street, New York, New York.

CLARENCE 13X was observed in attendance at an NOI meeting held on [Word redacted] at Wyandanche Community Center, Wyandanch, Long Island, New York.

CLARENCE 13X was observed in attendance at an NOI meeting held on [Word redacted] at Manhattan Center, 311 West 34th Street, New York City.

CLARENCE 13X was observed in attendance at two NOI meetings held on [Word redacted] and [Word redacted] at NOI Mosque #7C, 120 Madison Street, Brooklyn, New York.

At an NOI meeting held on [Word redacted] at NOI Mosque #7, 102 West 116th Street, New York, New York, in which CLARENCE 13X was in attendance, [Name redacted] said that when the so-called Negroes think of the white man as being wicked then they think of the white man as being a best. He said there are some good characteristics in the white man and also in a beast. He stated that the Honorable ELIJAH MUHAMMAD had taught that Allah has told him (MUHAMMAD) that the white man is the devil and when the so-called Negroes call a white man a devil then they call the white man by his true name. He said by nature the white man is a devil and cannot be any other way.

At an NOI meeting held on [Word redacted] at Mosque #7, 102 West 116th Street, New York, New York, in which CLARENCE 13X was in attendance, MALCOLM X said that the white man have proven themselves to be devils as the Honorable ELIJAH MUHAMMAD has taught that they were. He said he was tired of this devil and he hoped that Allah would take the so-called Negroes away from this earth.

At an NOI meeting held on [Word redacted] at Mosque #7, 102 West 116th Street, New York, New York, in which CLARENCE 13X was in attendance, MALCOLM X said that the courts would like to throw all the Muslims in jail, but he does not think the courts can. He said the Muslims are taught not to be the aggressor, but if an adversary aggresses on the Muslims, then the Muslims should kill the aggressor. He said the Muslim Mosque is a place of worship, not fighting, but if the Muslim Mosque is attacked then the attacker should be killed.

At an NOI meeting held on [Word redacted] at NOI Mosque #7, 102 West 116th Street, New York, New York, in which CLARENCE 13X was in attendance, [Name redacted] said that the white man, with all the soldiers, guns, tanks, rockets, bombs, police, FBI and Uncle Toms, are worried about the Muslims because the Muslims pray five times a day.

He said that today the Muslim God has the devil, the white man, in a deep freeze.

At an NOI meeting held on [Word redacted] at Mosque #7, 102 West 116th Street, New York, New York, in which CLARENCE 13X was in attendance, [Name redacted] said the so-called Negroes were kidnapped from their own land, brought to America and cast into slavery by the white man. He said that Allah has come to destroy America for what the white man has done to the so-called Negro.

At an NOI meeting held on [Word redacted] at NOI Mosque #7, 102 West 116th Street, New York City, in which CLARENCE 13X was in attendance, MALCOLM X said the so-called Negro leaders were not the cause of the race problems in America, that the Honorable ELIJAH MUHAMMAD was not the cause of this racial unrest, but it was the white man who has caused this racial unrest and it was the white man who has taught the so-called Negroes to hate. He said the white man has robbed the so—called Negroes of their language, religion, culture, and teach that the so-called Negroes were savages when taken from their native country.

At an NOI meeting held on [Word redacted] at NOI Mosque #7, 102 West 116th Street, New York, New York, in which CLARENCE 13X was in attendance, MALCOLM X said that what the white man is doing for integration today is only a trick to keep the people from listening to the Honorable ELIJAH MUHAMMAD. He said integration will not work and the so-called Negroes will not get freedom, justice and equality without bloodshed.

At an NOI meeting held on [Word redacted] at NOI Mosque #7, 102 West 116th Street, New York City, in which CLARENCE 13X was in attendance, [Name redacted] said that the white man has only three ounces of brains and this was all evil. He said there was no good in the white man, and it was the white man who caused Adam and Eve to sin.

At an NOI meeting held on [Word redacted] at NOI Mosque #7, 102 West 116th Street, New York, New York, in which CLARENCE 13X was in attendance, [Name redacted] said that the white man has used his number one tool, the Negro preacher, to teach the so-called Negro that there is life after death. He said it is better to be a living dog than a dead lion because the dead know nothing. He said the white man has been able to lynch and shoot Negroes because the Negroes think that there is another life. He said if the so-called Negroes had known differently then the so-called Negroes would know that the white man is the devil and that there is no good in the white man.

At an NOI meeting held on [Word redacted] at NOI Mosque #7, 102 West 116th Street, New York, New York, in which CLARENCE 13X was in attendance, [Name redacted] said that ELIJAH MUHAMMAD has taught that the white man is the devil.

B. Attendance at FOI Meetings

CLARENCE 13X was observed in attendance at [Word redacted] FOI meetings held on various dates from [XXXXXX] through [Word redacted] at NOI Mosque #7, 102 West 116th Street, New York, New York.

CLARENCE 13X was observed in attendance at an FOI meeting held on [Word redacted] at NOI Mosque #7C, 120 Madison Street, Brooklyn, New York.

CLARENCE 13X was observed in attendance at [Word redacted] FOI meetings held on various dates from [Word redacted] through [Word redacted] at NOI Mosque #7, 102 West 116th Street, New York, New York.

C. Attendance at NOI Rallies

CLARENCE 13X was observed in attendance at an NOI rally held on February 16, 1963 at 125th Street and Seventh Avenue, New York, New York.

At the above NOI rally, MALCOLM X said that the Muslims were tired of the injustice being handed their members in court action. He said the Muslims prefer holding their members in court action. He said the Muslims prefer holding their own court at the scene of an incident for their own cause.

At the above NOI rally held on February 16, 1963, MALCOLM X said that the so-called Negroes have helped the white man fight his wars, and that the so-called Negroes have died for the white man in Korea, Germany and Japan. He said it was time for the so-called Negroes to give their lives for their own freedom, and that the so-called Negroes should not have freedom in their vocabulary if they were not ready to fight and give their life for their freedom. He said that the so-called Negroes must let the white man know that the so-called Negroes are not afraid, and will fight and die for their freedom and will not die alone.

CLARENCE 13X attended an NOI rally held on June 29, 1963 at 115th Street and Lenox Avenue, New York, New York.

At the above NOI rally, MALCOLM X said that if the people had come to hear him teach non-violence, or to hear him say that they should love the white man, then they had come to the wrong place. He said Harlem is filled with all forms of vice and immoralities, and all of this is to be blamed on the white man. He said that dope is "pushed": in Harlem by the white man and that liquor stores in Harlem are owned by the white man.

CLARENCE 13 X attended an NOI rally held on September 7, 1963 at 115th Street and Lenox Avenue, New York, New York.

At the above NOI rally, MALCOLM X said that ELIJAH MUHAMMAD has taught the so-called Negroes that the white man is a devil and that there is no good in the white man.

CLARENCE 13X attended an NOI rally held on September 14, 1963 at 115th Street and Lenox Avenue, New York, New York.

CLARENCE 13X attended an NOI rally held on December 1, 1963 at NOI Mosque #7, 102 West 116th Street, New York, New York.

CLARENCE 13X attended an NOI rally held on June 28, 1964 at the 369th Regimental Armory, 142nd Street and fifth Avenue, New York, New York.

At the above NOI rally, ELIJAH MUHAMMAD spoke and said that the Negroes wants some territory where the Negroes can set up their own government. He said if the so-called Negroes do not get some territory, then Allah may have to remove the white man from this planet.

D. Attendance at NOI Unity Meetings

CLARENCE 13X attended two NOI Unity meetings of the [Word redacted] held on [Word redacted] and [Word redacted] at NOI Mosque #7, 102 West 116th Street, New York, New York.

Clarence 13X was observed in attendance at five NOI Unity meetings of the [Word redacted] held on various dates from [Word redacted] through [Word redacted] at NOI Mosque #7, 102 West 116th Street, New York, New York.

E. Attendance at NOI African-Asian Bazaars

CLARENCE 13X attended an NOI African-Asian Bazaar held on February 12, 1963 at Rockland Palace, 155th Street and Eight Avenue, New York, New York.

CLARENCE 13X was observed in attendance at an NOI African-Asian Bazaar held on September 21, 1963, at the 369th Regimental Armory, 142nd Street and Eighth Avenue, New York, New York.

CLARENCE 13X attended an NOI African-Asian Bazaar held on November 30, 1963 at the 369th Regimental Armory, 142nd Street and Fifth Avenue, New York, New York.

NOI Miscellaneous

CLARENCE 13X attended an NOI affair called "Muhammad Speaks" which was held on September 29, 1963 at the Philadelphia Arena, Philadelphia, Pennsylvania.

At the above NOI affair, ELIJAH MUHAMMAD spoke and said that the white man led the so-called Negroes to believe God is a spirit and that the so-called Negroes must die before they can see God. He said that the white man teaches that the snake tempted Eve. He said that we all know that a snake does not talk, so the scriptures only mean a people with a snake-like nature. He said the white man in America is of a snake-like nature and were created for the purpose of murdering black people.

On November 9, 1964, [Name redacted] BSS, NYCPD, advised SA [Name redacted] that in connection with an investigation by the NYCPD involving the death of an NOI member it was determined that CARENCE 13X SMITH of 21 West 112th Street, New York City, was an employee of the Earth Painters Improvement Company, 1087 Union Street, Brooklyn, New York, which is a company composed of NOI members.

Photograph with NYCPD Number B612230 is CLARENCE 13X SMITH who was, as late as the summer of 1964, an active member of the NOI in New York City.

[June 14, 1965]

Photograph bearing NYCPD Number B612230 is CLARENCE 13X also known as "Allah". CLARENCE 13X was a member of an NOI

Mosque #7, but he has not attended any NOI meetings for several months.

Photograph bearing NYCPD Number B612230 is identical to CLARENCE 13X. CLARENCE 13X had been a member of the NOI Mosque #7 for about two years, but left about the time MALCOLM X defected from the NOI. CLARENCE 13X has a family and several children, however, his current residence and employment are not known.

G. MMI Miscellaneous

On June 3, 1964, Detective [Name redacted] BSS, NYCPD, advised SA [Name redacted] that the NYCPD had determined that CLARENCE 13X had joined the MMI.

CLARENCE 13X, provided he is even a member in the MMI, holds no official position in the MMI.

Photograph bearing NYCPD Number B612230 is CLARENCE 13X SMITH. SMITH appeared to be associated with MALCOLM X. It is not known if SMITH was a member of the MMI or the OAAU, but was often seen around the Hotel Theresa, New York City, which is headquarters of the MMI and the OAAU and MALCOLM X's group.

III. AFFILIATION WITH THE "FIVE PERCENTERS"

On June 1, 1965, [Name redacted] BSS, NYCPD, advised SA [Name redacted] that at 9:15 PM, May 31, 1965, six Negro males were blocking the sidewalk and interfering with street traffic in front of the Hotel Theresa, 2090 Seventh Avenue, New York, New York. When told to move on by two police officers, they turned on the officers, called on bystanders to attack the officers and shouted anti-white and anti-police invectives. Additional police assistance was necessary to arrest these six Negro males.

[Name redacted] advised that the above six Negro males all had Muslim type names or aliases, but all denied being members of the NOI or the MMI. However, some of them appeared to have some knowledge of the NOI. They did claim to be members of the "Five Percenters", which they claim means the five per cent of Muslims who smoke and drink. According to [Name redacted] the "Five Percenters" have no headquarters and appear to be a loosely knit group that "hangs out" on Harlem street corners.

[Name redacted] advised that one of the above six Negro males who was arrested identified himself as "Allah" believed by the NYCPD to be identical to CLARENCE 13X SMITH. "Allah" was assigned NYCPD Number B612230. He was the ringleader of the above six who were arrested and was the self-proclaimed leader of the "Five Percenters."

[Name redacted] advised that all six were charged with felonious assault, conspiracy to commit same, resisting arrest, assault with a deadly weapon and disorderly conduct. In addition, "Allah" was charged with possession of a marijuana cigarette and malicious mischief.

[Name redacted] further advised that on June 1, 1965, all six were arraigned in Manhattan Felony Court, New York City and the case was adjourned until June 18, 1965. All six were incarcerated in lieu of bail ranging from $2,000 to $9,500, the latter being the bail for "Allah". During the hearing, "Allah" claimed that he was God and stated that the court could not charge them with anything since "you can't charge Allah". He also refused "white lawyers" when offered legal aid assistance.

On June 7, 1965, [Name redacted] BSS, NYCPD, advised SA [Name redacted] that "Allah", the recognized leader of the "Five Percenters" and one of the six Negro males arrested on May 31, 1965, by the NYCPD, has been identified by the NYCPD as CLARENCE 13X SMITH of 21 West 112th Street, Apartment 5E, New York, New York. SMITH is unemployed and "hangs out" on Harlem street corners in New York City where he contacts and indoctrinates the youth of the area.

[Name redacted] advised that the "Five Percenters", who are on occasion referred to as the "Brotherhood of Blackman" or the "Brotherhood of Allah", is a loosely knit group of Negro youth gangs in the Harlem section of New York City. He informed these youths are typical of the numerous street type gangs that exist in Harlem except that they have been influenced by CLARENCE 13X SMITH who refers to himself as "Allah" and who has indoctrinated these youths in the distorted Muslim teachings of NOI leader ELIJAH MUHAMMAD.

He informed that because of SMITH's influence over these youths, they like to consider themselves "Muslims" and many of them shave their heads and take Arabic sounding names. However, none of these youths follow the tenets of the orthodox Islamic religion nor do they actually belong to or follow the teachings of the NOI. These youths do, however, claim to be the "five per cent" of the followers of ELIJAH MUHAMMAD who believe in smoking and drinking.

[Name redacted] advised that investigation by the NYCPD has determined that the "Five Percenters" do not have any central meeting place or headquarters. Although each of the individual youth gangs formed from their respective neighborhoods has its own leader, they do not have an overall organizational setup other than to look up to SMITH as their teacher and "Allah".

IV. MISCELLANEOUS

The July 30, 1965, edition of the "New York World Telegram", a daily newspaper published in New York City, contained an article entitled "Harlem Knows 'Allah' as Puddin". This article read as follows:

"Allah claims he is God – but other Harlemites have different ideas".

"God? A barmaid once exclaimed."

"That ain't God. That's Puddin. That's what we always called him – Puddin."

"Allah is Clarence 13X Smith, 35, leader of a group of youths called the Five Percenters, 17 of whom were arrested last night."

"A man who knew him for 20 years, described him as a 'nice friendly guy, who used to work pushing trucks down in the garment district."

"But Allah hasn't worked since he formed his Muslim sect, which he claims has some 200 followers."

"That claim – as Allah's claim to divinity—is also questioned."

"That cat ain't got nothing but the blues, said another Harlem resident."

On September 9, 1965, [Name redacted] BSS, NYCPD, advised SA [Name redacted] that investigation by the NYCPD had determined that CLARENCE 13X SMITH had used the name of CLARENCE SMITH JOWARS in the past. However, it was not known at that time if subject's true last name was SMITH or JOWARS.

[An entire following paragraph is redacted]

During the investigation of the subject, several confidential sources familiar with various phases of activity and members of the NOI, MMI and the OAAU were contacted and could furnish no information concerning the subject.

DESCRIPTION

The following description of CLARENCE EDWARD SMITH was obtained from BSS, NYCPD; [XXXX] MPRC, St. Louis, Missouri; FBI

Identification Division, Washington, D.C.; and the State Bureau of Vital Statistics, Richmond, Virginia:

Name	CLARENCE EDWARD SMITH, Clarence Smith Jowars, Clarence Smith, Clarence 13X Smith, Clarence 13X, "Allah", "Puddin"
Race	Negro
Sex	Male
Date of birth	February 22, 1928
Place of birth	Danville, Pittsylvania County, Virginia
Height	5 feet 11 inches
Weight	162 pounds
Eyes	Brown
Hair	Black
Marital Status	Married
Education	Two Years High School
Occupation	Shines shoes and shipping clerk
Employment	Unemployed
Former Employment	Earth Painters Improvement Company. 1087 Union Street Brooklyn, New York
Address	Presently confined New York State Department of Mental Hygiene for an indefinite confinement.
Former Addresses	21 West 112th Street New York, New York.
Military Service	United States Army October 30, 1952 to August 21, 1954.
United States Army Serial Number	51-207-085
Selective Service Number	50-15-28-119
Social Security Number	228-28-0034
NYCPD Number	B612230

[Author's note: last few items have been blacked out per FBI]

DATE:	10/18/65
TO:	DIRECTOR, FBI
FROM:	SAC, NEW YORK (157-1489)

SUBJECT: **"FIVE PERCENTERS", aka**
Brotherhood of Blackmen,
Brotherhood of Allah
RACIAL MATTERS

Enclosed herewith for the Bureau are two newspaper articles, to wit: 1)10/ 15/ 65 edition of "The new York Times", page 1, captioned "Wingate Warns of Negro Revolt If Haryou's Program Is Curbed," and, 2)10/ 15/ 65 edition of the "New York Herald Tribune", page 1, captioned "Harlem '5 Percenters' – Terror Group Revealed.

Reference is made to NY airtel and LHM dated 6/ 2/ 65, captioned "DISTURBANCE BY GROUP CALLED 'FIVE PERCENTERS, HARLEM, NYC, 5/ 31/ 65, RACIAL MATTERS, "Nyairtel and LHM dated 6/ 9/ 65, above caption; Nyairtel and LHM dated 6/ 22/ 65, above caption; Nyairtel and LHM dated 7/ 9/ 65, above caption; Nyairtel and LHM dated 7/31/65, captioned, "DISTURBANCE BY GROUP CALLED 'FIVE PERCENTER', HARLEM, NYC, 7/ 29/ 65, RACIAL MATTERS."; Nyairtel and LHM dated 8/ 26/ 65, above caption; Nylet and LHM dated 9/20/65, above caption. (U)

The two enclosed articles deal primarily with a speech and subsequent impromptu press conference given by LIVINGSTON WINGATE on 10/ 14/ 65, before the eastern regional conference of the Urban League at the Belmont Plaza Hotel, New York City.

WINGATE is the Executive Director of the Harlem anti-poverty program known as Harlem Youth Opportunities Unlimited – Associated Community Teams (HARYOU-ACT). Both articles point out that WINGATE has been criticized for his handling of the program and that he is currently under investigation by the Manhattan District Attorney's Office and the Federal authorities following charges of fiscal mismanagement.

In his speech and press conference, according to these articles, WINGATE denied any fiscal wrongdoing and claimed the spending of certain monies on his part was necessary to avert racial violence in Harlem during the past summer. His main theme was that if anything happened to HARYOU-ACT there would definitely be racial violence. ON this latter point, WINGATE referred to a mysterious "armed" group of Negro youth who are "prepared to die" in a struggle against white people. He refused to identify by name this group stating he feared for his life if he talked too much. He further implied that only HARYOU-ACT was stopping this group from acting.

Both articles indicated that WINGATE WAS APPARENTLY SPEAKING OF A black Muslim-oriented extremist youth group known as the "Five Percenters." The "Tribute" article then set forth observations on this group which this paper developed in an "independent investigation" during the past three weeks.

It is noted that prior investigation by the NYO into the "Five Percenters" revealed that it was a Negro youth street gang in Harlem that has been influenced by CLARENCE SMITH JOWARS, aka (NY 100-150520), a former Nation of Islam (NOI) member who called himself "Allah". Under his influence and that of his associate, JAMES HOWELL these youths became indoctrinated in the perverted NOI form of Muslim ideology with anti-white racial overtones. Many of these youths have adopted Muslim names although investigation revealed that they were not members of or affiliated with the NOI, Muslim Mosque, Inc. (MMI) or the Organization of Afro-American Unity, Inc. (OAAU). JOWARS and HOWELL were arrested on 5/ 31/ 65, and continue to be incarcerated awaiting trial which has been delayed due to extensive psychiatric examinations of JOWARS, which had been ordered by the court. In asmuch as the gang was composed of teenagers without any real overall organizational setup or headquarters, the NYO conducted no extensive investigation of the group since they represented a local police problem.

In view of the publicity of the "Five Percenters" in the attached articles as a result of the WINGATE speech and, particularly, because of allegations outlined in the "Tribune" article, SA [name redacted] conferred on 10/15/65

[The following two paragraphs are redacted].

[Name redacted] has determined that there are approximately 200 "Five Percenters" in NYC, ranging in age from 12 to 21. Approximately 125 of them are centered in Harlem, around the 120 series of streets, bounded by 7th and Lenox Avenues. The remaining 75 youths are scattered over Bronx, Brooklyn and Queens, with the most concentrated in the Fort Greene area of Brooklyn and the St. Marys Park area of the Bronx. The gang is responsible for numerous assaults and muggings, chiefly aimed at whites on the fringe area of Harlem. However, if the gang is unable to find a white victim they have no reservations about choosing a Negro victim. The gang has also caused a great deal of trouble in schools, chiefly Junior High School #120 at Madison Avenue and 120th Street in Harlem, where they disrupt classes, demand to be called by their Muslim name and have assaulted some teachers.

The leaders of the "Five Percenters" was JOWARS assisted by HOWELL, both of whom are incarcerated and JOWARS is undergoing psychiatric examination. JOWARS is known to gang members as "Allah", CLARENCE 13X or "Puddin". [next 5 sentences are redacted]. There are no lother leaders of the gang although they do instruct each other in Muslim-type ideology and the practice of judo and karate.

The gang has no meeting place other than the street, school yards and public parks.

The current meaning of "Five Percent" is that 85% of Negroes are cattle, 10% are Uncle Toms and the remaining 5%, which they are, are the real leaders of the Negro people. The Muslim indoctrination they receive in addition to the adoption of a Muslim name is the memorization of the questions and answers put out by the NOI which NOI members must learn before receiving their "X" name. This list of questions and answers appears to have originated with JOWARS, who was an NOI member under the name of CLARENCE 13X SMITH, and he undoubtedly obtained it when he joined the NOI.

[The following 2 paragraphs are redacted]

With the exception of the above mentioned assaults and muggings of whites there is no definitive policy or activity by the gang of violence against whites. However, the overall attitude of gang members is one of anti-white insofar as the racial situation is concerned. Also, the gang has never engaged in any pre-mediated attacks on police officers. The one incident involving an assault of a police officer occurred when an officer was attempting to make a disorderly conduct arrest on 7/ 29/ 65. (See referenced airtel and letterhead memorandum dated 7/ 31/ 65.) No information has been developed that money obtained from muggings and assaults by gang members is turned over to any specific leader or fund.

Although a number of gang members have been arrested on numerous charges the incidents receiving the most publicity were the following:

The 5/ 31/ 65, arrest of JOWARS, HOWELL and four others. (See re NY airtels and letterhead memorandum dated 6/2/65 and 6/9/65.

The 6/ 18/ 65, arrest of eight gang members who were making Molotov cocktails. (See NY airtel and letterhead memorandum dated 6/22/65.)

The 7/ 29/ 65, arrest of 17 gang members for disorderly conduct and resisting arrest. (See NY airtel and letterhead memorandum dated 7/31/65.

[The following paragraph is redacted]

[Name redacted] described the "Five Percenters" as a particularly vicious type of street gang that has found in seems to unite and inspire them. [Next sentence is redacted].

In view of the fact that the "Five Percenters" is a teenage Negro type of street gang, its leaders are currently incarcerated [remaining sentence redacted] The NYO feels that it represents a local police problem and no investigation of the gang, itself is to be conducted. [next sentence is redacted].

In regard to the remarks of WINGATE, it appears that he is attempting to utilize the "Five Percenters" and the threat of past and future potential racial violence to neutralize criticism and possible criminal proceedings against him for his administration of HARYOU-ACT.

[U. S. GOVERNMENT MEMORANDUM LETTERHEAD]

New York, New York
November 4, 1965

Five Percenters
Racial Matters

The October 15, 1965 edition of "The New York Times" and the "New York Herald Tribune", daily New York City newspaper, both contained articles on page one dealing with a speech and impromptu press conference given by Livingstone Wingate on October 14, 1965, before the eastern regional conference of the Urban League at the Belmont Plaza Hotel, New York City. The two articles were respectively captioned "Wingate Warns of Negro Revolt If Haryou's Program Is Curbed" and "Harlem '5 Percenters'- Terror Group Revelaed". Wingate is the Executive Director of the Harlem anti-overty program known as Harlem Youth Opportunities Unlimited-Associated

Community Teams (HARYOU-ACT). Both articles point out that Wingate has been criticized for his handling of the program and that he is currently under investigation by the Manhattan District Attorney's Office and the Federal Authorities following charges of fiscal mismanagement.

According to these articles Wingate, in his speech and press conference, denied any fiscal wrongdoing and claimed that the spending of certain monies on his part was necessary to avert racial violence in Harlem during the past summer. Wingate's main theme was that if anything happened to HARYOU-ACT there would definitely be racial violence. On this latter point, he referred to a mysterious "armed" group of Negro youth who are "prepared to die" in a struggle against white people. Wingate refused to identify this group by name stating he feared for his life if he talked too much. He further implied that only HARYOU-ACT was stopping this group from acting.

Both of these articles further indicated that Wingate was apparently speaking of a Black Muslim-oriented extremist youth group known as the "Five Percenters".

On October 15, 1965, a confidential source who has furnished reliable information in the past, advised that the "Five Percenters" is a particularly vicious type of a street gang in New York City composed of Negro youths who have found in their Muslim form of indoctrination a mysterious ideology that seems to unite and inspire them. The gang is composed of approximately 200 youths in New York City ranging in age from 12 to 21. Approximately 125 of them are centered in the Harlem section of New York City around the 120 series of streets bounded by Seventh and Lenox Avenues. The remainder are scattered throughout the Bronx, Brooklyn and Queens with concentrations in the Fort Greene area of Brooklyn and the Saint Mary's Park section of the Bronx.

This same source advised that the original leader of the "Five Percenters" was one Clarence Smith Jowars, also known as (aka) Clarence 13X Smith, "Puddin", who was a former member of the Nation of Islam (NOI). Jowars is a 36 year old Negro male who was known to the "Five Percenters" as "Allah" and along with his associate James Howell, a 37 year old Negro male, indoctrinated these youths in the perverted NOI form of Muslim ideology with anti-white overtones. Jowars and Howell were arrested for felonious assault with four youthful "Five Percenters" in New York City on May 31, 1965, and both are still incarcerated in New York City on May 31, 1965, and both are still incarcerated awaiting trial which has been postponed due to a court ordered psychiatric examination of Jowars. Following the jailing of Jowars and Howell one Eugene White, aka "Hebeka", a Negro male age 22, assumed a leadership position with the "Five Percenters". However, on August 29, 1965, White was arrested for selling marijuana to one of the gang members and is currently awaiting sentencing after having entered a guilty plea.

A characterization of the NOI is attached hereto and all sources therein have furnished reliable information in the past.

On November 1, 1965, this same source advised that on October 19, 1965, White was sentenced to two years in prison by the Bronx County Supreme Court, New York, on the above mentioned charge.

On October 15, 1965, this source advised that the meaning of "Five Percent" is that 85% of the Negroes are cattle who just follow along, 10% are Uncle Toms while the remaining 5%, which they represent, are the real leaders of the Negro people. The Muslim type of indoctrination which they receive, in addition to the adoption of a Muslim name, is the memorization of the questions and answers put out by the NOI and which their new members must learn. This list of questions and answers appears to have originated with Jowars, who was an NOI member under the name of Clarence 13X Smith and undoubtedly obtained it when he joined the NOI.

This source further advised that the "five Percenters" have been responsible for numerous assaults and muggings, chiefly aimed at whites on the fringe area of Harlem. However, if a white victim cannot be located they have no reservation about choosing a Negro victim. They have also caused a great deal of trouble in schools, chiefly Junior High School number 120 at Madison Avenue and 120th Street in Harlem, where they disrupt classes, demand to be called by their Muslim names and have assaulted some teachers. Since the jailing of Jowars, Howell and White they have no overall leadership although they instruct each other in Muslim –type ideology and the practice of judo and karate. They have no meeting place other than the street, school yards and public parks. Although some members of the "Five Percenters" may have access to weapons, there is nothing to indicate that this gang is armed or has a cache of arms and weapons stored in Harlem. Also, there is nothing to indicate that they train in garroting or hand to hand killing methods.

Although the general attitude of the "Five Percenters" is one of anti-white, there is no definite policy or program of violence against whites other than the above mentioned assaults and muggings. The gang has never engaged in any pre-meditated attack on a police officer and the one incident involving an assault of a police officer in which they were involved grew out of a disorderly conduct arrest.

This source further advised that the "Five Percenters" are not known to have any direct ties with the NOI, Muslim Mosque, Incorporated (MMI), Organization of Afro-American Unity, Incorporated (OAAU), Revolutionary Action Movement (RAM), the individual arrested in 1965 for attempting to blow up the Statue of Liberty, or with the Castroite Cubans or Chinese Commmunists.

Characterizations of the MMI, OAAU, and RAM are attached hereto and all sources therein have furnished reliable information in the past.

[U. S. GOVERNMENT MEMORANDUM LETTERHEAD]

Date: 1/17/66
To: **DIRECTOR, FBI 100-444636**
From: **SAC, NEW YORK (100-150520)**

Subject: **CLARENCE EDWARD SMITH aka**
               SM-NOI
               (00 : NY)

Re NY Summary Report, dated and captioned as above.

It is recommended that a Security Index Card be prepared on the above captioned individual.

Residence Address Presently confined c/o New York State Department of Mental Hygiene.

Subject is being recommended for inclusion on the Security Index in view of his part affiliation with the NOI, his leadership of the Harlem Youth Gang known as "Five Percenters", his evidence of emotional instability, and his demonstrated propensity toward violence which resulted in his arrest and present confinement.

[In agent's handwriting] "There are approximately 200 members of the "Five Percenters" and subject is their leader. He had extensive activity in NOI from 9/ 60 to 3/ 23/ 65. He left NOI to follow Malcolm X and joined MMI. He presently indoctrinates his followers in a distorted version of Muslim teachings of ELIJAH MUHAMMAD.

[U. S. GOVERNMENT MEMORANDUM LETTERHEAD]

Date: 4/6/66
To: **DIRECTOR, FBI (100-444636**
From: **SAC, NEW YORK (100-150520) (C)**

Subject: **CLARENCE EDWARD SMITH aka**
                SM-NOI
                (00 : NY)

ReNY Summary Report of SA [Name redacted] 1/17/66.

On 3/ 9/ 66, [Sentence redacted] Matteawan State Hospital for the Criminally Insane, Beacon, NY, made available the institution file relating to the captioned subject.

A review of this file by SA [Name redacted] reflected that the subject, under the name of ALLAH aka Clarence Smith, was committed from NY County on 11/ 16/ 65, and admitted to Matteawan State Hospital on 11/ 26/ 65. His crime was described as assault, second degree.

Subject has been assigned Matteawan State Hospital Number E12915 and the file reflects that there are four warrants on file against him.

The subject indicated that he has never worked productively and has described himself as a master gambler. He states also that he has been a student of MUHAMMED since 1960. At the time of the subject's arrest on 5/31/65, he was in possession of marijuana.

The file reflects that the subject's original diagnosis was described as schizophrenic reaction, paranoid type. He expressed the dillusions of grandor of a religious nature and of persecution.

A stop was placed with [Name redacted] requesting that this office be notified when the subject is to be released.

[U. S. GOVERNMENT MEMORANDUM LETTERHEAD]

Date: 1/12/67
To: **DIRECTOR, FBI (100-444636**
From: **SAC, NEW YORK (100-150520) (C)**

Subject: **CLARENCE EDWARD SMITH aka**
                   SM-NOI
                   (00 : NY)

Rerep of SA [Name redacted] 1/ 17/ 66, at New York; and Nylet , 4/6/66.

On 1/ 5/ 67, [Sentenced redacted] Matteawan State Hospital for the Criminally Insane, Beacon, NY, advised SA [Name redacted] that subject continues to be confined to that hospital.

As subject has been in continuous confinement since rerep, there has been no reportable activity on his part.

In view of this, NY will not submit an annual report at this time. In the event subject is released from the hospital, this case will be reopened for appropriate investigation.

SAC, New York (100- not legible)
Director, [not legible]

CLARENCE EDWARD SMITH
SM-NOI

By letter dated 3/ 16/ 67, the [word is illegible] advised that the subject's name should be removed from the Security Index. This action has been taken at the Bureau and you should take similar action with respect to the subject's Security Index cards maintained in your office.

In view of the subject's background and his current mental condition, the Bureau feels that upon release from his incarceration at the Matteawan State Hospital for the Criminally Insane, Beacon, New York, you should determine his whereabouts and ascertain whether he resumes his participation in Black Nationalist activities. Therefore, New York should place a stop with appropriate officials at the above hospital, in order that you will be promptly advised of any action indicating that the subject may be released from confinement. Furnish any pertinent information received to the Bureau promptly in a form suitable for dissemination.

1 – 100-398030 (Emergency Detention Program)

NOTE: Subject was active in NOI affairs from 1961 to 1965. No leadership. He was, however, a leader of a teenage gang in New York City known as the "Five Percenters." He was arrested in New York City for felonious assault, resisting arrest, and other charges, and was remanded to custody of New York State Department of Mental Hygiene for indefinite confinement. Last report 1/ 17/ 66. Letter in lieu of report 1/12/67.

[FEDERAL BUREAU OF INVESTIGATION LETTERHEAD]
Date: May 16, 1967
Investigative Period: 3/17/67 – 5/8/67
Title of Case: CLARENCE   EDWARD   SMITH
Report Made By: [Name redacted]

REFERENCE:
Report of SA [Name redacted] 1/17/66, and Bulet, 3/23/67.

ADMINISTRATIVE:

A copy of this report has been furnished Secret Service, NYC, as the last information furnished reflects subject was in custody and his release might be of interest to Secret Service.

As subject does not meet any criteria for inclusion on the Security, he is not being recommended for inclusion on the Security Index.

This report is classified "Confidential" because of the information from [Name redacted] an informant of continuing value the unauthorized disclosure of which could compromise his future effectiveness and have an adverse effect on the national defense interests of the US.

[FEDERAL BUREAU OF INVESTIGATION LETTERHEAD]
Date: May 16, 1967
Copy to: Secret Service, NYC (RM)
Report of: [XXXXXX]
Title: CLARENCE EDWARD SMITH
Character: SECURITY   MATTER – NATION   OF
                      ISLAM

Synopsis:

Subject unemployed and has no permanent residence, but can be located on 127th St., NYC. Subject released from Matteawan State Hospital for the Criminally Insane on 3/ 6/ 67. He received a 3 month suspended sentence on 5/ 4/ 67, Criminal Court, NYC, for unlawful assembly, possession of marijuana and disorderly conduct.

-C-

DETAILS:

On June 1, 1965, [Name redacted] Bureau of Special Services (BSS) New York City Police Department (NYCPD), advised SA [Name redacted] that at 9:15 PM, May 31, 1965, six Negro males were blocking the sidewalk and interfering with street traffic in front of the Hotel Theresa, 2090 Seventh Avenue, New York City. When told to move on by two police officers these six turned on the officers, called on bystanders to attack the officers, and shouted anti-white and anti-police invectives. All six were arrested, one of whom was subject who identified himself as "Allah". He was charged with felonious assault, conspiracy to commit same, resisting arrest, assault with a deadly weapon, disorderly conduct, possession of a marijuana cigarette, and malicious mischief.

On November 16, 1965, [Name redacted] BSS, NYCPD, advised SA [Name redacted] that on November 16, 1965, subject appeared in New York Supreme Court, Part 30 (Felony), New York City, and was found "unable to understand the charges against him". On his date he was remanded to the custody of the New York State Department of Mental [Word redacted] (DMH) for an indefinite confinement.

On March 9, 1966, [Word redacted] Matteawan State Hospital for the Criminally Insane, Beacon, New York, made available to SA [Name redacted] the file for subject which reflected:

Subject was committed from New York County, November 16, 1965, and was admitted to Matteawan on November 26, 1965. His crime was described as assault, second degree. Subject indicated that he had never worked productively and had described himself as a master gambler and that he had been a student of Mohammed since 1960.

His original diagnosis was described as schizophrenic reaction, paranoid type. He expressed dillusions of grandeur of a religious nature and of persecution.

On March 6, 1967, [Name redacted] advised SA [Name redacted] that on that date, subject had been released from Matteawan and had been returned to the Manhattan House of Detention, 125 White Street, New York City, where he would stand trial on criminal charges against him.

On April 12, 1967, [Name redacted] BSS, NYCPD, advised that subject stood trial in Part 2B, Criminal Court, New York City, on April 5, 1967. He pled guilty to unlawful assembly, possession of a marijuana and disorderly conduct and received a three-month suspended sentence.

On May 4, 1967, [Name redacted] advised that he has been familiar with subject's activities since his release from the hospital. He stated subject is unemployed and has no permanent residence, but can almost always be located on 127th Street off Seventh Avenue, New York City.

[Name redacted] advised that since his release from the hospital, subject has not been in any difficulty with the police.

On March 28, 1967, subject was in the Hotel Theresa Coffee Shop, 125th Street and Seventh Avenue, New York City. [Next entire sentence is redacted]

New York sources familiar with many phases of "Black Nationalist" activity have not reported any additional activity on subject's part.

Concerning the [Word redacted] mentioned above the following is noted:
During February, 1967, [the next 4 sentences are redacted].
During 1966, [Name redacted] furnished information reflecting that [next 2 sentences redacted].
Characterization of the NOI and OAAU will be found in the appendix.

[Author's Note: The following FBI Memorandums is pertaining to the assassination of Clarence 13X Smith. More files on the assassination have yet to be released via the Freedom of Information Act. Some speculate that it is due to complexity and involvement of Bureau Informants.]

Domestic Intelligence Division

Date, 6/13/69.

Attached relates that a member of the Nation of Islam (NOI) was fatally shot in New York City on 6/13/69. He is a leader of a Negro youth group and a recent aide to New York Mayor John Lindsay. It is not known if there is any connection between this shooting and a previous slaying by gunshot of another member of the NOI recently.

Copy of attached sent Inter-Division Information Unit of Department, and pertinent portions of attached will be included in a teletype summary to White House and other interested agencies.

WA
FBI NEW YORK
9:45 PM URGENT 6-13-69 AWS

TO DIRECTOR (PLAIN)

Attention Domestic Intelligence Division
From New York

Killing of Clarence Thirteen X Smith, NYC,
Six Thirteen Sixty Nine RM- Racial Matter
New York City Police Department

On six thirteen sixtynine, representative of NYCPD advised that at three thirty am this date three unknown male Negroes shot and killed Clarence Thirteen X Smith, former member of the Nation of Islam (NOI). Leader or the Five Percenters, a Negro youth group and recent aide to mayor John Lindsay. Smith was killed in the doorway of his residence at twenty one west one hundred twelfth street, NYC.

His assailants fled in a white Chevrolet automobile which was parked a short distance away at one east one hundred twelfth street, NYC.

Smith was dead on arrival and his body is at the NYC morgue.

The identitities of assailants and the motive behind his murder are unknown.

It is not known if this has any connection with shooting of Charles Seven X Kenyatta on six seven, sixtynine.

Administrative:

Representative of NYCPD determined preliminary investigation elicited data Smith was en route to wife's apartment after winning at a crap game as it was his habit when he was a winner. Search of body failed to disclose any money in wallet but contained receipts which indicate Smith was on payroll of city (tension reduction fund). Even though Smith's wallet did not contain money, body did not give appearance of having been "rolled."

Selected informants given specific assignments to determine whether possible conspiracy exists and whether other repercussions will be forthcoming.

END
WA
SHD BE NUMBER 25
WA.... RDR R RELAY
FBI WASH DC

DATE:	**6/25/69**
TO:	**DIRECTOR, FBI**
FROM:	**SAC, NEW YORK (157-**

SUBJECT: **ALLEGED INVOLVEMENT OF MEMBERS OF FAIR PLAY COMMITTEE, 145 E. 149TH ST., NYC, IN SHOOTINGS OF CHARLES 37X KENYATTA AND CLARENCE 13X SMITH RACIAL MATTERS**

ReNYtel, 6/24/69.

The 6/24/69 issue of the New York "Daily News" carried an article which reported that NYCPD Chief of Detectives Frederick M. Lussen announced that CHARLES 37X KENYATTA and several other Negro leaders, recent shooting victims, may have been shot by a small group of extortionists who are "shaking down" businessmen in the NYC ghetto areas and "leaning" on anyone who opposes them. LUSSEN announced a 24 man investigation squad to investigate the group of extortionists who comprise 10 members and whom LUSSEN declined to identify.

On 6/24/69, [Name redacted] Special Services Division, NYCPD (conceal per request) advised that the NYCPD was conducting investigation into shooting of CHARLES 37X KENYATTA, American Mau Mau leader, 6/7/69, and into the fatal shooting of CLARENCE 13X SMITH on 6/13/69, and into the fatal shooting of ANTHONY REED, Jr., on 6/19/69, to determine if there was any connection between the three shootings.

- 402 -

Police investigation ascertained that REED was close associate of [Name redacted] and that [Name redacted] could be contacted through Fair Play Committee, 145 East 149th St., NYC.

Subsequent investigation determined that Fair Play Committee is also known as Vanguard Communications, Pride Magazine and Vital Press Information, all of which occupy space in converted brownstone building at above address.

Active in Fair Play Committee are [names redacted]. These account for 10 names referred to by Chief LUSSEN in his statement to the press.

On 6/22/69, [the rest of the paragraph is blacked out by FBI].
[Name redacted] stated shooting of [Name redacted] was a result of misidentity since [Name redacted] before shooting [Name redacted] asked "Are you [Name redacted]. NYCPD ascertained [Name redacted] an ex-convict lives within a block of shooting scene and possibly intended victim of [Name redacted].

NYCPD conjecture is that [Name redacted] and/or other members of Fair Play Committee hired REED to assassinate KENYATTA and SMITH and that REED called on [Name redacted] to assist him. Committee wanted SMITH and KENYATTA "out of the picture" because these two were either working for Mayor LINDSAY or "cutting into territory" of Committee in extorting money from local businessmen in Harlem area. Further conjecture is that REED was killed because he knew too much and [Name redacted] escaped shooting through misidentification.

[Name redacted] further advised that NYCPD conducted inquiry at Apollo Theatre, NYC, famous house for presentation of Negro artists in entertainment field. [next sentence is redacted]..... three Negro males who told him he had not done enough for the black community and that if he did not cooperate with them he might not leave the building alive. Two of the three Negro males subsequently identified as [Name redacted] and [Name redacted]. Unidentified person informed [Name redacted] he should cooperate with them as they had "offed" CHARLES KENYATTA and CLARENCE 13X SMITH.

[An entire paragraph is redacted]

[Name redacted] further advised that [Name redacted] radio station WLIB in NYC, which is located in Harlem, NYC.

[Name redacted] advised that [Name redacted] was formerly associated with the Revolutionary Action Movement (RAM) in NYC and the old Black Panther Party which is now defunct.

[Name redacted] requested that none of the above be disseminated outside the Bureau inasmuch as the NYCPD investigation into this matter is still pending and much of the information is to date unsubstantiated.

NYO will keep the Bureau advised of any further developments in captioned matter.

Appendix III
The Wisdom Of Allah:
Clarence 13X (Allah) Speaks!

Interview Conducted With Allah
At Otisville Training Institute For Boys
On November 15, 1967.

Allah: Protect the child. Show him where if he doesn't do right he is going to go to jail. Just like the Muslims. I'm not against anyone but they are really teaching their children not to smoke, drink or do anything to inquire other people to follow their standards. Now, I don't teach the child not to smoke— I teach him to get the understanding (what) of it.

Interviewer: Excuse me.

Allah: I am not against narcotics--because the only way to stop a narcotics pusher from bringing it into this country he must start using it his (what) self. Sending a person away that doesn't cure him. I used it. That didn't cure me. I stopped my (what) self!

So you got to keep the children together and you got to kill all religion. Other than that you are going to lose all fighting in them and they will not have the heart to kill. And you got to have the heart to kill! You've got to! Everyone has to have the heart to (what) kill! To continue a strong country. You can't tell me Russia is not strong because Russia is strong. Because the children here use drugs, they're going back to sleep. And now it's getting to your people. So they're using it. Sooner or later you're going to see the downfall. The hippies are losing the knowledge of themselves. You can't tell me they're not and they are.

Interviewer: Could you please explain?

Allah: They are losing the knowledge of themselves and their parents can't do anything about it. The only way their parents can get them home is to stop sending them money! And they will get hungry and they will go back home. Won't they? Won't they?

Interviewer: I don't know if they will.

Allah: They will go. They will go back home if they stop sending them money. And now they are asking the United States to help find their (what) children, because they are losing the knowledge of (what) themselves. When you lose knowledge of self-- the country got to fall. Why they leaving school? What's the matter? And the hippies-- what happened down there with Rush when he was making a speech the other day? Look at what happened. People don't want to fight and this is what other countries love to (what) hear. Whether you like it or not. If I had a bunch of men and they didn't want to fight, wouldn't another country like to hear that? Huh? Wouldn't you? If you was another country and you heard I didn't want to fight, wouldn't you want to hear that?

On Jesus

And the Five Percenters, I'm teaching them that they can't go on religion because religion has never did anything for them. Like my mother, she said, "Jesus, Jesus, Jesus," I know he over there in Jerusalem dead in the earth because he hasn't showed me nothing.

Now I was in the Army. I don't teach them not to go in the Army. I went and I came back. I saw action. I got the Bronze Star. I got all these medals. Now I came back home. I didn't benefit from it as by such as luxury, but I did benefit by knowing how to teach a man. To teach a man--to make a boy a man. This is what I did.

I don't teach them not to drink, I teach them to keep their mouth (what) shut! And listen and learn. Because I might tell them to drink to do exactly what I want them to do-- to get to that man I want to get to. Just like the United

States teach the FBI. I might make one a dope addict--if he strong he'll come out of it. Because there are many dope addicts that come amongst the people to catch who they want and not to use it. I know this.

I don't tell them not to fight for the country. They can. Fight! Now by me telling them children that all my people are against me because they thought that I was suppose to came out when I come from Matteawan to join them and I haven't joined any of them yet. And not going to join them because I'm civilized. We don't talk about nobody.

On Religion, Politics and War In The United States

Interviewer: Why not?

Allah: Because religious people fight against one another. You can't tell me they don't because they do. They'll tell me that why should you tell the child not to eat swine? I say why it's in your Bible in Leviticus & Deuteronomy. I'll show them where they are not even good religious people. And they say they believe in the scriptures that the prophets brought to people. You understand? This is not only hurting them but it hurts you it hurts everybody! These the kind of things you've got to keep away from your people, their people and my people to make a strong nation. And religious people don't believe in killing. I do. Years ago the people would form a vigilante to get the others that didn't want to go along with the rest of the people. Didn't they? If you hadn't did that, would you have built? No. You couldn't have built because someone was holding you down. I'm not against the United States for sitting over there in Vietnam. They should kill all of those people who do not want to build and become civilized and have a sanitary country. Because the earth is supposed to be built on. I'm not against it. Your people protesting against it. Now when your people protest against it, it gets all the rest of the people to protest (what) against it. Like Muhammad Ali said, "They burn their flag so why can't he [sic] it here."

Now where did this teaching come from? Did it come from me? Huh? Did it?

Interviewer: Did what?

Allah: Yes. Not fighting for their own country. Did it come from me?

Interviewer: Here is Mr. Belmont who heads the Division of Youth.

Allah: Glad to meet you.

Interviewer: He runs a start program and I will introduce you to the others that you don't know later, O.K. If you sit down you won't be able to get up.

Mr. Belmont: Thanks. I love you.

Allah: Didn't this come from your teaching? If not where did it come from?

Interviewer: It came from those who feel that way.

Allah: Feel like for what? How did they feel that way? You should have taught your child right and exact! How did they feel that way? You mean to tell me you don't know? You don't know who come in your country and plant a seed. This didn't happen a few years back did it?

Interviewer: Yes.

Allah: How many people?

Interviewer: They're called conscientious objectors.

Allah: Yeah, but how many? It wasn't public. No, not in 1945 it wasn't public.

Interviewer: People called the Quakers since the very beginning of this country.

Allah: That was the Quakers.

Interviewer: And it was public.

Allah: And if you was a cold-blooded country you should have stopped that. In another government if you don't go by the rules and regulations they kill you. You should have stopped that. Because I know for a fact when I was in Japan & Korea the people who disobeyed there something happened to them. Now if your country in danger and they disobey, shouldn't you do something to these people? Not only the Black but you'll now have to do it to your own. What kind of children you all raising? What's going to happen if there is no fighting in them? What's going to happen?

Interviewer: I don't know. I'm not a prophet.

Allah: Well you don't have to be a prophet to know that you will be the loser. Fighting, prophets know about that. Doesn't a man lead the way? Isn't a man a teacher? Well he's a prophet then. Isn't he?

Interviewer: Yes.

Allah: Well he's a prophet then isn't he?

Interviewer: In that sense.

Allah: In all sense. If United States don't wake up, then they going to lose. Because you got babies in the Army now and that's what you need in the Army, those seventeen and eighteen year old boys. That's what you need in the army. They got to be well qualified though. They got to be more tougher than they are. The United States are the most easiest people in the world because they live in luxury. Where other people eat one day and can last three. The Muslims taught me the same way. Eat one meal a day, one every other day or one every three days. And they can do it! They eat the proper foods to keep them strong.

Interviewer: Who does this? The Muslims?

Allah: I'm trying to teach those Five Percenters to do it. I do it. Because I go on a six to seven day fast. I don't eat nothing but drink water. Because if I don't, I'll dry up. I don't eat.

And Stokely Carmichael and H. Rap Brown they are really getting to the college students. Even your people because they really don't want to go to no war. And the other people are claiming that the United States of America are using the uneducated people to fight the (what) war.

Captains, Lieutenants And Private Soldiers

Interviewer: Do you think that's true?

Allah: Yes that's true. You can't send the captain into battle. He'll lead them into (what) battle. Because I was never patrolled by a captain. The lieutenant took me on patrol. Because knowledge kept him from going. Where as if they lose him, they'll have this one here. I wouldn't send the knowledge man into the Army. I would have him train them or lead them. Now today, you don't even have young generals in the Army. All of them are old. And they really don't know how to fight because they are losing too many men over there in Vietnam. And this is what they like because Russia is so very intelligent you fighting but they not losing their men. Are they? Are they?

Interviewer: No, not that I know of.

Allah: I'm telling you but you is. Now who in charge the most, you or Russia? Russia is very strong. And now Douglas, I read about him a little while ago and he pulled out and doesn't have much to do with the United States much more. Does he? Why? The United States have done a wonderful job. They have went all over the country and help build up for the lower class people. Because that's their duty.

Now my people are looking at it this way. They said if you can support the other countries, why can't you support the people that's in you own country? You can make all those people bear witness. Where so much propaganda won't get out of the country. Now pictures been got out of the country. Riots done started. Isn't this the downfall to any country? And those people come running out of the (sic). The educated only know how to tell the other low class people what the people in this country are doing to them? Now the people are making statements that you spend eight million dollars or a billion dollars for a rocket. And people here starving. This going all out now. They're sending pictures out that people got special privileges. And nothing stops it.

Show Love to the Children

Allah: The only thing that's going to stop it is the children will stop it by not listening to those (what) people. If you show some kind of love to the child you can stop it. And putting those laws in effect. When these people come here from different countries or different states put them in jail! That's the same if the government if they don't when they give these people (sic) money people don't want to pay for their children they should put him in (what) jail. And they gonna have to do it. They going to have to do it other than that they are going to lose the children and there is nothing I can do about it. Now they love me. There is so many Five Percenters it's something else. There still is nothing I can do if you don't show the child in different ways that you care about the child. If you don't-- H. Rap Brown going to get to them. Carl Stokely going to get to them or Kissick going to get to them. Many people going to get to them. Because what I'm telling you brother to the child if they shouldn't do it. The first thing their going to say is "see, you didn't get nothing any (what) anyway".

The Muslim View on War

Allah: And Muhammad Ali is sure showing a good example. Here is what he's fighting. Don't want to go to the army. He is a very intelligent man. There are many Muslims who went onto jail. He's fighting it. He's fighting to show the world that he gets not only recognition from the Muslim World but from your people too from all over the country. Because why? They want to see America fall whether you like it or not. They want to see America fall and you know it too. I don't have to tell you that. You know they want to see America fall.

And you got many people here that you think is on your side but is not. That's just like "The Invaders" a picture I saw the other night. We might look a-like but we may not be a-like. See un-alike attract and a-like repels. Now un-alike attract is between me and you. If we have the same mind together then it is not un-alike. It is a (what) like.

Supreme Mathematics And Supreme Alphabets

Allah: And I know the date is the 15th. That means knowledge and power. No one told me this. Tomorrow is the 16th, which means knowledge equality. Next day, knowledge god. Next day, is knowledge build or destroy. Next day, knowledge born. Because a child, must go through the birth record. When he one years old, he have knowledge. When he two years old, he has wisdom, he can talk. Three years old, he has the understanding. Four years old, he has his culture. Five years, he has his power. Six years, he has his equality; he's able to go to the bathroom. A man does not come into the understanding until he goes into his thirty years. Then he goes into the understanding. He goes into knowledge, wisdom, understanding all of this. No one told me this. I even know the teachings of your calendar. This month means Now Cipher Victory (NOV.). Next month is Divine Equality See (DEC.). No one told me this! That's why I don't talk. I listen. Many people like to talk, they like the spotlight. I don't like to talk. They didn't tell me how to master the twelve calendar. The twelve months only mean the government goes from knowledge to wisdom. That's all. They knowledge and (what) wisdom. In the Bible it teaches that Jesus had many disciples but they only had knowledge and wisdom. Jesus was the thirteenth--he had knowledge and understanding. He was the only one that they had to kill him. Because why? He had knowledge and (what) understanding! Where the other ones had the knowledge and wisdom they could go and get Jesus. He was the only healer. You understand that? Now this is the way it is. You can't do the wisdom until you have the knowledge, right? Right? When you go to school you got to have the knowledge before you could come out and put that into practice. And they don't know you got it until you go out and put it into practice. This is why I teach the child go out and get the knowledge, come back and put it into practice, then the people will get the (what) understanding. Then they'll know your culture. No one taught me this. And I'm telling you the knowledge now because this is the eleventh month means knowledge (what) knowledge. This is the eleventh month. The tenth month means knowledge add a (what) cipher. That means— if I had the knowledge and I tell you something and you didn't know it, I have a cipher. Didn't I? Didn't I? No one told me anything. And this is what you better do because I'm telling you.

The Babies Are The Greatest

Allah: To hold any nation together I read in a book what a white man said one time--and I take all book knowledge and use it to benefit myself. I don't care who I heard it from. He said the wealth of a country is the children-- not the money. Once upon a time there was no money. The wealth of any country is the children. And if you don't keep the young people strong how you going to win? The bombs can't do it. The bombs haven't made Vietnam submit. There has been no country in the world that bombs have been dropped on them more than Vietnam.

Interviewer: When you say strong. What do you mean strong?

Allah: You got to have the manpower!

Interviewer: How do you make them strong? In what way do you get the young people strong?

Allah: Feed them the right foods. Don't teach religion.

Interviewer: A lot of people think that helps make people strong.

Speaks On The Mayor Of New York

Allah: Well Mayor Wagner don't think so—I mean Mayor Lindsay don't think so. He said that the churches and the organizations have lost it! That they cannot control the children! Now where do they keep them at? That's why Mayor Lindsay is the greatest mayor that ever been. He tell the truth. He's a great mayor. He gets out with the people. Now he got a TV show so he make communication. Now he going out there in California. Mayor talking about "I got to meet Barry tonight to get off the telephone to make a special call to something else." Mayor Lindsay the greatest mayor who ever lived.

How To Eat To Live

Interviewer: What is the right foods you're talking about?

Allah: Don't eat the swine!

Interviewer: Everything else is all right?

Allah: No, everything else isn't all right. Don't eat no shrimp. Don't eat no crabs. Don't eat none of that food.

Interviewer: Crabs?

Allah: Lobsters.

Interviewer: Seafood you mean?

Allah: Yes. There's other seafood. Don't eat no buffalo fish because it doesn't have no scales. Anything bite it, the poison go right into it. If the fish has a scale, you bite it, the poison doesn't effect it because of the texture. Don't eat the old, eat the young. Because you shouldn't eat meat at all, period. Because you're taking on animal protein so you still spoil the human being system. If you are going to eat meat, eat the best. Not only is it good for you, it's good for me, too.

Interviewer: What's the best kind of meat?

Allah: Beef. Lamb. Fish, certain fishes. Don't eat buffalo fish because it has no protection. Something bite it the poison go right into the fish. If you bite a fish with a scale does the poison go into it? Don't eat tuna over 150 pounds but most tuna come over 150 pounds.

Interviewer: How do you know?

Allah: I'm telling you how it comes because civilized people know.

Interviewer: Are there any kinds of other foods?

Allah: There are many kinds. Don't eat butterbeans. Don't eat collard greens because it belongs to the weed family. Eat the white cauliflower because it melts in your mouth. The spinach (you eat that). The broccoli (you eat that). Cauliflower (you eat that). There are certain foods you have to eat. You've got to save your own (what) self! No medication can save you.

Interviewer: What about the people who do eat it?

Allah: Well that's their business. Don't worry about them, don't you eat it. That's why many of these women not built up they eating the wrong foods and can't hold a baby. Can't hold it. Don't worry about the other people. All you do is tell them. Save yourself. Live as long as you can. Now when I do stop eating meat I know I have to stop drinking wine. See?

Interviewer: Why can't you? Why so?

Allah: Because the liquor will have nothing to eat on. It will eat me up! There are many things you got to understand. This is why President Johnson got an operation on his hand. You know? And it won't heal. When they sewed it up, it wouldn't stay together. Why? Because it's decayed. You know what I mean by decaying? It won't stay (what) together. It's not solid. It's decayed. Because when you sew it together, you find some people they sew it together. They have a bad break in and it open, the thread keep pulling apart as it tighten up it come right on (what) through. It won't close up. Why? It's decayed. Why you think people get old? Do you think when you get old you call it a blessing? Do you call it a blessing when you get old? Huh? That's no blessing! That's long suffering!

Speaks On Age And Death

Interviewer: (Laughing) But everybody gets old.

Allah: Do they? I'm not going no more further! I'm 39 years old meaning understanding born. I'm not going no further. If I do want to go further than I know how to kill myself by taking on the wrong (what) foods. Doing the wrong (what) things. That's how you get old.

Interviewer: Do you think you're going to get older?

Allah: Not me! Not me!

Interviewer: You're not going to get older?

Allah: Not me!

Interviewer: How do you know that?

Allah: I know it!

Interviewer: How do you know?

Allah: Because I know what it do for me! I know what it do for me.

Interviewer: Then your body won't change?

Allah: Not mine. Because, I'm going to tell the truth. I'm not going to talk about no one. I'm just going to tell you what they do and you can't bring an accusation against me. I'm only telling you what they did because I'm studying them. And all things were brought forth before I became involved myself into the knowledge of self and let them know. I can tell them all about them but they can't tell me nothing about me because I'm a new breed that they don't know about. Now what they going to tell about me when I can tell them all about themselves? I can show a religious man that he never led anyone to God. Not the Pope or anyone. They all died. Now all the people in the Bible died. Now where are they? Where are they? The only way you will find God if you keep on reproducing. Until he make himself known. And the Pope he supposed to be a successor to God. Where they show the people? Have they? Elijah says W. D. Fard is God. Where is he?

On Religious Divisiveness

They make me [sic]. And religious people talk about one another. What's meant to be is meant to be. If it wasn't meant to be would it ever be? Would you see it? Huh? So don't talk about nothing! As life change you change. If you don't change you are going to die. Change with the young people. If you stay around young people you'll stay young. Two old people can't tell two people how to do. I don't want nothing old. I don't want an old woman. I'm going to keep young women. I don't know what you want. Do what you want to do. I don't want none. I don't want no old woman. You can have one if you want to. I don't want one. I want to be around young people. They will keep me active. And they always bringing me something to tell me. So, know what I do? I sit right there like Barry, he's the head of the task force and all his satellites go out and bring him back all the information. He just sitting right there. That's the same thing I do. They go out bring me back all the information tell me how you all treating them. That's good because they educate me don't they? Don't they? Just like the captain. He says, "Come on come say this time I ain't going to tell nobody". If you don't tell nobody they can't make it known to the people what people are (what) talking about can they? Sure can't.

On The Mayor's Man

Interviewer: Who is Barry?

Allah: Barry Gottehrer.

Interviewer: That's the mayor's aide?

Allah: He just sit there and all of them come with information. He sit right there. And he don't write nothing down. He's so intelligent he don't write nothing down. He puts it all into his mind. Now isn't that the most intelligent man? If I entrust a man with information he can't put it down on no paper. He must carry it in his mind because if someone took the paper they would have everything they want. Now if he don't tell them they won't know (what) nothing. This is why the U2 power is a disgrace to the United States of America. Because if he had everything they would take his life and they didn't do it. And he come back home and got a divorce from his wife. He going crazy. That's what he's going to go because he wasn't a man. It would have been better for him to take his life than be a disgrace. That's why his wife left him. Nobody else don't believe it but that's why she left him. He wasn't a man! He take on a job like that, then don't carry it through. He wasn't a man. You don't find many Russia people that will do that.

Marital Relationships In The United States

Allah: And the women are strong like the men. The women in the United States of America they dominate they men because they can put you in jail. Can't they? They put you in jail! And they got certain men that carry out their orders. Women are something else. Then the men wind up killing their women. Just pow! Blow their head off. A woman couldn't get me to kill her to make me go and suffer behind prison. I'll go have her arrested (you understand) and tell the woman to leave me (what) alone and I'll take care of the babies. Just get me a job. You think she can get me to kill her? Not me! Not me. That's why I tell all Five Percenters about this story in the Bible about Samson and Delilah. Boy, when he let that woman know what was happening she blind him boy. She turned him over to another government. He woke up and he find all of them. You understand that? Why? By telling that woman what's happening. And that government caused him—she caused him to lose his life. A woman can't tell me nothing, but just go there and cook. They don't need to tell me nothing. And I don't think it's right to put a woman over a man. That's why I agree with those people who were going to try to blow up the Statue of Liberty. Because she's holding the torch. That supposed to represent the woman holding a torch. Then they say justice is blind (laughs). Because, she has a thing around her neck around her eyes. Justice can't see (laughs). There is a sign to all these things. And the Liberty Bell is cracked. Liberty ain't got no crack in it. Liberty is the truth! Ain't no crack. All this is a sign. That woman knows that she's holding the torch. She can't do nothing to me, though. Can't do nothing to me. Because if I do something to her I will tell the judge, 'Yes I did and why I did it.' Then if he wants to give me any justice, I don't worry about it because I know nature is going to take its course.

On Matteawan

Allah: They sent me to Matteawan because I said I was Allah. Then they certified me out of Matteawan as Allah. I could have sued this city. But I don't want no money. I wouldn't give them any money because all they would do is sport and play. That's all children do with money is sport and play.

Let The Children Build A Nation

Interviewer: What do you want them to do?

Allah: I want them to live in America and help protect their country-- if the government does right by them. The ones that help protect the country-- the government should do right by these. The ones that don't-- the government should do away with them.

Interviewer: Besides them fighting how else could they protect themselves?

Allah: Unite. Let your children and them unite together and create new ideas. Where the world is building a square now it's going to be building a circle. And they don't need your ideas no more. Your ideas did what you was supposed to do. All you have to do is give them the basis because they'll do it them (what) selves. See you can see where ideas have traveled for many years cause when you first come to this country there were no houses. It went from the log cabin to this. So each generation brought this about right? So let the children bring about another new world.

Interviewer: Through education?

Allah: Or be destroyed.

Interviewer: Build an education?

Allah: I said build a nation or be destroyed. And if you stop them from mingling together it's over with. It's over.

Interviewer: What do you mean by that?

Allah: You can't accomplish nothing!

Interviewer: Stop mingling together?

Allah: The children.

Interviewer: I don't understand. Stop mingling together?

Allah: Why? Don't they supposed to give their knowledge to each other?

Interviewer: Always.

Allah: Well if you stop it, it is over because they will not have no ideas to build. They don't have it now. You don't see young men building. You see the old men building. What's going to happen when they can't do no building no more? Like your leg.

Interviewer: What about it?

Allah: It hurt right?

Interviewer: A little.

Allah: Not a little. A whole lot, because you got to have a crutch.

Interviewer: I guess.

Allah: But then you be the crutch for the young children until they are able to walk. You need that (crutch) to until you are able to walk. For the benefit of any country, certain people have to change. It's not a shame in change. There's not a shame. Because people now don't even want to walk in Harlem. They did it this year because I was home. That's why there was no riot in Harlem. They did this year and I'm going to stop it all.

I'm going to stop crime. Do you hear me? The houses and buildings that you all are in-- you going to have to give these to children as dormitories for the children. I'm going to stop crime. Hitting people in the head, killing people, that's a shame. This boy killed these two people-- a boy and a girl. Wasn't that a shame? What he kill them for? That sucker said that they have to sacrifice human life. Kill human life. He was an Uhura (Yoruba). Is that what he was?

Interviewer: Yoruba.

Allah: Don't you see where these people coming from? Now, people who even teach that doctrine should be eliminated. I can't do it because you'll put me in jail, or those other people will put me in jail. I can't do it. The government have to (what) do it. Then, if you eliminate these people the people will say where they gone? Got to kill humans for sacrifice? Now that lady lost her son, right? The other lady lost her daughter, right? Now the only thing they'll give that man is maybe 20 or 30 years. It will be life, but he still alive, right? And they don't have capital punishment in New York no more, unless killing a police. Now they been crying themselves. Now they done took their guns away from the police—really because he can't shoot nobody unless they attack (what) him. So you don't think that the United States is going backwards? Huh? You going to see. You going to see. You going backwards. Look at those people that went and killed those three brothers in the real estate business. Now when they catch them what they going to give them? Only life, right? That's all. And they might not even serve the time out if the United States don't act right. Because they going to lose and all prisoners will be set free. Because they know that these people came with the United States of America and they'll do anything to fight for their life. Won't they? United States better wake up.

On Homelessness

Interviewer: They are bringing the street pedestrians to New York on the 4th in order to free them.

Allah: I hope you keep them if they don't obey. Keep them. Isn't it best to keep them if they stagnant-- in chains? He sure should be. I wish you take all the people that are bums and put them in the jailhouse so that these children won't grow up and see them. Then they won't be a (what) bum. You hear me? Keep them all. Don't let them out in prison. Because I'll go directly to the Police and will help send them to prison if they don't say nothing. And this is exactly what you should do. And you shouldn't let them out in prison. They supposed to be (?). If I do something wrong it's the same thing. I supposed to be (?) myself.

Experience In Matteawan

Allah: I went through Matteawan and nobody did nothing. One officer hit me one time. The Doctor—if I would have told that doctor that officer hit me and I didn't do nothing to him, they would have fired that sucker. They tried. They said, "Where is he Allah? Let me know who he is,"— I wouldn't tell them. And the officer know he was wrong because I ain't do nothing to him, just enlightened him. And when he found out who I was he didn't do that no more. I didn't do nothing to him. And no one was supposed to be able to get me out of there because I was the law there.

I was under the Doctor and they had some very intelligent doctors there. Especially Dr. David P. Johnson, the Director. Because if I was to protest, I couldn't protest because they would send me to the court and the Deacon. And boy, whatever the Doctor say, that judge do not go against it. And I didn't have to go too sad. I didn't want for a thing in Matteawan. I didn't protest what they gave me to eat. If they gave me that meat, I didn't eat it. I had money and everything I want in Matteawan. I wouldn't buy no food. I wanted to show them exactly who I said I was and I was going to prove it. All I wanted was them was to do is ask the questions. And I know I was the only one that could give it to them. And they let me out of there. I could have sued New York City for putting seven charges against me and I hadn't did any of them. I didn't do a thing.

I had been shot with a double-barreled shotgun and a high powered rifle. And I don't run from no Muslims or nobody else. Because I know if I'm telling you the truth, if that don't stop you, then nothing else will. And them doctors let me right out of there. And now the officers are so friendly and intelligent and love me they expressed to me that I can go out by myself. And Matteawan is a place when you go there, they say you a criminal insane. Meaning that you cannot control your emotions. And I had just been--I hadn't been in the hospital too long.

Allah: The people been taking advantage of me ever since I said I was Allah. And I know when I said I was Allah, the Muslim whole world was (what) against me. I don't care. And now they really against me because I'm not anti-white nor pro-black. They really against me because everybody is against the white. Well, let me show you something. Who is man if he ain't man? Tell me. So this is up to you to make your country (what) God. It's up to you and if you don't teach the young right, you not hurting me you hurting yourself. Now I can gain power be even not turning them over to the law. Couldn't I? When they come to me about his stuff I can say no I don't know nothing about these gangs and 85'ers. Right? I don't want that kind of power, that's not power. Power comes through the truth. That's what power comes through. I don't want that kind of power so that these other so-called American Negroes are trying to gain. I don't want that kind of power.

And I don't recruit no old people. None! None! You can be of help and you got to know something. I don't recruit no old! I've got 4 or 5 old now. They give me they children. I don't recruit no old. And anybody can be a Five Percenter, white, I don't care who they are can be a Five Percenter. Because a Five Percenter is one that is civilized. We don't talk about nobody. And they mad because Barry Gottehrer is a Five Percenter. And his wife is getting a divorce from him just because of that. Ain't that something? But the man is a man because he know the truth is the (what) truth and this is the only thing that is going to bring the country together and make it strong. Now if he fall for his wife and 'baby don't you do this and don't you do that.' He'll be just like Samson in the Bible by letting that jive woman run him. And the country will fall because the woman can't go no further then equality and then she got to turn the babies to god to stay.

Like Father Like Son To Give Birth To A God

Allah: That's why the government-- he let a child quit school at 16, only even knowledge (what) equality. And then he seventeen, the child knowledge god. And that's his daddy. You can find any boy, if he don't know where his daddy at, all he got to do is look in the mirror and then he'll see him. Because he looking at him. Who is your son if he ain't you? Hmm? Can't you tell your son if someone come mess with your Earth? If you a apple and that's your orange. If he don't look like you, boy, he ain't you. That's somebody else's. That's a matter with your Earth. He not you. If a man can't— don't produce him a boy he not blessed because the woman done cultivated his seed into a girl. And he show you right there that he not blessed, the woman is (what) blessed.

Now me, I let the woman cultivate my seed if I fall in love with her a little bit, you know, but there is no such thing as love but y'all ain't made for it. Now I let her cultivate the seed a little bit. I let her [sic] but I'm blessing her. If I don't want her to cultivate that seed I don't do nothing, except make no love to her. I still go (unghh!) she can't cultivate my seed. Now if the woman continue to cultivate the seed isn't that there bringing destruction to man. Hmm? So if you don't continue to be men what's going to happen? She going to bring destruction to you because she's a cultivator. She's the Earth that you plant in. Just like this earth you build on. She'll bring destruction to you. Didn't you know that a woman's a cultivator? She'll turn you into a girl every time. And there are many men who don't have—yeah I'm about finnin' to go anyway, I'll take a pot to go please, I like mine regular (laughter). If a man don't become something, then a woman going to become man. Every one of his child is a (what), is a girl— and you don't have no girls in you. Man is (what) man. He's the creator of woman whether she like it or not.

And then you should—I know how to bring my own babies. I do. I do. After the birth, cut the thing then hit him bow they go ow! That's all to it. I don't need nobody to bring mine. Like the average woman go to the doctor— the man bring her to him she be like (sigh) Oh doctor! She give him all the love whether you like it or (what) not. Cause he right there and she there all the (what) time. That's why a man should treat his woman right.

On Polygamy

Allah: Now, to me for one, I'm not never going to have one woman —- because a poor rat got one hole. I found that out. I am not, you hear me woman? I'm not ever going to have one. Whoever love me, that's who I'm going to love. I'm not loving no more, they have to love (what) me. Because I found that out through my wife. She didn't write me a letter nor come to see me after 22 months. So now them young girls love me now. She say, 'I'm surprised at you'! I say 'Oh honey don't worry about them those just my blessings.' Because she saw me. And they young, too. I like that. And I can teach them myself. After I get through with her everything be alright because that means she not contaminate. Because I'll show you something. If your woman go to this church, right? And you go to another church, right? Isn't that wrong? Because I'll tell you something right now. Now, if you have to go to church for someone to teach your women— I'm not saying nothing about the Reverend or trying to make you feel bad or nothing like that because I'm only going to tell the truth. My wife wanted to teach me Elijah Muhammad. She tried to put my mind under the capture of that man. I said woman you crazy. She said, 'what, what, what,' I said 'what, what.' I'm not going to let my woman go up under this man when I'm a man myself and if I fall for that my children can never respect me. I don't need you to educate my child. It is my duty to educate my child my (what) self. You understand that?

Speaks About The Preachers

Allah: But the preachers are so far backwards that they have created teachings to educate that child. Don't you know if you take your child somewhere, and you don't have the knowledge of what that child is going up under, that person is taking your child's mind from you? He can control that child. I bear witness to this cause I know a man that went to get his child from church and wanted to speak to his child alone. You know what that child told that—told his daddy? 'You have to talk in front of the preacher.' What the? I would have (bam!). I would have knocked that sucker out! Telling me that he can't talk to me private and that's me. And another man has my mind and my child's mind? Boy, I would have hit that boy so hard I would have broke his jaw. So, if you grow up under someone else's indoctrination and you don't understand where that child is at or who that man is or what he's teaching that child. He going to take your child. I examine everything they teach mine. I go see the teacher and I look at him, is he a sucker or a man? You know I look at him. I look at him. I let him know, 'I'm looking at you sucker.' And I keep looking at him. And I watch his ways and actions because I don't want him to have no feminine ways whatsoever if he's teaching that boy!

This is what I like about they said Ron-- the method that the Governor up there in Reers. He fired everybody—he fired a lot of people out of his office or some of them because he said they were homo (what). He a homosexual. Now this man is a man. See a whole lot of people don't go for that but that man's a man. Because homosexuals brings on destruction to a (what) a nation. The man is right and a lot of people don't think the man is right but the man is what? he's right because homosexual bring destruction to a what? nation.

And when you produce a girl. (Silence. Cuts in and out as if tape is edited) Hmm, no don't kill her. I can't say that. I never said that. I never said that. I'm more [sic] then a non-violent man. I'm not violent. See, you got a word for something which is right, you might say it's non-violent. You understand? But see there is no such word as non-violent, you see, because I'm right in what I do. So to save my life I must survive. I don't care what you call it. If you had food in your house and you won't give it to me and I have to save my life I'm coming in there. And that's the way you should come in my house because you got to try and (what) survive. So if I'm trying to survive for my life you wouldn't call that violence would you? Hmm? Now you can't call that violence. I know if you got everything and I ain't got any. You gonna make me suffer. You got to kill me.

Interviewer: Are you talking about without having riots in the streets?

Allah: Do what? If I did something it wouldn't be a riot! I'd go to the government.

Interviewer: People would follow you.

Allah: I'd go to the government. You don't call that a riot! If the store got food in there and you own that store and don't give no food you not going to riot if I go in there and get some food.

Interviewer: But you said you would be (sic).

Allah: I'm civilized. All civilized people say that.

Interviewer: That what you want boys to follow you.

Allah: And I want them to obey your orders, too.

Interviewer: Use a cooperative approach.

Allah: If you try to force on them religion you can't win because the child must fight for the United States of America because he might make this (what) his home. And if you continue to teach that child about religion the first thing that boy going to be hollering out "Jesus Coming!" He ain't gonna fight. You don't want to get them like this because they don't want to pick up no what? arms. While this country is getting weak Russia is building up—and not only this country— building up the other countries. Now, I don't tell the children not to go to war because I'll go back with them. I enjoyed the army when I was in there. I enjoyed it. Because it's something to kill and not worry about it. Some people kill and have a conscious and go crazy behind it because they can't clear their mind up. Now, when I was in the army I know I was fighting for the country and also myself. And I was one to come back home with many units. And I'm reaping the benefits from it now whether I got anything or not. The United States of America taught me to be disciplined. They also done taught me how to raise me an army. They self educated me to lessen all my trials and tribulations. I have done messed with cocaine. I have done messed with everything but LSD and I'm not going to take any of those trips. Did I gain from using cocaine? Yes. I know what it do for me. I start bringing it on my ownself because I just had it because it freezed me. So, by you going to all these other countries getting all these results and bringing it back in. I know this because they made me a doctor. No [sic] did to me. Every doctor talking about that 'that's no understanding.' So, so it helped me in the Army. The only thing I need to know is where to get it at now. And also lily white come in (what) swaps. Because did it harm you or did it hurt you? It don't hurt do it?

Interviewer: What you do with it?

Allah: Well, alright then. It couldn't harm me.

Interviewer: I think one of your boys have a question.

Allah: Well, they can ask anything they want.

Interviewer: You can go ahead.

5%er Enrollee: (to interviewer) I know my Father.

Allah: And he's always coming with questions.

5%er Enrollee: Allah, you know like when we go to church on Sundays? Do we have to man?

Allah: Listen, son. I'm going to tell you something and I must say this. Listen, son. If you go without force, it is good to listen and learn. Now if you forced, don't go. Don't go. Because as a force it's gonna make you not to be able to protect this country. It's going to put you in a state of mind that if they don't get rid of this state of mind the country got to fall. And I don't want you under up nobody else's command. I want you to stay right here in the United States. If you go with anyone to church do exactly what they do—kneel. They didn't force me to go to church in Matteawan. They said Allah we don't have your service here. I said if you did—we don't have Muslim service here. I said if you did have Muslim service that is not my service. Because I don't have no religion. And they didn't force me to go. They put on my paper "very religious man" and I said, "No, I don't have no religion." They put on my paper that I was a leader and I said, "No, I'm not a leader." Because if I said I was a leader then I would hold records of you and they would come and ask for my records one day—so I don't have records. So that's when they come—if come ask me and they let me show no records of you. You understand that? So I say if you go. Go! Go! You'll benefit from it.

Interviewer: What about singing?

Allah: Plenty of singing. That's fine to sing. Sing!

Interviewer: It's almost Christmas time.

Allah: Listen. Barry Gottehrer was trying to get us a building so we could have a Christmas party. Now, Muslims don't believe in Christmas. I would like to have a Christmas party for the Five Percenters. You understand that? So if you want to go, go to church. You'll learn from it. You not going there—

Interviewer: And you say if you're not forced. Are we forcing you to go to church?

5%er Enrollee: I mean, there ain't no way we can get out of it.

Allah: Well go. Because I'm a show you why you have a right to go. Because if you hadn't did anything wrong, you wouldn't be there would you? All I know is that you didn't do anything wrong when it came to your mothers and I don't blame you because man don't have a mother. What is a mother? Man don't have no mother. Who is my daughter if she ain't my wife? I give her away if I want to. And in this country they'll say, "Oh you can't marry (off) your daughter." That's my seed, I'll give her away if I want to and not let nobody come in and try to steal her and contaminate my Earth. You understand that? And I feel exactly the way the Queen & them do of England. That's my Earth. I give her away if I (what) want to. Now, how many more concerns you have?

Interviewer: Thanks everyone.

Allah: Alright gentlemen.

Interviewer: Thank you very much.

Allah: All right, gentlemen. I'm not against nobody. I'm only trying to make the young people strong together so that they can keep the country safe because this is a new country. Isn't it? You don't keep it safe; you ain't going to

reap the benefits from it. Because it's a new country. You
know this is a new country.
[The End]

The Allah School In Mecca

Insights Into The Curriculum of The Allah School In Mecca

Young children in the computer lab at The Allah School In Mecca.

The Allah School In Mecca, located in Harlem, New York, has served as the Five Percenters National Headquarters over the past 40 years. Since it's inception, it has gone through various changes. Originally donated to the organization by the Urban League in 1967, it was christened as "The Urban League Street Academy" by its officials and the Mayor's administration. The original curriculum of the academy was oversaw by Urban League personnel along with Clarence 13X (Allah) and Akbar (Justice). The initial program faced challenges in its start since the neighborhood kids had issues with the Urban League's input and teachers. Conversely, the neighborhood children gravitated toward Allah and Akbar's methodologies and teachings. Sensing this was the case, the Urban League pulled their teachers out of the academy and the school was given to Allah for the exclusive use of the Five Percenters. The building was renamed "Allah's Street Academy" to reflect the new change in ownership.

Allah kept what he felt was the best part of the Urban League's program and infused it with the teachings and programs of the Five Percenters. He ran a viable productive program for the Five Percenters from the fall of '67 until the late spring of '69 when he was assassinated.

After Allah's departure, the once viable institution lost steam but it stayed safely with the Five Percenters because of the 20-year lease agreement between the group and the city. In 1970, the building became the rendezvous meeting spot for a group of Five Percenters that decided to kick-start the movement once again. The Five Percenters around the city sponsored different programs and the movement sprouted its legs post Clarence's departure.

Throughout the past four decades the school has had its ups and downs. The academy has been under constant threat by real estate developers attempting to take the land. The first attempt came in 1977 prior to the expiration of the lease and there have been several underhanded attempts since then to seize the property. The school and its clients are well aware of past and present ploys by the powers that be and their efforts to acquire the land.

On top of that there were two disastrous fires that occurred in the late eighties and early nineties that were major setbacks for the institution. Although they have faced organizational and management problems in the past, the Five Percenters have always rose to the occasion when it came to saving their edifice. Throughout its experience over the past 40 years, today the Five Percenters have assembled one of their most progressive administrations since the days of Allah and Justice. Today, The Allah School and its programs have come full circle. Allah B:

We have gone back to the original blueprint that Allah had when he was here. The school is currently being run in this manner and an emphasis is being placed on the original way and teachings especially as it pertains to the children.

One of the most welcomed initiatives is the continued targeting of youth in the neighborhood. Perhaps propelled by the most famous quote of understanding, "The Babies are the greatest!" The founder Allah publicly declared that the wealth of the nation is the children. It is within this realm that Sunez Allah, a teacher at the Allah School for the past 10 years, addresses the subject:

> The youth are the primary focus and education at our major institution. To note, our nation is not one based on a society, backed by an enforcing government, sequestering land and riches; rather, it is one of enlightened families actualizing their birthright of identity, proven mathematically and scientifically, where the Original man is being God and the Original woman is being Earth. Naturally being themselves, the pedagogical premise is on reaching the deeper reality of education's meaning. As revealed by its etymological root, *educare*, meaning to "draw out that which is within," our science of teaching is in simply showing our people whom they really are.[449]

One obvious characteristic of the Allah School personnel is their passion and commitment to their students. Each staff member takes their role seriously and understands the impact they will have on young peoples lives.

> While being a teacher of truth is seen as a duty, it continues to be best manifest as an honor, fulfilling one's nature to truly share what is needed and not merely appeasing a spiritual debt. A poor, righteous teacher is one who is willing to sacrifice everything he has to share a truth that may better others. Thus, our truths, self evident to us, are presented as unconditional offerings to the young for their complete, unbiased testing. The evangelical abilities one gains with taking supreme mathematics as a dialect to highlight one's constructed grandeur are constantly frowned upon.[450]

When you pair the mission statement of the institution and it's capable determined staff, it makes way for a fresh approach to learning. Never settling for traditional methods as the only way to learn, the student is given an opportunity to demonstrate their skills in a progressive manner.

Most essential to the framework of successfully sharing what one has known to be true, understood to be a fruitful culture and having built the loveliest family born, is the testing of all tradition, the denial of following any said doctrine and allowing for the new idea to become tomorrow's development. At this present time, this is no more exemplified than by the courses taking place at our root of civilization, Allah School in Mecca.[451]

The Allah School In Mecca has established a core syllabus for all its students and clientele. The itinerary could be best explained as 5 major parts to the overall curriculum. It consists of five major courses: (1) The Civilization Class (2) The "120" Course (3) The "Mathematical Buildup" Course (4) The Computer Laboratory Course and (5) The P.EA.C.E. Course.

One of the more longstanding courses has been the "Civilization" class. This is typically an exclusive class for Five Percenters and/ or strong sympathizers seeking to learn more about the Five Percent doctrine.

Traditionally, the coursework of our Nation is simplified as "the civilization class" where a group of "newborns," are newly introduced to the knowledge of themselves as revealed through our major teachings of supreme mathematics, its accompanying alphabet and the 120 lessons. The instructor would normally be the "enlightener" whom, in having revealed this knowledge to the newborn, has taken the duty to guide him or her through the process of living the teachings out with understanding. Sessions would include memorization of the lessons, accompanying techniques and exercises, historical sources referenced primarily from "plus lessons," those additional essays of sharings from older Gods and the works of the Honorable Elijah Muhammad available.[452]

The premise of the Civilization class can be viewed as the common denominator or the base for the rest of curriculum. This is extremely evident in the "120" class which is a review of the NOI lessons in a classroom setting.

> As tradition is emphatically unnecessary in conveying a truth, all of the instructors of Allah School in Mecca have taken this notice in their heart. Consequently, every course has the best part of the "civilization class" ethic at its core yet is a completely unique presentation of that instructor's experience, resources and sincerity. The closest any course comes to the traditional mode is the 120 course taught by a most respected elder, Um Allah. Equipping the students with the tools of the civilization class there is an immense effort added in revealing the need for embracing practicality, earnest application and camaraderie in learning and honoring the 120 lessons. Truly the public servant of highest caliber, Um Allah's experience in every facet of guidance, service and advocacy is relayed to students every week.[453]

The "Mathematical Buildup" course is an advanced study on how to apply Allah's (Clarence 13X) lesson Supreme Mathematics above and beyond its rhetorical qualities. This class establishes different ways to study and view these lessons that are held so dearly by the Five Percent Nation of Islam/ Nation of Gods and Earths.

> To lovingly reiterate the point of every sharing of understanding, the equality of every build, the power of everything born is the upliftment of all of our children. Clearly, this is no more evident than in the course taught by Wise Jamel Allah. Entitled "Mathematical Buildup," the course focuses on the use of supreme mathematics as more than a mere idiom for eliciting excitement from the unknowing but as a language that can express engaging ideas and detail solutions our hells entailed. Like Um Allah, Wise Jamel has the added experience and insight of having known Father Allah and the times that birthed our Nation. Their value in educating the young is clearly unquantifiable.[454]

One of the current signs to reflect the growth of the movement is its addition of a computer lab within the facility. There isn't any doubt that today's generation of children eagerly await to attend this class where they are allowed to work and play on computers. On hand are enthusiastic personnel who greet the children and aid them in their studies. This class is overseen by one of the Elders Allah B.

> A third elder, Allah B, instructs the newest course taught. It is a wonderfully constructed computer classroom offering all of the basics and necessities rendered along with assignments that cement our teaching's principles. As often as a student may learn something new, for instance, utilizing an internet search engine, they will also be given the assignment of researching the origins of the next holiday they may be about to haphazardly embrace. It is of note that our humble educational facilities are provided an upshot of quality of life with Allah B's diligence and dedication.[455]

Lastly, there is the class entitled The P.E.A.C.E. course. It is an acronym that stands for "Political Education And Civilization Enrichment." Sunez Allah, who teaches this class, outlines his spiritual approach:

> Finally, it is only with the principles of perfection, our culture, that I have come to teach my course, The P.E.A.C.E. course. A reality that witnesses no mistakes but is wonderfully filled with lessons. An ethos that does not pass judgment over illusionary perspectives of good or bad, but upholds justice for what is proven right, discarding all that is shown to be wrong. A way of life that sees no endings; rather, only constant reawakenings to the vignettes of enlightenment within us all. These principles of Originality, creativity expressing unique content, Honor, the natural manner of one's every word being our bond and a Full Uprightness, where each moment, one's every intention and forthcoming action shares one's vital understanding, are all I carry as the curriculum of every course session.[456]

Mr. Allah conveys the basic meaning and premise to the P.E.A.C.E. course that includes preparing children to face society:

> Embracing all the respectable tools of modernity to fulfill these prized principles of antiquity, the course of Political Education *And* Civilization Enrichment offers the student skills training

in dealing with the harsh hypocrisies and contradictions of the outside world *and* the sciences of everything in life. Acknowledging the unique dynamics I, myself, entail, I am the youngest teacher with the oldest current course, that has consecutively been run throughout this yet unfinished first decade of the twenty first century. With this said, the details of my fulfilling this immense honor may enlighten one as to the nature of our Nation's pedagogy.[457]

The staff at the Allah School In Mecca has embraced a revolutionary methodology that embraces the students and challenges the teachers. The ultimate aim is to prepare the children to be the future teachers and leaders of tomorrow.

...every student is taught as if he will never return. Everything shared must be to the best of the teacher's ability, a chosen lesson of worth for the student. The approach is always on the individual's needs while the classroom lecture is guided toward that student which knows the least. Those students who already know a particular lesson will have a review and a moment to study pedagogy itself, as it is displayed by the teacher. It is here where the next poor, righteous teachers begin their appropriate studies in the craft.[458]

In order to prepare, the students learn a variety of relevant subjects to enhance their studies. Utilizing the Five Percenter teachings as the foundation, the students delve into a broad range of subject matter.

The curriculum covers into all the disciplines necessary and conducive to learning the knowledge of oneself. From the root of Supreme mathematics utilizing the Supreme alphabet, the 120 lessons are studied as a subjective text filled with clear facts as well as abstract reasoning and insights needing of contemplative study and living experience. The primary tools offered become extensive reading training, research, writing and communication skills. Here, the student will use tools necessary in society and may draw his own talents out of such, if not mastering them as well. With special lessons ranging from bio-chemistry, quantum physics, the ancient esoteric texts of Asia and India, archaeology, exercise and fitness training, the martial arts of Shaolin Kung Fu as learnt from Grandmaster Sigung Bobby Whitaker, health protocols and the standards of a living foods diet, the reality of God and Earth is taught as wholistically as it truly is.[459]

In summing up the experience at The Allah School In Mecca for the students as well as the teachers, Sunez Allah offers his perspective on what he has learned from walking through the doors as a "new born" in 2000, to becoming a tenured teacher in the establishment for the past 7 years:

> In the years teaching, I have lectured over 200 students and have come to realize that it is not the truth that we offer that is unique. Our ancient ancestors from the magnificent architects of Kemit to the Taoists of China to the Sufis of India have all known it. Revealing that pristine interdependence of man, the supreme sole controller of the universe and woman, the supreme, nourishing and sustaining vessel live harmoniously as mathematics beckons their nature, that most definitive, completely fluid and liberating language.
> It is that the work of the Father and our elders has taken this truth to a most simplest form for the most savagely complex times. And unlike the sages that revealed themselves upon discovering the worthy student, we have donned beautiful universal flags and proclaimed our divinity as a gift to be shared. These poignant differences are not meant to lament the greats of our past. It is to remind us all that the saviors of the people, from the past, of the present and in the future, not only find the truth. They develop the pedagogy that that allows this liberation to be shared, embraced and enlightening to all.[460]

As evident in the above programs offered by The Allah School In Mecca, the institution has its eyes set for greater sights. With the advent of time many of its members have acquired credentials and the know-how to give back to their communities. In some cases the work is evident in other areas it may go unseen. In Islam, it said that the righteous walk the earth in humility. It is in this humble manner that the "poor righteous teachers" continue to "walk down the path that Allah made." It is through this spirit and memory that ALLAH LIVES.

Bibliography

Books

Allah, Almighty God Dawud. *The Secret of FreeMasonry*, 1997.

Allah, Shahid M. *Open It Up Yo!!: The Plot to Kill Clarence 13X*. Washington, DC: TKC Publishing, 1995.

Beynon, E.D. Prince –A– Cuba. *Detroit History*. Newport News: United Brothers & United Sisters Communications Systems, 1990.

Cuba, Prince A. *Our Mecca is Harlem: Clarence 13X (Allah) and the Five Percent*. Hampton: U. B. & U. S. Communications Systems, Inc, 1994.

Farrakhan, Louis. *7 Speeches*. Chicago: WKU & Final Call, Inc, 1992.

Gottehrer, Barry. *The Mayor's Man*. Garden City, NY: Doubleday, 1975. Out of Print.

Haley, Alex. *The Autobiography of Malcolm X*. New York: Ballantine Books, 1964.

Karim, Benjamin. Skutches, Peter. Gallen, David. *Remembering Malcolm* New York: Carroll & Graf, 1992.

Lincoln, C. Eric. *The Black Muslims in America*. Boston: Beacon Press, 1961.

Muhammad, Elijah. *How to Eat to Live*. Chicago: Final Call Publishing.

Muhammad, Elijah. *Message to the Black Man*. Atlanta: MEMPS, 1964.

Muhammad, Elijah. *Our Saviour Has Arrived*. Chicago: Final Call Publishing, 1974.

Muhammad, Elijah. *The Supreme Wisdom Vol. 1.* Atlanta: MEMPS, 1957.

Muhammad, Elijah. *The True History of Master Fard Muhammad.* Atlanta: MEMPS, 1996.

Muhammad, Jabril. *This is the One: The Most Honored Elijah Muhammad, We Need Not Look For Another, Volume 1.* Arizona: Book Company, 1993.

Magazines, Newsletters, Journals

ABG#7. "The Medina Heart." *Learn And Know Your History.* Undated.

ABG#7. "December 1964." *Learn And Know Your History Part 2.* Undated.

ABG#7. "October 1964." *Learn And Know Your History Part 2.* Undated.

"Allah School: Where to Now?", *The Five Percenter Newspaper*, January 1989 Issue.

"Allah School Is Not A Building", *The Five Percenter Newspaper*, January 1989 Issue.

Allah, Beautiful Life. "The First Born" *Learn And Know Your History Part 2.*

Allah's Born God. "In Memory of Allah." *The Sun of Man: A Five Percenter Digest,* June 2000.

Allah's Born God. "June 13th, 1969." *Learn And Know Your History.* Undated.

Allah, Born. "Allah's Essences." Sun of Man Newsletter, June 1990.

Allah, Born. "Allah's Show & Prove." Undated.

Allah, Dumar Wa'de. The National Statement 1996.

Allah, Gykee Mathematics. "The History of Medina." *Learn and Know Your History*. Undated.

Allah, Gykee Mathematics. "Our History in Medina." *Learn and Know Your History Part 2*. Undated.

Allah, Gykee Mathematics. "Wrongful Arrested." *Learn and Know Your History Part 2*. Undated.

Allah, Gykee Mathematics. "An Honorary Five Per-Center "1968"." *Learn and Know Your History Part 2*. Undated.

Allah, Gykee Mathematics. "Education And Working." *Learn and Know Your History Part 2*. Undated.

Allah, Gykee Mathematics. "This Was The Year Fourteen 1977." *Learn and Know Your History Part 2*. Undated.

Allah, Infinite Al'jaa'maar-U. "The History of Brownsville from 1967-1968." *The Black Family Show and Prove Special Edition Issue*, June 11, 2000.

Allah, Infinite Al'jaa'maar-U. "Some History On The First Born Muslims. *Learn And Know Your History Part 2*.

Allah, Know. "The Knowledge Being Born In Brownsville: Medina 1965-1966." *The Black Family Show and Prove Special Edition Issue*, June 11, 2000.

Allah, Shabazz Adew. "Study your Lessons." *The Five Percenter Newspaper*, Jan. 1996 Issue.

Allah, Shabazz Adew. "Unification is the Directive, Truth is the Criteria." *The Five Percenter Newspaper*, September 1996, Volume 2.1

Allah, Shahid M. "Imam Isa's Got A God Complex!." Atlanta: TKC Productions, 1991.

Allah, Wakeel. "Did The Most Honorable Elijah Muhammad Recognize The Five Percenters. *Learn And Know Your History Part 2.* Undated.

Allah, U. "The History of Pelan 1966-1972." *The Black Family Newspaper Vol. 1 Show and Prove Special Edition Issue,* June 11, 2000.

Azreal. "December 1965." *Learn and Know Your History Part 2.* Undated.

B., Allah. "I've Done My Time (On The Cross)." Article located on http://metalab.unc.edu/nge/4ban/

"Biography Article." *The Five Percenter Newspaper,* September 1995 Issue, 11.

Cuba, A. Prince. *"Black Gods of the Inner City."* Gnosis Magazine, Fall 1992.

"Dance With The Devil." *The Five Percenter Newspaper,* September 1996 Issue, 5.

Eye-God aka Amin. "The Harlem Six." *The Five Percenter Newspaper,* November 1995, Issue #4.

Eye God. "The Harlem Six." *Learning and Knowing Your History Part 1.* Undated

Islam, True. "Is Allah a Righteous Muslim?" Article on Allah Team Website, www.allahteam.com., 1998.

K7. "Give Off Light Not Lies." *The Five Percenter Newspaper,* February 1998 Issue, Volume 3.6.

K7. "1969 The Rifle." *The Five Percenter Newspaper*, May 1996 Issue.

Kalim, G. "Godism: Also Muslims & Muslim Sons." *The Five Percenter Newspaper*, August 1998 Issue.

Mathematics, Gykee. "The History of Medina." *Sun of Man Publications*, Article located on the Internet http://black7.org/archive.html.

Nuruddin, Yusuf. *"The Five Percenters: A Teenage Nation of Gods and Earths"*, *Muslim Communities in North America.* Albany: State University of NewYork Press, 1994 Chapter 5.

Sha Sha, *"Jimmy Jam The Old Man."* Article located on now defunct Oasis website.

Shaamguadd, U.S. "No Woman No Cry." *The Sun of Man*, Not dated.

Shaamguadd, U.S. "The Exact Expiration Date of The Devil's Civilization!" *Behold the Sun of Man*, Undated.

Shaamguadd, U.S. "Impressive Name Is No Guarantee Or Success For Fame." *Behold The Sun of Man*, 1985.

Shaamguadd, U.S. "Five Percenters – The Real Deal! Or Cleaning Up Yourself!." *Behold The Sun of Man*, 1984.

Shaamguadd, U.S. "In 1964." *Behold the Sun of Man.* Not dated.

Shaamguadd, U.S. "Allah Blessed America." *Behold the Sun of Man.* Not dated.

Shaamguadd, U.S. "The Snow Job or Needles and Pins." *Learn And Know Your History Part 2.* Not dated.

Shaamguadd, U.S. "The Ostrich Syndrome." *The Sun of Man*, July 1983 Issue.

Shaamguadd, U.S. "Exile!" *Behold the Sun of Man*, June 1983.

Shaamguadd, U.S. "The Science of Cain and Able." *Behold the Sun of Man*, Undated.

Shaamguadd, U.S. "Allah You Are The Greatest." *Behold the Sun of Man*, October 1986 Issue, 2.

Shaamguadd, U.S. "A Little Dessert For Those Of The Creative Thought." *Sun of Man Publication*, 1985.

Shaamguadd, U.S. "Excerpts from the Sun of Man#6." *The Sun of Man*, Not dated.

Shahid, Abu. "Let's Straighten It." Unpublished article. Undated.

Shahid, Abu. "From the Mind of the First Born." *Learn And Know Your History Part 2*. Undated.

Shahid, Abu. "How Are You Living." *The Five Percenter Newspaper*, March 1996 Issue.

Steinem, Gloria, and Lloyd Weaver, "The City on the Eve of Destruction." *New Yorker Magazine*, April 1968 Issue.

Newspaper Articles

Arnold, Martin. "2 Held in Killing Admit Another; Will Be Questioned on 2 More." *The New York Times*, May 2, 1964.

Farrell, William F. "Harlem Militants Offer Peace Vow." *The New York Times*, June 15, 1969.

Faso, Frank. "Kenyatta's Pal Killed; Cops See Muslim War." *The N.Y. Daily News,* June 14, 1969.

Griffin, Junius. "40 Negro Detectives Investigate Anti-White Gang." *The New York Times*, May 7, 1964.

Griffin, Junius. "Whites Are Target of Harlem Gang." *The New York Times*, May 3, 1964.

Griffin, Junius. "Anti-White Harlem Gang Reported to Number 400." *The New York Times*, May 6, 1964.

Jones, Theodore. "5 Percenters Called Hoodlums: Actions Blamed on Frustration." Article included in FBI HQ file on Clarence 13X and the Five Percenters.

Matthews, Les. "Allah Still Lives." *The N.Y. Amsterdam News*, June 21, 1969.

Mock, Brentin. "What If God Was One Of Us?" *The Pittsburgh City Paper*, October 16, 2002.

Robinson, Paul. "Born Allah: Positive Vibrations." *The Auburn Collective*, January 1983.

Roth, Jack. "Police Fill Court for Muslim Case." *The New York Times*, June 1, 1965.

Rustin, Bayard. "The Five Percenters." *The Amsterdam News: Brooklyn Section*, Sept. 9, 1967.

Sullivan, James. "Harlem '5 Percenters' – Terror Group Revealed." *The New York Tribune*, October 15, 1965.

Speeches, Audio Tapes, Documentaries

Allah (Clarence 13X). "Interview with Allah conducted at Otisville Training Institute For Boys." Nov. 15, 1967.

Farrakhan, Louis. *"Is the House Divided."* Lecture given in Phoenix, AZ, 1977.

Muhammad, Elijah. *"The Knowledge of God Himself."* Saviour's Day Speech, Feb. 26, 1969.

Muhammad, Elijah. *"The Theology of Time."* Lecture Series, 1972.

Muhammad, Dr. Khallid Abdul. *The Hypocrisy of Malcolm X*, Speech delivered in New York City, 1989.

"Nation History parts 1 & 2" Audio excerpts located on http://black7.org/archive.html, Undated.

Director: Woody King Jr., *"The Torture of Mothers: The Case of the Harlem Six"*, Narrated by Adolph Caesar featuring Ruby Dee, 1980.

Internet and the World Wide Web

Allah Team – A prestigious Five Percenter website that contains articles on Five Percenter teachings, books, products and events. (www.allahteam.org).

Allah Youth Center In Mecca – A website dedicated to the youth programs that are initiated in the Allah School In Mecca. (www.allahyouthcenter.org).

Black 7 – A Five Percenter website featuring the London, England Chapter. (http://black7.org/).

Final Call – The official website for the Final Call Newspaper published by Minister Louis Farrakhan. (www.finalcall.com).

Five Percent Nation of Islam – A website that contains articles, products and links to Five Percenter websites that cater to the Five Percent Nation of Islam doctrines. www.5percenters.net

Nation of Gods and Earths – A website that contains mostly links to other individual Five Percenter websites that cater to Nation of Gods and Earths doctrines. (www.ibiblio.org/nge/).

NGE Power – Official website of the NGE Power Periodical containing information on politics, business and health from the perspective of the Gods and Earths. (www.thengepower.com).

Nation of Islam – The official website of the Nation of Islam under the leadership of the Honorable Minister Louis Farrakhan. (www.noi.org).

Muhammad Speaks – A website that contains archives of Elijah Muhammad's teachings and is hosted by an offshoot of the Nation of Islam. (www.muhammadspeaks.com).

The Black God – A website that contains scholarly analysis and exegesis of the Honorable Elijah Muhammad's teachings. Primarily includes the work of Islamic scholar True Islam. (www.theblackgod.com).

---

[1] Author Unknown, The True History Of The Nation Of Islam, N.P., N.D.

[2] Ibid.

[3] Frederick Douglass, "What, To the American Slave, Is Your 4th of July," Speech given by Frederick Douglass on July 4, 1952 in Rochester, New York.

[4] Elijah Muhammad, *The Fall of America,* Chapter 16," Independence Day".

[5] Anonymous, The True History Of The Nation Of Islam, .N.P., N.D.

[6] Ibid.

[7] ibid.

[8] E. D. Beynon, "The Voodoo Cult Among Negro Migrants in Detroit," *American Journal of Sociology*, May 1938. Interview with Sister Denke Majied (formerly Mrs. Lawrence Adams).

[9] Beynon, "The Voodoo Cult," *American Journal of Sociology*, Interview with Brother Challar Sharrieff.

[10] C. Eric Lincoln, *The Black Muslims in America* (Boston: Beacon Press, 1961) xxv.

[11] Beynon, "The Voodoo Cult" *American Journal of Sociology*, Interview with Brother Yusef Muhammad.

[12] Beynon, "The Voodoo Cult," *American Journal of Sociology*, Interview with Brother Yusef Muhammad.

[13] Ibid.

[14] Anonymous, The True History Of The Nation Of Islam, .N.P., N.D.

[15] Ibid.

[16] Malu Halasa, *Black Americans of Achievement: Elijah Muhammad,* (Chelsea House Publishers, 1990) 20-21.

[17] Ibid.

[18] FBI Files on Fard.

[19] Ibid.

[20] Halasa, *Elijah Muhammad,* 42-43.

[21] Jabril Muhammad, *This is the One: The Most Honored Elijah Muhammad, We Need Not Look For Another, Volume 1.* (Arizona: Book Company, 1993) 163.

[22] Ibid.

[23] Elijah Muhammad, *Message to the Black Man* (Atlanta: MEMPS, 1964) 16-17

[24] J. Muhammad, *This is the One,* 163.

[25] J, Muhammad, *This is the One,* 164.

[26] E. Muhammad, *Message to the Black Man,* 16-17.

[27] E. Muhammad, *Message to the Black Man,* 281-282.

[28] Beynon, "The Voodoo Cult" *The American Journal of Sociology,* May 1938.

[29] Ibid.

[30] Anonymous,. Article contained in NOI Orientation Packet for processing Muslims. N.P., N.D.

[31] J. Muhammad, *This is the One,* 167.

[32] J. Muhammad, *This is the One,* 167.

[33] J. Muhammad, *This is the One,* 168.

[34] J. Muhammad, *This is the One,* 167 -168.

[35] Elijah Muhammad, *The True History of Master Fard Muhammad* (Atlanta: MEMPS, 1996) 50.

[36] Halasa, *Elijah Muhammad,* 50-51.

[37] Beynon, "The Voodoo Cult," *The American Journal of Sociology,* May 1938.

[38] Beynon, "The Voodoo Cult," *The American Journal of Sociology,* May 1938.

[39] Ibid.

[40] Detroit Free Press Newspaper

[41] E. D. Beynon, Prince –A- Cuba, *Detroit History* (Newport News: United Brothers & United Sisters Communications Systems, 1990) 6.

[42] E. Muhammad, *Message to the Black Man,* 16-17.

[43] Ibid.

[44] J. Muhammad, *This is the One,* 167.

[45] Elijah Muhammad, *"The Knowledge of God Himself",* Saviour's Day Speech, Feb. 26, 1969.

[46] *History,* Article located in NOI orientation packet for processing Muslims. Undated.

[47] J. Muhammad, *This is the One,* 173.

[48] J. Muhammad, *This is the One,* 176.

[49] J. Muhammad, *This is the One,* 173

[50] Ibid.

[51] J. Muhammad, *This is the One,* 176.

[52] Ibid.

[53] J. Muhammad, *This is the One,* 178.

[54] J. Muhammad, *This is the One,* 177.

[55] E. Muhammad, *Message to the Black Man,* 179…

[56] *History,* Article located in NOI orientation packet for processing Muslims. Undated.

[57] Author Unknown, The True History Of The Nation Of Islam, N.P., N.D.

[58] Alex Haley, *The Autobiography of Malcolm X* (New York: Ballantine Books, 1964) 202-203.

[59] Beloved Allah, "The Bomb: The Greatest Story Never Told", *The Word Newspaper*, 3-part series (July 1987, Aug./Sept. 1987).

[60] Les Matthews, "Allah Still Lives", *The N.Y. Amsterdam News,* June 21, 1969.

[61] Ibid.

[62] FBI HQ file on Clarence 13X and the Five Percenters.

[63] Ibid.

[64] Haley, *The Autobiography of Malcolm X* ,225.

[65] Ibid

[66] ibid.

[67] ibid.

[68] ibid.

[69] ibid.

[70] Elijah Muhammad, "What The Muslims Want." Muhammad Speaks Newspaper.

[71] Ibid.

[72] ibid.

[73] Elijah Muhammad, "What The Muslims Believe." Muhammad Speaks Newspaper.

[74] Ibid.

[75] ibid.

[76] ibid.

[77] ibid.

[78] ibid.

[79] Lincoln, *The Black Muslims in America*, 114.

[80] Master Fard Muhammad & Hon. Elijah Muhammad, The Student Enrollment, Questions and Answers (1-3). Undated.

[81] Lincoln, *The Black Muslims in America*, 15.

[82] Elijah Muhammad, *The Supreme Wisdom Vol. 1* (Atlanta: MEMPS, 1957) 21.

[83] Anonymous, in "Learn and Know Your History Part 2". 6.

[84] Haley, *The Autobiography of Malcolm X*, 231-232.

[85] Lincoln, *The Black Muslims in America* 225.

[86] Benjamin Karim, with Peter Skutches and David Gallen, *Remembering Malcolm* (New York: Carroll & Graf, 1992) 91.

[87] James 7X, Interview conducted by Author. April 1999.

[88] Master Fard Muhammad & Elijah Muhammad, *Lost-Found Muslim Lesson No. 2,* Questions 12-13, February 20, 1934.

[89] B. Karim, with P. Skutches and D. Gallen, *Remembering Malcolm*, 71-72.

[90] Lincoln, *The Black Muslims in America*, 224.

[91] Abu Shahid, *"Let's Straighten It"*, N.P., N.D.

[92] Ibid.

[93] Abu Shahid, Interview conducted by author on April 8, 2006.

[94] Ibid.

[95] Lincoln, *The Black Muslims in America*, 222.

[96] Louis Farrakhan, *7 Speeches* (Chicago: WKU & Final Call, Inc, 1992) 48.

[97] FBI HQ file on Clarence 13X and the Five Percenters.

[98] James 7X, Interview conducted by Author. April 1999.

[99] Les Matthews, "Allah Still Lives", *The N.Y. Amsterdam News*, June 21, 1969.

[100] Prince A. Cuba, *"Black Gods of the Inner City"*, Gnosis Magazine, Fall 1992, 61.

[101] Ramza Mahmud & James 7X, Interview conducted by Author. April 1999.

[102] Beloved Allah, "The Bomb: The Greatest Story Never Told", *The Word Newspaper*, 3-part series (July 1987, Aug./Sept. 1987).

[103] Yusuf Nuruddin, *"The Five Percenters: A Teenage Nation of Gods and Earths"*, *Muslim Communities in North America* (Albany: State University of New York Press, 1994) Chapter 5.

[104] Um Allah, Nation_History_part2, Audio excerpts located on http://black7.org/archive.html, Undated.

[105] Prince A. Cuba, *Our Mecca is Harlem: Clarence 13X(Allah) and the Five Percent* (Hampton: U. B. & U. S. Communications Systems, Inc, 1994) 6-7.

[106] Allah (Clarence 13X), Interview with Allah conducted at Otisville Training Institute For Boys, Nov. 15, 1967.

[107] Abdul Akbar Muhammad, Audio excerpt from "The History of Mosque #7 New York City." Speech delivered at Mosque #7, N.Y.C. May 18, 2005 Part 1.

[108] Louis Farrakhan, *Is the House Divided*, Lecture given in Phoenix, AZ, 1977.

[109] Dr. Khallid Abdul Muhammad, *The Hypocrisy of Malcolm X*, Speech delivered in New York City, 1989.

[110] Cuba, *Our Mecca is Harlem: Clarence 13X(Allah) and the Five Percent*, 48.

[111] Abu Shahid, Interview conducted by author on March 14, 2006.

[112] Abu Shahid, *"Let's Straighten It"*, Unpublished article. Undated.

[113] Ibid.

[114] Eye God, Interview with the Author on February 17, 2007.

[115] Um Allah, Nation_History_part1, Audio excerpts located on
http://black7.org/archive.html, Undated.

[116] Ibid.

[117] ibid.

[118] Dawud (Understanding Supreme) Allah, Nation_History_part1, Audio excerpts
located on http://black7.org/archive.html, Undated.

[119] Eye-God a.k.a. Amin, "The Harlem Six", *The Five Percenter Newspaper*, November
1995, Issue #4.

[120] Eye God a.k.a. Amin, "The Harlem Six" in Learn and Know Your History Part 1. 4-5.

[121] Ibid..

[122] ibid.

[123] ibid.

[124] ibid.

[125] Director: Woody King Jr., *"The Torture of Mothers: The Case of the Harlem Six"*,
Narrated by Adolph Caesar featuring Ruby Dee, 1980.

[126] Ibid.

[127] ibid.

[128] ibid.

[129] ibid.

[130] Eye God a.k.a. Amin, "The Harlem Six" in Learn and Know Your History Part 1. 4-5.

[131] Ibid.

[132] Martin Arnold, "2 Held in Killing Admit Another; Will Be Questioned on 2 More",
The New York Times, May 2, 1964.

[133] Junius Griffin, "Whites Are Target of Harlem Gang", *The New York Times*, May 3,
1964.

[134] Haley, *The Autobiography of Malcolm X*, 356.

[135] Eye God a.k.a. Amin, "The Harlem Six" in Learn and Know Your History Part 1. 4-5.

[136] Junius Griffin, "Anti-White Harlem Gang Reported to Number 400", *The New York
Times*, May 6, 1964.

[137] Junius Griffin, "40 Negro Detectives Investigate Anti-White Gang", *The New York
Times*, May 7, 1964.

[138] Haley, *The Autobiography of Malcolm X*, 367-368.

[139] Dawud (Understanding Supreme) Allah, Nation_History_part1, Audio excerpts
located on http://black7.org/archive.html, Undated.

[140] Allah B, Interview with the author on 5/2/06.

[141] Abu Shahid, *"Let's Straighten It"*, Unpublished article. Undated.

[142] ibid.

[143] Born Allah, "Allah's Essences", Sun of Man Newsletter, June 1990.

[144] Beloved Allah, "The Bomb: The Greatest Story Never Told", 1987.

[145] Allah (Clarence 13X), Interview with Allah conducted at Otisville Training Institute
For Boys, Nov. 15, 1967.

[146] US Shaamguadd, Behold the Sun of Man.

[147] "Introduction to the NGE", Audio excerpts located on http://black7.org/archive.html,
Undated.

[148] Shahid M. Allah, *Imam Isa's Got A God Complex!* (Atlanta: TKC Productions, 1990).

[149] Beautiful Life Allah, "The First Born" in Learn And Know Your History Part 2. 18,

[150] Allah B, Interview with the author on 5/2/06.

[151] ibid.

[152] Abu Shahid, "His Story" in Learn And Know Your History Part 2. 10-11. (Unpublished Manuscript).

[153] Master Fard Muhammad, Taken from the Supreme Wisdom Lesson called "The Problem Book", Question #13, Undated.

[154] Abu Shahid, "His Story" in Learn And Know Your History Part 2. 11. (Unpublished Manuscript).

[155] Abu Shahid, "How Are You Living", *The Five Percenter Newspaper*, March 1996 Issue.

[156] Nuruddin, *"The Five Percenters: A Teenage Nation of Gods and Earths"*, *Muslim Communities in North America*, 1994.

[157] US Shaamguadd, Behold the Sun of Man, Not dated.

[158] Nuruddin, *"The Five Percenters"* 1994.

[159] Barry Gottehrer, *The Mayor's Man* (Garden City, NY: Doubleday, 1975).

[160] US Shaamguadd, "Five Percenters – The Real Deal! Or Cleaning Up Yourself!" in Learn And Know Your History. 11–13.

[161] Ibid.

[162] ibid.

[163] ibid.

[164] US Shaamguadd, "No Woman No Cry", *The Sun of Man,* Not dated.

[165] Abu Shahid, Interview with the author on 3/14/07.

[166] US Shaamguadd, "The Exact Expiration Date of The Devil's Civilization!", *Behold the Sun of Man*, Undated.

[167] Lord Jamel God AK-BAR-U-ALLAH, "The History of W. F. Muhammad(1-20), Undated.

[168] US Shaamguadd, "In 1964", *Behold the Sun of Man*. Not dated.

[169] Allah, "The Revelation of Allah #1", Question #19, February 1974.

[170] US Shaamguadd, "Allah Blessed America", *Behold the Sun of Man*. Not dated.

[171] G. Kalim, "Godism: Also Muslims & Muslim Sons", *The Five Percenter Newspaper*, August 1998 Issue.

[172] True Islam, "Is Allah a Righteous Muslim?", Article on Allah Team Website, www.allahteam.com., 1998.

[173] Cuba, *Our Mecca is Harlem: Clarence 13X(Allah) and the Five Percent*, 7.

[174] Allah (Clarence 13X), Interview with Allah conducted at Otisville Training Institute For Boys, Nov. 15, 1967.

[175] Gottehrer, *The Mayor's Man*, 1975.

[176] US Shaamguadd, "Five Percenters – The Real Deal! Or Cleaning Up Yourself!" in Learn And Know Your History. 11–13.

[177] US Shaamguadd, "Five Percenters – The Real Deal! Or Cleaning Up Yourself!" in Learn And Know Your History. 11–13.

[178] Elijah Muhammad, *How to Eat to Live* (Chicago: Final Call Publishing).

[179] Allah (Clarence 13X), Interview with Allah conducted at Otisville Training Institute For Boys, Nov. 15, 1967.

[180] US Shaamguadd, "Five Percenters – The Real Deal! Or Cleaning Up Yourself!" in Learn And Know Your History. 11–13.

[181] Gykee Mathematics, "The History of Medina", *Sun of Man Publications*, Article located on the Internet http://black7.org/archive.html.

[182] *The Five Percenter Newspaper*

[183] Ibid.

[184] US Shaamguadd, "Exile!", *Behold the Sun of Man*, June 1983.

[185] ABG #7 Allah, "October 1964" in Learn And Know Your History Part 2. 27 (Unpublished Manuscript).

[186] Almighty God Dawud Allah, *The Secret of FreeMasonry*, 1997.

[187] US Shaamguadd, "Allah You Are The Greatest", *Behold the Sun of Man*, October 1986 Issue, 2.

[188] Allah (Clarence 13X), Interview with Allah conducted at Otisville Training Institute For Boys, Nov. 15, 1967.

[189] ABG #7 Allah's, "December 1964" in Learn And Know Your History Part 2. 27 (Unpublished Manuscript).

[190] Gottehrer, *The Mayor's Man*, 1975.

[191] Allah B., "I've Done My Time (On The Cross)", Article located on http://metalab.unc.edu/nge/4ban/

[192] Ibid.

[193] Beautiful Life Allah, "The First Born" in Learn and Know Your History Part 2. 20-22.

[194] Abu Shahid, *"Let's Straighten It"*, Unpublished article. Undated.

[195] Ibid.

[196] ibid.

[197] ibid.

[198] Allah's Born God, "In Memory of Allah", *The Sun of Man: A Five Percenter Digest*, June 2000.

[199] Ibid.

[200] In Learn and Know Your History

[201] Gykee Mathematics, "The History of Medina", *Sun of Man Publications*, Article located on the Internet http://black7.org/archive.html.

[202] ABG#7, "The Medina Heart," In Learn and Know Your History Part 2. 46.

[203] Ibid.

[204] Frank Paso, "Kenyatta's Pal Killed: Cops See Muslim War", *The N.Y. Daily News*, June 14, 1969.

[205] Allah (Clarence 13X), Interview with Allah conducted at Otisville Training Institute For Boys, Nov. 15, 1967.

[206] US Shaamguadd, "The Universal Flag!", *The Sun of Man*, Not dated.

[207] US Shaamguadd, "The Science of Cain and Able", *Behold the Sun of Man*, Undated.

[208] US Shaamguadd, Excerpts from the *Sun of Man* #6. Not dated.

[209] US Shaamguadd, "Allah Blessed America", *Behold the Sun of Man*. Not dated.

[210] Gykee Mathematics, "The History of Medina", *Sun of Man Publications*, Article located on the Internet http://black7.org/archive.html.

[211] Gykee M. Allah, "Wrongful Arrested" in Know and Learn Your History Part 2. 37 (Unpublished Manuscript).

[212] Allah (Clarence 13X), Interview with Allah conducted at Otisville Training Institute For Boys, Nov. 15, 1967.

[213] The Five Percenter Newspaper.

[214] FBI HQ file on Clarence 13X and the Five Percenters.

[215] Allah (Clarence 13X), Interview with Allah conducted at Otisville Training Institute For Boys, Nov. 15, 1967.

[216] FBI HQ file on Clarence 13X and the Five Percenters.

[217] Allah B., Interview with the author. May 2, 2007.

[218] Beautiful Life Allah, "The First Born" in Learn and Know Your History Part 2. 22

[219] Gykee Mathematics, "Our History In Medina" in Learn And Know Your History. (Unpublished Manuscript).

[220] Jack Roth, "Police Fill Court for Muslim Case", *The New York Times*, June 1, 1965.

[221] Ibid.

[222] Ibid.

[223] Gykee M. Allah, "Wrongful Arrested" in Learn and Know Your History. 37 (Unpublished Manuscript).

[224] Eye God a.k.a. Amin, "The Harlem Six" in Learn and Know Your History Part 1. 4-5.

[225] Theodore Jones, "5 Percenters Called Hoodlums: Actions Blamed on Frustration", Article included in FBI HQ file on Clarence 13X and the Five Percenters.

[226] Unknown Author, "Harlem Knows 'Allah' as Puddin", *New York World Telegram*, July 30, 1965.

[227] Theodore Jones, "5 Percenters Called Hoodlums: Actions Blamed on Frustration", Article included in FBI HQ file on Clarence 13X and the Five Percenters.

[228] FBI HQ file on Clarence 13X and the Five Percenters.

[229] Know-Allah, "The Knowledge Being Born In Brownsville: Medina 1965-1966", *The Black Family Show and Prove Special Edition Issue*, June 11, 2000.

[230] FBI HQ file on Clarence 13X and the Five Percenters.

[231] James Sullivan, "Harlem '5 Percenters' – Terror Group Revealed", *The New York Tribune*, October 15, 1965.

[232] Ibid.

[233] ibid.

[234] FBI HQ file on Clarence 13X and the Five Percenters.

[235] Ibid.

[236] James Sullivan, "Harlem '5 Percenters' – Terror Group Revealed", *The New York Tribune*, October 15, 1965.

[237] Shahid M. Allah, *Imam Isa's Got A God Complex!*, 1991.

[238] FBI HQ file on Clarence 13X and the Five Percenters.100-150520

[239] Beautiful Life Allah, "The First Born" in Learn and Know Your History Part 2. 23-24.

[240] Gykee Mathematics Allah, "Education And Working" The Year Three = 1966 in Learn and Know Your History. (Unpublished Manuscript).

[241] FBI HQ file on Clarence 13X and the Five Percenters.

[242] FBI HQ file on Clarence 13X and the Five Percenters. Director FBI 3/23/67.

[243] Allah (Clarence 13X), Interview with Allah conducted at Otisville Training Institute For Boys, Nov. 15, 1967.

[244] Les Matthews, "Allah Still Lives", *The N.Y. Amsterdam News*, June 21, 1969.

[245] Gykee Mathematics Allah, "Education and Working" The Year = 1966 in Learn and Know Your History Part 2. 41 (Unpublished Manuscript).

[246] Allah B., Interview with the Author.

[247] Allah (Clarence 13X), Interview with Allah conducted at Otisville Training Institute For Boys, Nov. 15, 1967.

[248] FBI HQ file on Clarence 13X and the Five Percenters. Director FBI (100-444636) 4/6/66

[249] Gykee M. Allah, "Our History in Medina" in Learn and Know Your History Part 2. 30-31 (Unpublished Manuscript).

[250] Ibid.

[251] U-Allah, "The History of Pelan" 1966-1972, *The Black Family Newspaper Vol. 1 Show and Prove Special Edition Issue*, June 11, 2000.

[252] Ibid.

[253] ibid.

[254] ibid.

[255] Allah B., Interview with the author.

[256] Anonymous, "Some History On The First Born Muslims" in Learn and Know Your History Part 2. 47 (Unpublished Manuscript).

[257] William F. Farrell, "Harlem Militants Offer Peace Vow", *The New York Times*, June 15, 1969.

[258] Azreal, "December 1965" in Learn and Know Your History Part 2. 35 (Unpublished Manuscript).

[259] Shahid M. Allah, *Open It Up Yo!!: The Plot to Kill Clarence 13X* (Washington, DC: TKC Publishing, 1995).

[260] ABG #7 Allah, "December 1964" in Learn And Know Your History Part 2. 28 (Unpublished Manuscript).

[261] Ibid.

[262] ibid.

[263] ibid.

[264] ibid.

[265] Gottehrer, *The Mayor's Man*, 1975.

[266] Ibid.

[267] FBI HQ file on Clarence 13X and the Five Percenters. 5/6/67.

[268] Ibid.

[269] Prince A. Cuba, *Our Mecca is Harlem: Clarence 13X(Allah) and the Five Percent*, 50.

[270] Allah's Born God#7, "June 13th, 1969", in Learn and Know Your History. 37-40.

[271] US Shaamguadd, "Exile!", *Behold the Sun of Man*, June 1983.

[272] Infinite Al'jaa'maar-U-Allah, "The History of Brownsville from 1967-1968, *The Black Family Show and Prove Special Edition Issue*, June 11, 2000.

[273] US Shaamguadd, "A Little Dessert For Those Of The Creative Thought", *Sun of Man Publication*, 1985.

[274] Gykee Mathematics Allah, "Education And Working" The Year Three = 1966 in Learn and Know Your History Part 2. 41-42(Unpublished Manuscript).

[275] Allah (Clarence 13X), Interview with Allah conducted at Otisville Training Institute For Boys, Nov. 15, 1967.

[276] US Shaamguadd, "Five Percenters – The Real Deal! Or Cleaning Up Yourself!" in Learn And Know Your History. 11–13.

[277] Untitled article appeared in *The Five Percenter Newspaper*, May 1996 Issue, page 3.

[278] Shahid M. Allah, *Open It Up Yo!!: The Plot to Kill Clarence 13X*, 1995.

[279] Beloved Allah, The Bomb: The Greatest Story Never Told.

[280] Abdul Akbar Muhammad, Audio excerpt from "The History of Mosque #7 New York City." Speech delivered at Mosque #7, N.Y.C. May 18, 2005 Part 1.

[281] Allah's Born God#7, "June 13, 1969," in Learn and Know Your History Part 1. 37 (Unpublished Manuscript).

[282] Gykee M. Allah, "Our History in Medina" in Learn and Know Your History Part 2. 32 (Unpublished Manuscript).

[283] Ibid.

[284] Gykee M. Allah, "This Was The Year Fourteen" 1977 in Learn and Know Your History Part 2. 57-58. (Unpublished Manuscript).

[285] Interview with Abu Shahid conducted by the author on April 8, 2004.

[286] US Shaamguadd, "Exile!", *Behold the Sun of Man*, June 1983.

[287] Um Allah, Nation_History_part1, Audio excerpts located on http://black7.org/archive.html, Undated.

[288] US Shaamguadd, "Impressive Name Is No Guarantee Or Success For Fame", *Behold The Sun of Man*, 1985.

[289] Elijah Muhammad, *The Supreme Wisdom Vol. 1* (Atlanta: MEMPS, 1957). 21.

[290] US Shaamguadd, "Allah You Are The Greatest", *Behold the Sun of Man*, October 1986 Issue, 2.

[291] US Shaamguadd, "Allah Blessed America", *Behold the Sun of Man*. Not dated.

[292] US Shaamguadd, "The Universal Flag!", *The Sun of Man*, Undated.

[293] ibid.

[294] Gykee M. Allah, "Our History in Medina" in Know and Learn Your History Part 2. 31 (Unpublished Manuscript).

[295] Gottehrer, *The Mayor's Man*, 1975.

[296] Ibid.

[297] Gottehrer, *The Mayor's Man*, 1975.

[298] Gykee Mathematics Allah, "An Honorary Five Percenter" "1968" in Learn and Know Your History Part 2. 40. (Unpublished Manuscript)

[299] Gottehrer, *The Mayor's Man*, 1975.

[300] Ibid.

[301] ibid.

[302] Allah's Born God#7, "June 13th, 1969", in Learn and Know Your History. 37-40.

[303] Ibid.

[304] ibid.

[305] ibid.

[306] ibid.

[307] K7, "Give Off Light Not Lies", *The Five Percenter Newspaper*, February 1998 Issue, Volume 3.6.

[308] Gottehrer, *The Mayor's Man*, 1975.

[309] Gykee Mathematics Allah, "An Honorary Five Per-center" "1968" in Learn and Know Your History Part 2. 40. (Unpublished Manuscript).

[310] Ibid.

[311] John P. Callahan, "Mayor, After a Walking Tour, Goes Aloft With 86 Harlem Youngsters" "Mayor Goes Aloft With Slum Group", *The New York Times,* August 6, 1967.

[312] Infinite Al'jaa'maar-U-Allah, "The History of Brownsville from 1967-1968", *The Black Family Show and Prove Special Edition Issue*, June 11, 2000.

[313] Shabazz Adew Allah, "Study your Lessons", *The Five Percenter Newspaper*, Jan. 1996 Issue.

[314] Abu Shahid, Interview with Author. Undated.

[315] Bayard Rustin, "The Five Percenters", *The Amsterdam News: Brooklyn Section*, Sept. 9, 1967, Reprinted in *The Five Percenter Newspaper*, July 1998 Issue.

[316] Ibid

[317] ibid.

[318] Allah (Clarence 13X), Interview with Allah conducted at Otisville Training Institute For Boys, Nov. 15, 1967.

[319] The Honorable Elijah Muhammad, *"The Theology of Time"*, Lecture Series, 1972.

[320] Ibid.

[321] Allah (Clarence 13X), 3 excerpts from interview with Allah conducted at Otisville Training Institute For Boys, Nov. 15, 1967.

[322] Elijah Muhammad, *"What the Muslims Believe"*, Point #10, Undated.

[323] Allah (Clarence 13X), Interview with Allah conducted at Otisville Training Institute For Boys, Nov. 15, 1967.

[324] Ibid.

[325] E. Muhammad, *Message to the Black Man*, 179, 323.

[326] Allah (Clarence 13X), Interview with Allah conducted at Otisville Training Institute For Boys, Nov. 15, 1967.

[327] Ibid.

[328] E. Muhammad, *The True History of Master Fard Muhammad*, 114.

[329] Allah (Clarence 13X), Interview with Allah conducted at Otisville Training Institute For Boys, Nov. 15, 1967.

[330] Shahid M. Allah, *Imam Isa's Got A God Complex!*, 1991.

[331] Allah (Clarence 13X), Interview with Allah conducted at Otisville Training Institute For Boys, Nov. 15, 1967.

[332] Gykee M. Allah, "Our History in Medina" in Learn and Know Your History Part 2. 32 (Unpublished Manuscript).

[333] US Shaamguadd, *"The Science of Cain and Able"*, Behold the Sun of Man. Undated.

[334] Frank Paso, "Kenyatta's Pal Killed: Cops See Muslim War", *The N.Y. Daily News*, June 14, 1969.

[335] Allah (Clarence 13X), Interview with Allah conducted at Otisville Training Institute For Boys, Nov. 15, 1967.

[336] Ibid.

[337] Elijah Muhammad, *History of The Nation of Islam"*(Cleveland: Secretarius Publication, 1993) 8-9.

[338] ibid.

[339] Gottehrer, *The Mayor's Man*, 1975.

[340] US Shaamguadd, "Allah You Are The Greatest", *Behold the Sun of Man*, October 1986 Issue, 2.

[341] Ibid.

[342] K7, "1969 The Rifle", *The Five Percenter Newspaper*, May 1996 Issue.

[343] Interview with David Garth, Pablo Guzman, Sid Davidoff and Barry Gottehrer that appeared in the New Yorker Magazine, April 1968 Issue.

[344] Ibid.

[345] ibid.

[346] Allah (Clarence 13X), Interview with Allah conducted at Otisville Training Institute For Boys, Nov. 15, 1967.

[347] Gloria Steinem and Lloyd Weaver, "The City on the Eve of Destruction", *New Yorker Magazine*, April 1968 Issue.

[348] Ibid

[349] ibid

[350] ibid

[351] ibid

[352] Gykee M. Allah, "An Honorary Five Per-center" "1968" in Learn and Know Your History. 39. (Unpublished Manuscript).

[353] Allah's Born God#7, "June 13th, 1969", in Learn and Know Your History. 37-40.

[354] Gloria Steinem and Lloyd Weaver, "The City on the Eve of Destruction", *New Yorker Magazine*, April 1968 Issue.

[355] Ibid

[356] Shabazz Adew Allah, "Peace", *The Five Percenter Newspaper*, October 1996 Issue.

[357] T. Evans, Judy Kaminski, *"Memorandum- To: Mr. Schwartz: RE: Allah Five Percent"*, July 25, 1968, Memorandum was reprinted in *The Five Percenter Newspaper*, Sept. 1995 Issue, 4.

[358] Ibid.

[359] ibid.

[360] ibid.

[361] Kathleen Teltsch, "City Acting to Reform Its Youth Detention Facilities", *The New York Times, Sep 22, 1968*.

[362] Abdul Akbar Muhammad, Audio excerpt from "The History of Mosque #7 New York City." Speech delivered at Mosque #7, N.Y.C. May 18, 2005 Part 1.

[363] Beloved Allah, "The Bomb: The Greatest Story Never Told", 1987.

[364] Louis Farrakhan, *Is the House Divided*, Lecture given in Phoenix, AZ, 1977.

[365] K7, "1969 The Rifle", *The Five Percenter Newspaper*, May 1996 Issue.

[366] U-Allah, "The History of Pelan" 1966-1972, *The Black Family Newspaper Vol. 1 Show and Prove Special Edition Issue*, June 11, 2000.

[367] K7, "1969 The Rifle", *The Five Percenter Newspaper*, May 1996 Issue.

[368] K7, Untitled Article, *The Five Percenter Newspaper*, June 1996 Issue 11.

[369] Ibid.

[370] Allah's Born God#7, "June 13th, 1969", in Learn and Know Your History. 37-40.

[371] Gottehrer, *The Mayor's Man*, 1975.

[372] Ibid.

[373] Frank Faso, Kenyatta's Pal Killed; Cops See Muslim War. Article appeared in The N.Y. Daily News. June 14, 1969

[374] Gottehrer, *The Mayor's Man*, 1975.

[375] William F. Farrell, "Harlem Militants Offer Peace Vow", *The New York Times*, June 15, 1969.

[376] Ibid.

[377] Gottehrer, *The Mayor's Man*, 1975.

[378] Ibid.

[379] ibid.

[380] Prince A. Cuba, *Our Mecca is Harlem: Clarence 13X(Allah) and the Five Percent*, 51-52.

[381] Gottehrer, *The Mayor's Man*, 1975.

[382] Ibid.

[383] Beloved Allah, "The Bomb: The Greatest Story Never Told", 1987.

[384] Gottehrer, *The Mayor's Man*, 1975.

[385] Prince A. Cuba, *Our Mecca is Harlem: Clarence 13X(Allah) and the Five Percent*, 50-51

[386] Shahid M. Allah, *Imam Isa's Got A God Complex!*, 1991.

[387] William F. Farrell, "Harlem Militants Offer Peace Vow", *The New York Times*, June 15, 1969.

[388] Ibid.

[389] ibid.

[390] Les Matthews, "Allah Still Lives", *The N.Y. Amsterdam News*, June 21, 1969.

[391] Ibid.

[392] ibid.

[393] ibid.

[394] U-Allah, "The History of Pelan" 1966-1972, *The Black Family Newspaper Vol. 1 Show and Prove Special Edition Issue*, June 11, 2000.

[395] Gottehrer, *The Mayor's Man*, 1975.

[396] Sha Sha, *"Jimmy Jam The Old Man"*, Article located on now defunct Oasis website.

[397] "Biography Article", *The Five Percenter Newspaper*, September 1995 Issue, 11.

[398] Brentin Mock, "What If God Was One Of Us?", *The Pittsburgh City Paper*, October 16, 2002.

[399] Anonymous, "Time To Teach" in Learn and Know Your History Part 2. 71. (Unpublished Manuscript).

[400] Beloved Allah, "The Bomb: The Greatest Story Never Told", 1987.

[401] Ibid.

[402] US Shaamguadd, "The Ostrich Syndrome", *The Sun of Man*, July 1983 Issue.

[403] Gykee Mathematics, "Our History in Medina" in Learn and Know Your History Part 2. 33 (Unpublished Manuscript).

[404] Anonymous, No Title in Learn and Know Your History Part 2. 36. (Unpublished Manuscript)

[405] Gykee Mathematics Allah, Untitled in Learn and Know Your History Part 2. 34 (Unpublished Manuscript).

[406] Shahid M. Allah, *Imam Isa's Got A God Complex!*, 1991.

[407] Anonymous, "Time To Teach" 2.000 in Learn and Know Your History Part 2. 70 (Unpublished Manuscript).

[408] Born Allah, "Allah's Show & Prove", Undated.

[409] Ibid

[410] ibid

[411] ibid

[412] ibid

[413] ibid

[414] Paul Robinson, "Born Allah: Positive Vibrations", *The Auburn Collective*, January 1983.

[415] Allah, "The Revelation of Allah #1", February 1974.

[416] Shahid M. Allah, *Imam Isa's Got A God Complex!*, 1991.

[417] "Dance With The Devil", *The Five Percenter Newspaper*, September 1996 Issue, 5.

[418] Louis Farrakhan, *Is the House Divided*, Lecture given in Phoenix, AZ, 1977.

[419] "Biography Article", *The Five Percenter Newspaper*, September 1995 Issue, 11.

[420] Shahid M. Allah, *Imam Isa's Got A God Complex!*, 1991.

[421] Nuruddin, *"The Five Percenters"*, 1994.

[422] Shahid M. Allah, *Imam Isa's Got A God Complex!*, 1991.

[423] Nuruddin, *"The Five Percenters"* 1994.

[424] Ibid.

[425] US Shaamguadd, "Allah You Are The Greatest", *Behold the Sun of Man*, October 1986 Issue, 4.

[426] Shabazz Adew Allah, "Unification is the Directive, Truth is the Criteria", *The Five Percenter Newspaper*, September 1996, Volume 2.1

[427] "Allah School: Where to Now?", *The Five Percenter Newspaper*, January 1989 Issue.

[428] "Allah School Is Not A Building", *The Five Percenter Newspaper*, January 1989 Issue.

[429] "The Million Man March", *The Five Percenter Newspaper*, Sept. 1995 Issue, 3.

[430] "Sweet Harmony", *The Five Percenter* Newspaper, Special Edition October 1995, 2.

[431] Brentin Mock, "What If God Was One Of Us?", *The Pittsburgh City Paper*, October 16, 2002.

[432] Interview with Abu Shahid on April 8, 2004 conducted by author.

[433] Paul von Zielbauer, "Inmates Are Free To Practice Black Supremacist Religion, Judge Rules", *The New York Times*, August 18, 2003.

[434] US Shaamguadd, "A Little Dessert For Those Of The Creative Thought", *Sun of Man Publication*, 1985.

[435] K7, "1969 THE RIFLE", The Five Percenter Newspaper, May 1996 Issue, 2.

[436] Beloved Allah, "The Bomb: The Greatest Story Never Told", 1987.

[437] ibid

[438] Cuba, *Our Mecca is Harlem: Clarence 13X(Allah) and the Five Percent*, 53.

[439] Dumar Wa'de Allah. The National Statement 1996.

[440] G. Kalim, "Godism: Also Muslims & Muslim Sons", *The Five Percenter Newspaper*, August 1998 Issue.

[441] Ibid. 6.

[442] Shabazz Adew Allah, "Study Your Lessons", The Five Percenter Newspaper, December 1995 Issue, 2.

[443] Cuba, *Our Mecca is Harlem: Clarence 13X(Allah) and the Five Percent*, 53.

[444] E. Muhammad, *The True History of Master Fard Muhammad*, 35.

[445] Charlie Ahearn, "The Five Percent Solution," SPIN Magazine, February 1991, 57

[446] Elijah Muhammad, *Our Saviour Has Arrived* (Chicago: Final Call Publishing, 1974) 56.

[447] Dumar Wad'e Allah. The National Statement Nov. 1996.

[448] True Islam, "Is Allah A Righteous Muslim?", April, 1998.

[449] Sunez Allah, "The Infinite Legacy of the 5%…Insights into the Pedagogy Employed at Allah School In Mecca." March, 2007.

[450] Ibid.

[451] ibid.

[452] ibid.

[453] ibid.

[454] ibid.

[455] ibid.

[456] ibid.

[457] ibid.

[458] ibid.
[459] ibid.
[460] ibid.

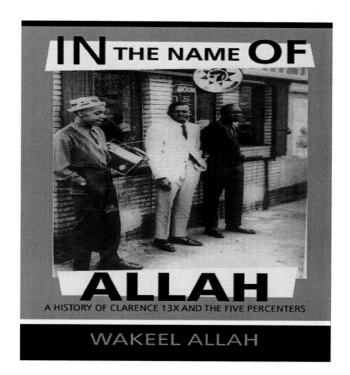

For More Information on the Book and its Subject:

www.InTheNameofAllahBook.com
www.myspace.com/fivepercenthistory
www.myspace.com/allahyouthcenterinmecca
www.5percenters.net
www.theblackgod.com
www.allahteam.org

Please forward all written correspondence to:

Wakeel Allah
P.O. Box 551036
Atlanta, GA 30355